THE CURIOUS DREAMER'S
DREAM
DICTIONARY

How to Interpret Dream Symbol
Meaning for Personal Growth

NANCY WAGAMAN

To the open-eyed and open-hearted
explorer within each of us.

Contents

About This Book

This dream dictionary is a companion to *The Curious Dreamer's Practical Guide to Dream Interpretation*, a dream-coach-in-a-book that shows step-by-step how to understand dreams and unlock their transformative power. This second book in the series continues the same focus on personal growth by presenting more than 1500 symbol descriptions to inspire your dream exploration and personal transformation process.

Stand-Alone or Companion Book

You can use this book as a stand-alone resource or to enhance the framework presented in *The Curious Dreamer's Practical Guide to Dream Interpretation.* For the most robust dream interpretation experience, I recommend using the two books together.

A Source of Possibilities

Because dream symbol meaning is personal to each dreamer, no dream dictionary can provide a single meaning of a dream symbol that's always true for every dreamer and every dream. Therefore, the symbol descriptions in this book are intended as a source of *possible ideas* about meanings, designed to enrich your own search for meaning. Each description provides suggestions intended to trigger your subconscious mind to confirm what it already knows about the symbol's meaning and what it says about you or your life.

Organization of This Book

This book contains three main parts followed by an index of symbols:

PART I: HOW TO FIND DREAM SYMBOL MEANING (p. 1)

Knowledge and tips about dream symbolism and interpretation to jumpstart your interpretation process and help you make the most of the dream symbol descriptions in this book.

PART II: SYMBOL CATEGORIES (p. 29)
Common categories of dream symbols, and how each category can provide more clues to symbol meaning because all of its symbols can be interpreted in a similar way.

PART III: SYMBOLS (p. 39)
More than 1500 dream symbol descriptions arranged alphabetically, each including possible meanings to assist in your exploration of meaning and to support your personal growth process.

PART IV: SYMBOL INDEX (p. 351)
A comprehensive list of the dream symbols in this book, including additional names by which the symbols are known.

How to Read This Book
I suggest you begin by reading " Part I: How To Find Dream Symbol Meaning" (p. 1). Then for each key dream symbol in your dream, read its category in " Part II: Symbol Categories" (p. 27) and its description in " Part III: Symbols" (p. 37). Use the index to quickly locate individual symbols, including by their alternative names.

Style and Usage Notes
This book's casual, conversational style is intended to make it easy to read and understand.

For the purposes of this book, "real life" refers to a person's waking life—although what happens in the dream state is technically also part of real life, in that it's one aspect of the dreamer's personal experience.

When this book discusses what a dream symbol might represent "in real life" or "in your life," this refers to anywhere in your current or past life (in any area such as home life, work life, relationships, etc.) or in your consciousness (in your mind, emotions, etc.).

In "Part III: Symbols" (p. 37), a symbol's "*See also*" section contains a list of related symbols as cross-references. In addition, within the text of some symbol descriptions are prompts to search for specific related symbols. For example, the symbol "Color" (p. 103) suggests, "See also the specific color name," prompting you to also read the symbol description for the particular color in your dream (such as "Purple" or "Red").

The Symbols
The dream symbol descriptions are listed in alphabetical order in "Chapter 3-2: The Symbols" (p. 45). Each symbol entry includes a description of possible meanings separated with periods. Any specific variations are

then noted in **bold,** followed by a "*See also*" list. The format is shown in the following example:

Hand

A person, humanness, or humanity in general. The ability to get things done, being "handy," or "handling things." The idea of holding on or letting go (physically, emotionally, or mentally). **A hand coming toward you with ill intent** could represent a feeling or fear of persecution, hostility, aggression, criticism, or being taken advantage of by someone or by people in general. **Holding hands or other positive interaction** with hands can represent good will or affection you feel toward someone, or that you believe someone feels toward you, or that you desire. Consider the context, whose hand it was, and what it was doing. *See also:* Finger; Touching; Fist; Body Part

PART I

HOW TO FIND DREAM SYMBOL MEANING

Chapter 1-1
Decoding Dream Symbols

In This Chapter:

The moment you wake up from a dream, you already know what it means. The answers lie deep within your consciousness where the dream and its symbolism were created, right where you left them when you woke up. The essence of the dreamer's quest is to coax those secrets out into the light of day to reveal dream meaning. This book shows you how to delve into those subconscious depths and retrieve that dream symbol treasure.

Unlocking the Power of Your Dreams

Dream interpretation provides powerful knowledge about yourself that you might not discover otherwise, if you can understand the language of dream symbols. Encoded within dream symbolism you can find clues to what makes you tick, answers that point you toward your ideal life, and insights to help you resolve past issues and move through the challenges ahead. In fact, dream symbolism is so potent that sometimes translating just one dream symbol can unlock the meaning of an entire life-transforming dream. This book teaches you how to translate dream symbol meaning and use it as the key to unlock the power of your dreams.

A Practical Goal

The practical goal of dream interpretation, as I see it, is to find the value in each dream so you can then apply it to improve yourself and your life. A dream's value may be profound and life changing, or as simple as the realization that eating sweets too close to bedtime can trigger nightmares. Whatever the content of a dream, you can learn from it. So as you explore your dreams, keep the following objective in mind:

Find the value in your dreams.

The Value in Dreams

Virtually every dream offers value, revealing some new understanding about yourself or your life. If you pay attention to your dreams, they can help you:

- Better understand yourself and your needs.
- Get answers to important questions.
- Clarify life purpose and direction.
- Discover creative ideas and visions.
- Help resolve issues from the past.
- Resolve fears and move ahead.
- Identify important health conditions.
- Learn how to reduce stress in your life.

Using This Book to Translate Symbols

This dream dictionary presents more than 1500 dream symbols defined for personal growth. You can use it as a stand-alone resource or as an enhancement to its companion book, *The Curious Dreamer's Practical Guide to Dream Interpretation.*

Translating Symbols

If you want to understand what a particular dream means, its individual dream symbols are an excellent place to begin exploring. The meanings of individual dream symbols can provide huge clues about the meaning of the whole dream. For example, once you recognize that an upward staircase in a dream represents an opportunity to "advance upward," it's a short leap to realizing that the dream was pointing to a real-life opportunity for career advancement.

Understanding a dream symbol's meaning requires you to translate its symbolism from the language of your subconscious mind into a language that your conscious mind can understand. When your subconscious mind creates a dream, it chooses particular symbols to tell a story in its own language of symbolism. However, once you're awake, you're no longer directly in touch with your subconscious mind. So, the challenge of dream symbol translation is discovering the meaning that your subconscious mind was "thinking" when it chose each dream symbol (in other words, discovering the symbol's true meaning).

There are many possible ways you might discover true dream symbol meaning. You could simply wake up with an intuitive understanding that you carried over from your dream state. You might catch a glimpse of true meaning as you analyze your symbol, or when you come across it in this book's description of the symbol. You might decide to follow the thread of embedded emotion in the dream symbol back to the original, real-life situation it represents.

There's no single or "best" way to discover dream symbol meaning. In fact, you can choose from many techniques and tips in the remainder of this chapter and in "Chapter 1-2: Jumpstarting Your Interpretation" (p. 17), plus many more in the first book of this series, *The Curious Dreamer's Practical Guide to Dream Interpretation.*

Possibilities, Not Answers

The meaning of each dream symbol in your dream is personal to you, as the dreamer of that dream. Because a dream symbol has no standard meaning in all dreams and for all dreamers, this dream dictionary offers *possibilities* for what the symbol could mean, rather than definitive translations. The symbol descriptions in this book are intended to inspire your exploration process in the hope that your intuition will alert you when you come across your subconscious mind's true meaning of your symbol (read more in "Recognizing Dream Symbol Meaning," p. 17).

Remember that you are the ultimate authority on your own dream. After all, you were there when the dream was created, and your subconscious mind already understands the dream and its symbols.

Learn Dream Symbol Language

Your dream and its symbols speak through the language of dream symbolism. Although that language shares similarities across dreamers, each dreamer's subconscious mind speaks in its own personal "dialect" of dream symbolism. So in this book you'll learn about the "standard" language of dream symbols (to the extent that there *is* a standard one), plus you'll learn how to decipher your own subconscious mind's personal symbol meanings (your personal "dialect"). The following three sections introduce the primary considerations about personal dream symbol translation to keep in mind as you explore the symbol descriptions in this book.

Personal Meaning

Because dream symbol meaning is subjective and personal to the dreamer, consider what the symbol means to you personally. To help yourself better understand its personal meaning, you could ask yourself:

- What thoughts and feelings come up when I think of this thing?
- How would I describe this thing to someone who has never seen it before? (See also "TOOL: Caveman Explanation," p. 14.)
- How would I feel about this thing if I actually saw it in real life?
- What would I say if someone asked for my impression of this thing?

Context

A dream symbol's meaning can be very specific to its context in the dream. So, think about how the symbol appeared in the dream and what that may convey about its meaning. For example, pay attention to:

- Where was the object?
- Was there anything unusual about its location or position?
- What was it near or surrounded by (objects, people, etc.)?
- What was its environment (indoor or outdoor, lighting, mood, weather, etc.)?
- (If an inanimate object) What was happening to it?
- (If a living being) What was it doing, how, where, and with whom?
- How were the characters (including you) viewing or relating to it?
- How did you feel about all of the above?

Look Beyond the Obvious

A dream symbol often represents something beyond its obvious meaning. A rose could represent a real-life rose, but it's much more likely to represent something else more symbolic (such as a feeling, characteristic, or event). So look beyond your symbol's literal meaning by asking yourself, "What else could this symbol mean?"

Let Intuition Be Your Guide

As you work toward understanding a dream symbol, the goal is for your intuition to recognize the symbol's true meaning. The process of reaching that goal is more of an adventure than a linear process. Although this book offers step-by-step tools to enhance your exploration, interpretation isn't as simple as completing a few steps that automatically lead to the symbol's meaning. So, allow your exploration to flow naturally, and follow your intuition when deciding the following:

- Which dream symbol to explore first, next, and so on.
- When to use a tool (and which one) to prompt your subconscious mind to reveal the symbol's meaning, and to give your intuition a chance to recognize the meaning when you see it.
- Whether a particular meaning from this book or elsewhere in your mind is the true meaning of your dream symbol.

(For more on intuition as a dream interpretation tool, see "Recognizing Dream Symbol Meaning," p. 17.)

Take the Winding Path

When you start down the path of exploring a particular dream symbol, be willing to persevere even if the path is a winding one. You may not always know which way to go, but your intuition will guide you if you pay attention to it.

Since your goal in symbol exploration is to intuitively recognize the symbol's true meaning, it's a good idea to give your mind a chance to encounter that meaning so your intuition can recognize it. Sometimes the true meaning simply comes forward within your consciousness and then your intuition confirms it. However, more often you'll need to put in a little more effort to discover it. If the true meaning isn't evident, you can use a technique that parades various possible meanings past your "inner intuitive eye," giving it a chance to confirm the true one. The technique can be as simple as mentally listing the meanings you associate with the symbol or reading the symbol's description in this book. You could also use a dream analysis tool that prompts your subconscious mind to reveal the meanings it associates with the symbol, such as "TOOL: Caveman Explanation" (p. 14), or many others in the Dream Analysis Toolkit in the first book of this series, *The Curious Dreamer's Practical Guide to Dream Interpretation*.

The Steps for Interpreting Symbols

The following tools provide two different step-by-step processes for using this dream dictionary to enhance your dream symbol exploration.

TOOL: Dream Dictionary

This technique shows how to use this book's description of your symbol to help you discover your true dream symbol meaning.

1. Choose a symbol from your dream that you want to explore, perhaps the one that stood out the most.
2. Find that symbol in the dream dictionary and consider the possible meanings listed. Notice which (if any) resonate with you intuitively.
3. While keeping the dictionary meanings in mind, consider:

   Personal meaning—What the dream symbol means to you, what it brings to mind for you, and feelings it triggers within you. (See more in "Personal Meaning," p. 6.)

   Context—How the dream symbol appears in the dream. For example, in a dream about a bird, consider what the bird was doing, how and where it was doing it, and how you felt about that. (See more in "Context," p. 6.)

   Look beyond the obvious—A dream is often about something other than its obvious meaning. For example, physical events in the dream can represent mental or emotional matters. (See more in "Look Beyond the Obvious," p. 6.)

4. Using what you discovered in Step 2 and Step 3, explore what the symbol represents on some level of your real life—physical, emotional, mental, spiritual, and so on. If a particular dictionary meaning resonated with you, explore it further by looking for more clues in the dream that point to something parallel in your real life.
5. Write your conclusions about the symbol's meaning in your dream journal, along with any other realizations about the dream.

Examples

The following examples illustrate how you might use this dream dictionary to assist you in discovering the meaning of a dream:

Example A:

In a dream, you watched a giraffe as she tried to eat some leaves high up in a tree, but she couldn't quite reach them. However, she was determined, and you knew she would eventually reach them.

You check the "Giraffe" symbol description in this book (p. 164) and it includes: reaching or stretching (for what you want, toward a goal, etc.); reaching beyond (beyond a perceived limitation, beyond what others can see or do, etc.); an ability to see things differently (differently than others, from a higher perspective, seeing both sides of an issue, etc.); being, feeling, or doing things differently than others. You keep these in mind as you consider the following:

Your personal meaning—When you think of a giraffe, you think of a very tall animal with a long neck who can reach things in high places.

Context—In this dream, the giraffe was trying to reach leaves high in the tree in order to eat them. She was stretching to get food because she needed nourishment, but was having trouble reaching it.

Look beyond the obvious—You haven't seen a giraffe or any references to a giraffe lately in your waking life, so you conclude that the giraffe probably represents something in your life other than an actual giraffe. You think about how perhaps you have stretched to get some kind of nourishment but couldn't quite reach it. You consider all the kinds of nourishment—physical, emotional, mental, spiritual, and so on—and you recognize that in real life you had planned to stretch yourself financially to take an art history class, but you decided it was too much of a stretch right now. You had been looking forward to the class because you're so interested in learning about art and artists from the past—a form of mental and emotional nourishment that would feed your own creative process. Your intuition confirms the dream dictionary's meaning of "reaching beyond," since you are determined to reach beyond your current financial shortcomings as you save money over the next few months so you can take the class. In your dream journal, you write your conclusions about the giraffe's meaning in your dream.

Example B:
Imagine that you dreamed you were enjoying yourself spending money at the mall when you remembered that you had to go home and take care of your dog, who needed to be fed and let outside. You were disappointed about having to leave, but you felt good about fulfilling your responsibility to the dog. In real life you don't have a dog.

The "Dog" symbol description in this book (p. 126) suggests that a dog can represent responsibility, protectiveness, security, unconditional love, loyalty, friendship, companionship, your inner child, or an actual dog.

You can't think of a real-life situation during which you had to interrupt a fun time because of someone who was protective, but the idea of responsibility feels on-target to you. In the dream you were leaving the mall to attend to your responsibility of caring for your dog. You keep this in mind as you consider the following:

Your personal meaning—The idea of a dog reminds you of responsibility because when you were a kid, taking care of your family's dog was your responsibility.

Context—In this dream, you knew you had to go home because you had a responsibility to go take care of your dog.

Look beyond the obvious—Because you don't have a dog, it seems that the dog probably represents something else in your life. You consider where in your life you've had to stop in the middle of a fun time to go take care of a responsibility, where you felt disappointed but knew you were doing the right thing by stopping. You recognize the disappointment you felt last month when you decided to stop going to the coffee shop every morning and buying expensive, calorie-laden drinks—and instead enjoying healthier morning beverages at home. Your intuition confirms that the dream portrays your pattern of overspending on expensive drinks you don't really need (represented by spending at the mall), which you stopped in order to fulfill your responsibility to yourself regarding your finances and your health (represented by your responsibility to the dog). You write your conclusions about this dream's meaning in your dream journal.

TOOL: Parallels Between Symbols and Real Life

This technique can help you discover what your symbol represents in your real life by giving your subconscious mind a chance to reveal what it already knows. The idea of this technique is to explore each symbol in a way that focuses your mind on it for a while to provide the time and space for a flash of recognition about its meaning.

1. Identify the key symbols in your dream—usually the characters or objects that stood out the most during the dream. Write a list of them in your dream journal or on a separate sheet of paper. Keeping notes will help when you get to the end of this process and it's time to pull together all of the clues.
2. For each key symbol, consider what stood out about it. Describe your first impression of it in a few words. Often, whatever you tend to notice about a symbol initially during the dream can tip you off as to what it represents, so make sure you note your first impression before you explore the dream symbol further. For more ideas, read the description for your symbol in "Chapter 3-2: The Symbols" (p. 45).
3. For each key symbol, explore the following aspects associated with it, looking for parallels between these aspects and aspects of your waking life.

Feelings—Consider your feelings about the symbol during the dream, and why—what was behind those feelings. Perhaps you recognize a certain time when you've felt that way in your real life. If so, consider what triggered those feelings in real life and how the symbol might represent that situation.

Physical Symbol—Take note of the symbol's physical characteristics, how it was placed or positioned, its context and attributes, and anything else physical that stood out about it or that seemed unusual or unexpected about it.

Setting—Consider the physical setting of the symbol. Think about where the symbol was located—in a kitchen, on a desk, on the lawn, in the air—and what else was around it. Pay attention to anything unusual or unexpected about its setting.

Environment—Notice the kind of environment around the symbol—season, weather, time of day, lighting, and so on. Consider how its environment reminds you of a situation or mood you've experienced in your waking life.

Actions—Consider the action(s) involved. If the symbol was an inanimate object, consider what happened to it and how the dream character(s) related to it. If the symbol is alive, consider its actions and motivations, and whether there was anything unusual or unexpected about them.

Wordplay—Think about what wordplay could tell you about what the symbol represents in your life. Wordplay includes puns, synonyms, sound-alike words or phrases, slang words, figures of speech, and so on.

4. Review all of your observations, and see if you notice a pattern that reminds you of an event or situation in your life, or an issue that's been on your mind. If the meanings you defined in Steps 1 through 3 don't match anything obvious in your real life, focus on the symbol and your feeling about it and see if another meaning comes forward that resonates with you. If you don't recognize a meaning that relates to your real life, the symbol may represent something in your mind—such as a hope, fear, desire, something

you're imagining, or some idea or experience your subconscious mind created during the dream state itself.

Examples

The following examples demonstrate how the Parallels Between Symbols and Real Life process can be used to explore dream symbol meaning:

Example A:

Imagine you dreamed that you were driving at night in an old car, when suddenly the steering failed, causing you to drive off the road. In Step 1 you determine that the car was the main symbol in this dream, and in Step 2 you summarize what stood out about the car as "An old car I was driving that went out of control." In Step 3 you look for parallels between aspects of the dream and aspects of your waking life. First, you describe your feelings during the dream as "I felt panic when I couldn't control the car and I was afraid of crashing." You realize that you recognize this feeling from your waking life—similar to the panic and out-of-control feeling regarding your finances lately, your fear of financial disaster. You describe the physical car symbol as "The car was old, rusty and in need of maintenance"—which you suspect may refer to your spending patterns that could use an overhaul. You describe the car's setting as "The car was traveling on a winding road"—which could represent an unpredictable process or journey somewhere in your life. You characterize the car's environment as "The car was driving at night"—which you suspect could imply something happening without your awareness— something about which you're "in the dark." You summarize the actions involving the car as "The car's steering stopped working and the car veered off the road and crashed"—which you think represents the time in real life when you stopped making wise decisions about spending, after which you experienced financial crisis. You don't see any obvious wordplay, so you move on to Step 4, in which you review your observations and explore the patterns that show parallels between your dream and your real life. When you review each dream element, your intuition flashes to the aspect of your waking life to which it refers. You recognize the out-of-control feeling in the car as similar to your out-of-control feelings about your finances. Veering off the winding road in the dark when the steering stopped working seems to represent your real life situation of poor decision making in the face of unpredictable financial demands, represented by the winding road. This is a pattern of which you've been unaware ("in the dark" about) until now, represented in the dream by the dark setting. The car needing maintenance seems to represent your financial patterns and decision making which need some attention and updating. You conclude that this dream portrays what you've been experiencing in the financial area of your life and the financial trouble that may occur if you don't take corrective action in that area.

Example B:

Imagine you dreamed that a bee that was pestering you. In Step 1, you identify the key symbol as the bee, and in Step 2 you summarize what immediately stood out about it as "The bee kept buzzing around my face." Looking for parallels with your real life in Step 3, you note that during the dream you experienced feelings of fear that the bee would sting you and frustration because it wouldn't leave you alone. You recognize these feelings as similar to a real life situation in which you're afraid of someone who has been pestering you at school. You note the bee's physical characteristic of being bigger than usual, which could imply a pest that "looms large" in your life or has a big effect on you. You note the bee's setting as the inside of your house—which could mean that whatever the bee represents has intruded into your personal space. You note the environment in which the bee appeared was during the daytime while you were trying to get things done—which could represent the idea of something that interferes with your day-to-day activities. You note the actions of the bee, which seemed to be taunting you, repeatedly flying near your face—which could represent someone repeatedly taunting or pestering you at school. You note the possible wordplay—a bee is a type of "bug"—so perhaps it represents something that is "bugging" you. In Step 4 you review your observations and conclude that the bee in the dream represents a girl at school who has been pestering you, intruding into your space when you are trying to focus on your schoolwork. She is relentless, and you are afraid that taking any action against her will result in you getting in trouble—getting "stung." You realize that this dream illustrates the situation from your waking life, but it does not provide any answer about what to do about it. So, you decide to talk it over with someone you trust to give you good advice, and then make a decision about what action to take.

If you've completed "TOOL: Dream Dictionary" (p. 7) and "TOOL: Parallels Between Symbols and Real Life" (p. 10) and you still need more clues to dream symbol meaning, consider other approaches. You'll find more suggestions in the next section ("If Your Symbol Is Not Listed") and many more in the first book of the series, *The Curious Dreamer's Practical Guide to Dream Interpretation*.

If Your Symbol Is Not Listed

If you can't find your symbol in this book, consider these two other ways to explore symbol meaning. (These can also be helpful even if your symbol *is* listed in this book.)

Find the Symbol Category

Read the description for your symbol's category in "Chapter 2-2: The Symbol Categories" (p. 31), which may help you better understand how to interpret your symbol. For example, if an unusual insect appeared in your dream, you'll find that its category description ("Insects," p. 34) provides ideas for interpreting the meaning of any insect or bug-like creature.

TOOL: Caveman Explanation

The following technique can help you to deep-dive into the meanings that your subconscious mind associates with the symbol:

1. Choose a symbol from your dream, and imagine that you are explaining what it is to someone who is not familiar with it—such as a caveman, young child, or alien from another planet. The person has no idea what the thing is, how it works, what it does, what it's known for, or anything else about it. Start from the beginning with the most basic explanation.
2. Write the meanings that you used to explain the symbol.
3. Consider which meaning resonates intuitively with you as the meaning of your dream symbol, or which meaning relates to a matter that you've experienced in your real life or that's been on your mind.

Examples

Here are some examples of using the Caveman Explanation technique to reveal your own personal meanings of a particular dream symbol:

Example A:

Consider a dream in which you were making a phone call to your father, but you couldn't get through because of a bad connection. You might imagine explaining a phone to a caveman this way:

"Okay, Caveman, here's what a phone is. It's a device I can use to talk with other people. I can call them on the phone when I want to talk, or they can call me when they want to talk. A phone lets us talk as if we are standing right next to each other, even if we are far apart. I can also use a phone to call for help."

So, based on your explanation of a phone, the phone in your dream might represent one or more of the following, which you write down:

- Communication, or a desire to communicate.
- One person's availability to another person, such as to talk or listen.
- Bridging the (physical, emotional, or mental) distance between two people.
- A need to speak or be heard.
- Wanting or needing help.

The idea of a phone as a means of communication really resonates with you. In your dream you kept getting a bad connection when trying to reach your father, so you consider how in real life you might be experiencing a "bad connection" when trying to communicate with your father. You realize that you and he haven't been seeing eye-to-eye about how to handle a certain matter. You conclude that the dream was portraying your subconscious mind's view of your disagreement with your father, and you note this in your dream journal.

Example B:

If you dreamed about an apple growing very quickly, you might explore its possible meanings by imagining that you're describing it to an alien from another planet:

"Mr. Alien, let me explain what an apple is. It's red and round, and it grows on trees. It's good to eat, and it's nourishing and healthy. Apples are fruits that take a long time to develop before they are ready. Each apple contains seeds that can grow a whole new generation of apple trees, which can then produce their own apples."

So, based on the way you described an apple, you write the following possible meanings:

- Roundness or redness.
- Something that is created by something else, since an apple is produced by a tree.
- Nourishment—such as mental, emotional, or spiritual nourishment.
- A process, or something that takes time to develop, as an apple does.
- "Seeds" (such as ideas or actions) that can "grow to fruition" and produce desirable results in the future.

In your dream, the apple grew from tiny and green to large, red, and ripe in just a few seconds, so you suspect that the apple may represent a process being completed more quickly than expected. When you think about where in your real life a process went more quickly than expected, you realize that the apple's quick growth represents your financial investment growing more quickly than expected because several of the stocks you chose did very well in a short time. You note this conclusion in your dream journal.

If you still haven't discovered your dream symbol meaning after completing this technique and reading the suggestions in "Search Tips" (p. 42), you can find more in-depth help in "Chapter 1-2: Jumpstarting Your Interpretation" (p. 17).

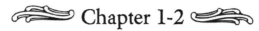 Chapter 1-2 ⤇

Jumpstarting Your Interpretation

In This Chapter:

I n dream symbol analysis you intuitively examine a dream's symbols for clues to what the dream is saying about you and your life. Much like a detective, you're "searching the scene" of the dream for clues, and each dream symbol provides an important clue about dream meaning. And just like fingerprints or DNA at a crime scene, dream symbols tend to convey meaning through specific patterns. Learn those patterns, and your dream interpretation process becomes much easier.

(Note: This chapter is intended to get you started in your dream interpretation process. To learn about these topics in much greater depth, refer to the first book of this series, The Curious Dreamer's Practical Guide to Dream Interpretation.*)*

Recognizing Dream Symbol Meaning

When you're trying to understand the meaning of a dream symbol, what you're really looking for is what that symbol means for you (not for someone else) in its current context in this particular dream (not in someone else's dream or another dream you had ten years ago). I use the term "true meaning" to refer to the accurate translation of what your subconscious mind was portraying in the dream. The true meaning is usually the one that resonates with you as you're considering various possible meanings, the one that rings true according to your intuition, and the one that your subconscious mind recognizes as the original meaning.

Intuition Is Your Dream Translator

Your intuition is your own personal translator of dream meaning. Intuition is key in understanding both the meaning of the overall dream and the meanings of its individual symbols because your intuition is the part of you that recognizes the truth.

Explore Until Your Intuition Says Yes

Rather than working in a linear or logical way (like when you're solving a math problem), your intuition may require you to spend some time mulling over your dream symbol before an intuitive insight comes forward. So try looking at your dream symbol in different ways and considering different meanings until your intuition says, "Aha! That's the one." Keep exploring until you experience a flash of intuitive recognition, a sudden sense that everything within you is in alignment, or a sense of peace and completion. (You'll learn to recognize this intuitive sense as you encounter it more often.)

Tips for Translating Dream Symbolism

Dream symbol meaning is specific to each dreamer, and it can even vary from dream to dream for the same dreamer. As your subconscious mind chooses particular dream symbols to portray particular aspects of your waking life, it may be influenced by many factors and may follow certain patterns. At the same time, all of our subconscious minds seem to use a set of similar approaches to encode meaning into dream symbols. Understanding these personal and general factors (discussed in the next sections) could provide a shortcut to discovering dream symbol meaning.

Dreams Are About You

Because dreams occur within a deep part of yourself, it's not surprising that most of what they convey pertains to yourself and your life.

Dreams Tell About You and Your Life

Dreams very often portray a snapshot of some part of your daily life or something on your mind, presented from the perspective of (and in the language of) your subconscious mind. As you examine each dream, you can often find a parallel between each element in the dream and a certain element of your waking life or mind.

Dreams Show Your Perspective

In most dreams, everything in the dream (all the elements, people, settings, etc.) pertains to you personally. More specifically, most dreams portray your thoughts and feelings about things, rather than portraying the things themselves. Each dream symbol tends to represent your perspective of something from real life, rather than the actual thing. For example, your sister in a dream likely portrays your experience of her (rather than her, herself), your perception of something she said (rather than what she actually said or meant), or your assumption about what she was thinking (rather than her actual thoughts).

Dreams Convey a Distorted Reality

Because dreams portray people and things the way you view or interpret them, you can't rely on a dream for an accurate representation of reality. Every dream has been filtered through the distorting lens of your subconscious mind and often infused with subconscious fears, desires, and imaginings. Therefore, it's unwise to base a decision solely on a dream, which would mean blindly following the whims of your subconscious mind.

Subconscious Influences on Dream Symbolism

When considering what a particular dream symbol means, it may help to imagine what may have led your subconscious mind to chose that particular symbol to portray a certain thing from your real life or mind. Those influences could include the following.

Shared Influences

Many influences are common among all humans, or at least among all humans with a certain shared experience, such as the following ones (on which the symbol descriptions in this book are primarily based):

- Traditional meanings of the symbol.
- Cultural or regional meanings of the symbol.
- Logical meanings of the symbol.
- Parallel meanings of the symbol.
- Meanings based on the context of the symbol in a certain situation.

For example, the traditional meaning of a shamrock is good luck, a crossroads might logically represent a decision, and a heavy physical burden like a boulder could parallel a heavy mental burden such as responsibility in your real life.

Personal Influences

Other influences on dream symbol meaning may be more personal and individual to you, including:

- Your past personal experiences with the symbol.
- Your perceptions and preconceptions about the symbol.
- Things (ideas, people, places, etc.) you associate with the symbol.
- Feelings you associate with the symbol or that it triggers within you.
- Your personality and preferences.
- Your intuitive understanding of the symbol.

For example, you may associate the symbol of bread primarily with your mother because it brings to mind the sandwiches she used to make you (based on your past experience with the symbol), and a brightly colored jacket might represent cheerfulness because that's the feeling the jacket triggers within you.

Contextual Influences

Your inner environment during the dream and the content of the dream itself could also affect the way dream symbols are chosen. Some of these influences include:

- Your current thoughts and feelings at the time of the dream.
- Your mood, memories, or reactions still lingering from experiences earlier in the day.
- The content and context of the particular dream.

For example, if your day's experience was very busy, your subconscious mind might choose a bee to represent busy-ness, whereas if your day was filled with sweet experiences a bee might be chosen to represent "gathering sweet experiences" (because it gathers sweet nectar). If the dream begins its story in a forest setting, your subconscious mind might be more likely to choose a bear than a shark to represent strength.

Follow the Emotion

Your feelings about a dream symbol during the dream can provide a huge clue to meaning, since they are likely the same as your feelings about whatever the symbol represents in your real life. Although whatever the symbol represents in your real life may look different in the dream, the emotion about it often feels the same as in real life. That's one reason emotions are so valuable in dream interpretation: you can trace the emotion from the dream back to real life by considering when you've actually felt that emotion before, perhaps revealing what the symbol represents in your life.

Symbolism Patterns

Dream symbols often mean something beyond the obvious, sometimes far beyond the obvious. However, dream symbolism also sometimes follows particular patterns that can help you decipher their meanings. For example, consider the following patterns that your dream symbol may use to represent something in your life or mind.

Time Frame

A dream symbol can symbolize a particular time frame in your life, or a particular memory or person from that time frame. For example, red sneakers might represent seventh grade, when you wore that kind of shoes. So when exploring your dream symbol, consider which time frame it might point to in your real life.

A symbol can also represent something in the present, such as something that happened earlier in the day and is still on your mind (an overflowing river could represent the coffee you spilled this morning), or even something happening in your body or mind at the time you're dreaming (a hot desert scene could reflect feeling physically overheated because it's too hot in the room).

Sometimes a symbol represents something you expect or imagine might happen in the future—perhaps something that you wish would happen (an airplane might represent a vacation you'd like to take), you fear happening (a boat sinking could represent fear of a project failing), or something your subconscious mind imagined happening as it mocked-up a best-case or worst-case scenario (winning the lottery or your child getting lost).

Hierarchical

Sometimes a dream symbol's meaning is based on the symbol itself, such as a carrot representing something happening secretly (because carrots grow underground). However, sometimes a symbol's meaning is based on a more general category within which the symbol falls (a carrot falls into the more general category of food, which could represent something that nourishes you). And sometimes a symbol represents something more specific based on its details (a carrot with a rotten spot could represent a good situation gone bad).

So, think of the more specific and less specific versions of your dream symbol and what each of those might represent in your real life. To do this, start by considering what the symbol itself might represent. Then consider what a more general idea of it might represent (for example the category within which it falls), and then what a more specific version might represent.

For example, consider a dream in which the Golden Gate Bridge was swaying due to heavy winds. The most general version of the symbol (something that connects things) could represent something very different from the most specific version of the bridge (specifically the Golden Gate Bridge swaying due to heavy winds). Here's how you might think through various possibilities within the hierarchy of meanings, from most general to most specific:

- (Very general) **Something that connects things** could represent communication between two people.
- (General) **A bridge** could represent a transition from one phase to the next in your life because a bridge is a transition from one place to another.
- (More specific) **The Golden Gate Bridge** could represent strong self-support because it's a "self-supporting" bridge.
- (Very specific) **The Golden Gate Bridge swaying due to heavy winds** could represent a challenging situation that's "shaking you up."

Levels of Existence

A dream symbol can represent its literal equal in real life, such as a wedding representing an actual wedding you attended last month. However, a dream symbol often symbolizes something on a different level of existence in your waking life, such as a wedding representing a new beginning in your life or a desire to be in love. Determining which level of existence a dream symbol is portraying in your real life can help you understand its deeper meaning.

We experience life on multiple levels (including physical, emotional, mental, and spiritual levels), and dreams include symbols on all these same levels. Symbols in dreams can be physical (such as objects or people), mental (such as decisions or judgments), emotional (such as fear or anger), and spiritual (such as spiritual experiences). What's tricky is that a dream symbol on one level in a dream doesn't always represent something on the corresponding level in real life. For example, a blue flower (a physical symbol in the dream) might represent something in real life on the physical level (a blue blouse your friend was wearing yesterday), emotional level (sadness), or mental level (your decision to choose an insurance company with "blue" in its name).

Multiple Meanings

A dream symbol can convey more than one meaning simultaneously. Sometimes the subconscious mind cleverly weaves together a dream in which several issues or concerns are "stacked together" in a way where one symbol represents two or more aspects of your waking life. For example, a dream about trying to walk to work with an injured foot could represent your real-life foot problem as well as your difficulty in "moving forward" in your career (since your feet move your body forward physically). So consider whether your symbol could be pointing to more than one aspect of your life or mind.

Consider Common Dream Symbolism First

If there's any such thing as a shortcut to finding dream meaning, this is it. The majority of dreams convey meaning using one of just a few forms of symbolism. So, chances are that your dream symbol represents something in your life or mind in one of the following ways, which you'll begin to recognize as you interpret more dreams. When searching for a symbol's meaning, always consider these most common forms of symbolism first.

Literal Translation

If the dream symbol (person, event, object, action, setting, etc.) exists in your real life, it might represent that actual element of your waking life. For example, your mother who was hugging you might represent a particular time she hugged you, or her affection toward you in general. Consider whether the dream symbol might represent the same thing in your current life, past, or imagined future, and whether your feelings about the dream symbol remind you of feelings you felt about something in your real life (perhaps recently).

Emotions

The emotions you feel regarding the dream symbol are probably the same as the emotions you feel about whatever the symbol represents in your real life. For example, if you feel overwhelmed by a swarm of insects in a dream, the swarm might represent your to-do list that feels overwhelming in real life. (See more about emotions in the "Emotions" symbol category, p. 33.)

Abundance or Lack

A dream symbol can represent something that you feel you have too much of, do too much of, or want less of in your real life. Alternatively, your dream symbol could represent something that you feel you lack, do too little of, or want more of. If your dream contained a pleasant experience (such as relaxing on a beach), your subconscious mind could be pointing to your desire for more relaxation in your life. If your dream was unpleasant (such as someone judging you), your subconscious mind may have been focused on trying to avoid that kind of experience in real life.

Personal Symbolism

A dream symbol may convey meaning that you personally associate with it based on your experiences, feelings, and other influences (as described in "Subconscious Influences on Dream Symbolism," p. 19). For example, one person might associate a baby with vulnerability and someone else might associate it with growth.

A particular dream symbol may bring more than one meaning to mind for you. For example, money might bring to mind how fun it is to spend, but you might also think of money as power or a solution to financial problems. If the first meaning that comes to mind doesn't seem to relate to anything in your real life and doesn't resonate intuitively, explore additional meanings ("TOOL: Caveman Explanation," p. 14, is helpful for this).

Importance

The symbols you tend to notice in a dream are often the most important ones. So a good place to start when exploring your dream is with the symbols that stood out. Symbols may stand out because they're so huge you can't miss them (like a boulder falling on your house) or they could be small details that happen to stand out in your mind (like the chipped rim of a teacup). Sometimes an important symbol is highlighted in the dream with a bright color, illuminated with light, pointed to with an arrow, or emphasized in some other way.

Urgency

If there's a sense of urgency involved in the dream, the dream might represent an urgent matter that you feel needs attention in your real life (or one that you fear or imagine needing attention). For example, a dream about trying to put out a fire at work could point to a real-life problem that arose suddenly at work that you feel requires quick action to avoid catastrophe.

Subject Context

A dream might be about you or it could represent your perception of a friend or a recent situation—even in the media, on TV, or in a movie. For example, in a dream about a girl wearing a cheerful flowered dress, the girl could represent a happier version of yourself or your desire to feel more cheerful. Alternatively, she might represent a friend who was in a happy mood when you saw her yesterday, an upbeat song you just heard, or an optimistic character you saw in a TV show last night.

Time Context

A dream symbol could represent something in your past, present, or imagined future. Look for elements that bring to mind a particular time frame, either in the characteristics of the symbol itself or in the other things associated with it in the dream (people, activities, clothes, places, music, books, etc.). Time-related cues could include things like hair or clothing styles, a person appearing younger or older than their current age in real life, technologies of a different era, or personal cues such as the cowboy boots you wore in at age seven.

Emotional Exaggeration

When a dream portrays a real-life situation that's particularly emotional for the dreamer, sometimes the situation shows up as exaggerated in the dream. In other words, the subconscious mind may amplify the real-life situation, "making a mountain out of a molehill," expressing how strongly you feel about the dream's subject matter. For example, if in real life you saw a baby snake in your yard, and you're very afraid of snakes, the snake might show up in a dream as a huge serpent attacking you. So, consider whether a particular dream symbol could represent a similar but less extreme situation in your waking life, about which you feel strong emotion.

PART II

SYMBOL CATEGORIES

~ Chapter 2-1 ~
How to Use These Symbol Categories

In This Chapter:

About Symbol Categories 29
Working with Symbol Categories 29

A dream symbol category is a group of dream symbols that are similar somehow or that share something in common. This part of the book presents top dream symbol categories along with suggestions for interpreting the symbols in each.

About Symbol Categories

When considering a particular symbol from your dream, its category can help you understand how to interpret the symbol's meaning. Often all the symbols in a particular category provide similar kinds of clues to meaning or can be interpreted using the same approach. For example, all of the dream symbols in the "Animals" category (p. 32) (bear, cat, horse, etc.) can represent something in your life that reminds you of that animal, one of its characteristics, or its action during the dream.

Working with Symbol Categories

For each dream symbol you're exploring, read both the description for its category (in "Chapter 2-2: The Symbol Categories," p. 31) and the description for the symbol itself (in "Chapter 3-2: The Symbols," p. 45). The category description provides tips for translating any symbol in that category, while the symbol description suggests possible meanings for the individual symbol.

A particular symbol might fall into more than one category. For example, red could fall into Colors (as in the color red), Attributes (as in red hair), or Conditions (as in being "red in the face"). So consider the entries for all of the categories that pertain to your symbol based on the symbol's context in the dream.

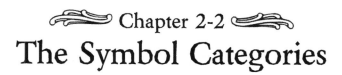

Chapter 2-2

The Symbol Categories

In This Chapter:

Activities

A particular activity or task in a dream can represent something in which you've participated in real life (perhaps something that you've done recently or that you imagine doing). Very often an activity in a dream represents something completely different in real life, but with some similar characteristic. For example, trimming a hedge might represent trimming your beard, and picking apples in an orchard might represent grocery shopping. An activity in a dream is almost never a prediction of the future, so dreaming that you're a guest on a talk show doesn't necessarily mean you're going to be on TV. More often an activity represents a recent real-life activity or a feared, desired, or imagined version a particular activity. (See also the symbol "Activity," p. 48.)

Animals

Dreaming about a particular animal often means that a certain quality of that animal is significant to you right now. Think about what that kind of animal symbolizes to you personally (such as a turtle representing your responsibility for a childhood pet turtle) and the traditional ideas about the animal (for example, a mule is often thought of as stubborn). Notice what the animal was doing in the dream and how it was doing it (for example, a dog digging a hole may represent the idea of needing to "dig" to find what you're looking for). Also pay attention to anything else that stood out about the animal, such its mood, mannerisms, surroundings, or anything unusual about it. (See also the symbol "Animal," p. 54.)

Attributes

A attribute of something often represents something noteworthy or important to you about whatever the thing itself represents in your real life (or at least something your subconscious mind considers noteworthy or important). Whenever a certain attribute stands out, consider both the attribute's meaning and the meaning of the thing displaying that attribute (the person who's tall, the place that's deserted, etc.). Also pay attention to anything that stood out about the attribute (big hair, timid voice, slow swagger, etc.) or any incongruence or inconsistency (such as someone wearing sunglasses at night or your mother appearing younger than she is in real life). The attributes of a dream setting (such as the temperature, weather, level of light, dirty, new, etc.) can also provide clues about what that setting represents in your real life. (See also the specific attribute and the symbol "Attribute," p. 61.)

Body Parts

A part of the body (leg, head, etc.) often represents one of the main functions of that body part, or the symbolic version of that function in your real life. For example, a shoulder might represent comforting someone (as in having "a shoulder to cry on"). A broken leg might represent having trouble moving forward in your life, since your legs literally move you forward when walking. Occasionally, a dream about a particular body part can be triggered by an actual physical sensation (pain, pressure, etc.) in that area while you're sleeping. For example, a headache while you're sleeping might trigger a dream in which an elf is hitting you over the head with a big mallet. (See also the symbol "Body Part," p. 78.)

32

Colors

Colors that stand out in a dream often convey significant meaning. A color can represent a mood, an emotion, or your sense or assumption about the object that displays that color. For instance, a person wearing all black can indicate that your subconscious mind is portraying that person as sad or mourning a loss, or as very formal in their manner. Consider also the hue and brightness of the color. For example, a bright green could convey a different meaning than a drab green or a pastel green. (See also the symbol "Color," p. 103.)

Conditions

The condition of something or someone in a dream can convey important meaning, sometimes just as important as the meaning of the object itself. For example, in a dream about a broken headlight, the condition of the headlight (broken) is the key factor regarding the headlight. If the headlight represents your ability to see the road ahead, a broken headlight could mean that you're feeling unclear about your future somehow. Your brother's condition of laryngitis could represent your sense that he was unable to speak up for himself in a certain situation. (See also the symbol "Condition," p. 104.)

Emotions

An emotion in a dream often represents a similar emotion in your real life. For instance, if you're feeling angry during a dream, you're also likely angry about the real-life situation the dream was portraying.

Someone else's emotion can represent an emotion you saw that person express in the past or that you imagine, expect, or fear from them. For example, a coworker's anger at you might represent your fear of their anger in real life if you were late finishing the work they need.

Someone else's (especially a stranger's) emotion in a dream can also represent your view of "people" or "the world," such as a generous stranger representing your feeling that people are generous in general.

An emotion can also show up when it's been on your mind recently, such as because you've felt it or witnessed it (in person, on TV, etc.).

Another kind of emotion you might experience during a dream is the mood of the dream or its scenes (happy, eerie, boring, etc.). The mood in a dream often parallels your mood regarding the real-life situation being portrayed, which can provide a helpful clue about meaning.

Emotional reactions during a dream can also provide clues to meaning, since your or others' reactions may be the same in the dream as in the real-life situation being portrayed. For example, your surprise in a dream when a cat gave birth to kittens in your kitchen could represent your surprise at your sister dropping off her children last week to babysit on the spur of the moment. (See also the symbol "Feeling," p. 147.)

Events

An event in a dream can represent an actual event in your life, perhaps one that's already happened or perhaps one you're imagining in the future. A series of events in a dream can represent a parallel series of events in your real life, with each dream event including the telltale signs of similar dynamics and feelings as in real life.

Many different types of events can show up in dreams. For example, an event can involve a character taking an action, such as an action you take (walking out your front door representing a new beginning), an action someone else takes (a friend handing you a gift representing an opportunity), or an action another entity takes (the power company sending you an overdue bill notice representing your fear of being late). A dream event can also be an occurrence not initiated by a person or other entity (the wind blowing away your napkin representing an inability to clean up a problem, or a mudslide covering your house representing extreme overwhelm). Other kinds of dream events include a one-time event (such as a wedding representing a party you attended) or a repeating event (such as each wave reaching the shore representing the fresh start of each day). (See also the symbol "Event," p. 140.)

Insects

An insect (or other bug) as a dream symbol can represent something in your real life or mind that you associate with the insect or with one of its characteristics, actions, tendencies, or traditional meanings. Consider what comes to mind when you think of that type of insect (for example, a fly is often considered a nuisance). Notice anything that stood out about the insect or that wasn't as expected, as well as the insect's motivations, actions, and their effects. For example, a fly watching you might represent cautiousness, whereas a fly buzzing around your head might represent a nuisance or something that's "bugging" you. (See also the symbol "Insect," p. 189.)

Objects

An object in a dream often represents a characteristic you associate with that object, something it usually brings to mind, or something that stood out about it in the dream. For example, a watch that kept stopping might represent "stops," delays, or interruptions in your life lately. Alternatively, the significance of an object in a dream might be based on its context, such as where it was placed, how it was used, or what was happening to it. For example, an object that was out of place or in an unusual place could represent something in real life that feels "out of place" or "off" (such as a chair on the ceiling representing your inability to find an opportunity to rest lately). Also keep in mind that a physical object in a dream can represent something tangible (an object, person, location, etc.) or intangible (an emotion, decision, intention, etc.) in real life. (See also the symbol "Object," p. 237.)

People

A person in a dream can represent that actual person, another person, or something the person tends to bring to mind for you. The significance of a person in a dream might not be their identity, but instead what they're doing or how, or their attitude or motivation. For example, if you dream about your boss who is always in a hurry, he might represent himself or the idea of hurrying too much. Also keep in mind that a person can represent a real person you know, a real stranger, an imaginary person, a group, or something intangible such as a characteristic, concept (such as a set of beliefs), activity, time frame, location, or almost anything else. Pay special attention to anything that stood out about the person, including anything unusual or unexpected. (See also the symbols "Person You Know," p. 249, and "Person Unknown," p. 248.)

Places

A place in a dream can represent a real-life place or something you associate with one. A place can also represent something intangible such as a mood, memory, desire, activity, or attitude. For example, your home often represents your life or one aspect of it (home life, relationships, etc.). A graveyard could represent a solemn or eerie mood. A pro-football stadium might represent an actual game you watched or a competitive activity or attitude. Whether or not you recognize a location in a dream, there's a good chance it represents something in your life or on your mind. For more clues to meaning, consider your feelings about the location and consider where or when you've experienced those feelings in real life. (See also the symbol "Location," p. 211.)

Sensory Cues

Sensory cues in dreams can include visuals, sounds, smells, tastes, physical sensations, textures, and other things related to the senses. These cues can simply be part of the dream story (such as the smell of breakfast cooking in a scene that represents your morning routine) or they can convey significant meaning (such as the smell of smoke representing an urgent problem at work). Consider the meaning of the sensory cue, its source, and how it was delivered. For example, if someone was speaking in a garbled way, consider the meanings of "Hearing," "Communication," and "Garbled." Sense-related dream elements can also be triggered by physical triggers during sleep, such as external noises or pain from an awkward sleeping position. (See also the symbols "Vision," p. 332, "Hearing," p. 175, "Smell," p. 291, "Tasting," p. 309, and "Touching," p. 319.)

Time Frames

Time frame can show up in many forms in a dream. The dream may depict a certain time period in your life (third grade, the time you worked for a certain company, etc.). A dream also might use a certain historic era to convey the feeling of a real-life situation (the Victorian era to depict your grandmother's conservative sensibilities). Look for time frame indicators that suggest what period of your life the dream depicts, such as someone's age or a certain era of clothing (your father appearing to be in his 20s representing your early childhood, or bell-bottom jeans representing the years you were in junior high). (See also the symbol "Time Frame," p. 316.)

Words and Numbers

Words, letters, or numbers can appear in many different contexts in dreams. For example, you might experience words that are spoken or written, a street address on a house, or an alphabet letter on a report card. Numbers can also show up in conceptual ways, such as seeing three apples or five horses. Keep in mind that a number may or may not have any significant meaning itself. Often a number's meaning is reflected more in its context, such as trying to solve a math problem representing your effort to solve a problem at work (rather than having to do with the numbers themselves), or reading garbled words representing your difficulty understanding a Shakespeare play in real life. (See also the symbols "Words," p. 344, "Letter (Alphabet)," p. 206, and "Number," p. 236.)

PART III

SYMBOLS

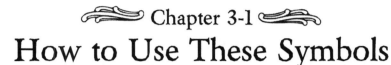

Chapter 3-1

How to Use These Symbols

In This Chapter:

W hen using the symbol descriptions in "Chapter 3-2: The Symbols"
(p. 45), remember that they provide *possible meanings* rather than
definitive answers about your dream symbol's meaning. Use these
descriptions as a springboard for your own interpretation process.

Remember also that you are the ultimate authority on your own
dream. Your subconscious mind already knows your dream's meaning,
and your intuition will recognize that meaning. The hope is that as you
review possible dream symbol meanings, you'll experience an intuitive
flash of recognition when you encounter the one that's true for your
symbol in your particular dream.

Prerequisites

Before working with the symbols in "Chapter 3-2: The Symbols" (p. 45),
it's strongly recommended that you read these previous sections in "Part I:
How to Find Dream Symbol Meaning":

  • The Steps for Interpreting Symbols (p. 7)
  • Consider Common Dream Symbolism First (p. 23)

Working With These Symbols

The following information is very important to apply as you read the symbol descriptions in "Chapter 3-2: The Symbols" (p. 45). These are contexts that apply to every symbol but weren't repeated in each description for the sake of brevity. The descriptions include such wording where it's particularly relevant, but you'll need to always keep these in your mind as you're reading symbol descriptions.

Imagine These Words Before Each Meaning

In your mind, add the following words before each suggested meaning in a symbol description.

"Your Subconscious Mind's Version Of"

A dream symbol very often portrays your subconscious mind's version of whatever the symbol represents in real life (as if your subconscious mind was painting a portrait of it), rather than an accurate representation of the thing. So, insert the words "your subconscious mind's version of" before every suggested symbol meaning. For example, when the description for the "Event" symbol says an event can represent "an actual event in your life," it means it can represent "your subconscious mind's version of an actual event in your life." Your subconscious mind's version can show a view through a different "lens" or "memory filter," coloring things according to your thoughts and feelings about it, perhaps emphasizing the emotional aspects (such as portraying a tiny spider as a huge monster, or a leaky pipe as a flood).

"Your Perception Of"

Each dream symbol portrays your perception of something rather than a straight-on view of the real thing. So, insert the words "your perception of" before every suggested meaning. For example, when the description for the "House" symbol says a house can represent "you or your life," it means it can represent "your perception of you and your life," and when the description for the "Food" symbol says food can represent "nourishment," it means "your perception of nourishment." Your perception can include any personal understandings, assumptions, biases, curiosities, fears, desires, imaginings, or anything else in your consciousness regarding the real-life thing the dream symbol represents.

Imagine These Words After Each Meaning

In your mind, add the following words after each symbol description.

"Consider What Comes to Mind"

Because dream symbol meaning is so personal, each symbol likely represents something that you already associate with it (at least subconsciously). So, in addition to the possible meanings listed in the symbol's description, "consider what comes to mind" when you think of the dream symbol. For example, if you dreamed about a tree, think about the word "tree" and see what shows up in your mind. It might be a specific tree or a memory of one, an event that happened near a tree, or something else. You can also try a technique designed to prompt your subconscious mind to share the meanings it already associates with the symbol, such as "TOOL: Caveman Explanation" (p. 14).

"Or Something Else"

Because the meanings listed for each symbol are merely possibilities to jumpstart your exploration, add the words "or something else" after each dream description you read. Your personal meaning of your symbol could be almost anything, and the options are not limited to the ones listed in this book.

Consider Each Symbol's Focus

A dream symbol can convey symbolism through one or more of the following focuses (or more specifically, "your subconscious mind's version of" "your perception of" the following):

- Something in your real life.
- Something you participated in, observed, or otherwise experienced in the past (saw firsthand, read about, saw on TV, etc.).
- Something perceived, desired, feared, or imagined.
- Something in your past, present, or expected or imagined future.
- Something on the physical, emotional, mental, or spiritual level.
- Something regarding yourself or someone else.

Special Wording in Symbol Descriptions

The following particular words and phrases are used often in the symbol descriptions to convey specific meanings.

"Physical, Emotional, Mental, or Spiritual"

"Physical, emotional, mental, or spiritual" refers to different levels of your personal experience. "Physical" refers to your physical body, physical environment, tactile experiences, and so on. "Emotional" refers to your emotional experiences such as cheerfulness or anger. "Mental" refers to your mental experiences or dynamics such as thoughts, beliefs, judgments, or doubts. Each of these can also refer to activities or any-

41

thing else on each of these levels, such as financial, conversational, or other mode of activity.

"A Feeling or Fear Of"

In "a feeling or fear of" something, "a feeling of" refers to an actual experience you've had in real life and "fear of" refers to a fear within you. (For example, in "a feeling or fear of abandonment," "a feeling of abandonment" means something that happened in real life that you experienced as abandonment, and "a fear of abandonment" means a fear of being abandoned.)

"A Feeling of or Desire For"

In "a feeling of or desire for" something, "a feeling of" refers to an experience you've had in real life and "desire for" refers to a desire within you. (For example, in "a feeling of or desire for safety," "a feeling of safety" means safety you experienced in real life, and "a desire for safety" means wanting to be safe.)

"Perceived"

"Perceived" refers to the way you see or interpret something in real life. (For example, "perceived perfection" would point to something you consider to be perfect according to your definition of perfection, whether or not it would be considered perfect according to anyone else's definitions.)

"God"

"God" refers to the highest power, which you might choose to think of as the holiest of holies, creator, source of pure love, or some other name. As you read, you can substitute the name with which you feel most comfortable, according to your personal preference.

Search Tips

Use the following tips to help locate the symbol you're looking for in "Chapter 3-2: The Symbols" (p. 45).

Symbol Name Guidelines

Symbol names in "Chapter 3-2: The Symbols" (p. 45) tend to follow these guidelines, so make sure you're searching for these forms of the words:

- Verbs are usually listed in **present tense ending in "-ing"** ("eating" instead of "eat" or "ate" or "eaten").
- Nouns are usually listed in **singular form** ("foot" instead of "feet").

Broad Symbols

Some symbols are "umbrella terms," each of which covers a broad group of specific symbols that all convey meaning in a similar way. For example, the "Feeling" symbol (p. 147) covers all the different kinds of feelings (happy, angry, sad, etc.) because they're all interpreted in a similar way. Likewise, the "Agreement" symbol (p. 50) covers all forms of agreements (contract, promise, vow, etc.). Examples of these "broad symbols" include:

Agreement
Activity
Animal
Attribute
Authority Figure
Body Part
Color
Condition
Cooking Vessel
Event
Feeling
Insect
Limit or Boundary
Person Unknown
Person You Know
Plant
Object
Relative
Storage
Vehicle
Water, Body of

If You Can't Find Your Symbol

If you can't find a particular symbol, first check " Part IV: Symbol Index" (p. 349) and then try searching for the following instead:

- Another form of the word (such as "falling" instead of "fell").
- Synonyms of the symbol (such as "road" instead of "street").
- Different wording to describe the symbol (such as "last minute" instead of "waiting too long").
- A more general version of the symbol (such as "problem" instead of "flat tire").

- A more specific version of the symbol (such as "tie" instead of "neckwear").
- A related symbol, and then look through its "*See also*" symbols to find your symbol.

If your symbol isn't listed, revisit "If Your Symbol Is Not Listed" (p. 14) for other options to explore its meaning.

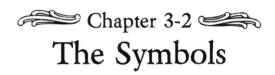

Chapter 3-2
The Symbols

Abandonment

An issue of trust, integrity, support, or self-support. A feeling or fear of abandonment on some level in your life, including physical (such as your best friend relocating to another state), emotional (such as your partner withdrawing emotional support), mental (such as friends refusing to talk to you), spiritual (such as feeling that God has abandoned you), financial (your parents refusing to help you financially), or otherwise. The idea of being let down, being left behind, or losing someone or something in real life. Abandoning yourself somehow (such as not standing up for yourself). **You abandoning someone** can represent: a feeling or fear of letting someone down, breaking a promise, or neglecting a responsibility to that person; an emotional reaction to that person or their behavior; the idea of giving up on someone; a desire to get away from someone or something; abandoning yourself. *See also:* Rejection; Betrayed, Being; Leaving a Person; Breaking Up; Left, Being; Agreement, Breaking an; Helpless

Abduction

An issue of power, control, personal boundaries, authority, or abuse of authority. **Abducting someone** can represent: trying to force your will or motives onto another person; attempting to victimize, manipulate, or take power away from another person. **Being abducted** can represent: a feeling or fear of someone forcing their will on you, abusing their authority, or (especially if the person is a friend or loved one) removing you from your comfort zone; a fear of losing control or feeling helpless somehow in your life. *See also:* Hostage; Missing Person; Taking From; Stealing

Above

Feeling or being above something or someone, or imagining what that would be like. Considering yourself "too good for" involvement with a certain activity or person. Believing that you're an exception or you're not subject to general rules (such as feeling "above the law"). Feeling more advanced or evolved than others. Also consider the meaning of what's below the object that's "above" in the dream. *See also:* Climbing; High; Under; Top

Abscess

Something that "festers" within you (such as a grudge, lingering judgment, or long-term blame of others). Getting rid of unwanted or undesirable things, or detoxing or cleansing in some aspect of your life (such as decluttering your schedule). An attempt at damage control or containment. A nuisance or situation that slowly builds before you're finally forced to deal with it. *See also:* Infection; Acne; Eruption; Skin

Absorbing

Dealing with, finding a solution for, or making something go away. Assimilating or taking into your own circle, space, life, or area of responsibility (as in taking on someone else's responsibilities or letting someone join your group). Receiving or using (as in absorbing information, ideas, or nourishment). Making disappear (as in "cleaning up" a problem). *See also:* Towel; Eating; Cleaning; Dry Up

Abuse

A feeling or fear of (physical, emotional, or mental) abuse, manipulation, someone trying to gain power over you, someone taking advantage of you, or other ill will. Something in your past that was (or felt) abusive. Perceiving someone in your life as hurtful or disrespectful. *See also:* Tormented; Attacked, Being; Attacking; Judgment or Disapproval; Hurt, Being; Weird

Abyss

A huge challenge, obstacle, or "unknown" in your life. A fear. Infinity or oblivion. Something unfathomable or too "deep" to understand. Feelings of overwhelm. Depth of feelings, beliefs, etc. *See also:* Canal; Valley

Accelerator

An accelerator or gas pedal (or something else that feeds fuel to an engine) can represent: Your ability to move forward and make progress in life. The idea of making quicker progress toward a goal. A desire to escape a situation more quickly. **An accelerator that's not working** can represent a perceived obstacle or a lack of empowerment, motivation, or energy. **An accelerator stuck in the "full-on" position** can represent feeling out of control or not able to slow down in some aspect of your life. *See also:* Fuel; Feeding; Fast; Fire; Driving; Starting an Engine; Vehicle; Propeller

Accent

Someone speaking with an accent can represent: The idea of that person (or whatever they represent) seeming foreign or different from you (or from others) in some way. A characteristic you attribute to that person that reminds you of the culture or area associated with the accent (such as a Swedish accent representing a talent at creative design, if that's what you associate with Sweden). *See also:* Language

Accident

Being in an accident (such as in a car or airplane) can represent feeling or fearing: a surprise, a threat, something catastrophic that's out of your control, or things not going your way or according to your schedule. **Being hit by a vehicle** can represent: a wake-up call about something you need to be aware of or change in your life; the idea of a sudden challenge in real life, such as a feared, expected, or imagined change; feeling taken by surprise or blindsided by something. *See also:* Problem; Injured; Hurt, Being; Disaster; Driving; Rear Ended; Failure; Breaking; Destroying

Accumulating

Accumulating, saving, or stocking up on things can represent an actual, desired, or feared: Situation of having plenty or too much of something (such as money, possessions, or love). Shortage of something, or a desire to avoid or compensate for one. Preparedness (or lack of it) for the future. Procrastination or postponing, as in "letting things stack up" while delaying action. Letting things pile up emotionally (such as grudges, blame, or judgments) by not working through them. Hoarding or keeping things for yourself (such as money) or to yourself (such as secrets). *See also:* Increasing; Many; Group; Storage; Shelf; Container; Finances; Money

Ache

A physical ache in a dream might point to an actual imbalance in the body, or it might represent: Physical, emotional, or mental pain, or a person or situation triggering pain within you. A yearning or desire for something. **An ache in a specific area of your body** could represent feeling challenged in whatever area the body part represents (such as a back ache representing feeling tired having to stand up for yourself in a certain situation). *See also:* Pain; Hurt, Being; Injured; Headache

Acne

Putting up with nuisances. Letting things "get under your skin" and bother you (but perhaps not doing anything about them). Repressed anger. The feeling or fear that a situation in your life is "coming to a head" (that something will soon demand your attention or become a crisis you must deal with). A physical, emotional, or mental reaction to something (such as to a substance, event, or situation). *See also:* Infection; Eruption; Rash; Abscess; Skin; Immune System

Activity

A particular activity or task can represent: That actual activity in your life, or your thoughts and feelings about it. A completely different activity, but with a similar characteristic (such as sitting in a class representing sitting in a meeting at work yesterday). A fear or hope of participating in something similar in real life, or your subconscious mind exploring what it would be like. *See also:* Working; Phase or Process; Task; Event; Activities (the category)

Address

A street address, house number, ZIP code, or other address can represent: A specific location you associate with that address. A specific place that's on your mind (whether or not it has that address). The address number or its individual digits could also have significance (such as representing a friend who has those digits in her phone number). *See also:* House; Location

Admitting

Someone admitting or confessing something can represent: A desire to know the truth regarding that person or a related situation. Suspecting that the person may not be what they seem or may not be telling the truth in real life. A desire for that person to be honest (or a fear that they will be). A desire for peace or harmony with that person, or for everything to be out in the open between the two of you. Wanting or needing to admit something to someone (or to yourself). The idea of honesty being on your mind right now for some reason. *See also:* Confronted, Being; Confronting; Denying; Blaming; Blamed, Being; Confiding

Adoption

Adopting a child or pet can represent: Responsibility, or the desire or intention to take responsibility for or "take on" whatever is represented by whomever is being adopted. Feelings of nurturing, or the desire to love, nurture, care for, or support someone else. **Being adopted (when**

you weren't in real life) can represent someone who has taken responsibility for you in real life (or a desire for that); feeling dissimilar from (such as in beliefs or attitude) one or both of your parents; feeling love for or loved by a parent-like figure. *See also:* Mother; Father; Family

Adultery

Your partner committing adultery can represent: Feeling insecure about your ability to hold your partner's interest. A feeling or fear of betrayal (such as by your partner, a friend, God, or yourself). Jealousy about a loved one spending time on something other than you (such as work or a hobby). *See also:* Cheating; Betraying; Betrayed, Being

Adventure

A feeling of excitement, interest, or involvement in your life (or a desire for more of such). A past event that felt like an adventure. An adventurous, exploratory, or curious attitude toward life or toward a certain aspect of it. *See also:* Traveling; Trip or Vacation

Advice or Opinion

Giving advice or an opinion can represent a desire to help, express yourself, or control another person by getting them to agree with you or do things your way. **Asking someone for advice** can represent: feeling confused or not sure of yourself; a desire for help or support; a desire to connect with the person you're asking for advice (or with whatever they represent). **Receiving unwanted advice** can represent: a feeling or fear of someone doing that in real life (or doing it too much or too forcefully); a feeling or fear of disapproval, intrusion, or interference. *See also:* Therapist; Judgment or Disapproval; Right or Wrong; Approval; Attacked, Being; Hurt, Being

After

One event that happens after another event often represents a similar order of events in real life, so look for a parallel series of events, thoughts, decisions, feelings, or other things in your past (especially your recent past). **The order of people or things** can represent real or perceived priority, importance, ranking, or good will (as in one person standing behind another in a queue, or letting someone else proceed through a doorway first). *See also:* Before; Time Passing; Chasing; Following a Procedure; Future; Following a Path; Result; Following (Trailing Behind)

Afternoon

The time frame when the event represented in the dream took place in real life. Productivity. Rest or relaxation (as in an afternoon nap). Sunshine or bright light. Also consider what afternoons mean to you personally, such as how you usually feel and what you do then. *See also:* Time of Day; Sun

Age

Your age in a dream, if different than your current age, can represent a specific time frame depicted (or imagined) in the dream. **Lying about your age** might represent: a wish to be older or younger (or to at least appear that way); a judgment against yourself or your age; a concern about others' opinions. **The age of another person** may provide clues to whom or what they represent in your real life. For example, if you dream about someone who's 95, consider who you know who's that age (or whom you think of as elderly). If the person is someone you know and their age in the dream is different than their real age, this might indicate that you think of them as younger ("young at heart" or immature) or older (more mature) than their actual age implies. *See also:* Aging; Time Frame; Baby; Child; Old Person

Aging

Aging or maturing during a dream can represent: Moving forward through time or within a process. The passage of time in your life, whether or not it's related to aging. Learning, growing, or maturing personally. Actual aging, or issues or concerns about it. *See also:* Age; Time Passing; Bigger, Getting; Old Person

Agreement

A commitment, promise, contract, vow, or other form of agreement can represent a real or desired: Commitment, or feeling committed toward something or someone. Specific agreement in your life, or a feeling of agreeability. Peace. Solution to a problem or discord. Trustworthiness, or questioning whether someone is trustworthy. *See also:* Agreement, Breaking an; Decision, Someone Else's; Decision, Your; Joining; Secret; Engagement; Trust; Negotiating

Agreement, Breaking an

Someone breaking a commitment, agreement, or promise can represent feeling or fearing: Someone being dishonest in real life. Breaking a promise to yourself. God or "life" breaking a promise or not "delivering"

50

the way you expect or want. *See also:* Betrayed, Being; Agreement; Trust; Decision, Someone Else's; Decision, Your; Negotiating

Air

Breathing or sustenance. Survival (physical, emotional, mental, or otherwise). Life energy. Lightness or airiness. Fluid motion, flexibility, or adaptability. **Seeing only air where you expected something else** could represent nothingness, emptiness, lack, or surprise somewhere in your life (or a fear of such). *See also:* Wind; High; Sky; Breathing; Bubble; Balloon

Airplane

An actual or imagined airplane, such as one you've flown on recently, expect to fly on, or heard about on the news. A shared experience, such as an event or life experience you had in common with a group of people in which you were "all in the same boat." For example, a sports team on an airplane that's experiencing turbulence might represent the challenging meeting your project team had yesterday. *See also:* Vehicle; Flying; Traveling; Airport; Helicopter; Rocket

Airport

The beginning or end of a process, phase, or journey in your life. A past or imagined trip. The idea of trying to "get somewhere" in life, make progress, get ahead, or solve a problem. A real-life public place. A group or a process you participated in with other people. A desire to get away, take a break, or escape from something. A desire to go somewhere specific. For more clues, consider the events at the airport and your feelings about them. *See also:* Station; Traveling; Airplane

Alarm Clock

A "wake-up call" about something, or an indicator that a certain issue or situation in your life needs your attention. The end or beginning of a process (since an alarm clock ends your sleep and begins your waking time). Something or someone that interrupted a process in your life (or that tends to do so). **The alarm clock not going off** can represent: fear of neglecting a responsibility and facing the consequences; the importance you place on a certain upcoming event; not trusting others to alert you when something is wrong; a feeling or fear of missing out on something. *See also:* Waking Up; Morning; Clock; Time; Late; Missing an Event

Albino

Something or someone you see as different than others somehow. A rarity or exception somewhere in your life. A perceived lack of personality, vigor, or some other characteristic (represented by the physical attribute of paleness). *See also:* Bleach; White; Person You Know; Person Unknown

Alcohol

Drinking an alcoholic beverage can represent: Wanting to escape, change your reality, feel more relaxed or more interactive, go along with the crowd, or have more fun or excitement (perhaps to the detriment of yourself or your integrity). A different form of addiction (such as to another substance, activity, habit, or way of thinking). For more clues, consider your feelings before and while you were drinking in the dream. *See also:* Drunk; Drug; Bar or Night Club

Alert

Dreaming that you are (or someone is) alert, awake, or conscious could represent awareness, paying attention, mental focus, or a thought process (or perhaps your belief that you or someone else needs more of such). **Receiving an alert or notification** (such as on your phone) can represent communication, news, a change, or something that needs your attention (or a desire for or fear of such). *See also:* Waking Up; Alive or Exists; Communication; Text; Email; Voicemail; Phone

Alien

The idea of aliens. A stranger or person you don't know. A visitor from an area of the world other than where you live. Something in your life that seems alien, strange, or new. The unknown. A person or group you don't know or don't understand, or whom you perceive as thinking or living differently than you. A fear or curiosity about someone or something. **An alien coming after you** can indicate that you were having a Toxic Dream (p. 320), or it could represent a feeling or fear of a (physical, emotional, or mental) threat in your real life. *See also:* Person Unknown; UFO; Space, Outer; Weird

Alive or Exists

You or someone else existing or being alive can represent: Perseverance. Reliability. A purpose or activity. Recognizing the life-force, spirit, or soul within that person. The person being on your mind right now for some reason. **Dreaming that a deceased loved one is alive** can mean they're on your mind, perhaps because you miss them or feel that you have unfinished business with them. *See also:* Life; Light (Spiritual); Moving Around; Life Force; Alert; Surviving

Allergy

A defense mechanism, or an overactive defense mechanism. Vigilance. A desire or tendency to distance yourself in real life from some person, situation, or experience. *See also:* Protecting; Protected, Being; Inflammation; Breathing; Itch; Indigestion; Fight

Alley

An indirect, secret, or out-of-the-way route, either literally or figuratively (as in a hidden course of action). An alternative or unusual way to access something or someone. A shortcut. A tangent, or going off-course somehow. **A dark or scary alley** could represent a feeling or fear of danger or the unknown. *See also:* Passageway; Road

Alligator

Primal. Stealth, or making oneself less than obvious. Direct or blunt. Quick action or haste. Monstrous, or having the ability to hurt someone without regret or compassion. Dreaming of this animal can represent too much or not enough of one of those qualities, or someone or something you associate with the quality or animal. Consider also the animal's actions, context, and your feelings about it. *See also:* Animal; Crocodile

Almost

The idea of "almost" or "not quite" can represent: A feeling of falling short (as in feeling not quite good enough, qualified enough, or valued enough). A near miss (such as almost driving off the road), which could represent a course correction in your life. Feeling you're ready for something (such as ready to act like an adult). Consider also the meaning of whatever or whoever was "almost." *See also:* Missing an Event; Inferior; Second Place; Failure

Altering

Someone altering or changing something can represent: Change in real life, or a desire for it. An unmet need or desire, or an attempt to fulfill one. Adaptability or resourcefulness. **Something that is altering or changing unpredictably** could represent a surprise, a change in plans, or a lack of reliability or predictability. *See also:* Changing; Variety; Repeating; Starting Over

53

Ambulance

A feeling or fear of crisis or emergency. A source of help. Someone or something coming to the rescue, or a desire for that. A person whom you feel tends to rescue others of to be codependent. *See also:* Help, Calling for; Rescuing; Rescued, Being; Paramedic; Firefighting; Emergency Room

Amnesia

A feeling or fear of losing whatever you lost in the dream due to amnesia, such as yourself or your identity. Escaping from your life or something in it, such as responsibilities or challenges. Forgetting or escaping something in your past. *See also:* Forgetting

Amusement Park

A particular place or environment (perhaps one you've visited lately, like a vacation destination). A real-life environment with a lot going on. Your view of your current life that includes many activities, tasks, or opportunities. Fun, adventure, or variety (or a desire for more of such). Consider the context and events there, and your feelings about them. *See also:* Ride; Merry-Go-Round; Ferris Wheel; Zoo; Festival or Carnival

Anchor

Something or someone you consider a source of security, steadiness, or support. Something or someone you perceive as a source of burden, delay, or limitation. A feeling or fear of being hindered in a process. Getting in your own way or holding yourself back. *See also:* Boat; Heavy; Interfering; Slow; Dock

Angel

An angel or other spiritual helper can represent the idea of receiving guidance, support, or comfort (whether from a human or a spiritual source). Perhaps you'd like help or you feel helpless somehow, or perhaps you're remembering a time when you received help in the past. *See also:* Paranormal; Religious Figure; Light (Spiritual); Messenger; God; Mythological Character

Animal

A particular quality of that animal. Something or someone you (at least subconsciously) associate with that type of animal in general. Consider also the animal's characteristics, actions, and what stood out about it during the dream. For example, a cold and slimy frog might represent someone you think of as "cold and slimy." If frogs remind you of Prince

Charming in disguise, a frog could represent someone you consider a "hidden gem." A frog making a big jump could represent the idea of quick progress in your life. See also the specific animal. *See also:* Baby; Animal Noise; Insect; Animals (the category)

Animal Noise

A noise an animal makes (such as a dog bark or a rooster crow) can represent: A traditional or cultural meaning of that sound or that animal, such as a rooster crow representing dawn. The animal that makes that sound, or one of its characteristics. The situation or feeling associated with the particular sound, such as a dog's whimper representing sadness or an unmet need. A personal experience you associate with that animal or its sound (such as a sheep's "baa" representing your recent trip to Scotland). *See also:* Communication; Crying; Noise; Animal

Animation

Animation, anime, or a cartoon format can represent: The idea of something that doesn't seem real or that you're not taking seriously. Your own creativity, active imagination, or desire to be more creative. An aspect of a dream in which the message is the point, rather than how the message is portrayed. *See also:* Cartoon; Alive or Exists; Moving Around

Ankle

Your ability to move forward and make progress in life. Your ability to adapt or "take things in stride" as you go along. Something that connects things together (since the ankle connects the foot to the leg). **An injured ankle** can represent: feeling hindered in one of the areas just mentioned; feeling a need to slow down for your own well-being. *See also:* Leg; Foot

Ant

Industriousness, work, or working with others through teamwork. Discipline. Society or social organization. Playing by the rules for the benefit of the greater good. Altruism, or otherwise sacrificing your own needs for the benefit of others. Dreaming of this insect can represent too much or not enough of one of those qualities, or someone or something you associate with the quality. Consider also the insect's actions, context, and your feelings about it. *See also:* Insect

Antelope

Speed in moving ahead or making progress. Quickness (such as quick to react, judge, etc.). Fear or anxiety. Watchfulness or vigilance. Gracefulness. Dreaming of this animal can represent too much or not enough of one of those qualities, or someone or something you associate with the quality or animal. Consider also the animal's actions, context, and your feelings about it. *See also:* Animal

Antique

The past. Age, or the idea of aging. Endurance. Sentimentality or reminiscing. For more clues, consider the type of item, its context and owner, the era from which it originated, and your feelings about the item. *See also:* Museum; Aging; Past; Time Frame

Anus

Self-control or regulation (such as monitoring or controlling your own behavior). Guilt. Ability or inability to release old or toxic issues (such as judgments, grudges, or outdated beliefs). *See also:* Buttocks; Digestion; Feces

Apocalypse

The end of a phase in your life or the world, perhaps which you feel completely changes everything or changes the rules (such as losing your job, or a major change in government). A feeling or fear of overwhelm, loss of control, chaos, or destruction, especially as a result of external circumstances. A real or imagined loss of control by an established authority (such as government, military, police, etc.). A possible indicator of a Toxic Dream (p. 320). Consider also the event that caused the apocalypse. *See also:* Disaster; Ending

Apology

Regret or remorse. A desire for peace, harmony, or reconciliation. Self-righteousness. **Making an apology** can represent a guilty feeling; a sense that you owe someone an apology; a real-life apology you've made or you're thinking about. **Someone else apologizing to you** can represent: an apology you've received in real life or you'd like to receive; your belief that someone owes you an apology; perceiving or imagining that someone is feeling guilty. *See also:* Feeling; Forgiving; Blamed, Being; Blaming; Confronting; Confronted, Being; Denying

Applause

Approval, recognition, validation, acceptance, or appreciation somewhere in your life (or a desire for such). An indication of enjoyment or being entertained. *See also:* Audience; Performing; Theater; Standing Up; Bowing; Love

Apple

Wholeness, or perfection in wholeness. A characteristic of the apple, such as the color red or its ripeness. The result of a process, or something that takes time to develop. Temptation. A location, season, or something else you associate with apples. *See also:* Fruit; Food

Appliance

A tool, approach, method, or source of assistance that helps you accomplish something more easily or quickly. See also the specific type of appliance. *See also:* Tool; Machine or Robot; Furniture; Electric

Appointment

A commitment or promise. A real or imagined planned event, such as an appointment, meeting, or party. An issue in your real life regarding scheduling or activities. *See also:* Calendar; Dates on a Calendar; Visiting; Interview; Meeting; Schedule

Approval

Approval you've experienced in real life. A desire for or expectation of approval. Experiencing or fearing disapproval somehow in real life. *See also:* Liking; Decision, Someone Else's; Decision, Your; Good; Advice or Opinion

Aquarium

A self-contained world that's separate from reality. Feeling like you're "living in a vacuum," artificial environment, or a situation that feels like a mock-up rather than reality. Forcing physical or mental imprisonment or limitations upon someone. A feeling or fear of hopelessness or being unable to change your situation. Creating a contrived situation (such as an artificial circumstance or a context that's different than where the situation would usually occur). **Keeping living beings in an aquarium** can represent observation; security; providing a healthy or safe environment; limiting or manipulating others for your own entertainment or motives, or "playing God." *See also:* Pool; Fish; Water, Body of

Arcade

An area with many different games can represent: A real-life situation with a variety of activities or choices (such as all the different hobbies you pursue, or the choices of activities at a resort you visited recently). A real-life setting with many different activities. A situation that involves many different challenges, such as your multiple roles, responsibilities, commitments, and activities. *See also:* Game; Video Game; Shopping Center

Arena or Auditorium

The idea of lots of attention being focused on one thing or in one direction (such as on a person, event, or story). Demand, or the idea of "popular demand." Performing or being seen (or a desire for such). A particular real-life venue (such as an auditorium, movie theater, a concert, a room where you watch TV, or a classroom). *See also:* Stage or Screen; Theater; Audience; Show or Movie; Music

Arguing

Arguing with someone can represent: Emotion. Disagreement. Feeling the need to express something to that person (possibly something that they're not willing to hear in real life). A desire to engage or connect with that person. Your own inner conflict. An effort to understand opposing arguments or points of view. *See also:* Fight; Negotiating; Judgment or Disapproval; Violence

Arm

Effectiveness in life. Accomplishing or arranging things, or the ability to do so. Embracing or accepting. The ability to hold onto, retain, or keep. **Not being able to use your arms or having no arms** might represent a feeling or fear of being helpless or ineffective somehow in your life. *See also:* Hand; Wrist; Cuddle; Hug; Holding a Person; Branch

Armadillo

Self-protection. Indifference to your environment. Being impervious to or unaffected by outside events (such as changes or others' actions or opinions). Dreaming of this animal can represent too much or not enough of one of those qualities, or someone or something you associate with the quality or animal. Consider also the animal's actions, context, and your feelings about it. *See also:* Animal

Armor or Shield

A feeling or fear of a threat, discomfort, embarrassment, or other unpleasantness. A desire for protection in your life somehow. Protecting yourself from outside influences, opinions, criticism, or judgments, perhaps through physical, emotional, or mental distancing. An antagonistic attitude, a fighting mentality, or a mood of hostility. A desire to avoid being affected by others, the world, or a specific influence. Isolation. Guarding a hidden identity. A characteristic you associate with a character or type of character who wears armor (such as a knight or warrior).

Consider also the meaning of the part of the body that the armor or shield is protecting. *See also:* Protected, Being; Helmet; Cover; Protecting; Soldier; Knight

Armpit

Something in your life (or something about yourself) you consider undesirable or unwanted, or you'd like to avoid or hide. Stress, or the way you show stress. *See also:* Smell; Deodorant; Body Part

Arriving

Arriving at a destination can represent: Meeting a goal, or the desire to do so. Feeling successful, or wanting success in a particular aspect of your life. An ending. Completing a process, project, journey, or something else in your life. *See also:* Visiting; Succeeding

Arrow

Direction. Focus or attention. A focal point of emotion, intention, or action. **Shooting an arrow** can represent having a goal or focus, or making progress toward a goal. **Shooting an arrow at someone** can represent ill will, anger, or an attempt to victimize or take power away from someone. **An arrow symbol or pointer** could indicate something in the dream that's important, or it could represent a desire for help with direction, problem solving, or next steps in some area of your life. *See also:* Sharp; Symbol; Turning; Path

Arthritis

Dreaming that you have arthritis when you don't in real life can represent: Feeling less adaptable, responsive, or flexible somehow in your life (physically, emotionally, or mentally). The idea of self-sabotage or holding yourself back from progress or success. Feeling that you're being too hard on yourself mentally (judging yourself) or physically (expecting too much of your body). Feeling old, tired, or weak right now. *See also:* Joint; Pain; Aging; Age; Illness

Artwork

The person, place, or thing depicted in the artwork, or the idea of attention being focused on the featured subject. Feeling distanced from what's represented in the artwork, perhaps a feeling that it's unattainable (since art is a representation rather than reality). An opinion, belief, or other expression (as expressed by the artist). Creativity. For more clues to meaning, consider the subject and context of the piece, and how you felt about it. **Creating art** can represent: expression, creativity, communication, freedom, releasing inhibitions (or the need for more of such); extra focus on or thought about the person or topic portrayed in the art; feeling particularly creative during the dream state. *See also:* Photo; Painting; Statue; Shaping; Performing; Creativity

Ashes

The end of a phase or cycle. The result or by-product of a process. The results of destruction. **Someone's cremated ashes** might represent that person, something you associate with that person, or an ending in a phase of their life. *See also:* Fire; Destroying; Cigarette; Fireplace; Smoke; Dirt

Asleep

Dreaming that you're asleep may mean that you're extra tired or sleeping very deeply. Dreaming that you're asleep and can't make yourself wake up can be an indication of a Toxic Dream (p. 320). *See also:* Resting; Lying Down; Waking Up

Astrology

Astrology, horoscopes, numerology, or similar systems can represent: A desire to explain or predict the unknown. A desire to characterize or figure out a person, relationship, or event. A wish to better understand yourself or your life. Feeling like you could use some assistance in decision making. **An astrological sign (such as Pisces or Scorpio)** can represent something you associate with that sign (such as a specific person, quality or personality characteristic, or time of year). *See also:* Paranormal; Sign

Astronaut

The idea of exploring (such as new places, situations, opportunities, etc.). Curiosity, a desire, or a need for adventure or fun. *See also:* Space, Outer; Rocket; Flying; Adventure

Attached

Something attached to something else could represent: A feeling that the two belong together, are involved with each other, or are part of each other in some way. Neediness. Companionship, or a desire for it. *See also:* Joining; Joining Together; Touching; Next To

Attacked, Being

Being attacked, beaten, or otherwise harmed can represent: A feeling or fear of persecution, hostility, aggression, criticism, or other hurtful expression by someone else. A situation in which you feel or fear your boundaries being invaded or your integrity being compromised by someone else. *See also:* Injured; Killed, Being; Invaded, Being; Attacking; Torment-ed; Abuse; Violence; Fight; Terrorism; Shot, Being; Weapon; Knife; Criminal; Soldier; Enemy; Bully; Helpless; Surprise

Attacking

If you dream that you're attacking someone (physically, emotionally, or mentally), consider your feelings during the dream: If you're attacking because you're angry at the person, you may be angry at them or some-thing associated with them in real life. If you're attacking to defend your-self, you may feel threatened in real life by that person's criticism, hostili-ty, ambition, etc. *See also:* Killing; Abuse; Enemy; Criminal; Crime; Violence; Bully; Invading; Fight; Terrorism; Weapon; Injured; Knife; Pushing; Bitten; Surprise; Attacked, Being

Attorney

Taking sides. Seeing things in a one-sided way, as in "right or wrong" or "black or white." Argument or debate. Defense or prosecution, or pro-tagonism or antagonism. Unconditional or "blind" support, such as for a person, cause, or belief. Support given in return for something (such as money, reciprocal support, or affection). *See also:* Justice; Court; Trial; Judge; Blaming; Blamed, Being; Arguing

Attractive

Considering something or someone to be attractive can represent a de-sire for whatever that thing or person represents to you. Be careful, be-cause you might not want that actual thing or person, but rather the ex-perience or feeling you think you'd have with them. Consider also the meaning of the person or object itself, and see also the specific attribute you find attractive. *See also:* Beauty; Wanting; Crush, Having a; Ro-mance; Expensive

Attribute

An attribute or characteristic of someone or something can represent: Your perception of an aspect of yourself (such as a powerful magnifying glass representing your "powerful" eye for detail). Your perception of a certain aspect of another person, group, activity, experience, etc. (such as energetic puppies representing the boisterous activity in your child's pre-school class). Consider also the details and context of the attribute. For example, if you dream about a dog, consider his color, demeanor, what he was doing and how, whether his tail was wagging, how healthy he looked, etc. A defensive dog could represent something completely dif-ferent than a friendly dog. **An attribute that stands out** can represent an amplified version of your feelings or impression of whatever the thing with the attribute represents in your life, or something you feel is important to pay attention to. **An attribute that seems unusual or out of place** can represent something or someone that seems unusual, "off," or out of place in your life. *See also:* Attributes (the category)

Audience

Observation, or being observed. Focus or attention. A group activity. **Being in front of an audience** can represent: a feeling of self-consciousness; being observed or focused on by others (or a desire for or fear of that); a heightened concern about others' opinions, or a need for others' approval. **Being a member of an audience** can represent the idea of watching other people live their lives; feeling like a passive observer rather than a participant in life; viewing your life (or some aspect of it) from an objective or unbiased perspective. *See also:* Theater; Crowd; TV, Being On; Show or Movie; Talk Show; Performing; Audition; Applause

Audition

An actual, expected, or imagined audition (or something similar, like a job interview). An application process (such as for a job, university, etc.). The idea of participating in a competition. Trying to make a certain impression on others. A feeling or fear of being tested. Feeling evaluated, judged, or "put on the spot" by others. Wanting approval from others. *See also:* Audience; Performing; Dancing; Singing; Interview

Aunt

A real-life aunt. Someone who reminds you of an aunt (such as older, wiser, kind, protective, or trustworthy). Consider what comes to mind when you think of an aunt or the particular aunt in your dream. *See also:* Family; Person You Know

Authority Figure

An authority figure can represent someone or something in your real life whom you allow to have power over you somehow, or to whose opinions you listen. **Being an authority figure when you're not in real life** can mean that you're discovering your personal power, or you'd like to feel more empowered, respected, or needed. See also the specific kind of authority figure. *See also:* Manager; Leader; Rule or Law; Religious Figure; Demanding; Superior; Obeying

Autumn

Maturity of a person, project, relationship, or anything that goes through a life cycle. The "winding down" of a phase or cycle. The beginning of a learning process, a new job, a new activity or project, or something else (since autumn is often a time of new beginnings, such as the school year). Wistfulness, reminiscing, or inner reflection. Consider also the events in the dream and what autumn means to you personally. *See also:* Time of Year; Time Frame; Weather

Avalanche

A real, imagined, or feared situation that feels chaotic or out of control, that is worsening or involves escalation of a problem, that seems overwhelming, that you feel you need to escape, or that you feel threatens you with negative physical, emotional, or mental consequences. *See also:* Flood; Disaster; Snow; Cover; Trapped; Escaping; Descending

Avoiding

Trying to avoid something undesirable or unpleasant can represent avoiding (or wanting to avoid) something in real life. For example, avoiding a friend could represent anger at them or fear of them asking you for something you don't want to give. Consider also the meaning of whatever you're avoiding in the dream. **Avoiding someone with ill intent toward you** could represent a feeling or fear of being manipulated, taken advantage of, or threatened (physically, emotionally, or mentally). **Someone trying to avoid you** may represent a feeling or fear of that person avoiding or abandoning you in real life (for more clues, consider why they're avoiding you in the dream). *See also:* Hiding; Escaping; Warning

Award

Validation, recognition, or fame (or a desire for such). Receiving an award can represent feeling celebrated, recognized for your talents, rewarded for your hard work, or other validation. **Attending an awards ceremony** and mingling with the celebrities can represent a desire to associate with people you perceive as important, elevate your social status or people's perception of you, or experience that kind of fun activity. *See also:* Celebrity; Succeeding; Competition; Winning

Baby

A baby (or baby-related items) can represent: responsibility, a new beginning, vulnerability, innocence, or needs (such as for basic care or attention). **Being a parent to a baby when you aren't in real life** can represent a responsibility, perhaps a new one that has shown up in your life; your responsibility for your own needs (such as for self-nurturing or

63

basic care); your feelings about having a baby or spending time around young children. *See also:* Child; Pregnancy; Birth, Giving; Baby Animal

Baby Animal

Promise or potential. A new beginning. Hope. Vulnerability. Innocence. The need for care and nurturing. See also the particular type of animal. *See also:* Puppy; Kitten; Baby; Animal

Babysitter

An authority figure or person whom you feel is responsible for supervising or taking care of others. Responsibility for others (perhaps you feel there's too much or too little of it in your life). *See also:* Watching; Authority Figure

Back Seat

The back seat of a vehicle (or a seat that's not near the driver) can represent: Being or feeling away from the main action or events. Being an observer in a group process rather than a full participant or decision maker. Following others or "just along for the ride." Secondary or inferior, or feeling that way. Consider the context and the intention of the person in the back seat. If they're trying to direct the driver, they could represent a desire for more control in a particular situation. If happily riding, they could represent someone who was present but not a primary player in the real-life events represented in the dream. *See also:* Vehicle; Seat; Riding

Backward

Something that is backward or opposite of what you expect can represent: Something in your real life that seems amiss or not quite right. Something you tend to confuse or get backward (such as the names of two people). **Moving or stepping backward** could represent: fear, retreating from something, or avoiding something (or a desire to do so); regressing or losing progress. **Walking backward or retracing your steps on a path** could represent a desire to revisit, reevaluate, or redo something in your past. *See also:* Moving Around; Repeating; Returning

Backyard

A backyard, back porch, or back patio can represent: A similar casual setting in real life. The idea of home, familiarity, casualness, relaxation, downtime, social interaction, or play. The private part of your home life or family life (since a backyard is often hidden behind a house and not easily visible to outsiders). *See also:* Lawn; House; Outdoors; Porch

Bad

An event that you consider to be bad can represent something real or imagined that you consider undesirable. **Considering a person or their actions to be bad can mean:** you've (consciously or subconsciously) labelled them as "bad"; you're feeling threatened by them physically, emotionally, or mentally; you're feeling insecure, possibly from comparing yourself to them; you're attempting to make yourself feel better by judging them; you're trying to distance yourself from them mentally or emotionally. When you consider something or someone to be bad, be careful that your judgments and mental labels aren't keeping you from seeing the true meaning or value (such as the real person and their value, or the usefulness or lesson in the situation). *See also:* Catching Someone; Evil; Problem; Inferior; Disobeying; Luck; Judgment or Disapproval; Right or Wrong

Badge

A badge (such as a sheriff's or one that grants access to an area) can represent authority or permission. **Wearing a badge** can represent a feeling of belonging; permission to do something; a desire to feel more empowered, accepted, or "official." **A person wearing a badge** can represent: an actual authority figure in your life (such as your parent, teacher, or supervisor); a feeling or fear of that person taking charge or having power or authority over you. *See also:* Authority Figure; Police; Investigator

Badger

Tenacity or perseverance. The ability to dig and keep digging until you get to the bottom of things (or to the truth). Dreaming of this animal can represent too much or not enough of one of those qualities, or someone or something you associate with the quality or animal. Consider also the animal's actions, context, and your feelings about it. *See also:* Animal; Beaver; Wolverine

Bag

A bag (such as a purse, backpack, or tote) can represent: Necessities, or your needs in your daily life. The amount of effort it takes to maintain yourself, your lifestyle, or your daily requirements. Things you "carry around with you," such as emotional baggage, judgments, biases, or other things that weigh you down emotionally or mentally. Your ability to accomplish things out in the world, or the essentials you rely on to do so, such as your identity and skills (consider the meanings of the individual items in the bag). Your responsibilities (such as financial, self, or family). **Losing your bag** can represent a feeling or fear of: neglecting a responsibility; "losing out" because you're not paying attention; losing something tangible or intangible. **Someone stealing your bag** can represent a feeling or fear of victimization that interferes with your ability to accomplish things in the world. *See also:* Container; Suitcase; Wallet; Packing; Losing an Item; Stolen Item

Bakery

A setting or situation in which things are created, "cooked up," or completed. Something physically, emotionally, or mentally nourishing (such as a place, situation, activity, person, or relationship). A feeling you associate with a bakery, such as happiness, guilt, or treating yourself. An actual place in your real life (such as a restaurant, store, or cafeteria at work). *See also:* Restaurant; Dessert; Store; Dough; Food; Cooking

Balancing

Balancing an object or yourself (such as on a tightrope) can represent: Maintaining a balance among the important areas of your life. Managing your priorities or your schedule. A feeling of balance within your consciousness (such as peace, calm thoughts and feelings, or an absence of inner conflict). Feeling a need for more balance somehow in your life or consciousness. The idea of precariousness or needing to be cautious. Fairness or equity. Stasis, self-managing, or self-correcting. *See also:* Measure; Evenness; Steady

Balcony

A higher perspective or a view from above. An elevated consciousness or heightened awareness. Feelings of great insight or clarity. A sense of being "above it all," "above the crowd," or "above the fray." Feeling superior to others (or otherwise distanced from them). Feeling like a passive observer in life rather than a participant. *See also:* Upstairs; Audience; Theater; Arena or Auditorium

Ball

A ball can represent: Roundness. Bounciness or resilience. A game, or some aspect of your life that seems like one. **People tossing a ball back and forth to each other** can represent the back-and-forth in a dialogue. **Bouncing a ball alone** could represent a mental process, such as trying to make a decision or figure something out. *See also:* Bouncing; Circle; Game; Dancing; Special Occasion

Balloon

Lightness (such as of mood or substance). Pressure, or someone or something that's under pressure. Emptiness. Something that ends up amounting to nothing (such as a worry). Fullness or abundance. **A balloon floating in the air** can represent lightness, happiness, or the ability to "rise above it all." **A deflating balloon** could represent: a loss of momentum; the end of a process; a downturn in mood or events; a deflated ego or loss of self-esteem. **Popping a balloon** could represent shattering an illusion or dashing someone's expectations. *See also:* Bubble; Air; Bursting; Swelling

Band

Playing in a band, orchestra, or other ensemble can represent: Relationships or group events in your life. Teamwork, or cooperating or creating with others in your life. An actual musical activity, or a desire to be involved in one. *See also:* Group; Music

Baptism

Birth or rebirth. A new beginning (or a desire for one). Accepting beliefs or rules. Another ritual or ceremony in your life (such as a graduation). **Being baptized** could represent accepting someone else's beliefs as your own; joining or being accepted into a larger group; being forced to participate or pressured to adopt certain beliefs (if in the dream you didn't asked to be baptized). *See also:* Ritual or Tradition; Religion; God; Water

Bar or Night Club

A bar, night club, dance club, or similar location can represent: A place or activity in your life where you interact with others, especially with a casual or upbeat feeling. Letting go and having fun with others (or a desire for such). A past situation that involved meeting new people or interacting with strangers (such as a party or shopping at a busy store). For more clues, pay attention to the people and events in this setting, and how you felt about them. *See also:* Drinking; Dancing; Weapon

Barefoot

Freedom, or a desire for it. Feeling casual or comfortable. Being open and honest with others. Feeling exposed, vulnerable, or unprotected or choosing to be vulnerable with others. Going without or feeling deprived. Being inappropriate or feeling unprepared in a particular situation or environment. Consider how you felt about the lack of shoes during the dream. *See also:* Foot; Toe; Heel; Shoe; Sock

Barn

A barn or other outbuilding can represent: An actual barn. A real-life setting that reminds you of a barn. Something you associate with barns (such as hard work, protection, security, or storage). An aspect of your life or a role you play (such as animal owner, cultivator, "muckraker," or "problem cleanup"). **See also:** Building; Animal; Farming; House; Storage; Hut

Basement

Your subconscious mind. Subconscious or basic instincts or desires. Something that you keep hidden or that's not intended for public knowledge. Storing or holding onto things long term (such as grudges or outdated beliefs). For more clues, consider what was going on in the basement and how you felt about it. **See also:** Upstairs; Floor; House; Building; Underground; Descending; Stairs; Low; Under; Storage

Bat

Stealth. Having a special gift or "secret weapon" (as bats use echolocation). Having a higher perspective or understanding. The ability to adapt in order to excel. Dreaming of this animal can represent too much or not enough of one of those qualities, or someone or something you associate with the quality or animal. Consider also the animal's actions, context, and your feelings about it. **See also:** Animal; Weapon

Bathroom

The very personal and private aspects of your life that you don't share with anyone else. The health and well-being of your body or consciousness, especially through cleansing-and-releasing of outdated, decaying, or self-defeating elements in your life. **A bathroom that's messy or in disrepair** can indicate a need for more attention to self-maintenance, or a need to clean out or reorganize your consciousness (thoughts, emotions, beliefs, judgments, etc.). **Interacting with someone in a restroom** can represent a frank, straightforward interaction, or perhaps an awkward one about a personal matter. **See also:** Drain; Sink; Bathtub or Shower; Toilet; Soap; Towel; House; Room

Bathtub or Shower

Cleanliness of body, emotions, mind, intentions, or other aspects of yourself. Getting rid of something you consider undesirable (or a desire to do so). Starting fresh, or a desire for a new beginning. A secret, your secret thoughts, or your feelings about them (since a bathtub is one of the most personal areas of your living space). Relaxing or luxuriating (or a wish to do so). **See also:** Bathroom; Sink; Soap; Towel; Cleaning; Faucet; Drain; Container

Battery

A battery or other stored source of energy can represent: A source of energy, fuel, motivation, or inspiration in your life (or a desire for such). Perseverance or the ability to keep going. **A low or dead battery can represent:** low energy, fuel, motivation, or inspiration; exhaustion, overwhelm, or trying to do too much; the need to recharge, refresh, or start anew; the end of a phase, cycle, event, project, or something else. *See also:* Fuel; Magnet; Attacked, Being; Attacking

Beach

Fun, relaxation, play, warmth, vacation, or escape. A boundary or edge in space or time (the edge of a state or country, the end of a phase or project), since the beach is a boundary between land and water. Changeability or a shifting environment (as sand and shoreline are easily changed by the action of the water). *See also:* Sand; Water, Body of; Limit or Boundary; Edge, Coming to an; Divider; Suntan

Bear

Power, or a power imbalance. The use of power to accomplish something, such as in protection or aggression. Personal empowerment. Strength or assertiveness. Dreaming of this animal can represent too much or not enough of one of those qualities, or someone or something you associate with the quality or animal. Consider also the animal's actions, context, and your feelings about it. *See also:* Animal

Beard

A characteristic or tendency you associate with masculinity. **A beard on a woman** can represent a fear being perceived as (or perceiving yourself as) less feminine or more masculine; a personality characteristic you associate with masculinity; something unusual about whomever the woman represents in your life, or something that's inconsistent with your view of that person otherwise; a blurring or overlooking of gender boundaries. *See also:* Hair; Face; Chin

Beauty

Beauty or handsomeness can represent any desirable or pleasant concept, such as physical attractiveness, kindness, personal warmth, compassion, inner beauty, happiness, or trustworthiness. Consider also your feelings about the beauty. *See also:* Attractive; Face; Liking

Beaver

The ability to build or create. Embracing the idea of working in order to accomplish things. The ability to start with things of little value or substance and use them to create something grand. Dreaming of this animal can represent too much or not enough of one of those qualities, or someone or something you associate with the quality or animal. Consider also the animal's actions, context, and your feelings about it. *See also:* Animal; Otter; Badger; Weasel

Bed

Your inner thought process or your relationship with yourself. Security and safety, especially on the emotional level. If you share a bed with someone else in real life, a bed could represent your relationship with that person, especially communication, openness, and mental and emotional intimacy within the relationship. The idea of rest, relaxation, downtime, or sleeping. *See also:* Communication; Furniture; Asleep

Bee

The sweetness of life, or the idea of focusing on that. Productivity. Community or cooperation. Good communication (perhaps nonverbal, since bees use nonverbal cues). A perceived threat, or a hidden or underestimated danger. Flying, or something it represents to you. Dreaming of this insect can represent too much or not enough of one of those qualities, or someone or something you associate with the quality. Consider also the insect's actions, context, and your feelings about it. *See also:* Insect; Honey; Sting

Beetle

Heartiness, durability, or longevity. Steady progress. Activity or damage of which you're not aware. Wisdom. Royalty, or a sense of self-value. Dreaming of this insect can represent too much or not enough of one of those qualities, or someone or something you associate with the quality. Consider also the insect's actions, context, and your feelings about it. *See also:* Insect; Firefly

Before

One event that happens before another often represents a similar order of events in real life, so look for a parallel series of events, thoughts, decisions, feelings, or other things in your past (especially your recent past). An event that actually happened before another in real life (look for a parallel series of events, thoughts, decisions, or feelings in your past). **Allowing someone to go first** (such as through a door) can represent respect, kindness, honor, or a recognition of perceived importance or superior rank. **Putting your needs before others** can represent urgency, disrespect, or arrogance. *See also:* Past; Time Passing; Cause; Early

Beginning

An actual or imagined situation in which something began or in which you began a process or phase. A fresh start you've experienced or you desire. A feeling that the time is right or you're ready for something to begin. For more clues, consider the context (expected or a surprise, etc.), your reasons for beginning, your feelings about it, and who or what was involved. Consider also the meaning of the specific type of process that was beginning. *See also:* Phase or Process; Entering; Starting Over

Beheading

Loss of identity, self, authority, or the authority figure of a group (such as a company's president being fired), or a fear of such. **You being beheaded** can represent a feeling or fear of: the end of a phase in your life; losing your identity, your ego, some aspect of your life or yourself, or your authority over your own decisions. **You beheading someone else** might represent your anger toward, fear of, or some other feeling toward whomever or whatever the person represents in your life. For more clues, consider the motivation behind the action. *See also:* Execution; Head; Killed, Being; Killing; Killer; Dying; Death of You; Life Force; Authority Figure

Beige

The color beige or tan can represent: Neutral. Natural. Relaxing. Simple, plain, or basic. Subtlety. Formality. Someone's conservative personality or beliefs. Consider also the context of this color within the dream. *See also:* Brown; Color; Suntan

Belly Button

Nourishment or nurturing. Being human or mortal. Your connection with or dependence on those who came before you (such as your parents and grandparents). **Someone or something sucking energy out of you near the belly button** can represent an "energy sucker" or someone you think wants to have power or control over you (possibly through a promise to nurture or take care of you). *See also:* Stomach

Belt

A belt or suspenders can represent: Support, especially self-support. An embellishment or expression of self. A personality characteristic of the wearer, from the point of view of your subconscious mind. *See also:* Clothes; Decoration

Bench
"Sitting it out" or observing the action. Not participating, or waiting to participate. Rest. Idleness. Peace. A desire for more (or less) of one of those things in real life. *See also:* Sitting; Resting; Seat; Sofa

Betrayed, Being
Dreaming that someone has betrayed you or is a traitor can represent feeling suspicious of them in real life, exploring a worst-case scenario, or feeling paranoid in general. **Your loved one betraying you** can represent: insecurity about your ability to hold their interest, or fear of them cheating on you; jealousy about your loved one paying attention to a pastime other than you (having nothing to do with actual cheating). **Someone other than a romantic partner betraying you** can represent someone in your life you don't trust or you feel has betrayed you (such as a person, yourself, or God). *See also:* Interfering; Lied To, Being; Agreement, Breaking an; Dishonest; Trust; Telling on Someone; Sabotaged, Being; Abandonment; Catching Someone; Leaving a Person; Cheating; Trickery

Betraying
Betraying someone can represent: An issue of trust or of trusting yourself. A past betrayal of someone (that perhaps you still feel guilty about). A desire to make up for betraying someone in the past. **Betraying a loved one** could represent: a desire to break or change your current agreement with them; a reminder to yourself how important it is to you *not* to betray them. *See also:* Lying; Dishonest; Agreement, Breaking an; Telling on Someone; Sabotaging; Abandonment; Caught, Being; Leaving a Person; Cheating; Betrayed, Being

Between
Something positioned between two other things can represent: Feeling or needing protection or comforting. The idea of being "in the middle" (of the action, of an argument, etc.). Feeling conflicted, such as trying to choose between two options or opinions. Feeling confined, restricted, or limited. Experiencing a challenging situation in which you feel your options are limited (as in being "between a rock and a hard place"). *See also:* Next To; Crowd; Center

Bicycle

Riding a bicycle can represent: The way you're "running your life" or an aspect of it (now or in the past). Making progress (or a lack of progress, if the bicycle is slow or it has a problem). Maintaining balance in your everyday life or in a particular process. *See also:* Riding; Driving; Vehicle; Exercising; Motorcycle

Big

Power or strength. Protectiveness. A feeling of overwhelm or of things being out of control. For more clues, consider what the big object or person represents. The big size may represent "a greater amount" or "an extreme" of whatever the object or person represents. For example, if a flower represents love, a huge flower might represent huge feelings of love or adoration. If a car represents personal power, an oversized car might represent an enhanced feeling of personal power. *See also:* Bigger, Getting; Size; High; Heavy; Measure; Fat; Infinite; Many

Bigger, Getting

Something or someone getting bigger or growing can represent: Gaining more power or strength. Growing more important or more prominent in your mind. Becoming more overwhelming. Maturing or getting older. The passage of time. Becoming more of whatever is represented by the thing that's increasing in size. *See also:* Big; Sprout; Aging; Increasing; Swelling; Many

Bills

A bill (such as from the power company) can represent: A promise or commitment (since a bill follows up on a commitment you've made to pay a certain company). A demand on you, your time, or your energy. A feeling of someone expecting or demanding something from you. A feeling of obligation or indebtedness to someone. Someone asking you to fulfill a promise or offer you made in the past. **Paying bills or people demanding money** can represent a feeling that life seems very demanding right now or that someone (or people in general) wants something from you. *See also:* Paying; Owing; Finances; Buying; Debt; Scarcity

Bird

A bird can represent: A particular quality of that bird. Something or someone you (at least subconsciously) associate with that kind of animal. Consider also the bird's characteristics, actions, and what stood out about it during the dream. For example, a flying bird might represent freedom, soaring, or meaningful success. A bird rising high above a problematic area might represent an ability to "rise above" problems or others' negativity. A bird's sharp vision could represent an ability to see clearly or understand (such as to see the "big picture" or understand the truth). See also the specific kind of bird. *See also:* Animal

Birth Control

Actual birth control. Feeling the need for protection, precautions, or security measures somewhere in your life. Feeling that you need to pay special attention or manage things carefully right now to help ensure the outcome you want. *See also:* Protecting; Protected, Being; Cover; Security; Armor or Shield; Blockage or Obstacle

Birth, Giving

A new beginning or phase in your life or a particular aspect of it (such as a new relationship, job, etc.). Creating something new (such as an idea, a work of art, or a business). A new or additional responsibility. Your subconscious mind exploring what it would be like to actually give birth or have the responsibility of a baby. *See also:* Fetus; Baby; Pregnancy

Birthday

An actual birthday. The idea of celebrating or honoring a person, or giving them positive attention or good will. The idea of giving or receiving tangible or intangible gifts (things that are valuable to you). **Someone throwing you a birthday party** could represent a real-life party or other event; good will you've received somewhere in real life; a desire for more positive attention or appreciation. *See also:* Special Occasion; Birthday Cake; Dates on a Calendar; Calendar

Birthday Cake

Someone giving you a birthday cake can represent feeling celebrated, recognized, validated, or paid special attention (or a desire to feel such). A real-life experience that felt emotionally or mentally nourishing. *See also:* Birthday; Cake; Dessert; Food; Party; Special Occasion

Bison

Strength through gentleness and moderation. Ruggedness. Sturdiness. Ability to persevere. Dreaming of this animal can represent too much or not enough of one of those qualities, or someone or something you associate with the quality or animal. Consider also the animal's actions, context, and your feelings about it. *See also:* Animal; Buffalo; Bull; Cow

74

Biting

Biting into food to take it into your body might represent: The idea of taking what you want or need from the world around you (or the idea of taking *only* what you need). Your ability to accomplish tasks in your life (as in "biting off more than you can chew"). Feeling a need for mental, emotional, or spiritual nourishment. Trying something new. "Taking something in" mentally, such as a new idea or suggestion. Actively participating in the world around you. **Biting someone in aggression** could represent self protection, or anger or fear regarding something in your real life. **"Love bites" (such as playful nips from a puppy)** might represent affection, playfulness, or a gesture of good will. *See also:* Tooth; Mouth; Food; Eating; Chewing; Tasting; Bitten; Attacking; Insect; Fragment

Bitten

Being bitten by an insect or animal can represent a nuisance, fear, or something else that's "gnawing at you" or "eating you up." See also the specific insect or animal. *See also:* Biting; Attacked, Being; Sting; Insect; Parasite; Eating; Sucking

Black

The color black can represent: Solemnity or formality. Authority. "Dark" emotions. Mourning a loss. Basic or conservative. Night, darkness, or stealth. The unknown. The absence of light, color, or emotion. *See also:* Darkness; Color; Night

Black and White

Dreaming about something in black and white (instead of in color) can mean you perceive whatever that "something" represents as having no "color," no life, no vitality, or as boring, dreary, hopeless, or cold. For more clues, consider your feelings during the dream. **Something printed in black and white** (such as text on a page) could represent communication or clarity, or a desire for such. **Dreaming in extra-sharp black and white** can represent the idea of over-clarification, over-thinking, or feeling you're the victim of someone else's logical decision (perhaps one lacking compassion). *See also:* Color; Black; White; Text

Blackbird

Watchfulness. Insight (such as into the mysteries of life). The idea of timelessness, commonalities passed down through generations, history, or ancient tradition. Humbleness, or being content with what you're given. Dreaming of this animal can represent too much or not enough of one of those qualities, or someone or something you associate with the quality or animal. Consider also the animal's actions, context, and your feelings about it. *See also:* Bird; Raven; Crow

Blamed, Being

An issue of responsibility or blame. **Being blamed when you actually were at fault** can represent: a willingness to take responsibility for your actions; your perception of a particular person or environment as fair. **Being or feeling falsely accused** can represent: a real, feared, or imagined situation in which you felt blamed for something you didn't do; a denial of or failure to accept responsibility for something you did; a feeling that someone is refusing to take responsibility or is trying to shift blame away from themselves. *See also:* Blaming; Apology; Forgiving; Confronted, Being; Caught, Being; Denying; Admitting; Judgment or Disapproval; Rule or Law; Crime; Suing; Bully

Blaming

Blaming someone can represent: An effort to understand a situation or identify the cause. An unwillingness to take responsibility for events in your own life. **Suing someone** could represent an exaggerated or vengeful form of blaming. *See also:* Blamed, Being; Apology; Forgiving; Confronting; Confronted, Being; Denying; Admitting; Judgment or Disapproval; Rule or Law; Crime; Revenge

Bleach

The idea of removing, reducing, or getting rid of something (such as perceived flaws, mistakes, differences, evidence, etc.). The idea of purifying or purging. Concern about what other people think of you, or an attempt to avoid being judged or blamed by others (such as by hiding or changing something). *See also:* Soap; Cleaning; Deodorant; White; Dyeing; Pale

Blind

Impaired eyesight (when you can see well in real life) can represent: Feeling lost or disoriented. A lack of mental or emotional clarity, such as about your life or direction. An inability or unwillingness to see something in your life, or a tendency to deny something. **Going blind** can represent: fear, overwhelm, or a desire to shut out reality; an unwillingness to understand or accept something; a feeling or fear of isolation or abandonment; deprivation of information, social connection, or other connection with the world. *See also:* Eye; Vision; Can't See; Disabled

Blinking

Blinking your eyes can represent: A desire to see or understand something more clearly. A hesitation or pause. A desire to temporarily protect or isolate yourself, perhaps due to overwhelm or threat. A brief moment, or the idea of something happening quickly. A fresh start, wiping off, or cleaning out (since a blink clears and restores the surface of the eye). **A blinking light** can represent importance, urgency, or warning; safety or visibility; a means of creating orderliness or controlling a flow (as in a blinking traffic light). *See also:* Eye; Reflective Light; Sparkle; Cleaning; Sign

Blockage or Obstacle

An impediment to your progress. An obstacle to meeting a goal. Control, especially of a flow or process (as a valve controls the flow of water by blocking it). Lack of control (as a blocked water pipe causes a loss of control that results in flooding). A stoppage or holdup in a process (such as "writer's block"). A way to fix a leak (such as of information) or stop a loss (such as of wasted effort). *See also:* Breakwater; Divider; Interrupting; Interfering; Sabotaged, Being; Closing; Problem; Denying; Tight; Closed

Blood

Life force or life energy. The essence of humanity. Connectedness. Loyalty. **Someone being injured and losing blood** can represent a situation in your real life in which you feel someone is in a weakened state. **You bleeding** can represent feeling weak or tired (emotionally, mentally, or physically) or that something is sapping your energy, time, or attention. **Bleeding as a result of someone injuring you** can represent a real or imagined threat (emotional, mental, or physical), or it can be an indication of a Toxic Dream (p. 320). *See also:* Vein; Body; Flow or River; Family

Blue

Honesty or sincerity (as in "true blue"). Average or "regular" (as in "blue jeans" or "blue collar"). Relaxation. Royalty or distinction (as in "blue blood"). Spirituality. *See also:* Color; Attribute

Bluebird

Optimism, happiness, contentment, or well-being. Dreaming of this animal can represent too much or not enough of one of those qualities, or someone or something you associate with the quality or animal. Consider also the animal's actions, context, and your feelings about it. *See also:* Bird

Boar

Fierce. Independent. Volatile or easy to anger. Stubborn. Dreaming of this animal can represent too much or not enough of one of those qualities, or someone or something you associate with the quality or animal. Consider also the animal's actions, context, and your feelings about it. *See also:* Animal; Pig

Boat

The means by which you move forward in your life, or the course or direction you take in your life (or in some aspect of it). **Traveling on a boat** can represent: change; progress toward a goal; "skimming along the surface" of life but not participating fully; feeling protected from possible threats (as a boat protects you from threats below). *See also:* Vehicle; Traveling; Driving; Dock; Oar; Propeller

Bobcat

Solitary. Stealthy or silent. Instinctive. Opportunistic. Dreaming of this animal can represent too much or not enough of one of those qualities, or someone or something you associate with the quality or animal. Consider also the animal's actions, context, and your feelings about it. *See also:* Cat; Animal

Body

A person in your life. An unknown, idealized, or feared person. Humanness or humanity. Identity. Consider also the context of the body, what's noteworthy about it, and how you felt about it. See also any specific body parts you noticed in the dream. *See also:* Body Part; Dead Body; Person Unknown

Body Part

The main function of the body part (such as hands "handling situations" or teeth "biting off more than you can chew"). Something the body part allows you to do, or a way it allows you be (such as a joint representing your ability to be flexible, compromise, or adapt to different circumstances). A characteristic of the body part (such as a soft lap representing comfort, or an elbow representing an "elbow nudge" to pay attention). Consider the body part's context in the dream and what stood out about. See also the specific body part. *See also:* Body Parts (the category)

Bomb

Perceived or imagined hostility or ill will. A feeling or fear of domination or victimization by an authority (legitimate or otherwise). Feeling helpless or victimized in some aspect of your life due to misuse of authority or power. An indication that you were having a Toxic Dream (p. 320). *See also:* Weapon; Explosion; Nuclear; Attacked, Being; Attacking; Terrorism; Rocket; Missile

Bond

A bond or closeness between people can represent an actual, desired, or imagined closeness in real life. The people in the dream may represent themselves or other people in real life, imaginary people, or a general ideal (such as the idea of "someone trustworthy" or "someone caring"). *See also:* Relationship; Feeling; Love; Liking; Chemistry

Bone

Support of self. Ability to stand and persevere. Personal integrity. Strength of character (as in being a "solid person"). Something that is felt or experienced deeply (as in "I've got a feeling in my bones"). See also the particular area of the body. *See also:* Spine; Broken Bone; Body Part

Book

Information, answers, knowledge, or understanding (or a desire for such). Expression or communication (since a book is an expression of the author). The topic of the book or a related activity, person, location, etc. The idea of reading or studying. A different form of entertainment, relaxation, or story (such as the movie you watched last night). *See also:* Text; Communication; Story; Following a Procedure; Library; Notebook; Journal

Borrowing

Borrowing something from someone can represent a feeling that you've taken something (tangible or intangible) from that person and you owe them something back. For example, maybe in real life the person did you a favor and you intend to return the favor sometime. *See also:* Debt; Owing; Loaning; Giving; Agreement; Finances; Money; Receiving

Bothered, Being

Someone bothering you can represent someone or something bothering you in real life or in your mind, such as a person, problem, stressful situation, or feeling (such as guilt or something "nagging at you"). *See also:* Interfering; Bothering; Interrupting; Invaded, Being; Problem; Tormented

Bothering

You bothering someone else could represent: A feeling or fear that you're bothering or pestering someone in real life. Wanting something from that person in real life (such as an object, information, approval, or feedback). Feeling a need for something that person represents (for example, bothering a police officer could represent a desire for protection). Also consider the context and your feelings about and motivation for bothering the person. *See also:* Interfering; Bothered, Being; Interrupting; Invading; Problem; Tormented

Bottle

A container or dispenser for liquid (such as a bottle, jug, or pitcher) can represent: Drinking, quenching, or satisfying. Containment or control. Abundance. The idea of generosity or something else "pouring forth." The idea of flowing, free-flow, or controlled flow (such as of a process or activity). Consider also the meaning of whatever's inside the container, and the role of the container with respect to it. *See also:* Drinking; Liquid; Container

Bottom

Getting to the root or origin of something, such as a problem or personal issue. Discovering the truth about something. Reaching the end of a process. A limit or an extreme somewhere in your life (such as "the slowest" or "the fewest problems"). Down-to-earth, grounded, or practical. *See also:* Failure; Low; Under; Inferior; Ground; Valley; Descending; Limit or Boundary; Basement; Buttocks

Boulder

Obstacle, challenge, or threat. **A moving or rolling boulder** might represent momentum, critical mass, overwhelm, or the idea of being out of control. Consider also the context of the boulder and how you felt about it. *See also:* Stone; Hard Object; Big; Blockage or Obstacle

Bouncing

Energy or enthusiasm. Playfulness. A person, object, or situation that seems active, reactive, flexible, or resilient. **Repeated bouncing** (such as dribbling a basketball) can represent repetition or control. **Something ricocheting** might represent a change in direction or plan (such as due to an obstacle or external force) or an unexpected complication. **An object bouncing back to you** can represent: something you gave away in real life that has come back; something you expect to get back; the return of something (such as a relationship partner, your turn in a dialogue, or a bounced check). *See also:* Ball; Check (Money)

Bowing

Honor toward or recognition of the person or thing being bowed to. Gratitude for something that's being given. A greeting or introduction.

An intention to leave or finish, as in "bowing out." Subservience, or an indication that the person bowing is acting as if they are "less than" the person they are bowing to. *See also:* Crouching; Applause

Boy

A particular characteristic that you noticed about the boy. A stereotypical characteristic of boys. A responsibility in your life. Your inner child. Your playfulness or need for fun. A child or adult you know in real life, or the role that person plays in your life (friend, boyfriend, son, etc.). Your vulnerability or your need for support or empathy. Consider also the context of the boy and your feelings about him. *See also:* Child; Baby; Son; Person You Know; Person Unknown; Male; Man; Romantic Partner

Bracelet

A decoration or embellishment, perhaps one conveys a characteristic you associate with the wearer in real life. A reminder. A commitment or agreement. **Someone giving you a bracelet** can represent your bond with that person or the idea of them expressing admiration (real or imagined). *See also:* Jewelry; Wrist

Brain

A person's brain can represent their mind or something in it (such as their ability to think or their beliefs, thoughts, judgments, perceptions, or imagination). **Problems with the brain** can represent real or imagined trouble of a mental nature (trouble solving a problem, making a decision, or thinking clearly). **A brain that's not part of a body** can represent the meanings just mentioned or the following: the self, soul, or identity of a person; the end of a life or of another process. *See also:* Head; Body Part; Person You Know; Person Unknown

Brakes

The brakes in your car or other vehicle can represent: Self-control or caution, or the ability to exercise it. Slowing, stopping, or a delay in some aspect of your life (real, feared, or desired). **Using the brakes too much** can represent feeling hesitant or overly cautious, or holding yourself back somehow in your life. **The brakes being stuck in the "on" position** (for example, the emergency brake being on) can represent someone or something you perceive to be holding back your progress. **Your brakes suddenly not working** can represent a feeling or fear of losing control or security somehow in your life. *See also:* Stop Sign; Accelerator; Vehicle

81

Branch

A branch, offshoot, or the branching out of something can represent: One portion of something larger (such as a branch of a company). A divergence or diversification. Proliferation or multiplication. Multiples of something (projects, attempts, generations, iterations, etc.). Variation. The idea of things getting more complicated (as in one branch sprouting several smaller branches). Cause and effect, or one thing leading to another. A decision or choice. A tangent or "offshoot" (such as a detour or an aside). *See also:* Plant; Tree; Stem or Trunk; Crossroads; Path; Arm; Leg

Bread

Abundance or sharing. Basic physical, emotional, or mental nourishment, or the means by which nourishment is provided to you. **Being given only bread to eat** can represent a feeling or fear of deprivation, or of only your most basic needs being met. *See also:* Food

Breaking

An ending (such as of a process, relationship, or team effort). A transition, or a feeling that something will never be the same again. **Accidentally breaking an object** can represent a feeling or fear of making a mistake or ruining something. **Breaking an object in anger** can represent strong feelings (frustration, resentment, etc.), perhaps toward whatever is represented by the object. **Breaking an object on purpose when not feeling angry** could represent a desire or decision to be free of or finished with whatever that object represents in your life. *See also:* Broken Object; Bursting; Hole; Accident; Destroying; Throwing; Fragment; Agreement, Breaking an

Breaking Up

A relationship coming to an end (such as a breakup or divorce) can represent: An actual, desired, feared, or imagined breakup. The end of a process, phase, agreement, or arrangement in any area of your life. A change in the mode of a relationship or friendship (such as when it becomes a long-distance one). The end of an interaction phase (such as a work team disbanding when a project is finished or a sports team going separate ways at the end of the season). *See also:* Ending; Relationship; Romantic Partner; Ex; Abandonment; Leaving a Person

Breakwater

A breakwater, jetty, or other protective water barrier can represent: Protection against trouble, challenges, or chaos. Something that separates or distances you from "what's out there" in your life. An extension from one environment or world into another (since a breakwater often extends from land into water). *See also:* Divider; Water, Body of; Dock; Fishing; Blockage or Obstacle

Breast

Physical, emotional, mental, or spiritual nourishment. Femininity or female sexuality. Motherhood or motherly love. **Breastfeeding** might also represent: responsibility for another person's needs; the idea of having a baby, or perhaps spending time mentally or emotionally nurturing young children. **The individual who's being breastfed** can represent dependency, neediness, or someone in need of nurturing. *See also:* Gland; Nipple; Chest; Heart; Feeding; Milk; Secretion

Breathing

Life or life force. The ability to survive or thrive. For more clues, pay attention to the quality of the breathing. Fast, shallow breathing could represent fear or stress, and a pause in breathing could represent suspense or waiting (as in "holding your breath" for something). **Trouble breathing** can represent: fear or panic; feeling smothered in some situation in your life; feeling unable or not allowed to express yourself; feeling unable or unwilling to participate fully in life (to "breathe deeply and live fully"). *See also:* Air; Rib; Lung; Coughing

Brick

A brick, block, stone, or other building component can represent: Strength, solidity, reliability, or rigidity. A resource used to create or build. The process of establishing or building something. An input to a creative process (such as ideas, designs, or information). The process of breaking something down into its smallest components (such as to examine or understand it). Weight, load, burden, or feeling weighed down. Consider also the context of the brick and how it's being used. *See also:* Stone; Divider; Building; House

Bride

A commitment or connection (romantic or otherwise). The beginning of a new phase, process, or lifestyle. A feeling or fear of being put "on the spot" or being the center of attention somehow. The idea of a wedding, party, or other gathering. A desire for, fear of, or curiosity about being in a committed relationship or marriage. Reflecting on a certain romantic relationship (past or present). *See also:* Wedding; Relationship; Marriage; Veil; Wedding Dress

Bridge

A passage from one phase to another in your life, or a transition into a new beginning. The ability to rise above a challenge in your life or escape certain difficulties (as in a bridge that allows you cross dangerous waters). The idea of taking a shortcut or a more direct route somehow in your life. A connection from one dream area to the next. A transition from one point in time to another in your real life. The way you transition back and forth between different aspects of your life (such as between your role as a parent and as an employee). A connection between you and another person. Consider also the meaning of the two areas the bridge was connecting, what the bridge was crossing over, the role it played, and how you felt about it. *See also:* Road; Path; Tracks, Railroad

Broken Bone

A broken limb or other body part can represent a perceived or real problem or challenge in whatever area of your life that body part represents. For example, if a leg represents your ability to make progress in life, then a broken leg might represent something you feel is impeding your progress somehow. If a toe represents trying something new (as in "dipping your toe into the water"), then a broken toe might represent getting your feelings hurt when you tried something new in real life. *See also:* Broken Object; Breaking; Leg; Body Part

Broken Object

A broken or damaged object can represent a less than perfect, impaired, less effective, or useless version of whatever the object represents. For example, a broken steering wheel could mean you're feeling less than effective at staying on track in your life right now. A broken wedding ring could represent a feeling that your marriage is going through challenges and could use some "repair." *See also:* Depleted; Breaking; Bursting; Flood; Inferior; Hole; Leg; Destroying; Disabled

Brown

The color brown can represent: Earthy or natural. Plain or basic. Autumn, or the winding down of a phase or cycle. Chocolate or other food. Soil or dirt. *See also:* Color; Beige

Bruise

Emotional hurt, or the way you've reacted to it within your consciousness. A feeling or fear of someone hurting you. **Self-inflicted bruises** (such as from accidentally bumping into objects) can represent: allowing your boundaries to be crossed or your integrity to be compromised; subconscious self-sabotage; an opportunity for greater self-care. *See also:* Hurt, Being; Injured

Bubble

An enclosed or self-contained environment. Isolation or ignorance, as in "he's living in a bubble and doesn't know what's going on." Protection. A void or hole (such as an air bubble in Swiss cheese). A short-lived or temporary process (since bubbles often don't last long). **Bubbles in a liquid can represent:** fun or relaxation; lightness or airiness; a feeling of celebration; stimulation, interest, activity, or productivity. **Blowing a bubble** can represent a process or project. **A bubble bursting** can represent: the end of a process or project; disappointment; destruction. *See also:* Gum, Chewing; Air, Balloon; Soap; Hole

Bucket or Basket

Containing, controlling, holding, reining in, or restraining (as a bucket or basket does to whatever is inside it). Inclusion, or including things or people all together. A process of carrying, bringing, gathering, or helping. *See also:* Cleaning; Water; Wet; Container; Carrying

Buffalo

Ruggedness. Sturdiness. Strength, perhaps through gentleness or moderation. Strength in groups, or finding safety in a crowd. Dreaming of this animal can represent too much or not enough of one of those qualities, or someone or something you associate with the quality or animal. Consider also the animal's actions, context, and your feelings about it. *See also:* Animal; Bison; Bull; Cow

Building

A building or other similar structure can represent: You, your life, or a certain aspect of your life (such as an office building representing your work life). A building can convey the setting, atmosphere, tone, or mood you associate with whatever its dream events represent in your real life (for example, a school might represent a recent life lesson you learned, or a desire to learn). Consider also the floors of the building (for example, a basement can represent your subconscious mind, the top floor your spirituality, and the middle floors the main areas of your life or consciousness). See also the type of building (house, store, hotel, etc.). *See also:* Location; Main Floor; Upstairs; Basement; Roof; Making or Building

Bull

Aggressiveness, assertiveness, or a no-nonsense attitude. Virility or masculinity. Strength or force. Tenacity or stubbornness. Dreaming of this animal can represent too much or not enough of one of those qualities, or someone or something you associate with the quality or animal. Consider also the animal's actions, context, and your feelings about it. *See also:* Animal; Cow

Bully

Actual, feared, or imagined abuse of power or authority. Someone who continues a cycle of abuse passed to them from someone around them. Perceived lack of compassion or ill will. *See also:* Violence; Attacked, Being; Abuse; Attacking; Hurt, Being

Bursting

Something that bursts or ruptures (such as a water balloon or a dam) can represent: Experiencing too much physical, emotional, or mental pressure in your life. The end of a process or project. Destruction. Disappointment. *See also:* Breaking; Broken Object; Explosion; Squirting; Opening; Eruption; Flow or River

Burying

Burying an object can represent: An unwillingness to deal with or a desire to avoid whatever that object represents. Hiding something or being dishonest. Ending a phase, putting something to rest, or putting something behind you. *See also:* Hiding; Cover; Grave; Coffin; Cemetery; Dead Body; Dead Acquaintance; Funeral

Business

A business, company, or other commercial entity could represent: A group or community, especially one with shared goals or shared experience. Productivity or accomplishment. Organization. Your work, job, career, or work income. A system for tangible or intangible trading. A real-life company you've dealt with or are thinking about doing business with. Something you associate with the business, such as its purpose, products, reputation, or your personal experience with it. *See also:* Organization, Membership; Factory; Processing; Store; Shopping Center; Entrepreneur; Restaurant; Workplace

Butterfly

Transformation, transition, or a series of phases. Carefree joy or freedom. Spiritual maturity or self-actualization. Perceived beauty or inner beauty. The idea of flitting from one thing to the next, or a non-linear process. Dreaming of this insect can represent too much or not enough of one of those qualities, or someone or something you associate with the quality. Consider also the insect's actions, context, and your feelings about it. *See also:* Moth; Insect

Buttocks

Ability to make strong progress, get ahead, or "make strides" in life. Procrastination or inactivity (as in "just sitting around"). Resting or taking a break. "Sitting it out" or refusing to participate. A person's foundation, such as their beliefs and values. *See also:* Sitting; Hip; Anus; Bottom; Seat; Body Part

Buying

An actual recent purchase or something you'd like to purchase. Exchanging one thing of value for another thing of value (whether tangible or intangible), such as people helping each other or exchanging ideas. A situation in which work or effort is exchanged for something of value, such as money, thanks, or praise. An exchange or agreement within a relationship. *See also:* Paying; Store; Sale or Discount; Finances; Investment; Rich; Finances

Cabinet

Things you keep, store, or stash away (such as memories, personal issues, or other things within your consciousness). The extent to which you, your life, or your mind are organized. Hiding or concealing things from others or from yourself. **Looking for something in a cabinet** can represent seeking something you need, you've lost, or you've been neglecting in real life. **An upper cabinet** can represent a spiritual or "lofty" matter that needs your attention. **A lower cabinet** can represent a basic matter (physical, practical, logical, etc.) that needs your attention. **Reorganizing your cabinets** can represent the idea of physical, emotional, or mental "cleaning out" or re-prioritizing (or a need for such). *See also:* Container; Storage; Drawer; Knob; Locker

Cake

A special occasion. Fun, happiness, or "sweet times." Actually feeling hungry or craving sweets. *See also:* Birthday Cake; Dessert; Sugar; Food; Eating

Calculator

Real or desired assistance in solving problems. The idea of a shortcut or a way to make something easier. Another technological tool (such as a computer or smartphone). A real-life activity involving a calculator, computer, or other similar device. *See also:* Math; Tool; Computer

Calendar

Time or schedule. The passage of time. The idea of past or future. A specific time period. *See also:* Dates on a Calendar; Time Passing; Time of Year; Time Frame; Month; Appointment; Schedule

Camel

Endurance. Stamina. Patience. Ability to "hang in there" for the long run. Reaching long term goals. Resourcefulness, conservation, or the ability to make the best use of what you have (as a camel makes very efficient use of water). Carrying things for others (such as responsibilities or burdens). Dreaming of this animal can represent too much or not enough of one of those qualities, or someone or something you associate with the quality or animal. Consider also the animal's actions, context, and your feelings about it. *See also:* Animal; Desert

Camera

Watching, observing, or witnessing something. The idea of being watched, or an issue regarding privacy. Attention or focus (or a fear of it or desire for it). A desire to preserve or remember an experience. Security or proof. **Someone taking your picture or videoing you against your will** can represent a feeling or fear of someone compromising your boundaries. **A photo or video taken without your awareness** can represent a feeling or fear of boundary violation, victimization, betrayal, dishonesty, or manipulative motives. *See also:* Photo; TV, Being On

Camping

A period or event in your life that takes place away from home, or that differs from your normal activity or personality (since your home often represents you or your life). The idea of being out of your comfort zone. Having to get by on less, or without certain luxuries or advantages. A real or desired vacation or change of pace. Freedom from authority or from the usual societal structure. *See also:* Trip or Vacation; House

Canal

A canal, ditch, or other water channel can represent: A context in which events happen or a process progresses (since a canal is a channel through which water progresses from one place to another). A means of movement forward in your life. Movement away from something (a situation, the past, etc.), or getting rid of something. Movement toward something (a goal, the future, etc.). A connection, such as between people, situations, or events. A transition, such as between one phase and the next. *See also:* Passageway; Flow or River; Water, Body of; Abyss; Drain

Canary

Sensitivity or vulnerability. The power of personal voice and "singing your own song." Restriction or limitation, or wanting more freedom (since canaries are sometimes kept in cages). Dreaming of this animal can represent too much or not enough of one of those qualities, or someone or something you associate with the quality or animal. Consider also the animal's actions, context, and your feelings about it. *See also:* Bird

Candle

Mood or romance. Spirituality or the idea of the presence of God. Religion or ritual. Clarity, understanding, or "shedding some light" on a particular subject. Using energy (as in the flame converting wax to energy). *See also:* Light (Illumination); Fire

Can't Move

Being unable to move physically can represent: Feeling oppressed, held back, or challenged (physically, emotionally, or mentally). Feeling overwhelmed or unempowered. Feeling stuck, unable to make progress, or unable to make a change in a certain area of your life. Indecision or lack of clarity about what course to take or how to proceed. Consider also what was hindering your movement in the dream and why. *See also:* Paralysis; Numb; Moving Around; Problem; Helpless; Disabled; Can't Speak

Can't See

Not being able to see, or your vision or view being obscured, can represent: Feeling unable to understand or see something clearly in your life (perhaps a problem for which you can't see a solution). Feeling that something is hidden from you or that someone is hiding something. Not wanting to know, discover, accept, understand, or take responsibility for something in your life. *See also:* Blind; Vision

Can't Speak

An inability or unwillingness to communicate or express yourself. Consider the reason you couldn't speak. **A throat problem** could represent an unwillingness or inability to express yourself or speak for yourself. **Laryngitis** could represent the idea of talking too much or expressing a lot (or not enough). **Being overcome by emotion** might represent actual emotion you feel about something in your real life, or an in-the-moment reaction to an event in the dream. **Someone else stopping you from speaking** might represent a feeling or fear of a challenge, victimization, or oppression. **Being "tongue tied"** might represent an issue of overwhelm, pride, nervousness, or self-sabotage. For more clues, consider your feelings, the context, what you were trying to say, and to whom. *See also:* Voice; Paralysis; Problem; Helpless; Illness; Help, Calling for; Quiet

Cape

A cape or cloak can represent: Concealment or mystery. Questionable or suspicious intent. Protection. The idea of all-encompassing inclusion (as a cape surrounds the body). *See also:* Cover; Clothes; Superhero

Car

Movement forward through life. **A car owned or driven by you** can represent: you, as you proceeded through the period of your life depicted in the dream, or as you move forward through your life in general; the personal context (your mind, perceptions, etc.) within which you grow personally, make decisions, and learn; your personal integrity and the whole of who you are (the "sum of all your parts," including your knowledge, intentions, abilities, etc.) during the real-life period portrayed in the dream. **A car owned or driven by someone else** can represent: a person in your life (usually the car's owner or driver in the dream) or that person's life; a stranger, group, idea, or action you've experienced (in real life, on TV, etc.). **Your car being stolen** can represent a feeling or fear of your integrity being compromised, someone taking advantage of you, or someone taking something from you in a way that impedes your progress. *See also:* Wheel; Vehicle; Driving; Riding; Steering; Accelerator; Engine; Fuel; Headlight; License Plate; Back Seat; Windshield; Brakes

Cardinal (Bird)

Well-adjusted, happy, cheerful, or content. Bringing interest, joy, or lightness to those around you. Beauty (or inner beauty) without vanity. Dreaming of this animal can represent too much or not enough of one of those qualities, or someone or something you associate with the quality or animal. Consider also the animal's actions, context, and your feelings about it. *See also:* Bird; Religious Figure

Cargo

Cargo or a cargo vehicle (such as a truck, barge, or cargo train) can represent: "Hauling around" personal baggage or issues. Having or needing help, or being supported or "carried" by someone or something. The ability to help others. Movement of people or things from one place to another, or forward through time in their life processes. Bulk, mass, abundance, or the idea of "many." *See also:* Boat; Carrying; Towing; Bag; Suitcase

Carnation

Good thoughts or good will. A vague expression of feelings. Consider also how you feel about carnations. For example, if they remind you of a fond memory, they might represent that period in your past or a sentimental feeling about it. If you think of them as cheap, they might represent an empty or meaningless gesture. *See also:* Flower; Plant

Carried, Being

Support, responsibility, or delivery. **You being carried by someone else** can represent: receiving help or assistance; someone else taking responsibility for you or taking on your responsibilities; the idea of being a burden to someone else. *See also:* Carrying; Supporting; Traveling

Carrying

Helping, taking responsibility for, or delivering something (such as value, a message, or a gift). **Carrying a person or animal** can represent helping or taking responsibility for someone or something in your life. **Carrying something heavy** can represent feeling burdened, bogged down, or overloaded in your life. **Trying to carry too many things** can represent trying to focus on or do too many things in your life. *See also:* Grasping; Bucket or Basket; Pulling; Towing; Heavy; Walking; Cart; Cargo; Messenger; Delivery; Pregnancy; Carried, Being

Cart

Carrying or supporting, or a means of doing so. Emotional issues or baggage. Gathering things (such as items or experiences), or a means of gathering them. Consider the context, purpose, and condition of the cart. *See also:* Vehicle; Carrying; Container; Following (Trailing Behind); Store

Cartoon

A story, joke, or something funny. A situation or scenario in your life that doesn't seem quite real. Consider the context and what the particular cartoon means to you. *See also:* Animation

Cat

Responsibility. Independence. Having strong ideas about how things should be. Lithe and adaptable (physically, emotionally, or mentally). Making huge leaps (of progress, logic, or something else). Mysterious. Stealthy or quiet. Prone to surprises. Dreaming of this animal can represent too much or not enough of one of those qualities, or someone or something you associate with the quality or animal. Consider also the animal's actions, context, and your feelings about it. See also the specific kind of cat. ***See also:*** Pet; Animal

Catching Someone

Catching someone doing something that you think they shouldn't can represent: Feeling watchful or suspicious somehow in your life. The idea of having power over the person (or a desire for such). A desire for justice or to see that person get into trouble. Feeling the need or responsibility to monitor others' actions. Vigilance or over-vigilance. Nosiness or inserting yourself into others' business (consider your motives). **Catching someone when they're falling** can represent: providing physical, emotional, mental, or spiritual support or protection; a perceived need for support or security (yours or someone else's). ***See also:*** Caught, Being; Police; Chased, Being; Betrayed, Being; Cheating; Trickery; Dishonest; Lied To, Being; Bad; Thief; Criminal; Crime; Adultery; Searching; Rescuing; Protecting

Catching Something

Catching something (for example, a fish) could represent finding something you've been wanting or looking for. **Catching an object that was thrown to you** (such as a ball) could represent: accepting an invitation to dialogue, play, or otherwise participate with the thrower; something in real life that you perceive as a game; receiving authority or something else that's handed off to you (as in "now the ball is in your court"); communication, or receiving a message; completing a process; an event that you consider a success. ***See also:*** Receiving; Ending; Succeeding; Throwing; Net; Hunting; Fishing; Caught, Being

Caterpillar

Potential. The early stage of a life transition (since a caterpillar is the larval stage of an insect). Gradual, consistent progress. Dreaming of this creature can represent too much or not enough of one of those qualities, or someone or something you associate with the quality or creature. Consider also the creature's actions, context, and your feelings about it. ***See also:*** Larva; Cocoon; Butterfly; Moth

Caught, Being

Someone catching you doing something you shouldn't can represent: Feeling guilty somehow in your life (perhaps you've compromised your integrity). Fear of an authority figure (or of authority in general) or of their perceived power over you. A feeling or fear of being falsely accused. **Someone catching you when you're falling** can represent: receiving physical, emotional, mental, or spiritual support or protection from someone; a perceived need for support or security (yours or someone else's). *See also:* Blamed, Being; Chased, Being; Catching Someone; Police; Security; Cheating; Trickery; Dishonest; Stealing; Lying; Stalking; Crime; Adultery

Cause

A cause, trigger, or stimulus (as in a "cause and effect") can represent a real, imagined, or feared cause in your life (for example, a compliment that results in a smile, or a transgression that results in a punishment). For more clues, consider what the cause and its effect might represent in your life (or in your fears or imagination), paying special attention to your feelings about them. *See also:* Result; Before; Supporting

Ceiling

A limitation or perceived limitation (such as on how high you believe you can climb, or how much progress you think you can make). An elevated mood or perspective. Power or ambition. Something that seems "over your head" or unattainable. Protection from something "above," such as from an authority or from something "falling on you out of the blue." *See also:* Roof; Climbing; High; Floor; Building; House; Upstairs

Celebrity

Talking to or being friends with a celebrity can mean that your subconscious mind considers the celebrity a friend because you "interact" with them often by watching them in the media. (The subconscious mind may not see much difference between encountering a person in the media and interacting with them in person.) **Dreaming that you're a celebrity when you're not** can represent (real or imagined) attention, recognition, respect, acceptance, approval, or something else you associate with fame or a particular celebrity. *See also:* Character; Show or Movie; Talk Show; Royalty; TV, Being On; Model, Fashion

Cemetery

A feeling or mood (such as solemn or scary). Sentimentality or focusing on the past. A feeling or fear of a phase or activity coming to an end. A feeling or fear of loss or change. *See also:* Grave; Dead Body; Dead Acquaintance; Death of You; Safe or Vault; Funeral

Center

The center (such as standing in the center of a circle) can represent: Being the center of attention. Feeling "put on the spot." Being in the middle of the action. Experiencing the "heart" or innermost part of something.

Protecting yourself (as in hiding in the middle of a crowd). *See also:* Between; Crowd; Rotating; Shopping Center; Medical Office

Centipede

Activity or busy-ness. Smooth progress forward. Harmony (with others or within yourself). Coordinating well with others. Redundancy or contingency planning (since a centipede has lots of "backup" legs). Dreaming of this creature can represent too much or not enough of one of those qualities, or someone or something you associate with the quality or creature. Consider also the creature's actions, context, and your feelings about it. *See also:* Animal; Spider

Changing

Something changing or transforming can represent a past, expected, or imagined changed in your life. For example, a tree becoming stronger can represent strengthening, or a caterpillar transforming into a butterfly can represent a transition in your life. For more clues, consider what is changing and how, and your feelings about the change. *See also:* Shaping; Soft; Different; Altering; Starting Over; New

Chaos

An actual chaotic situation in your real life or within your consciousness. A feeling or fear of overwhelm or losing control somehow in your real life. Disorganized thinking or irrational thought processes. Having trouble making a decision, or feeling ambivalent. *See also:* Moving Around; Dizzy; Circles, Going in; Disaster; Problem; Wild; Storm

Character

A familiar character (such as from a book, movie, or TV show) might represent: A characteristic you attribute to that person (for example, if you consider Harry Potter courageous, he might represent courage within yourself or someone else). The idea of fame, validation, respect, or recognition by others. A particular celebrity who portrayed that character. For more clues, consider the character's actions, demeanor, characteristics, your feelings about them, and what the character signifies to you in real life. *See also:* Person You Know; Person Unknown; Celebrity; Superhero

Chased, Being

If you dream someone is chasing you, consider the context. **If the chaser wants to harm you,** this could represent: a feeling or fear of persecution, hostility, aggression, criticism, or other harm by another person (or by others in general); a real-life situation in which you feel your boundaries have been crossed or your integrity has been compromised. **Someone**

playfully chasing you could represent the idea of that person interacting with you or your feeling of friendliness toward them. *See also:* Escaping; Attacked, Being; Catching Someone; Killing; Hunting; Stalking; Chasing

Chasing

If you dream you're chasing someone, consider the context. For example, if you're angry at the person you're chasing, the chasing may represent that anger. **Chasing someone who has stolen something from you** can represent your desire to set right a situation in which you feel someone has taken advantage of you. **Playfully chasing someone you like** could represent your fond feelings toward them or a desire to interact with them. *See also:* Catching Someone; Following (Trailing Behind); Attacking; After; Hunting; Stalking; Chased, Being

Cheating

Cheating (such as on a test, on taxes, or in a game) can represent: The idea of unethical shortcuts, dishonesty, or stealing (possibly relating to a real-life situation). Resentment of someone whom you feel is attempting to control you. Rebellion against an authority. Feeling unwilling to put in the required effort, or preferring to take a shortcut somewhere in your life. Dreading or lacking interest in something you have to do. Feeling dishonest, or considering cheating or its consequences. *See also:* Stealing; Thief; Criminal; Crime; Inferior; Adultery; Betrayed, Being; Dishonest; Lying; Trickery

Check (Money)

Something that represents something else valuable, or that stands in for something valuable (as a check stands in for cash). A promise or an "IOU" (such as for a favor, support, etc.). **Cashing a check** can represent collecting on a promise or debt; something given in return for something received (both could be tangible or intangible in real life). *See also:* Money; Finances; Giving; Paying

Cheek

Bravado or nerve. Rejection. Neutrality or non-reactivity (as in "turning the other cheek"). Beauty (as in "rosy-cheeked"). Purity. *See also:* Face

Chemistry

The idea of two or more components working together, how well they work together, or the results of their combination (for example, compatibility, rapport, cooperation, synergy, or a catalyst effect). Dreaming that a real-life relationship has "good chemistry" can represent your perception of, imagination of, or desire for such. *See also:* Mixing; Science; Laboratory; Lubricant or Catalyst; Crush, Having a; Liking

Chest

Courage, bravado, or resiliency. Love, passion, or compassion. Emotion, the ability to feel emotion, or a specific emotion that was expressed in the dream. *See also:* Breast; Lung; Heart; Furniture

Chewing

Processing or breaking down something into smaller pieces, perhaps in an attempt to use or understand it better. Trying to "take in," understand, or accept something. The process of making a decision, forming an opinion, or mulling something over. A repetitive action or continuous process, perhaps just to pass the time (such as "chewing the fat"). *See also:* Eating; Biting; Food; Tooth; Jaw

Chicken

Fertility. The power of creativity or the feminine. Fear or cowardice. Caution or skepticism. Common sense (or a need for more of it). Dreaming of this animal can represent too much or not enough of one of those qualities, or someone or something you associate with the quality or animal. Consider also the animal's actions, context, and your feelings about it. *See also:* Rooster; Bird

Child

An actual child or child-like person in your life. An adult who's been acting like a child, or one with the emotional disposition of a child. Your inner child. The need for self-nurturing or taking responsibility for yourself. **Dreaming you have a child when you don't in real life** can represent: responsibility for something or someone in your life; responsibility for yourself or your needs. Consider also what stood out about the child, such as age, actions, or a characteristic that reminds you of a real person in your life (child or adult). *See also:* Baby; Daughter; Son; Birth, Giving; Age

Chimes

The sound of chimes (such as wind chimes blowing in the breeze) can represent: The existence of life. The passage of time. The presence of God or the desire for support by God. The idea of soul, or existence beyond the realm of the physical body. *See also:* Ringing; Alert; Noise

Chimpanzee

Playfulness. Rambunctiousness. Resourcefulness. Companionship or community. Nonverbal communication or unspoken language. Basic human skills. Humanity or human-like qualities (such as sentience or compassion). Dreaming of this animal can represent too much or not enough of one of those qualities, or someone or something you associate with the quality or animal. Consider also the animal's actions, context, and your feelings about it. *See also:* Animal; Monkey; Gorilla or Ape; Orangutan

Chin

Determination. Perseverance or resolve (as in the attitude of "chin up!" or "stick out your chin"). The aspect of a person that handles or suffers from challenges (as in to "take it on the chin"). Spilling, spilling over, or messy side effects during a process (as when food is dribbled onto the chin while eating). Also, pay attention to its particular characteristics (such as tension or a dimple) and what they suggest to you. *See also:* Face; Head; Jaw

Chipmunk

Playfulness. Quickness (as in a quick wit or quick thinking). Curiosity, trust, or the balance between trust and caution. Darting from side to side (as in being open minded or able to see both sides of an issue). Dreaming of this animal can represent too much or not enough of one of those qualities, or someone or something you associate with the quality or animal. Consider also the animal's actions, context, and your feelings about it. *See also:* Animal; Squirrel

Chocolate

Indulgence, or feeling a need for an emotional or mental "treat" (such as feeling special or appreciated, or soothing emotional pain). "Sweet times" or a pleasant event. Richness or fullness. Actual hunger or craving. *See also:* Dessert

Choir

Teamwork. A shared voice or opinion, or the expression of a shared opinion as a group. A shared or group process, co-creativity, or cooperation with others. Shared effort, or working toward a common goal or cause. The joining of diverse people or things to create an integrated whole (as in "the whole is greater than the sum of its parts"). The idea of "singing from the same sheet of music" or everyone being in agreement, harmony, or peace with each other. *See also:* Performing; Singing; Music; Voice

Church

A place of worship (church, temple, mosque, etc.) can represent: God or spirituality. The spiritual or religious aspects of your life. The importance of a spiritual connection. Ritual or tradition. A mental or superficial focus on spirituality (such as saying the words of a prayer without meaning them). Consider also the dream events in this setting and your feelings about them. *See also:* Religious Symbol; Religion; Business; Organization, Membership

Cigar

Perceived grandeur or status (or a desire for such). Celebration. Masculinity. Noxiousness or toxicity. Dependency or addiction (such as to a substance, activity, habit, or way of thinking). *See also:* Cigarette; Smoke; Ashes; Fire; Destroying

Cigarette

The idea of an addiction or a nervous habit (possibly to different substance, activity, habit, or way of thinking). A source of physical, emotional, or mental toxicity in your life. Self-sabotage. Rebellion. A desire for more independence or a stronger sense of identity. **A cigarette burning** can represent the exhaustion or "burning up" of resources, energy, or time somehow in your life. Consider what the idea of smoking brings to mind for you personally. *See also:* Ashes; Fire; Destroying; Cigar; Smoke

Cigarette Butt

The end of a phase or process (as a cigarette butt is the end of the cigarette-burning process). Something or someone you consider old, used up, discarded, ignored, or valueless. A certain person who smokes, or evidence of that person's presence. **Cigarette butt litter** can represent: someone else's discard; being affected by someone else's issues, carelessness, or disregard for others; a littered or messy (physical, emotional, or mental) environment. *See also:* Ashes; Fire; Cigarette; Smoke; Garbage

Circle

Whole or wholeness. Inclusion or exclusion. Femininity. Perfection. Well-roundedness. For more clues, consider the context, what stood out about the circle, and what it brings to mind for you. **A group of people in a circle formation** can represent connectedness or intercommunication. *See also:* Circles, Going in; Shape; Ball; Ring (Jewelry); Zero; Curve

Circles, Going in

Traveling in circles (such as running or driving in circles) can represent: Repeating the same actions or thoughts while making no progress. A certain repeated pattern (such as isolating yourself rather than reaching out) or habit (such as buying coffee every morning). Randomness or chaos. Lack of direction, or feeling lost. *See also:* Repeating; Circle; Dizzy; Erratic; Chaos; Corner; Curve; Rotating

City

An organization or group of people sharing something in common (such as location, goals, beliefs, culture, or background). The actual city or place, or people who live there. An event or memory that happened there, or that brings the city to mind. A characteristic, mood, event, or something else you associate with this city or some other city. *See also:* Region; Location

Class

A class, seminar, or training can represent: A class or similar situation in real life. Learning or being taught. Self-improvement, personal growth, evolution, or an attitude of learning. Life lessons or learning through experience. A group of people in a shared process. The era of your life when you attended the school in your dream, or something from that era (a relationship, an experience, unfinished business, etc.). Anything else you associate with a classroom situation (interesting topics, boredom, friendships, getting into trouble, teachers, etc.). Consider also the class's purpose, teacher, participants, types of activities, and your feelings about being there. *See also:* School; Meeting; Teacher; Homework; Book

Claws

Attacking or being attacked. Ability to grasp, hold onto, or keep something. Security. Greed. A desire for or fear of keeping someone close. **Claws trying to harm you** can represent a real, perceived, or imagined threat in your life. See also the symbols for the type of animal and its action in the dream. *See also:* Fingernail; Attacking; Attacked, Being; Pulling; Taking From; Reaching For; Animal

Clay

Changeability or malleability (such as a volatile situation or a person whose opinions or beliefs are easily changed). Wide-open opportunity or potential. An opportunity for creativity or vision. Immature or undeveloped. *See also:* Shaping; Artwork; Creativity; Changing

Cleaning

Cleaning (such as washing, sweeping, wiping up, or polishing) can represent: Getting rid of unwanted things such as feelings, thoughts, situations, or relationships (or a desire to do so). Making an improvement in your life or making things more orderly in your physical, emotional, or mental world. Fixing a mistake (or a desire to do so). Denial, trying to "erase" facts, or trying to get rid of feelings or evidence. **Cleaning up after someone else** can represent: fixing their problems, coming to their rescue, taking responsibility for them, or supporting their irresponsibility. Consider also the context, who's cleaning what, their motivation, and your feelings about what's happening. *See also:* Water; Soap; Sink; Cleaning Person; Washing Yourself; Napkin; Towel; Absorbing; Bleach

Cleaning Person

A feeling or fear of having to clean up other people's messes, fix their problems, or come to their rescue. A person in your life who tends to clean up after you or others, or whom you expect to do so. *See also:* Cleaning

Climbing

Making progress or "getting somewhere" in your life or a certain aspect of it. Working toward a goal. Moving forward or upward in life through your own effort. Improving yourself or your situation. A desire for one of the things previously listed. For more clues, consider what is climbing or rising, how easily or quickly, and your feelings about it. *See also:* Increasing; High; Stairs; Hill; Ladder; Above; Superior; Sky

Clock

The idea of time in general. The passage of time. Being late or early, short of time, or having too much time (or a fear of such). The idea of adhering to a schedule or other regimen. A particular time of day, or a certain event or activity you associate with it. **An oversized clock** might represent feeling overwhelmed by time demands (such as schedules, restrictions, or too much to do in an allotted time frame). *See also:* Alarm Clock; Time

Closed

Something that's closed or sealed (such as a door or a box) can represent: An obstacle or challenge to moving forward somehow in your life. Perceived inaccessibility or unavailability. A feeling that you lack permission (such as to do something, say something, or access something). Safety, security, or protection. The end of a phase, where something has "come

100

to a close" or "a door has closed" in your life. *See also:* Tight; Closing; Lock; Hill; Blockage or Obstacle

Closing

Closing something (such as a door or a suitcase) can represent: The end of a process, phase, opportunity, etc. A decision or wish to end something. The end of a discussion or topic (as in "case closed"). Satisfaction. An effort to avoid, distance yourself from, or protect yourself from something on the other side of whatever you're closing (such as a door). Consider also what's represented by the thing being closed, who is closing it, and why. *See also:* Ending; Blockage or Obstacle; Repairing; Lock; Opening; Next To

Clothes

Self-expression. Your perception of the wearer's self-image or attempt to control other's impressions (such as kids "dressing older" to be treated as older by others). A role the person plays (as in a uniform) or would like to play (as in children playing dress up). Protection, such as from being judged or taken advantage of (for example, cold-weather clothing that represents protection from "cold" behavior). A characteristic associated with the type of clothing (culture, age, or personality type, etc.). A real-life setting (swimwear representing a real-life event at the beach), mood (a black suit representing solemnity), or timeline (saddle shoes representing the 1950s). See also the specific items of clothing. *See also:* Costume; Nightclothes; Fashionable; Jewelry

Cloud

Interpretation or subjectivity. The forces of nature. The presence of God. Creativity. A dream or goal. For more clues, consider the cloud's shape, color, and context. **A cloud blocking the sun** can represent a disruption in something constant; temporary relief; a temporary obstacle; an emotion. **Clouds that are moving or changing** can represent change, transformation over time, or the passage of time. **Dark storm clouds** can represent a feeling or fear of a challenge in your life; or "dark" emotions (such as depression, anger, or despair). *See also:* Sky; Weather; Fog; Rain; High; Storm

Clown

Fun or enjoyment. Comic relief. Someone who plays the role of entertainer or jokester. Disguise, anonymity, concealment of identity, or mystery. Consider the context, actions, motivations, and your feelings about the clown. *See also:* Performing

Coat

Self-protection, such as protecting yourself from people's "coldness" or harshness (as a coat protects you from cold temperatures). Self-nurturing, self-care, or survival measures. **A coat that disguises or that covers much of the body** can represent stealth, hiding something, or a secret motive (or a fear of such). *See also:* Cover; Cape; Fur

Cockroach

A perceived pest, or something that pesters you. Things that invade your life, your space, or your to-do list. Judging something as inferior, distasteful, or negative. Neglect (such as of responsibilities, yourself, or your environment). Dreaming of this insect can represent too much or not enough of one of those qualities, or someone or something you associate with the quality. Consider also the insect's actions, context, and your feelings about it. *See also:* Insect; Beetle

Cocoon

A transition in your life (since a cocoon is an insect's transition between larval and adult phases). Progress or development that isn't visible or of which you're not aware (as in a larva developing inside its cocoon). A lull in a process before progress resumes. Feeling cozy, comfortable, or secure. A period of rest, recuperation, revitalization, or nurturing (or a need for such). *See also:* Insect; Larva; Caterpillar

Code

Communicating in code can represent: Secrecy, or fear of others learning certain information. A desire to maintain power or keep the upper hand. Purposely being vague, making your message hard to understand, or wanting to hold back information. *See also:* Symbol; Secret; Password; Help, Calling for; Communication; Text; Letter (Alphabet); Number; Computer; Garbled; Unknown Thing

Coffin

The end of a phase, process, or project. Death, dying, or the afterlife (or fear of such). A scary or spooky feeling. Feeling limited, trapped, or at a "dead end" somehow in your life. *See also:* Death of You; Killed, Being; Dead Body; Dead Acquaintance; Hearse

Cold

Cold weather or feeling cold can represent: Less excitement or low energy (as molecules vibrate more slowly at cold temperatures). Less activity, or feeling that more activity is needed. Perceived harshness (as cold temperatures feel physically harsh). Something energizing or invigorating (as in a brisk day or cold shower). A wake-up call or attention grabber (as in a "cold slap in the face"). Lack of compassion or caring (as in a "cold" person). Feelings or characteristics you associate with the natural environment during cold weather (dull, lifeless, beautiful, peaceful, etc.). *See also:* Weather; Ice; Winter; Time of Year; Decreasing; Virus; Coughing; Condition

Color

A perceived characteristic of the person or thing with that color (such as orange representing cheerful or purple representing regal). Your mood, feeling, or sense about the object or situation where the color appeared. Something specific you tend to associate with the particular color (such as green representing your office that's green, or blue representing peace). For more clues, consider your reaction to the color and feelings about it during the dream. See also the specific color. *See also:* Pale; Vivid Color; Colors (the category)

Comb

A comb or hairbrush can represent: Self-care. Attention to yourself or your physical, emotional, or mental well-being. Neatening or organizing an aspect of yourself or your life. Attention to or concern about the impression you make on others. *See also:* Hair; Organizing

Communication

Feeling that you need to say or express something, or that someone else needs to hear or understand something. A need to be heard. The way the communicator in the dream tends to interact with others (for example, someone speaking gently could represent a person you consider to be gentle with others). An actual communication from your past (perhaps portrayed in a different form), or a desired, imagined, or feared communication. Consider also the dynamics between the communicator and the recipient. *See also:* Words; Writing; Voice; Listening; Phone; Text; Email; Letter (Message); Typing; Texting; Help, Calling for; Confiding

Compass

Finding a direction or a path. Orienting yourself physically, emotionally, mentally, or spiritually (such as by examining your priorities or reevaluating your beliefs). Looking for a solution to a problem, an answer to a question, or a way to achieve a certain result. **Having trouble reading a compass** can represent feeling confused or frustrated in terms of direction. *See also:* Map or Directions; Direction; Traveling

Competition

A real-life challenge such as a test, race, performance, or other situation in which you're judged or compared to others. Competitiveness, motivation, or teamwork with others. Cooperation and harmony with yourself, or feeling aligned with your goals. Feeling motivated to do well or to improve. Wanting to win. Wanting to feel superior, feed an ego or insecurity, or wanting someone else to lose (indicating an opportunity to work through an underlying issue). *See also:* Game; Test; Winning; Succeeding; Superior; Inferior; Enemy; Decision, Someone Else's; Running

Computer

The ability to accomplish things or figure things out. Connection. You or your mind, brain, or mental ability. **Communicating with others by computer** can represent actual or imagined communications with those people. **Your computer crashing** can represent: feeling challenged, unable to get things done, or out of touch with others; experiencing a loss of self or of some aspect of your life. *See also:* Communication; Login; Internet; Typing

Condiment

A condiment (ketchup, sauce, syrup, etc.) can represent a real or imagined: Improvement or enhancement. Something extra (such as "the icing on the cake"). An afterthought. *See also:* Food; Spice; Decoration

Condition

The condition or state of something can represent: The actual condition of the thing in real life. A feeling or assumption about the thing. Your perception or impression of the thing, or the direction in which you think it's going (such as a ripening apple representing your son maturing into an adult). A fear regarding the thing (such as a damaged car representing your fear of getting into an accident). A desire (such as a renovated version of your house representing improvements you'd like to make to it). See also the specific condition. *See also:* Conditions (the category)

Confiding

Confiding in someone can represent: The idea of trust or feeling comfortable with that person. A particular matter that you'd like to share, vent about, get guidance on, or ask for assistance with. A desire to feel closer to someone. The idea of confiding too much or not enough. **Someone confiding in you** can also mean there's something you'd like to know or understand from that person. *See also:* Trust; Admitting; Secret; Communication; Betraying; Betrayed, Being

Confronted, Being

A feeling or fear of others' suspicions, accusations, or of being confronted about something. Defensiveness, or feeling the need to be defensive. Feeling guilty about something. *See also:* Blaming; Blamed, Being; Forgiving; Apology; Confronting; Denying; Admitting

Confronting

Confronting someone can represent: Wanting to know the truth about something, or wanting the other person to admit the truth or agree with you. An actual, imagined, or desired clearing of the air, resolution of a conflict, or acceptance of responsibility. *See also:* Blaming; Blamed, Being; Apology; Forgiving; Confronted, Being; Denying; Admitting

Confused

Dreaming that you can't think clearly can reflect an actual unclear mental state during the dream, or it can represent trouble making a decision or figuring something out in real life. *See also:* Fog; Garbled; Mentally Unstable; Forgetting; Decision, Your

Constipated

A real or imagined blockage or delay in a process. Holding on to the old (such as grudges, the past, or outdated beliefs, ideas, or agreements). Holding on to something too long, perhaps due to mental or emotional factors such as a fear of letting go. *See also:* Blockage or Obstacle; Digestion; Feces; Problem

Container

Control or restraint (physical, emotional, or mental). Being or feeling contained, restrained, or not allowed freedom. A category or other "container" within which to organize thoughts, feelings, opinions, to-do list items, etc. Being or feeling organized or neat, especially as it pertains to your state of mind (orderly or logical thinking). Keeping or grouping certain things together in your mind (such as objects, people, or ideas). Safety, security, or safe-keeping. See also the type of container. *See also:* Package

Controlled, Being

Someone trying to take power or control over you can represent: A real-life person or situation you feel is crossing your boundaries, manipulating or overpowering you, or taking more time or energy than you're willing to give. Fear of powerlessness, victimization, or loss of personal power. *See also:* Controlling; Stalking; Invaded, Being; Trickery

Controlling

Trying to control or have power over a person or situation can represent: Compensating for a feeling of powerlessness, victimization, loss of personal power, or fear of losing control of a situation in your life. A wish for more control due to a situation feeling out of control or overwhelming. Anger or vengefulness toward the person or situation (indicating an opportunity to work through an underlying issue). *See also:* Controlled, Being; Interfering; Interrupting; Invading; Stalking; Trickery; Bothering; Attacking; Privacy; Violence

Cooking

Preparing or obtaining physical, emotional, mental, or spiritual nourishment or inspiration. Nurturing, love, or devotion to family. Creating or creativity. A process or project. What's going on or what's current (as in "What's cooking?"). The idea of heat, hot, or burning (literally or figuratively). *See also:* Making or Building; Meal; Food; Cooking Vessel; Stove; Hot; Warm; Mixing; Eating; Fire; Fireplace

Cooking Vessel

A cooking vessel such as a pot or pan might represent: Preparing or obtaining physical, emotional, mental, or spiritual nourishment or inspiration. Starting something or "stirring things up." An environment for creating or preparing. *See also:* Container; Dish; Cooking

Cooperating

Cooperating, partnering, or teaming with others could represent: A similar dynamic in real life. A desire to join forces with others somehow. The idea that "the whole is greater than the sum of its parts." A desire for belonging or acceptance by others. *See also:* Joining Together; Game

Copying

Multiplying. Mimicking. **Something that multiplies quickly** (such as a problem) can represent an amplified or multiplied version of whatever the original represents in your life. **Copying someone else** can mean there's an aspect of that person that you admire or respect. **Copying someone else's work** (such as a test or something they've created) can represent stealing, shirking responsibility, or feeling unprepared or inadequate. **Using a copy machine** can represent: having something you want to express or share with others; the idea of things multiplying or growing (such as your to-do list); repeating messages; work, your job, or an office environment in general. *See also:* Cheating; Fake; Repeating; Increasing

Corner

The meaning of a corner can depend on the type of corner and its context. **Turning a corner** when you're walking or traveling can represent a change or the start of a new phase. **Not being able to see what's around a corner** can represent looking toward the future, feeling like you don't know what lies ahead, or the idea of something that's hidden or inaccessible. **Someone hiding around a corner** can represent a feeling that they have hidden motives or are withholding information. **Being stuck in a corner** can represent feeling limited in your options or powerless somehow in your life. **Being cornered** by someone can represent feeling pressured or even attacked somehow. **Being sent to a corner as punishment** can represent the idea of punishment, accusation, rejection, or isolation from others (real or feared). *See also:* Crossroads; Turning; Circles, Going in; Erratic; Traveling; Driving; Walking; Curve

Costume

Pretend or playfulness. A role you play, want to play, are considering (such as a new job), or want others to think you play. The impression you want to give or the kind of self-image you desire. A disguise, a wish to be disguised, or a desire to not be recognized or seen. Hiding or deceit (or an intent for such). *See also:* Clothes; Hat; Makeup; Hiding; Cover

Coughing

Coughing a lot can represent: A feeling or fear of having trouble expressing yourself or speaking up for yourself. Something that's bothering you or that you refuse to accept (as in having something "stuck in your craw"). Feeling that something is keeping you from living life fully. *See also:* Breathing; Lung; Cold; Mucus

Country

A (real or imagined) country or nation can represent: An actual place or people. A real or imagined group with something in common, such as location, goals, beliefs, or culture (for example, a region, organization, industry, religion, or political party). An entity with boundaries, or a group that separates itself from others or considers themselves different from others. Againstness, or one side in an argument (as a country can represent one side in a war between two countries). **A foreign country** could also represent a feeling of unfamiliarity, strangeness, or difference from what you're used to. **A specific nation** can represent something you associate with that nation or its people, culture, language, resources, etc. *See also:* Region; Nationality; Location; Flag; Unknown Thing

Court

A real or imagined decision by an authority figure. **Being judged by a judge or jury in court** can represent: feeling subject to scrutiny or judgment by others in some aspect of your life (perhaps because you've done something that could get you into trouble); feeling guilty, the need to explain or defend yourself, or the need to apologize or make amends for something. *See also:* Trial; Judge; Courtroom; Justice; Jury; Authority Figure

Courtroom

An area, setting, situation, or aspect in your life in which you feel judged or subject to the authority of others. *See also:* Court; Trial; Judge; Justice; Jury; Authority Figure

Cousin

Your actual cousin (or other relative), or something that comes to mind when you think of that person. Someone else with whom you're very close. Someone who feels like family or gives you the feeling of family (such as trustworthy, friendly, supportive, etc.). Someone with whom you have something in common. *See also:* Person You Know; Family

Cover

A cover, or something that covers, can represent: An obscured view or limited understanding (as in an obstructed view through the window that represents feeling uninformed about events in the world). Concealment or hiding (as in a concealed gun that represents a hidden motive to overpower others). Protection (as in a blanket representing protection from harsh conditions). Misrepresentation or dishonesty (as in a picture covering a damaged wall that represents an attempt to hide the truth). Denial or dishonesty to yourself (as in a layer of beautiful snow representing a misrepresentation of the landscape underneath). *See also:* Hiding; Burying; Curtain; Secret; Protected, Being; Protecting; Quiet; Veil; Under; Masked or Hooded; Painting; Quilt; Coat; Cape; Hat

Cow

Femininity. Feminine or motherly nurturing (physical, emotional, mental, or spiritual), as in cows giving milk as nourishment. Contentment or satisfaction. Simplicity. Innocence. A relaxed or easy-going attitude. Dreaming of this animal can represent too much or not enough of one of those qualities, or someone or something you associate with the quality or animal. Consider also the animal's actions, context, and your feelings about it. *See also:* Animal; Bull

Cowboy

A person who manages others or keeps them in line. An activity you associate with a cowboy (managing, gathering, guiding, etc.). Freedom or independence. A certain geographic region or time period. Romantic ideals. Consider what comes to mind when you think of a cowboy or cowgirl. *See also:* Person Unknown; Person Unknown; Hat; Clothes

Coworker

An actual coworker, past or present. Your work or workplace. Team-work, or your typical dynamics with that person (such as cooperation, competition, or animosity). **A coworker from a past job** could repre-sent that person, that job, or that time period in your life. *See also:* Person You Know; Workplace; Manager; Working; Time Frame; Past

Coyote

Wiliness. Taking advantage of a situation or person. Taking action qui-etly or without others' knowledge. The "balance of nature" or "a natural balance." Dreaming of this animal can represent too much or not enough of one of those qualities, or someone or something you associate with the quality or animal. Consider also the animal's actions, context, and your feelings about it. *See also:* Animal; Wolf; Fox

CPR

Cardiopulmonary resuscitation (CPR) can represent: Physical, emotion-al, mental, or spiritual rescue or assistance (or a desire for it, or a fear that you might need it). The idea of re-starting a process, project, or ac-tivity. *See also:* Rescued, Being; Rescuing; Help, Calling for; Paramedic; Medical Treatment; Dying; Alive or Exists

Crab

Grabby, stingy, or needy. Holding onto something or someone. Grump-iness or irritability. Emotionally well-protected or distanced. Defensive-ness, or defending yourself. Dreaming of this animal can represent too much or not enough of one of those qualities, or someone or something you associate with the quality or animal. Consider also the animal's actions, context, and your feelings about it. *See also:* Animal; Claws

Cramp

Overwhelm. Frustration, or something else you need to express. Holding on or refusing to let go. Getting hung up on something in your life, or getting in your own way somehow. Trying to get rid of something. Feeling unable to take action or move forward. *See also:* Muscle; Pain

Crane

Strength through uniqueness or individuality. Having a higher perspective. Persistence through challenges. Stretching yourself (such as to get what you want, or beyond your comfort zone). Dreaming of this animal can represent too much or not enough of one of those qualities, or someone or something you associate with the quality or animal. Consider also the animal's actions, context, and your feelings about it. *See also:* Bird; Heron; Flamingo; Stork

Crawling

Consider the reason for crawling. **Crawling because you're struggling to move forward** could represent a feeling of struggling to move ahead, get somewhere, or reach a goal in your life (mentally, emotionally, or physically). **Crawling because you're injured** can represent feeling a lack of well-being, something out of balance, or feeling under attack somehow in your life. **Crawling toward a hiding place** could represent a feeling of fear or avoidance somewhere in your life. **Crawling to sneak up on someone** could represent the idea of mental, emotional, or physical stealth, covert action, or hidden intentions. Consider who or what is crawling, why how, and where, and your feelings about it. *See also:* Walking; Injured; Low; Hiding; Attacked, Being; Invaded, Being; Person You Know; Person Unknown; Animal

Creativity

A particular creative person or process in your real life. A process of creativity or self-expression, or your desire for it or appreciation of it. *See also:* Making or Building; Painting; Artwork; Performing; Music; Problem; Poetry; Song; Shaping; New.

Cremation

An ending (such as of a phase of life, a phase of a relationship, a job, or an activity). A feeling or fear of losing a person, a relationship, a job, a project or activity, an experience, a way of being, or something else. *See also:* Dead Body; Dead Acquaintance; Death of a Loved One; Funeral; Fire

Cricket

Moving forward in occasional, large leaps rather than making constant progress. Moving toward a goal in a way other than a straight line (such as through trial and error). Expressing yourself without caring what others think. Expressing yourself differently than other people. Nocturnal, or something nighttime represents (such as stealth, or shining at times when others do not). Dreaming of this insect can represent too much or not enough of one of those qualities, or someone or something you associate with the quality. Consider also the insect's actions, context, and your feelings about it. *See also:* Insect; Grasshopper

Crime

Breaking a rule or law. Behavior you perceive as unacceptable or going against a societal norm. Accusation or blame. Feeling guilty, whether or not you are. Consider also who is committing the crime, why, and your feelings about it. See also the type of crime. *See also:* Criminal; Catching Someone; Police; Attacked, Being; Attacking; Justice; Rule or Law; Blamed, Being; Blaming; Violence; Disobeying; Dishonest; Evil; Weapon

Criminal

Laws or societal rules. Perceived "right or wrong." Blame or accusation. **A criminal attacking you** could represent a feeling or fear of victimization somehow in your life. **A criminal in jail** could represent justice or punishment for misconduct (or a desire for that or fear of that). **A criminal on trial** could represent feeling judged or evaluated. **Being a criminal** could represent feeling guilty, angry, deprived, or powerless. *See also:* Catching Someone; Dishonest; Attacked, Being; Attacking; Menacing; Thief; Cheating; Crime; Evil; Weapon

Crocodile

Primal. Stealth. Lack of regret or compassion. Taking what you want. Devouring (as in devouring information or tackling a project with great enthusiasm). Dreaming of this animal can represent too much or not enough of one of those qualities, or someone or something you associate with the quality or animal. Consider also the animal's actions, context, and your feelings about it. *See also:* Animal; Alligator

Crossing

Crossing a street, river, or other boundary can represent: Passing from one phase to another in your life. A new beginning or fresh start. **Crossing a large area** (such as a desert) can represent making progress through a phase or process. **An illegal or unpermitted crossing** (such as a property line or international border) can represent a feeling or fear of doing something wrong, "crossing a line," or getting caught. *See also:* Road; Bridge; Crossroads; Entering; Invading; Crime

Crossroads

Being at an intersection or crossroads can represent: A decision point, or feeling the need to choose a course of action somewhere in your life. Interaction or cooperation among people according to a set of agreed-upon rules (like at a real intersection). **Someone going out of turn at a traffic intersection** can represent feeling someone has acted "out of turn" in real life. **Not knowing which way to go or not being able to decide** can represent confusion or stress about a real-life decision, or needing more information before you decide. *See also:* Decision, Someone Else's; Decision, Your; Road; Traveling; Driving; Walking; Path; Branch

Crouching

Consider the motivation for crouching. **Crouching to get past an obstacle** (such as a tree branch) can represent the idea of handling a challenge in order to continue making progress in your life. **Crouching to avoid harm or injury** can represent a real-life feeling or fear of a physical, emotional, or mental threat. **Crouching to hide** can represent feeling the need for self-protection, or the idea of doing something secretive, manipulative, or dishonest (such as lying). *See also:* Avoiding; Low; Crawling; Hiding

Crow

A message bearer, or the idea of a message or guidance. A feeling of foreboding. A perceived nuisance. Intelligence, resourcefulness, or ability to solve problems. Dreaming of this animal can represent too much or not enough of one of those qualities, or someone or something you associate with the quality or animal. Consider also the animal's actions, context, and your feelings about it. *See also:* Bird; Blackbird; Raven

Crowd

A recent time when you were actually in a crowd. Feeling that you "fit in" with others (or a desire for such). Enjoying or feeling comfortable around other people. Feeling insignificant in the world. Feeling overwhelmed, perhaps by others' needs or demands on you. For more clues, consider how you felt about the crowd. *See also:* Group; Audience; Many; Person Unknown

Crown

A feeling of (or a desire to feel): Specialness. Royalty. Power or authority. Recognition. Validation. *See also:* Royalty

Crush, Having a

Recognizing the specialness or uniqueness in someone (or your ability to do so). Experiencing or hoping for a feeling of connection with someone. Projecting an ideal on someone or something. Infatuation, obsessiveness, or over-focusing. Attachment, objectification, or self-centered desire. A desire for a certain kind of experience you're imagining as positive. Looking outside yourself for happiness, when in actuality you are responsible for your own happiness. *See also:* Liking; Wanting; Attractive; Stalking; Chemistry; Breaking

Crutch

A crutch, brace, cane, or other structural aid can represent: Needing help in order to get along or function, literally or figuratively (or fearing that you might). A dependency, or something physical, emotional, or mental on which you're dependent. **Someone using a crutch** might represent you perceiving or imagining that the person needs help or support. *See also:* Injured; Wheelchair; Disabled; Pain

Crying

Expression of emotion (such as of sadness, anger, or frustration). An indication that something within your consciousness or your life needs attention (as when a baby cries, it often needs help or support). Consider your feelings during the crying and whether they indicate an underlying issue in need of further attention. *See also:* Feeling

Cuckoo

Announcement or alert. The heralding of a change. An interruption or surprise. Being present in the current moment. The idea of time, or awareness of the passage of time. Isolation, whether or not by choice. The idea of home or coziness. Chaos or craziness. Dreaming of this animal can represent too much or not enough of one of those qualities, or someone or something you associate with the quality or animal. Consider also the animal's actions, context, and your feelings about it. *See also:* Bird; Mockingbird

Cuddle

Affection, familiarity, closeness, trust, security, or sharing. Being close to or in touch with someone (physically, emotionally, or mentally). Feeling that in real life you have (or want) whatever you associate with the cuddling. Consider the motivation for and your feelings about the cuddling. *See also:* Holding a Person; Hug; Kissing; Arm; Touching

113

Cult

A group you feel has strong influences, such as on beliefs or decisions (such as a religion, political party, or school). Someone's attempt for power or control over others, possibly to feed an ego, insecurity, low-self esteem, or a feeling of powerlessness. A misdirected attempt to help. A group you feel is misleading, purposely or otherwise. Feeling tricked, getting "sucked in," or buying into an illusion. The idea of changing your beliefs in an attempt to fill a void within yourself (such as for validation or acceptance). *See also:* Religion; Church; Religious Symbol; Religious Figure; Organization, Membership

Curse

A curse (as in witchcraft) can represent: Power or control over others, whether real or imagined. Blaming outside sources instead of taking responsibility for yourself and your life. An attempt to explain something you can't otherwise explain. **Putting a curse on someone** can represent fear of a perceived threat; anger toward or a judgment of someone (indicating an opportunity for you to work through an underlying issue). *See also:* Attacked, Being; Attacking; Bad; Blaming; Magic; Spell; Swearing

Curtain

A division or dividing line between areas or "worlds" (as a curtain is a divider between the stage and the audience, or between patient areas in a hospital). Privacy, protection, or personal boundaries (such as a house with no curtains that represents feeling emotionally exposed or vulnerable). Mystery or the element of surprise (as in someone hiding behind a curtain). **Opening your curtains** could represent a mental or emotional accessibility to others or the world. **Closing your curtains** could represent: distancing yourself from others or the world; a desire for privacy or solitude; a need to maintain your personal boundaries. *See also:* Cover; Window; Hiding; Privacy; Stage or Screen; House

Curve

Fluidity, flexibility, softness, or femininity. Fun, flair, adventure, or an artistic sensibility. **A curve in a road** can represent a real-life turning point or turn of events. **A curvy road** can represent a process or journey with lots of twists and turns. *See also:* Corner; Circles, Going in; Erratic; Circle; Shape; Rotating

Cut Off

Stopping a process or a flow (as in cutting off the electricity). A desire to get rid of, be free from, or not have to deal with something. A feeling or fear of threat. A perceived power imbalance. Consider the context and what is cut off. *See also:* Ending; Interrupting; Scissors; Knife; Disabled

Daffodil

Renewal or a new beginning, especially after a long resting period or a hardship (since daffodils are some of the earliest blooming flowers in the spring). Cheerfulness, or something else daffodils bring to mind for you. *See also:* Flower; Plant

Daisy

Friendship, good will, happiness, fun, or something else you associate with daisies. *See also:* Flower; Plant

Dancing

Actual or desired self-expression, creativity, or communication. Happiness, joy, or other emotion. **Dancing with a partner** can represent a relationship, bond, or interaction (such as a conversation or time spent together), getting along well, or being in agreement with each other. *See also:* Stage or Screen; Creativity; Performing; Audition

Danger

A feeling of caution, risk, or threat regarding something in your life or mind (such as a fear or doubt). Something dangerous you witnessed (firsthand, on TV, in the media, etc. *See also:* Feeling; Threat; Evil; Warning

Darkness

Mystery, uncertainty, or the unknown. Stealth, or hidden activity. Subconscious dynamics. Something of a suspicious or questionable nature. **Something happening in the dark** can represent: something in your life happening without others finding out, or without full knowledge or understanding; something in your life that you keep to yourself or keep secret (as in keeping others "in the dark"). *See also:* Night; Time of Day; Hiding; Shadow; Gloomy

Dates on a Calendar

Certain events, milestones, points in time, or periods in your life. Awareness of or concern about your schedule. Planning, scheduling, expecting, or looking forward to something. Remembering something from the past. The personal significance of a particular date (such as your mother's birthdate representing your mother). *See also:* Calendar; Time Passing; Time Frame; Time of Year; Month; Appointment; Holiday; Meeting; Birthday; Past; Future

Daughter

Your real-life daughter. Someone who feels like a daughter to you. Someone whom you feel protective of or parental toward. *See also:* Family; Child

Daytime

An event happening in the daytime or "in broad daylight" can represent a real-life event you feel is intended to be open, obvious, public, or for all to see. Productivity or activity (since daytime is their usual time frame). *See also:* Time Frame; Time of Day; Light (Illumination)

Dead Acquaintance

Seeing a person in a dream who has passed away in real life can represent that person, your memory of them, a characteristic of theirs (optimism, creativity, etc.), or something else you associate with them. The person might be on your mind because you've been thinking about them, you're missing them, a significant date such as a birthday is approaching, you're curious how they're doing or what they'd think about something in your life (or some other reason). *See also:* Person You Know; Dead Body; Death of a Loved One; Dying

Dead Body

The end of a phase in some area of your life. The physical body in general, or the idea that it's just a physical "shell" in which a person lives during the course of their life. **If the body is someone you know,** perhaps you consider that person to be reaching the end of a phase before beginning a new one, or perhaps you're afraid of that person dying or becoming less unavailable to you (or at least not available to you in same way as before). *See also:* Dead Acquaintance; Ending; Dying; Death of a Loved One; Ghost; Coffin

Deaf

Dreaming that someone is deaf (or hard of hearing) when they aren't in real life can represent: An unwillingness or inability to hear something, someone, or your own inner wisdom. Denial, or being unwilling to accept something or admit that it's true. *See also:* Hearing; Ear; Disabled

Death of a Loved One

A feeling of loss, grief, loneliness, or isolation. Grieving a specific loss or change in your life (losing a loved one, losing a job, etc.). A fear or feeling of abandonment (whether due to death or some other reason). Someone in your life who has experienced a loss or significant change.

See also: Dead Acquaintance; Dead Body; Feeling; Death of You; Dying; Abandonment

Death of You

The end of a phase of your life before entering another one. Some aspect of your life situation coming to an end (or a fear of or desire for such). A fear, expectation, or curiosity about an ending or about death. Feeling physically, emotionally, or mentally tired or overwhelmed (such as from trying to deal with too much). The "death" of a process, habit, or your ego. For more clues, consider the circumstances of your death in the dream. For example, death as a result of being attacked could represent a feeling or fear of victimization. Death can also be an indication that you were having a Toxic Dream (p. 320). *See also:* Dying; Life Force; Killed, Being; Ending; Death of a Loved One; Heaven

Debt

A feeling or fear of "owing" or feeling indebted to someone. A demand on you in real life (financial or otherwise). An unfulfilled promise or other unfinished business. **Someone owing you money** can represent feeling that the person "owes you" or is indebted to you somehow, or feeling that you've given more to this person than you've received from them. *See also:* Debt; Owing; Borrowing; Money; Scarcity

Decision, Someone Else's

Someone's actual decision in real life, or one that you expect, desire, or fear. An issue involving control, authority, or personal boundaries. A feeling or fear of someone else having authority over you. The idea of letting someone else make your decisions or take away your decision-making power. Exploring your boundaries in terms of what you are or aren't willing to allow, or how much control you're willingly giving someone else. *See also:* Decision, Your; Interview; Competition; Judge; Authority Figure; Approval; Judgment or Disapproval; Rule or Law; Agreement; Crossroads

Decision, Your

Deciding (or trying to decide) can represent: Exploring your thoughts and feelings about a particular real-life decision. Feeling decisive or confident. Feeling indecisive or unsure. A feeling or fear of making a decision you'll regret later. An issue involving direction, life decisions, or which path to take. A desire to be in charge of your own decisions, manage them well, or take responsibility for the ones you've made. *See also:* Decision, Someone Else's; Problem; Crossroads

Decoration

Embellishment, personalization, expression, or creativity. For more clues to meaning, pay attention to the characteristics of the decorations, such as color (perhaps representing a certain holiday or team), texture (lace representing femininity), and type (china representing a formal occasion). Also pay attention to the motivation behind the decorations. For example, they may represent a desire to enhance something, communicate a message, cheer someone up, show affection, or acknowledge a person or milestone. *See also:* Jewelry; Party; Special Occasion; Holiday; Wedding; Festival or Carnival; Creativity; Award; Furniture; House

Decreasing

The idea of less. Deterioration. Improving or worsening (depending on what is decreasing). Minimizing or downplaying. Becoming less urgent or less important in your mind. For more clues, consider what's represented by the thing that was decreasing, why it was decreasing and the resulting effects, and your feelings. *See also:* Disappearing; Deterioration; Descending; Smaller, Getting; Size; Eroding; Depleted; Empty; Inferior

Deer

Innocence. Sensitivity, heightened awareness, or intuition. Gentleness. Instinct. **A stag** might represent masculinity, assertiveness, or aggression. Dreaming of this animal can represent too much or not enough of one of those qualities, or someone or something you associate with the quality or animal. Consider also the animal's actions, context, and your feelings about it. *See also:* Animal; Elk

Deflating

Deflation (such as a deflating balloon, tire, or ball) could represent: The idea of "less than before." The ending of a process or phase. A challenge or obstacle. A downturn in mood or events. A loss of energy or momentum. A deflated ego or loss of self-esteem. *See also:* Decreasing; Smaller, Getting; Disappearing; Descending; Eroding; Depleted; Empty; Scarcity; Air; Breathing; Lung

Deformity

A deformity, or the idea of something that has mutated, can represent: Someone or something that's different or unexpected (or a fear of such). The idea of being different or of being seen as different than others. Change, or fear of change. Feeling affected in the area symbolized by the deformed body part (such as a deformed hand representing feeling less able to handle matters in your life). *See also:* Different; Shape; Tumor; Disabled; Illness; Monster; Weird

Delivery

Receiving a delivery can represent: Something or someone that has just shown up in your life (a person, opportunity, information, etc.). An event you imagine, desire, or fear happening in your life. Feeling like you've received or been "given to" somehow. The beginning of a process, or the ending of a process leading up to the delivery. **A delivery person** can represent a (real, expected, desired, or feared) communication, message, or gift. *See also:* Package; Receiving; Carrying; Messenger; Letter (Message); Giving; Communication; Birth, Giving

Demanding

Demanding something can represent: A strong desire or need for whatever you're demanding, or for the experience you think it will provide you. An attempt to gain power or control or make yourself feel more important than others. Exercising power that you've already been given. Feeling powerless, desperate, or a sense of self-righteousness. An indication that you could benefit from further developing your interpersonal skills. *See also:* Wanting; Taking From; Controlling; Requesting; Pulling; Obeying; Rule or Law; Authority Figure

Dentist

Seeking help or answers. The importance you place on being able to achieve, handle things, or cope in your life (or a desire for help in improving those abilities). A desire to improve your support of self (such as through self-expression or emotional nourishment). A feeling or fear of (physical, emotional, or mental) discomfort. Fear of intimacy, or of intimacy in a particular situation. An issue involving trust, vulnerability, or accepting help from others. *See also:* Doctor; Healer; Mouth; Tooth; Pain; Medical Office

Denying

Denying an accusation can represent: Feeling guilty or afraid of being accused. A feeling or fear of being persecuted, blamed, or needing to defend yourself somehow in real life. **Someone else denying something you know to be true** can represent a sense that they're being dishonest or there's something "off" about them in real life. **Someone else denying something when you don't know the truth** could represent a denial in real life, or a desire to understand or clarify a situation. **Someone being denied something** (such as denied entry or an opportunity) can represent a feeling or fear of control, authority, or deprivation. **Someone being in denial** (not willing to accept or admit the truth) can represent your perception of dishonesty or irresponsibility, or your blaming the person for a particular problem. For more clues, consider the context and your feelings about the denial. *See also:* Blaming; Blamed, Being; Lying; Lied To, Being; Confronting; Confronted, Being; Admitting; Rejection; Scarcity; Blockage or Obstacle

Deodorant

Deodorant or deodorizer can represent: A desire to change something about yourself or your environment (a habit, an irritating person, etc.), perhaps to make it seem more pleasant or tolerable. A desire to obscure or hide something unpleasant or unacceptable (perhaps the truth, or a perceived flaw). A desire to present yourself or a situation in the best light, control the image you project, or to avoid judgment by others. For more clues, consider the meaning of the area or thing being deodorized. *See also:* Armpit; Smell; Fragrance; Soap; Cleaning; Bathtub or Shower

Depleted

A resource being depleted can represent: A feeling or fear of something in your life being depleted (such as money, energy, health, free time, freedom, personal resources, or social support). A real or imagined need (yours or someone else's). See also the meaning of whatever was depleted. *See also:* Decreasing; Smaller, Getting; Scarcity; Sparse; Broken Object; Empty; Leaking; Hole; Deterioration

Descending

Descending or going downhill could represent: A feeling of losing progress, moving backward or downward in life, or the idea of things getting worse (as in a "downward spiral"). Things getting easier or making easy progress (as walking downhill is easier than walking uphill). The idea of something decreasing (such as energy, stress, or money). Descending into the subconscious level. Becoming more relaxed. *See also:* Falling; Low; Bottom; Stairs; Floor; Under; Underground; Diving; Decreasing; Sliding

Desert

A mentally or emotionally harsh environment. A characteristic you associate with deserts or with a particular desert (hot, dry, lifeless, empty, interesting, exotic, etc.). Something with a desert-like characteristic (such as an empty landscape or a person with a dry sense of humor). *See also:* Landscape; Hot; Dry; Dry Up; Sand; Dust; Depleted; Sparse; Scarcity; Rural; Region; Location

Design or Plan

A design, plan, or strategy can represent: An actual plan in real life, or feeling the need for one. Intentions or motivations. Forethought or planning. Creativity. Preparedness. Thoughtfulness. Problem solving. *See also:* Making or Building; Shaping; Problem; Creativity; Manager; Leader; Cooking; Sewing

Desk

Diligence, work, study, or anything that feels like that (such as your job, schoolwork, or paying bills). A desire for, need for, or dislike of one of the activities just mentioned. The idea of organizing or preparing in order to be more productive. *See also:* Furniture; Working; Workplace; Business; Homework; Writing; Sitting

Dessert

Something "sweet" (a pleasant experience, a kind gesture, etc.). A treat, or the idea of treating yourself. An indulgence, self-reward, or self-soothing. An indication of actual hunger or a craving for sweets. **The dessert course of a meal** could represent the ending of an interaction, process, or phase. *See also:* Cake; Ice Cream Sugar; Food

Destroying

A destructive act can represent a feeling or fear of: Aggression. Anger (perhaps indicating that the person isn't accepting responsibility for their own feelings). Persecution. Hostility. Criticism, judgment, or againstness. **Destroying evidence** can represent hiding, denying the truth, refusing to take responsibility, or a fear of blame or punishment somewhere in your life. *See also:* Attacking; Killing; Abuse; Enemy; Violence; Fire; Ashes; Broken Object; Breaking; Explosion; Bursting; Accident; Eroding; Weapon; Fight; Denying

Deterioration

Atrophy, corrosion, or other natural deterioration can represent: Inattention or neglect, or the result of it. The result of an active destructive force or adversarial action (such as criticism that deteriorates a relationship). A gradual change or general decline, perhaps of which you're not aware. A tendency toward disorder. A tendency toward the natural order of things, or nature taking its course. *See also:* Rotten; Eroding; Smaller, Getting; Decreasing; Disappearing; Depleted; Inferior; Sparse; Scarcity

Diamond Shape

Something diamond-shaped might represent: High quality or value (as in a diamond jewel or a rating). Chance or risk (as in playing cards, which include a diamond symbol). Consider the context and what the shape means to you personally. *See also:* Shape; Jewelry; Gem; Game

Diarrhea

Rejection or getting rid of something. Oversensitivity or heightened personal boundaries (physical, emotional, or mental). Denying yourself love, nurturing, or nourishment (such as for body, mind, or spirit). Feeling afraid of the world, people, or situations around you. *See also:* Rejection; Indigestion; Stomach; Illness; Infection; Digestion; Anus; Body Part; Depleted; Toilet; Drain

Dice

A risk or gamble, or leaving something to chance. Feeling lucky or unlucky. Something in your life that feels like a game. Recreation or fun (or a desire for more). *See also:* Risking; Game

Different

Something that appears differently in a dream than in real life (such as a woman who appears as a man) can represent: Your perception of something in real life as "different than expected." The different characteristic itself (such as a bold red sweater representing a bold person). A feeling that the "different" thing is important, desirable, undesirable, or is on your mind right now for some other reason. *See also:* Changing; Variety; Many; Weird; New; Discovering; Good; Bad

Digestion

Digestion or the intestines can represent: The ability to take in or accept something (such as support, encouragement, or other emotional, mental, or spiritual nourishment). Processing something (as in thinking or mulling something over, or "letting a problem digest"). *See also:* Food; Eating; Biting; Chewing; Absorbing; Indigestion; Mouth; Stomach; Body Part

Digging

Searching for or trying to recover something. Delving into matters from the past. Trying to understand or discover the truth about something. Trying to hide or escape. *See also:* Discovering; Searching; Rescuing; Shovel; Quarry; Underground; Hole; Tunnel; Nest or Dwelling

Dinosaur

A large or overwhelming presence. Basic or primitive, or the idea of "back to basics." Something or someone from the past (perhaps gone now). Something that's outdated. Finding value in the past or learning from your past. Something that seems mythical or unattainable. Dreaming of this animal can represent too much or not enough of one of those qualities, or someone or something you associate with the quality or animal. Consider also the animal's actions, context, and your feelings about it. *See also:* Animal; Lizard; Bird; Depleted

Direction

A direction (such as west or NNW) can represent: A specific direction on your life path. A desire for more clarity about direction. A place, person, or event that you sense is in that direction from you in the dream. A concept you associate with the direction, such as north representing "higher" or south representing "warmer." Something specific you associate with that direction (such as a location, city, country, person, activity, or culture). Consider also your feeling about the direction and what's supposed to be in that direction in the dream (such as a threat or something you want). *See also:* Map or Directions; Turning; Compass; Traveling

Director

Leadership, guidance, authority, or vision. **Being a director when you aren't in real life** can represent: taking more personal control over your own life or a certain aspect of it (or a desire to do so); a desire to be a leader (perhaps in a way that involves creative and visionary thinking); a desire to feel more "in charge" or powerful; feeling less than powerful somehow in your life. *See also:* Authority Figure; Manager; Leader; Show or Movie; Stage or Screen; Celebrity; Theater; Audience; TV

Dirt

Dirt on an object, you, your clothes, or something else can represent: The intrusion of the outside world into your world. The result of participating "out in the world" or interacting with others (since the world or the people in it can "rub off" on you or have an effect on you, whether desired or undesired). A perceived imperfection or mistake. A feeling or fear of being judged or embarrassed, or a situation being spoiled. Feeling less than perfect, or getting caught up in perfectionism or a false sense of self value. **Getting dirty and feeling okay about it** can represent: letting go of inhibitions; feeling free to enjoy life despite its problems; accepting yourself or someone else as they are. *See also:* Ground; Problem;

Accident; Ashes; Mud; Dust; Germs; Failure; Sabotaged, Being; Rejection

Disabled

Someone who's disabled when they're not in real life can represent a feeling or fear of that person experiencing a challenge in their life. Pay attention to the type of disability and any type of supportive equipment the person is using. For example, the inability to walk might represent your feeling that the person is having trouble making progress in their life. A mental disability might represent your feeling that the person isn't thinking clearly or is affected mentally somehow (such as by a mood, alcohol, etc.). See also the specific type of disability. *See also:* Injured; Illness; Broken Object

Disappearing

Something or someone who disappears can represent: A sudden lack of availability, accessibility, or understanding of whatever is represented by the thing that disappeared. A decrease in importance or perceived importance (such as a fierce wolf that disappeared representing a threat that has subsided in real life). A wish to disappear or not be seen, or to avoid responsibilities, blame, embarrassment, or some other undesired experience. *See also:* Transparent; Eroding; Deterioration; Smaller, Getting; Decreasing; Depleted; Sparse; Scarcity; Rotten; Powers

Disaster

A feeling or fear of (physical, emotional, or mental) overwhelm, loss of control, victimization, or destruction. *See also:* Storm; Tornado; Flood; Earthquake; Apocalypse; Landslide; Avalanche; Problem; Chaos; Failure; Accident; Event; Fire; Firefighting

Discovering

Discovering something in real life (such as a situation, an opportunity, or the truth). An imagined, desired, or feared discovery. An insight that occurred to you during the dream. **Discovering an item you lost** can represent regaining something you've lost in real life, such as a relationship, happiness, or a source of income (or a desire for or fear of regaining something). *See also:* Searching; New; Surprise; Treasure; Opening; Digging; Exposed (Object)

Dish

The mode by which you receive emotional, mental or spiritual nourishment (for example, a plate presented to you that represents an opportunity for learning or enrichment). Consider also the context, how the dish is being used, what it contains, and your feelings about it. *See also:* Glass, Drinking; Container; Cooking Vessel; Silverware; Food; Eating

Dishonest

Someone being dishonest (or taking dishonest or unethical action) can represent: A feeling or fear of someone being dishonest, unethical, or not telling the whole truth in real life. Feeling or fearing that the world is generally dishonest or untrustworthy. Feeling that you are dishonest, unethical, guilty (or afraid you might be in the future). Compromising your integrity or not being honest with yourself somehow. For more clues, consider the motive for the dishonesty. *See also:* Betrayed, Being; Catching Someone; Criminal; Crime; Lied To, Being; Lying; Cheating; Trickery

Dishwasher

Renewal or a fresh start. Cleaning up after yourself in your life (such as dealing with the consequences of your actions, accepting responsibility for your decisions, or repairing relationships). Cleaning up after someone else (such as dealing with a problem they created or a responsibility they've neglected). Letting someone else "clean up" problems, or expecting them to do so. **A broken dishwasher** can represent an opportunity to "repair" the renewal or "cleaning up" aspect of your life. *See also:* Appliance; Cleaning; Dish; Silverware; Food

Disobeying

Disobedience or misbehaving can represent: A person's will or strength of will. An effort to maintain your sense of power or control, or your own personal empowerment. Independence or independent thinking. Following your own inner guidance. Consider also the motives for disobeying. *See also:* Sabotaging; Crime; Dishonest; Betraying; Bad; Problem; Right or Wrong; Rule or Law; Rigid

Distance

Distance between things or people can represent: Physical, emotional, or mental distance or remoteness. Separation. Isolation or privacy. The differences between people (opinions, beliefs, cultures, etc.) *See also:* Different; Divider; Between; Limit or Boundary; Privacy; Next To; Touching

Divider

A wall, fence, or other divider or barrier could represent: An obstacle or challenge. Something that keeps people apart, such as a disagreement or distance. Protection, separation, or an attempt to distance yourself from another person or situation (as in "putting walls up"). An attempt to keep things out. An attempt to keep things in, contained, or controlled. **A wall in a house** can represent a separation or boundary between different aspects of your life. Consider the divider's context, purpose, and how you felt about it. *See also:* Blockage or Obstacle; Privacy; Limit or Boundary

Diving

Diving into water can represent: A new beginning, starting a new process or project, or entering into a new phase or area in your life. Becoming deeply involved in something. An ending, an escape, or leaving something behind you (or a desire to do so). **Diving gear** (such as mask or swim fins) can represent preparing to "be immersed" in a new, different, or challenging situation or environment. Consider the individual items' functions (such as a mask protecting or clarifying, or fins enabling you to make progress). *See also:* Falling; Jumping; Descending; Underwater; Water; Swimming

Dizzy

Vertigo or dizziness in a dream (when you don't actually have it) can represent: Feeling confused or "off" somehow. Feeling overwhelmed or that things are out of control somehow in your life. *See also:* Confused; Circles, Going in; Chaos; Mentally Unstable

Dock

A place to stop, rest, find security, or take refuge from the elements (or a person or situation that provides such). An entrance, exit, or other transition. A beginning or ending place, as in a process, story, or journey (such as the departure point for a journey). *See also:* Boat; Anchor; Breakwater

Doctor

A doctor, therapist, or other healing professional can represent healing, fixing, or a type of assistance. **Visiting a doctor for help for a health problem** can represent a desire for help or answers regarding a problem in your life (physical or otherwise). **A doctor harming, controlling, or giving you questionable advice** can be an indication of a Toxic Dream (p. 320). *See also:* Medical Treatment; Healer; Healing; Health; Illness; Injured; Paramedic; Surgery; Hospital; Medical Office; Therapist; Nurse; Problem; Rescued, Being; Rescuing

Dog

Responsibility. Protectiveness or security. Unconditional love. Loyalty. Friendship or companionship. Your inner child. An actual dog in your life. Dreaming of this animal can represent too much or not enough of one of those qualities, or someone or something you associate with the quality or animal. Consider also the animal's actions, context, and your feelings about it. *See also:* Animal; Pet; Wolf; Coyote; Fox

Doll

Childhood, children, or your inner child. Innocence. Creativity, imagination, or playfulness. Parental nurturing. **A specific doll** from your past can point to something regarding that time in your past. **An acquaintance who turns into a doll** could represent a desire to change or control that person, resentment of their attempts to control you, or feeling unempowered in general. **Choosing outfits for a doll** could represent creativity, image, or a particular mood. *See also:* Toy

Dolphin

Fun or playfulness. Intuition. Tuning into non-verbal communication or cues. Connecting with someone who's different from yourself, or the willingness or ability to do so. Dreaming of this animal can represent too much or not enough of one of those qualities, or someone or something you associate with the quality or animal. Consider also the animal's actions, context, and your feelings about it. *See also:* Animal; Whale; Fish

Donkey

Working hard, or the willingness or ability to do so (perhaps without much payback or gratitude). Productivity. Carrying things for others (such as responsibilities or burdens). Humbleness. The idea of being "a regular person," average, or not fancy. Dreaming of this animal can represent too much or not enough of one of those qualities, or someone or something you associate with the quality or animal. Consider also the animal's actions, context, and your feelings about it. *See also:* Animal; Mule; Horse

Door or Entrance

A door, gate, portal, or other entrance or exit can represent a passage or transition from one area of space or time to another, such as: A new beginning, or a transition from one phase to another in your life. Access to a different reality such as "the other side" or "another world." A dream cue that indicates the dream story shifting from one setting or time frame to the next. **A door inside a house** might represent a connection between two aspects of your life. **A house's front door** might represent a transition from your public life to your personal life. **Not being able to open a door** can represent feeling stuck or unempowered, or a belief that you're being held back (by a circumstance, a person, God, etc.). **A door that provides access** (such as on a refrigerator or a safe) could represent the idea of access or permission to access something (an area, person, certain information, money, etc.). **A revolving door** can represent a speedy or smooth transition; an obstacle or delay (if you got stuck); "going in circles" or being stuck in a pattern (if you went around and around). *See also:* Passageway; Opening; Gatekeeper; Room; Entering; Lock; Faucet; Valve; Knocking; Knock, Hearing a; Password

Doorknob

Taking action, or an intention to act. Searching. Beginning a process. Feeling open to opportunity or progress. Consider the doorknob's context and your feelings about whatever was on the other side of the door. **Grabbing a doorknob to open a door** can represent: feeling confident or ready for whatever's next in your life; searching for information, answers, or greater understanding. **A missing or broken doorknob** can represent a feeling or fear of being unable to act, escape, or access an opportunity in your life somehow. *See also:* Door or Entrance; Knob; Entering; Opening; Key; Lock

Doormat

The threshold of something new (real or imagined). Preparing for a transition or change. Your feelings (optimism, dread, etc.) about a certain aspect of your life or about what's coming next in your life. The idea of feeling welcome or welcoming others. The idea of homeor the feeling of home. A feeling or fear of being taken advantage of ("treated like a doormat"). **Wiping your feet on a doormat** can represent letting go of old issues and baggage before starting fresh. *See also:* Door or Entrance; Porch; Entering; Flooring

Dough

An early stage of a process. Opportunity or potential. Naive, immature, or premature. **Dough rising** can represent growth or potential for growth; the idea of allowing time enough time for a process to occur; a process with a useful by-product (as in the yeast creating bubbles in the dough); a desire for warmth (physical, emotional, or spiritual). *See also:* Food; Bakery

Dove

Peace. Hope. Commitment or loyal partnership. A promise. Optimism. Dreaming of this animal can represent too much or not enough of one of those qualities, or someone or something you associate with the quality or animal. Consider also the animal's actions, context, and your feelings about it. *See also:* Bird; Pigeon

Dragon

Power, or power that seems magical or "bigger than life" (or a wish for such). A challenge, problem, quest, or goal. Consider the type of dragon, its actions, what stood out about it, and how you felt about it (for example, a friendly dragon might represent personal power or the importance of friendship, whereas a fire-breathing dragon might represent self-protection or aggression). *See also:* Mythological Character; Dinosaur

Dragonfly

Ability to "rise above" or maneuver in your life. Different or other-worldly. Observation or perspective. "Magic," or a wish for it. Intuition, inner guidance, or spiritual assistance. Dreaming of this insect can represent too much or not enough of one of those qualities, or someone or something you associate with the quality. Consider also the insect's actions, context, and your feelings about it. *See also:* Insect

Drain

The idea of something "going down the drain," being wasted, flowing out, or disappearing. Something being lost or gone (such as time or energy) like "water down the drain." The idea of getting rid of something (as in "washing your hands of" a particular matter). Movement within a process, across space, or through time. **A blocked or backed up drain** can represent a stalled process, or trouble stopping or getting rid of something. *See also:* Sink; Pipe; Flow or River; Hose; Water; Vent; Valley; Canal; Passageway; Toilet; Funnel; Faucet; Blockage or Obstacle; Cleaning

Drawer

A drawer (such as in a dresser or cabinet) can represent: The idea of keeping or holding on to things. The way you organize things in your life or in your mind. A certain area of your consciousness or the things in it (such as thoughts, beliefs, or memories). The idea of having (or not having) enough space or time in your life. **Looking in a drawer** can represent: seeking knowledge, information, or answers; revisiting something from the past (such as a memory or unresolved issue); trying to regain something that you've lost (or that you fear you've lost). *See also:* Cabinet; Furniture; Container; Storage; Under; Darkness; Light (Illumination)

Drinking

Drinking any beverage might represent: "Taking in" (as in admiring a view or absorbing an idea). Gaining understanding or knowledge (as in "drinking from the fountain of knowledge"). Satisfying a yearning or need. Restoring or refueling yourself physically, emotionally, mentally, or spiritually. See also the type of beverage you were drinking, and consider your feelings and motivations (for example, tea might represent relaxation or thirst-quenching, while coffee might represent energy). **Drinking an alcoholic beverage** can represent: a desire to "numb out" or escape a problem; a desire to feel more relaxed or more interactive; a desire to be accepted or go along with the crowd; a habitual form of behavior or thinking. *See also:* Glass, Drinking; Liquid; Bottle; Sucking; Straw, Drinking; Bar or Night Club; Drunk; Alcohol; Drug

Driver's License

A driver's license, I.D., or other form of identification can represent: The idea of being official, approved, or validated by an authority. Your identity or the way you think of yourself. Permission to participate in or access a particular experience. **Misplacing your driver's license** can represent a feeling or fear of: not being permitted or "officially approved"; a loss of identity; losing or being denied the ability to make progress in your life (represented in the dream by not being allowed to drive). **Your driver's license being taken away by authorities** can represent an issue relating to responsibility, authority, rules, or societal norms. *See also:* License; Driving; Wallet

Driveway

A driveway can represent: An actual access route. A symbolic access route or a means of approaching a person, place, situation, or something else. The degree of accessibility of something (for example, a celebrity's driveway being very steep might represent how difficult you think it would be to meet that person). Your own driveway could represent the way you interact with people who approach you (if your house represents you). *See also:* Door or Entrance; Driving; Car; Porch

Driving

Driving a vehicle can represent how you "run your life," or did in the past. **Driving well** can represent taking charge of your life, making good decisions, or staying on track. **Crashing** can represent a feeling or fear of a disaster or inability to handle things in your life. **A driver other than yourself** can represent an authority figure or someone you've allowed to make decisions for you; someone who was in charge of a certain process that's represented by the vehicle's movement (such as the leader of your project team, or your friend who took you to dinner). *See* *also:* Traveling; Vehicle; Car; Steering; Road; Riding; Fast; Leader; Driver's License; Windshield; Accident

Drowning

A feeling or fear of overwhelming circumstances, helplessness, hopelessness, or loss of control, or of an important need being denied. The idea of "too much," "going overboard" or "getting in over your head." A desire for help or rescue. *See also:* Underwater; Breathing; Death of You; Flood

Drug

A drug can represent actual or desired: Solving or relieving of a physical, emotional, or mental problem. Changing the course of a process in a positive way (as a medication can change the course of an illness). Consider the context, type of drug, and motivation and feelings associated with taking the drug. **Using illegal drugs (when you don't in real life)** can be an indication of a Toxic Dream (p. 320) or can represent: feeling "out of it" or not quite yourself; a feeling or fear of being out of control of yourself; taking a risk; a desire to escape something painful or unpleasant; rejecting yourself or neglecting responsibilities; a desire to change something about yourself or to try something new. **Someone trying to get you to use illegal drugs** can represent a feeling or fear of: questionable motives; manipulation; being tempted into a harmful habit; or someone trying to "bring you down to their level." **Forgetting to take or losing your prescription drugs** can represent a feeling or fear of neglecting a responsibility in your life or not having something you need. *See also:* Medicine; Alcohol; Sugar

Drunk

Dreaming that you're drunk (when you're actually not) can represent: Not feeling quite right or feeling "out of it." A current or past desire to escape something unpleasant. An indicator that you were experiencing a Toxic Dream (p. 320). *See also:* Alcohol; Medicine

Dry

Drying due to natural evaporation can represent: Loss or disappearance. Shrinkage. Transformation. A process of reduction, or a dwindling supply of something. *See also:* Dry Up; Dryer; Absorbing; Desert; Hard Object; Eroding; Decreasing; Depleted; Sparse

Dry Up

Drying due to evaporation can represent: Loss or disappearance. Shrinkage. Transformation. A process of reduction or a dwindling supply of something. **Something that is dried up,** or that has lost all of its moisture, can represent: dormancy or a rest period; the end of a process or the loss of potential; non-productive; the idea of failure. *See also:* Dry; Absorbing; Desert; Hard Object; Eroding; Deterioration; Smaller, Getting; Decreasing; Depleted; Sparse; Scarcity

Dryer

Finishing a cycle or completing something before you begin anew. Lightness or taking the "weight" out of a situation (as a dryer removes the water weight from clothing), like using humor in a tense situation. *See also:* Dry; Dry Up; Absorbing; Appliance; Warm; Hot; Cleaning

Duck

Family, emotional security, nurturing, or bonding. Remaining impervious to negativity from others. Making a certain activity look easy. Projecting a calm demeanor. Quirkiness. Dreaming of this animal can represent too much or not enough of one of those qualities, or someone or something you associate with the quality or animal. Consider also the animal's actions, context, and your feelings about it. *See also:* Bird; Goose

Dust

A dusty house or object could represent: Neglect or lack of attention in some area of your life. Unused, unoccupied, resting, or dormant. The passage of time. A neglected responsibility, or apathy. The idea of dryness (as in a dry, dusty landscape). Impediments to your inner process, or an outdated way of thinking. **Dusting off an object** can represent: revisiting a matter from your past; a desire to see or understand more clearly; clearing out judgments, self-limiting beliefs, or other dynamics from your consciousness. *See also:* Cover; Dirt; Dry; Cleaning

Dyeing

A change, change of pace, or distraction (or a desire for such). An attempt to disguise. An effort to conceal something you judge as undesirable. **Dyeing your hair** can also represent: exploring the idea of a change in personality or identity; seeing yourself differently or in a new light; a desire for others to see or react to you differently; feeling not quite yourself somehow. Consider also the color of the dye and your motivation for using it. *See also:* Hair; Hair Product; Bleach; Color; Wig

Dying

Someone dying can represent: A feeling of low "life energy" or a weariness in your life, perhaps due to an emotionally or mentally sapping situation or a physical tiring condition. The end of a phase (such as of childhood, career, or a certain lifestyle). The idea of "dying" mentally, emotionally, or spiritually, such as due to lack of nourishment, inspiration, or fulfillment on that level. An indicator that you were having a Toxic Dream (p. 320). *See also:* Death of You; Dead Acquaintance; Life Force; Killed, Being; Ending; Death of a Loved One; Heaven

Eagle

Strength (such as in spirit or character). Independence. Personal growth or healing (as in "soaring to new heights"). Adventure. Dreaming of this animal can represent too much or not enough of one of those qualities, or someone or something you associate with the quality or animal. Consider also the animal's actions, context, and your feelings about it. *See also:* Bird; Hawk; Falcon

Ear

The idea of hearing, listening, or understanding. Desired, feared, or imagined communication (such as hearing good news). A willingness (or unwillingness) to listen or to accept something. Consider the context of the ear in the dream story, and what is being heard or not heard. *See also:* Listening; Hearing

Early

A real life event that was early. An early point in a real-life process. Sooner than expected. Preparedness. **Arriving early for something** can represent: the perceived importance of whatever you were early for in the dream; feeling extra-responsible, eager, or impatient about something in your life; a feeling or fear of your timing being off somehow in your life. For more clues, consider the motivation for and your feelings about the earliness. *See also:* Before; Age; Time Frame

Earrings

Adornment. Self-expression. **Someone giving you earrings** can represent receiving a gift or something else of value (such as love, appreciation, thoughtfulness, or good will), or a desire for such. *See also:* Jewelry; Decoration; Gold; Clothes

Earthquake

Loss of control, or fear of losing control. A fear of threat from external circumstances. Feeling or fearing a threat to your inner foundation (such as to a long-held belief or something else you've always taken for granted). Feeling "on shaky ground" somehow in your life. Experiencing a shake-up in your life (such as in your beliefs, finances, relationship, job, or routine). *See also:* Unstable; Disaster; Ground; Trembling

Eating

Nourishing yourself physically, emotionally, mentally, or spiritual (or otherwise). Acquiring something, "taking it in," or making it your own (such as an idea, suggestion, or belief). Giving to yourself or treating yourself. Actual hunger or cravings. Consider the type of food, your feelings, and the context. *See also:* Food; Meal; Tasting; Biting; Chewing; Cooking; Absorbing; Gluttony; Feeding; Mouth; Tooth; Stomach

Eavesdropping

Eavesdropping on someone can represent curiosity about a certain person, situation, or the motives of others. **Someone eavesdropping on you** can represent a feeling or fear of personal boundaries being invaded, loss of privacy, or a secret being revealed. *See also:* Listening; Telescope; Secret; Privacy

Edge, Coming to an

A transition, such as within a process or between two phases. Being forced to change, adapt, or take action of some kind in your life. Feeling as if your options are very limited. An obstacle or challenge. Feeling pushed to an extreme or limit. A sudden loss of support from others (perhaps giving you the opportunity to "fly" on your own somehow). *See also:* Ledge or Cliff; Limit or Boundary; Sharp

Eel

Stealthy, slippery. Questioning your or someone else's motives. The element of surprise, or waiting for the best timing in order to be most effective. Flexible or adaptable. Dreaming of this animal can represent too much or not enough of one of those qualities, or someone or something you associate with the quality or animal. Consider also the animal's actions, context, and your feelings about it. *See also:* Animal; Snake; Worm

Egg, Bird

A new beginning somewhere in your life. A nurturing or all-inclusive environment. **An egg that's cracked or rotten** can represent a problematic situation that you feel needs attention or action. *See also:* Bird; Ovum; Fetus; Baby Animal

Eight

Perceived perfection (such as perfectly balanced). Spirituality. Something else you associate with eight, such as an octet, octagon, time frame, someone's age, or your family. *See also:* Number; Age; Time Frame

Eighteen

A certain time frame or phase in your life. Revisiting the past or looking forward to the future. **Dreaming that you're 18 when you're not** can represent newness or beginning a phase; responsibility, freedom, self-sufficiency, or validation; learning through experience or "the hard way." *See also:* Number; Age; Time Frame

Elbow

Effort or hard work. Discipline, follow-through, or perseverance. Flexibility, agility, or adaptability (physical, emotional, or mental). *See also:* Joint; Body Part

Electric

Something that is electric or electronic could represent: The idea of being or seeming robotic, inanimate, or inhuman. Efficiency. Intelligence, as in advanced technology. Assistance, or a tool that assists. The idea of automation or something that takes place without awareness. *See also:* Electricity; Machine or Robot; Appliance; Music; Electrocute; Lightning

Electricity

Energy, life, or vigor. Excitement. Flow, movement, or a process. Activity or action. Harshness. Surprise or shock (mental or emotional). Consider the context of the electricity and how you felt about it (such as whether you consider it helpful or harmful). *See also:* Electric; Wire; Flow or River; Electrocute; Lightning; Fuel

Electrocute

An accidental electrocution can represent: An emotional "shock" or trauma that feels overwhelming. A "jolting" wake-up call that brings a certain realization. The result of an unwise decision. The power of nature. "Short circuiting" or overwhelming the body, one of its systems, the mind, or the emotions (such as when you ate way too much sugar and it overloaded your system). *See also:* Electric; Electricity; Lightning; Execution

Elephant

Sheer strength and power, or elegant strength. Strong presence. Royalty. Honoring or elevating someone. Slowness. An issue of size or amount. An unusual or highly developed ability (as elephants are skilled at using their trunks). Communication that's stealthy or that certain groups can't understand or aren't aware of (as in the low-frequency elephant communications that humans can't hear). Dreaming of this animal can represent too much or not enough of one of those qualities, or someone or something you associate with the quality or animal. Consider also the animal's actions, context, and your feelings about it. *See also:* Animal

Elevator

Ability or mobility in life, especially ability to make progress (or succeed or fail) quickly. Shifting between the areas within your consciousness (such as subconscious, conscious, emotional, or mental), as represented by the various floors. Switching between areas of your life (such as work, relationships, or hobbies). Consider also the context and what the elevator is doing. **Moving upward** might represent moving forward or making progress somehow in your life. **Moving downward** might represent a perceived loss of progress, or an ending (represented by exiting the building). **Getting stuck** might represent feeling stuck, held back, or delayed somehow in your life. *See also:* Floor; Building; Climbing; Descending; High; Low; Basement; Upstairs; Main Floor; Stairs; Levitating

Eleven

The idea of luck, or the perception of it or desire for it. High-minded, spiritually evolved, or a deep connection with God. Something else you associate with eleven, such as a time frame, someone's age, or your family. *See also:* Number; Age; Time Frame

Elk

Graceful strength. Versatile. Noble. Kindness, charity, justice, or protection (based on the fraternal organization associated with this name). Dreaming of this animal can represent too much or not enough of one of those qualities, or someone or something you associate with the quality or animal. Consider also the animal's actions, context, and your feelings about it. *See also:* Animal; Deer; Moose

Email

Communication. An actual, imagined, desired, or feared message. A desire to communicate with a particular person, or to feel more heard in general. Help or support (or a desire for it). Consider also the content and timing of the email, identity of the sender and receiver, and how you felt about the message. *See also:* Communication; Computer; Texting; Voicemail; Typing; Words; Phone

Emergency Room

Actual, feared, or imagined crisis or trauma. The idea of needing help or feeling helpless. The availability of support, such as for problem solving.

See also: Medical Treatment; Help, Calling for; Rescued, Being; Rescuing; Doctor; Hospital; Ambulance; Paramedic; Medical Office; Illness; Injured

Empty

A void, an empty space, or nothingness can represent: Openness, freedom, potential, or endless possibility (as in an empty canvas or empty space). Feeling emotionally empty, missing something or someone, or lacking something specific. An unmet need or expectation (as in expecting something but getting nothing). Meaningless or insincere (as in "empty praise"). *See also:* Zero; Depleted; Wanting; Vacuum; Container; Hole; Scarcity; Sparse; Leaking

Emu

Well-grounded, practical, or down-to-earth (since emus don't fly). Contrary or cocky. Kicking, self-defense, or "kicking the habit." Using your feet to your advantage, literally or figuratively (as in making progress, or moving on after a challenge). Stretching or reaching for what you want. Dreaming of this animal can represent too much or not enough of one of those qualities, or someone or something you associate with the quality or animal. Consider also the animal's actions, context, and your feelings about it. *See also:* Bird; Ostrich

Ending

The ending of a process or activity can represent an actual, feared, expected, or imagined situation in which something ends. Consider the context (such as whether the ending was expected or a surprise), who or what was involved, and your feelings about the ending. **If you were the one ending the process,** consider your motivation (which could point to a desire to end something, feeling a need or obligation to do so, or a belief that the activity has run its course). See also the specific type of process that's ending. *See also:* Quitting; Interrupting; Failure; Breaking Up; Death of You; Ex; Phase or Process; Dying; Dead Acquaintance; Graduation; Starting Over; Closing

Enemy

An enemy (someone who is "against" you or whom you're "against") can represent: A real, imagined, or feared person in your life. A general concept that you're against or afraid of, or that you feel is antagonistic to you or your well-being. **Feeling "against something" or "against someone" (feeling ill will toward them)** can mean you feel that way about them in real life. Consider what you're feeling "against" in the dream and what those feelings might represent in your real life or your mind, such as:

feeling angry at or disliking the person; wanting them to do poorly in order for you to gain something; seeing yourself as different from them; wanting to distance yourself from them; judging characteristics in them because you actually judge those characteristics in yourself. *See also:* Feeling; Revenge; Competition; Attacked, Being; Attacking

Engagement

Getting engaged can represent a romantic or non-romantic: Agreement or commitment. Exclusive partner. Beginning or milestone. *See also:* Proposal; Ring (Jewelry); Agreement; Marriage; Appointment

Engine

An engine, motor, or other source of mechanical power could represent: Work or effort. How well something works (as in a "well-tuned engine"), such as your body, or you in a certain environment or relationship. Ability to move forward in your life. Strength, skill, or other resource required to make progress. *See also:* Car; Vehicle; Machine or Robot; Locomotive; Fuel; Lubricant or Catalyst

Enough

Having enough or a satisfactory amount of something can represent: Feeling satisfied in real life. Wishing you had more of something (tangible or intangible). *See also:* Extra; Many; Big; Infinite; Rich; Scarcity

Entering

Entering an area or structure (such as walking through a door) can represent: A transition from one space or time to another. Change. A new beginning, phase, project, or mode. Making an agreement. **Entering into an area where you're not allowed** can represent: a fear or respect for authority; a feeling or fear of making a poor choice. **Entering someone else's property or personal space** can represent: compromising personal boundaries or integrity; disrespect, betrayal, anger, or an intent to harm. Consider also your feelings, intent, and motivations for entering. *See also:* Crossing; Edge, Coming to an; Limit or Boundary; Knocking; Door or Entrance; Doorknob; Opening; Traveling; Driving; Walking; Passageway; Bridge; Invading; Starting Over; Agreement; Joining

Entrepreneur

Self-sufficiency. Autonomy or freedom. Resourcefulness or creativity. Flexibility. Isolation. Your work, job, career, or income. Tangible or intangible trading with others. Consider also what comes to mind when you think of running your own business. *See also:* Business; Working

Eroding

Eroding, wearing off, or wearing away can represent: A process of loss or degradation of something tangible or intangible (such as of communication, a relationship, integrity, or resistance to temptation). The passage of time. Usage over time. *See also:* Deterioration; Rotten; Smaller, Getting; Decreasing; Disappearing; Depleted; Inferior; Sparse; Scarcity; Descending

Erratic

An erratic or zigzag shape or pattern might represent randomness or chaos. **Something moving in a zigzag pattern** could represent: high energy; a process of searching or exploration. Consider the context of the action or shape and the motivation behind it. *See also:* Chaos; Circles, Going in; Shape; Corner; Unstable; Curve; Mentally Unstable; Nomad

Eruption

Something erupting (such as a volcano or a fight) can represent: A buildup and then explosion of emotion (as when someone bottles up their anger). A problem that builds and builds until it must be dealt with. An experience or fear of sudden and unavoidable crisis in your life. *See also:* Explosion, Bursting, Flood

Escalator

Assistance to move forward or upward, or to accomplish what you want in life. Movement between aspects of your consciousness (subconscious, conscious, spiritual, etc.), represented by the different floors. *See also:* Stairs; Descending; Climbing; Elevator; High; Low; Floor

Escaping

Escaping or running away from an undesirable situation can represent a real-life escape (or a desire for such). **Escaping from jail** could represent escaping punishment, or escaping limitations within your environment or your own consciousness. **Escaping from someone with ill intent** could represent a feeling or fear of being manipulated, taken advantage of, or threatened (physically, emotionally, or mentally). *See also:* Running; Attacked, Being; Missing Person; Leaving a Person; Avoiding

Evening

An ending, or something winding down. A beginning (such as of a hidden process or period of unawareness). A pause or period of relaxation. An activity or mood that tends to occur in the evening. *See also:* Time of Day; Time Frame; Night; Twilight; Sunset

Evenness

Two or more things that are even, balanced, or symmetrical could represent: Fairness. Equity among many (such equal rights). Balance. Symmetry. An issue of abundance, scarcity, or injustice. A desire for or fear of action intended to "even things out." *See also:* Balancing; Fairness; Quiet

Event

An actual event in your life, perhaps a recent one or one that happened long ago. A desire for or fear of something similar happening in real life. An exploration of an imagined scenario (best-case, worst-case, etc.) by your subconscious mind. Curiosity about how a certain experience might feel and how you would react to it or handle it. A desire to avoid or be prepared for a particular kind of challenge. Events in dreams are almost never predictions of real life events (in the author's experience). *See also:* Activity; Phase or Process; Disaster; Special Occasion; Events (the category)

Evil

Something evil (such as "the devil") trying to harm you can indicate that you were having a Toxic Dream (p. 320), or it can represent: A feeling or fear of "ill will" in real life (such as a mean or violent action, a story on the news, or a scary movie). Labelling something as "evil" according to your own assumptions, observations, judgments, or some other mental process. *See also:* Threat; Bad; Criminal; Right or Wrong

Ex

A former romantic partner, boss, or other "ex" can represent: Your current romantic partner or someone else currently in your life. A feeling of unfinished business with your ex, such as something left incomplete, unresolved, or unspoken. Fond memories of your time with that person, perhaps the kinds of feelings you'd like to experience more of in your current life (but not necessarily with that person). Remembering something unpleasant about your relationship, perhaps that you'd like to avoid in another relationship or something from which you can learn. An imagined or desired relationship or partner (romantic or otherwise). *See also:* Relationship; Breaking Up; Ending; X

Execution

The forcible end of a process or phase in your real life or imagination (such as getting fired from your job or expelled from school). Fear of a process or project ending. A desire to escape or to get rid of a problem. **Executing someone as punishment for a past deed** can represent: a

140

feeling of self-righteousness; needing to feel right or needing to consider another person wrong; feeling critical, or wanting your opinion to seem more important or carry more weight; an opportunity to resolve an issue involving your judgment of self or others. *See also:* Killing; Beheading; Killed, Being; Death of You; Death of a Loved One

Exercise Equipment

Exercise equipment (such as a treadmill or stationary bike) might represent: Exerting yourself with the intention of self-improvement (such as learning or bettering yourself) or a particular goal (such as changing a habit). Making an effort without making any real progress (such as "treading water" or "running in place" somehow in your life). Self-sufficiency. Isolation. An artificial environment or activity (such as "busy work"). *See also:* Exercising; Bicycle

Exercising

The idea of improving through practice, repetition, or consistent effort. Physical, emotional, or mental improvement or personal growth (or the desire or intention for such). Work or effort, perhaps toward a specific goal or result. Activity or busy-ness. *See also:* Moving Around; Exercise Equipment; Game; Martial Arts

Exhaust

By-products and fumes from a fire (or a vehicle, furnace, or something else involving combustion) can represent: The "by-products," results, or effects of a process or action. The results from an interaction between people. Venting something undesired, such as toxic emotions or judgments. *See also:* Smoke; Engine; Vehicle; Vent; Fuel

Exorcism

A wish to escape something that's scary, or that feels out of control or unpredictable. A desire to escape the effects of someone else on you (such as their opinions, judgments, beliefs, etc.). A desire to escape your own feelings, beliefs, judgments, or another aspect of yourself. A desire for spiritual or other assistance. An effort to get rid of something the person conducting the exorcism is afraid of or judges in real life. *See also:* Possessed; Controlled, Being; Evil; Religious Figure; Authority Figure

Expensive

An expensive item can represent: Something for which you'd have to pay a high price (such as money, effort, or your integrity). Something you value or really want. Something you feel others value. Something you consider a goal in your life. A thing, relationship, or experience you consider unattainable. *See also:* Rich; Money; Treasure; Good; Wanting; Attractive

Experimented On

Being experimented on can indicate a Toxic Dream (p. 320), or it can represent a feeling or fear of vulnerability, manipulation, or victimization. *See also:* Laboratory; Medical Office; Abuse; Attacked, Being

Explosion

A feeling or fear of: Destruction. Loss. Chaos or loss of control. Victimization or ill will. A sudden, unavoidable challenge in your life. A sudden and severe expression of negativity, such as anger or frustration. *See also:* Bursting; Eruption; Fire; Smoke; Destroying; Breaking; Accident; Bomb; Flood

Exposed (Body)

A part of the body that is exposed could represent: Vulnerability. Obviousness or a desire for attention from others. Aggressive intimacy or an attempt to act too familiarly with others. Casualness, a relaxed mood, or a lack of concern about appearance. *See also:* Naked; Underwear; Body Part; Cold; Discovering; Exposed (Object)

Exposed (Object)

An object that is exposed could represent: Visible or obvious. Vulnerability. Honesty or being straightforward. **An object that is visible when you feel it should not be** can represent: carelessness or oversight; a secret exposed; a particular intention on the part of whomever left the object exposed. *See also:* Discovering; Seeing; Cold; Exposed (Body)

Extra

Abundance. More than enough or too much of something in your life. Something that you feel doesn't fit in. **Having extra of something you like** can represent abundance in your life (or a desire for more). **Having too much of something you don't want** can represent feeling burdened or oppressed somehow (or a fear of such). **Feeling like an extra person or "fifth wheel"** might represent feeling left out or superfluous in your life somehow. **Playing an extra in a movie** can represent feeling you have no meaningful role in the real-life process represented in the dream. *See also:* Many; Enough; Leftovers; Orphan; Increasing; Enough; Storage; Fat; Rich; Variety; Infinite; Big; Bigger, Getting

Eye

Vision, or the ability to see or perceive. Awareness or clarity. Inner wisdom. Ability to understand. Inner vision, knowing, or a connection with God (a higher power). Self-expression. A person's soul or essence. **Seeing someone's eyes** can represent connecting with that person, or feeling watched or criticized in real life (depending on your feelings). **Seeing isolated eyes looking at you** can mean you're feeling watched, intruded upon, or aware of how others see you. Seemingly random "eyes looking at you" can appear when you're dropping off to sleep or waking up, although they often have no significant meaning and are best ignored. *See also:* Vision; Eyelashes; Eyebrow; Blinking; Body Part

Eyebrow

Expression, such as of feelings, thoughts, or opinions. How or whether you express yourself in the world. Questioning or doubting (as in a raised eyebrow). *See also:* Eye; Vision; Eyelashes; Body Part

Eyelashes

Protection of vision or perception, as in protecting your viewpoint from bias or influence by others. Femininity. Persuasion. Perceived attractiveness. The idea of "many." *See also:* Eye; Vision; Protecting; Protected, Being; Hair; Body Part

Fabric

The fabric of a garment, curtain, or other object made from cloth can represent: The image conveyed by the particular type of fabric (for example, velvet as luxurious or cotton as comfortable). A characteristic conveyed by the fabric's color, weave, pattern, condition, weight, or otherwise (for example, flowered fabric representing cheerfulness or dirty fabric representing neglecting yourself). A characteristic associated with the item that's constructed of the fabric (for example, denoting a particular climate, generation, culture, nationality, or hobby). **Unused fabric** can represent: the raw materials for or input to a creative process; potential, possibility, or opportunity. *See also:* Clothes; Woven; Thread; Sewing

Face

Identity. The way a person presents himself, or what he chooses to show to the world. If a person's face looks different in a dream than in reality, consider how it's different (which may say something about how you view that person). For example, your mother's face appearing 30 years younger than her actual age could mean that you think of her as young at heart, or that the dream refers to a past event. Seemingly random faces can appear when you're dropping off to sleep or waking up that can seem important at the time, although they are best ignored. *See also:* Head; Forehead; Cheek; Mouth; Lips; Eye; Eyebrow; Eyelashes; Nose; Jaw; Chin; Body Part

Factory

Creating or making things, especially combining basic building blocks to make something "greater than the sum of its parts." Productivity. Organization. Automation. Your work, job, career, or income. *See also:* Business; Processing; Making or Building; Workplace; Machine or Robot

Failing a Test

Failing or missing a test can represent: Fear or expectation of a challenge (past or future). Real or imagined criticism (feeling like you don't meet others' criteria or don't pass their "tests"). The importance you place on whatever the test represents in your real life (something at which you don't want to fail). *See also:* Test; Competition; Failure; School

Failure

Judging yourself as failing or as a failure could represent: A feeling or fear of failure or of falling short of expectations. An attempt to prepare mentally for a challenge ahead. Judging or labelling yourself negatively, or feeling or imagining others doing so. **Judging someone or something as a failure** can represent a judgment of that person or yourself (providing an opportunity to work through your underlying issue). *See also:* Ending; Disaster; Second Place; Accident; Bad

Fainting

Extreme fear, trauma, or other emotion. A desire to escape a particular experience. The idea that there's something you're unwilling to see, admit, or deal with in your life. For more clues, consider what was happening in the dream right before you fainted and how you felt about it. *See also:* Falling; Tired

Fairness

The idea of fairness or equitability somewhere in your life, perhaps a desire for it or a fear of not having it. **Something that feels unfair** can represent a feeling or fear of judgment, injustice, victimization, being falsely accused, or witnessing something unfair (in person, in the media, on TV, etc.). For more clues, consider the context and how you felt about the actions and people involved. *See also:* Judge; Justice; Evenness

Fake

Something that's fake or a person faking something can represent: Deceit or lying. A fear of being fooled. Doubt or a lack of trust in whatever the fake or faker represents. A sense that something's not quite right or not as it seems. Empty or invalid. A lack of something (such as a scarecrow lacking any sign of life or humanity). A replacement of something with something else less real, valuable, or meaningful (such as a "chocolate flavored" candy made with artificial flavor, which could represent pretending to be happy rather than expressing authentic feelings). *See also:* Pretending; Performing; Dishonest; Lied To, Being; Lying; Statue; Wig; Copying; Trickery

Falcon

Vision or watchfulness. Power. Speed or agility. Pursuit or perseverance. Inspiring awe in others. Maneuverability, or ability to adapt in the middle of a process. Dreaming of this animal can represent too much or not enough of one of those qualities, or someone or something you associate with the quality or animal. Consider also the animal's actions, context, and your feelings about it. *See also:* Bird; Hawk

Falling

A feeling or fear of losing a sense of security or control. A sudden lack of foundation in your life, such as a situation in which "the rug is pulled out from under you." Experiencing or fearing abandonment, especially by someone or something that provides critical support (a partner, employer, God, etc.). **An object falling** can represent: a loss (or loss of control) of whatever that object represents in your life; the idea of "coming back down to Earth" or facing reality; the idea of an unseen force in action (such as a belief that "grounds" your behavior). *See also:* Descending; Decreasing; Jumping Off; Tripping; High; Ledge or Cliff; Slipping

Family

Your real family, whether or not the they look like themselves. Another group with whom you interact in real life, such as friends or coworkers. An ideal imaginary family or group, perhaps triggered by issues with your actual family. *See also:* Relative; Mother; Father; Son; Daughter; Grandparent; Aunt; Uncle; Cousin; Person You Know; Person Unknown

Famished

Feeling deprived of happiness, life energy, or "the good things in life." Feeling deprived (or depriving yourself) of basic emotional nourishment, such as love or support. Actual hunger or cravings. *See also:* Hunger; Thirst; Scarcity; Depleted; Empty

Fangs

Feeling threatened somehow in your real life. A feeling or fear of someone intruding on you, crossing your boundaries, compromising your integrity, or attacking you (physically, emotionally, or mentally). A feeling or fear of a person or situation "getting under your skin," perhaps with a lasting effect (as an animal bite can lead to an infection). See also the type of creature. *See also:* Bitten; Biting; Attacked, Being; Animal

Farming

Farming, growing plants, or raising animals on a farm can represent a real-life activity that involves investing time or resources in a process that yields delayed results or a long-term gain (such as nurturing a child as they grow up, or managing your stock portfolio). *See also:* Field; Plant; Planting; Reaping; Sprout; Orchard; Garden; Animal; Barn

Fashionable

Something that's fashionable (or that's a trend or fad) can represent: A desire to be like others or to follow the lead of someone else. Copying others somewhere in your life. The way a person comes across in interactions with others (their demeanor, mood, personality, etc.). Something that you feel is a norm, generally accepted, or approved of by "everyone" (such as a popular belief or behavior). A desire to be accepted, avoid being judged, or otherwise control others' opinions of you. A desire to feel better about yourself or express yourself (in verbal or non-verbal communication). *See also:* New; Clothes; Jewelry; Decoration; Approval

Fast

Going fast (such as driving fast) can represent: Progressing quickly or easily somehow in your life (or a desire to do so). Wanting to move faster through life or a particular situation. The idea of being in a hurry, taking a risk, or being reckless. *See also:* Competition; Driving; Accelerator

Fat

Abundant or plenty (as in a "fat" wallet). Rich or valuable. The idea of having "enough." Stored energy or unused potential. The idea of holding on to things such as emotional baggage or outdated beliefs. Fear of loss, or a desire to get rid of something you don't want. *See also:* Big; Skinny

Father

Your real-life father. An authority or caretaker figure (such as your employer). A masculine role model or inspiration. The idea of fatherhood, fatherly qualities, or parenthood in general. Your spiritual parent (God). *See also:* Family; Person You Know

Faucet

Flow, such as of time or a process. Control of flow, including stopping, starting, or regulating when and how fast something is allowed to proceed. The idea of abundance or an endless supply. The idea of convenience or ready availability of something. *See also:* Valve; Flow or River; Water; Controlling; Gatekeeper; Sink; Drain; Passageway

Feather

Light or airy. Flying or soaring. Playfulness, fun, or color. Characteristics or symbolism of birds. Dusting or housework (as in a feather duster). A by-product, or something previously used but no longer needed (as a bird occasionally drops feathers). See also the type of bird from which the feather came. *See also:* Bird; Lightweight; Decoration

Feces

Something in your life that you consider to be undesirable. A by-product of a process. Something that you no longer need or that no longer benefits you (such as outdated beliefs or toxic thoughts). **Someone else's feces affecting you** can represent disrespect, or being affected by someone else's problems or issues. *See also:* Bathroom; Urinating

Feeding

Feeding someone can represent: Physical, emotional, mental, or spiritual nourishment. A responsibility, or the idea of fulfilling a commitment. The action or idea of giving, especially where there is a need. Generosity, love, or caring. Encouraging someone or something (an idea, a motive, a habit, etc.). Enabling something or someone to do more or to thrive (such as feeding a fire or feeding a car engine by pressing the accelerator). *See also:* Food; Cooking; Giving; Fuel; Accelerator

Feeling

Feelings in dreams often represent themselves, meaning that whatever you're feeling about the dream situation is likely the same way you feel about whatever the situation represents in your life. **Another person's feelings** can represent feelings you've seen that person express, or the way you imagine or fear that person feels. **An angry person** could represent: a real-life event during which you experienced someone's anger; a feeling that the world is an aggressive or negative place; your own anger. *See also:* Trembling; Gratitude; Helpless; Supporting; Hurt, Being; Jealousy; Forgiving; Touching; Unfeeling; Emotions (the category)

Female

Someone or something that's female can represent: A person in your real life. Femininity. Female self-image or related issues. Motherhood or your relationship with your mother. Your inner child (whether you're female or male). Creativity or creation. Stereotypical female characteristics, emotions, or dynamics. Something you personally associate with being female. **A problem with the female reproductive system** can represent a perceived issue regarding one of the above topics. *See also:* Woman; Person You Know; Person Unknown; Body Part

Ferris Wheel

Fun or participation (or a desire for more of it). Having or wanting a new perspective or change of pace. Ability to see the "big picture." The idea of going around and around (such as circular logic or a feeling of "getting nowhere"). Repeated chances (such as to resolve an issue, or to notice or understand something). **Being stuck on a Ferris wheel** might represent feeling stranded, or being stuck in a never-ending situation or cycle. *See also:* Ride; Merry-Go-Round; Amusement Park; Festival or Carnival

Festival or Carnival

A place or situation in your real life with lots of different things going on (the different activities might represent different aspects of your life, such as relationships, projects, pursuits, or challenges). Fun, variety, or excitement (or a desire for more of such). Consider also your feelings and the events there. *See also:* Ride; Ferris Wheel; Merry-Go-Round; Amusement Park; Zoo; Party; Parade; Holiday

Fetus

A fetus, embryo, or other early stage of life can represent: An early stage of a process or project. Responsibility for someone or something, especially a new responsibility. Responsibility for self or for your inner child. Perceived fragility or vulnerability. The idea of pregnancy, creating something, or bonding with another human being (of any age). A desire to be of value to others, or a need to feel needed by someone else. *See also:* Ovum; Baby; Birth, Giving; Pregnancy

Field

A natural field or meadow can represent: Freedom. Remoteness or privacy. Nature, or its beauty or power. Feeling removed from society or its rules. **A crop field** might represent: food or food preparation; physical, emotional, or mental nourishment; farming or a particular farmer you know of; long-term gain, such as investing energy in order to "harvest" benefits later. For more clues, consider your feelings and what you noticed about the field. *See also:* Plant; Planting; Farming; Orchard; Garden; Reaping; Sprout

Fight

A fight, battle, or war can represent: An opportunity to resolve a problem somewhere in your life. A feeling or fear of (physical, emotional, or mental) aggression or needing to defend yourself. A combative environment somewhere in your life (or in a movie, the media, or a video game). Your own inner conflict. An effort to understand two opposing arguments or points of view. A real or imagined situation that triggers feelings of anger, againstness, or self-righteousness. A one-sided perspective, taking a stance of "us vs. them," or feeling threatened by differences you perceive in someone else. Desperation, perhaps due failure of diplomatic or social skills. Compassionless action, bravado, or immaturity. The idea of your immune system battling against an infection or something else. *See also:* Arguing; Violence; Invading; Invaded, Being; Attacking; Attacked, Being; Surviving; Immune System; Allergy

Filing Cabinet

Physical organization or appearance. A system or method. A logical way of thinking. Mental organization or neatness (such as of your thoughts or your life). The idea of storing memories. **Filing something away** can represent the idea of putting something out of your mind, saving it for the future, or completing a task. *See also:* Folder; Organizing; Furniture; Drawer

Finances

Finances (and especially the flow of money) can represent the flow of something that's given and received in your life (such as time, effort, support, or something else of value). **A savings account** with a high balance can represent something you've saved or "banked" (such as good will, favors that people owe you, or good karma). **Wasting money** can represent wasting something valuable (such as time, energy, or effort). For more clues to meaning, consider the flow of money, the context and motivations involved, and your feelings about it. *See also:* Money; Check

(Money); Paying; Buying; Accumulating; Bills; Debt; Owing; Loaning; Borrowing; Rich; Investment

Finch

Activity, busy-ness, talkativeness. Flighty, frenetic, or moving quickly. Having great insight into the world around you. Exotic or interesting. Restriction or limitation, or wanting more freedom (since finches are often kept in cages). Dreaming of this animal can represent too much or not enough of one of those qualities, or someone or something you associate with the quality or animal. Consider also the animal's actions, context, and your feelings about it. *See also:* Bird; Canary; Wren

Finding a Lost Item

Regaining something you've lost in real life (a relationship, happiness, your source of income, etc.), or a desire to regain it. Consider your feelings about losing the item and also about finding it. See also the item you lost. *See also:* Losing an Item; Discovering; Catching Someone

Finger

Dealing with the details in life. Dexterity in handling life's tasks and challenges. Capability, ability, or adeptness. **A finger pointing at you** can represent a feeling or fear of blame, attack, or attention. *See also:* Thumb; Fingernail; Joint; Hand; Body Part; Blaming

Fingernail

Protection, especially self-defense. Abrasiveness or an abrasive personality (as in "fingernails on a chalkboard"). Consider also what stood out about the fingernails and their context. Your perception of someone's personality (such as long fingernails representing femininity, or dirty fingernails representing hard work or lack of hygiene). *See also:* Finger; Thumb; Manicure; Claws; Hand; Body Part

Fire

Fire can represent: Life or your "internal light." Light (as in illumination or awareness). Heat. Destruction. Cleansing. The end of a process, perhaps before a new one begins. **A fire igniting** can represent a trigger, or the beginning of a process. **A flame** (such as a burning candle) can represent the soul, spirit, or essence of a person, or the idea of eternity or infinity. For more clues, consider what started the fire, its context and purpose, and how you felt about it. *See also:* Destroying; Light (Illumination); Lamp or Light; Fireplace; Furnace; Smoke; Ashes; Cigarette; Accelerator; Fuel; Firefighting

Firefighting

Reacting to a crisis or situation that needs immediate attention, perhaps to the extent of neglecting other responsibilities. Solving problems or fixing things. Rescuing or saving (or a tendency toward these). *See also:* Fire; Hose; Water; Rescued, Being; Ambulance; Disaster; Destroying; Smoke; Paramedic

Firefly

A feeling of magic or specialness. The ability to make your own "light," happiness, or enthusiasm. A beacon or a bright spot in the dark. Guidance in your life, or a desire for it. Doing something that's seen in a positive way by others, such as finding an "opportunity to shine." Uniqueness, being yourself, or "doing your own thing in your own way." Dreaming of this insect can represent too much or not enough of one of those qualities, or someone or something you associate with the quality. Consider also the insect's actions, context, and your feelings about it. *See also:* Insect; Beetle

Fireplace

Home, or feelings of home. Heat. Luxury. Romance. Fire or destruction. For more clues, consider your feelings about the fireplace. *See also:* Fire; Hot; Warm; Cooking; Ashes; Smoke; House

Fireworks

Actual fireworks that you've seen, or that you're expecting or imagining. The idea of spectacle, celebration, or a sense of magic. A particular event, time of year, or person you associate with fireworks. *See also:* Holiday; Special Occasion; New Year

Fish

Adept in a certain environment or a particular pursuit (as in a fish's great ability to thrive in water). Not overly emotional. Simple or basic (such as in style or approach). Dreaming of this animal can represent too much or not enough of one of those qualities, or someone or something you associate with the quality or animal. Consider also the animal's actions, context, and your feelings about it. *See also:* Animal; Fishing; Religious Symbol

Fishing

Seeking (or being open to) ideas, opinions, advice, opportunities, new experiences, relationships, or something else. Trying to find or catch something. Offering an incentive or enticement. An attempt to feel more powerful by dominating those you consider less powerful. A perceived disregard for life or insensitivity to others. *See also:* Fish; Hunting; Searching; Catching Something; Caught, Being; Breakwater

Fist

A hand in the form of a fist can represent: Aggression. Power, or a desire for power. Encouragement or support. Tension. Holding on to something (beliefs, ideas, etc.). *See also:* Hand; Finger; Grasping; Tight; Body Part

Five

Excellence or popularity (as in a five-star restaurant). The idea of a full set (as in five fingers or five toes). A certain time frame. Something else you associate with five, such as a quintet, pentagon, time frame, someone's age, or your family. *See also:* Number; Age; Time Frame

Flag

An identity (such as identifying with a certain nationality or religion). A message or signal (such as a warning, or the start or end of a race). An occasion (such as a celebration). Consider the type of flag, any specific symbols or colors, and the flag's role in the dream. *See also:* Country; Nationality; Region; Symbol

Flamingo

Having a higher perspective or understanding. Having greater insight into the world around you. "Rising above" or having an advantage (such as maturity or feeling more secure about yourself). Exotic or interesting. Dreaming of this animal can represent too much or not enough of one of those qualities, or someone or something you associate with the quality or animal. Consider also the animal's actions, context, and your feelings about it. *See also:* Bird; Crane; Heron; Stork; Pelican

Flesh

The soft tissues of the body can represent: Physical existence or your physical level. Everything that goes along with having a physical body (feelings, experiences, rules, etc.). The idea that the body is merely a vehicle within which the soul resides. Physically, emotionally, or mentally vulnerable areas (feelings, ego, etc.). The fragility of life. A personality characteristic or aspect of the associated person. See also the specific part of the body being portrayed. *See also:* Body; Body Part; Skin; Muscle

Flirting

Friendliness or good will. Interest in a person (romantic or nonromantic). Focusing on the positive, admirable attributes in another per-

152

son. Manipulation (such as an ulterior motive or an attempt to control others' impressions). Consider the motivations behind the flirting and how you felt about it. *See also:* Friendly; Liking; Attractive; Crush, Having a; Chemistry; Romance

Floating

You floating (such as in a body of water) can represent a feeling of or desire for: Freedom. Feeling unburdened, unlimited, or without a worry. The idea of buoyancy or "rising above." Escape or detachment from physical reality. **An object floating** might represent freedom, abandonment, or rejection. For more clues, consider what is floating and how you felt about it. *See also:* Water, Body of; Swimming; Levitating

Flood

A body of water flooding or rising can represent: Overwhelm (such due to a crisis, challenge, or a long to-do list). Feeling or fearing being "in over your head" or things being out of control. A "flood" of emotions or thoughts. *See also:* Water; Water, Body of; Overflowing; Leaking; Increasing; Underwater; Storm; Disaster; Wet; Eruption; Mud

Floor

The floor of a room can represent: The setting of the real-life events that are represented in the dream. A starting place. A minimum or lower limit. The idea of lowness, disrespect or humiliation (such as groveling on the floor). **The floors or levels of a house** can represent the areas of yourself or your life. For example, a basement can represent your subconscious mind, the top floor might represent your spirituality, and the floors in between might represent other areas of your consciousness or your daily life. *See also:* House; Building; Upstairs; Main Floor; Roof; Room; Elevator; Flooring; Low

Flooring

A floor covering (such as carpet, tile, or linoleum) can represent: A covering, or something that covers something up. A veneer or mask. A fresh start or new beginning (since a carpet gives a floor a "new look"). An attempt to control your appearance or the impression you make. **A mat on the floor** (on which you sit, sleep, do yoga, etc.) can represent: the setting for a real-life activity or event, or something that's represented by the activity for which the mat is intended (such as a welcome mat representing hospitality). **An area rug** can represent: self-expression or personality, or a desire to cover up or deny something you judge or fear others will judge. Consider also the color or other attribute of the flooring (dirty, clean, business-like, fun, etc.) and what it signifies to you. *See also:* Cover; Floor; Doormat

Flow or River

The course, path, or flow of something (such as your life, or a particular process, project, or relationship in your life). The passage of time. The "path of least resistance" (since that's the path water usually takes). **A river that's flowing well** can represent things flowing well or going easily somewhere in your life. **You floating in or flowing with a river** can represent peace, contentment, "going with the flow," an attitude of acceptance, surrendering to a higher power, cooperating, or using your current circumstances to your benefit. **Fighting against the current or trying to go upstream** can represent "going against the flow" somehow in your life. **A dry riverbed** can represent challenging circumstances, especially ones that hinder your progress. *See also:* Water, Body of; Flood; Canal; Waves; Fountain; Squirting; Leaking; Wind; Swirl or Eddy; Valve

Flower

Beauty or femininity. Producing or creating. Something that produces useful results (as a flower produces a fruit and seeds). Life force or life cycle. **A healthy flower** might represent vitality within you or within a certain aspect of your life. **A wilted flower** might represent low energy or life force, or the end of a process. For more clues, consider what stood out about the flower and what comes to mind when you think of the flower. See also the specific flower type. *See also:* Plant; Smell; Fragrance

Flower Bulb

Potential. Stored energy. Someone or something that needs time to unfold and become its full self. An early version of something that doesn't exist fully yet or hasn't matured (such as a person, idea, or project). A cycle that repeats (since many bulbs bloom repeatedly). *See also:* Flower; Seed; Root Vegetable; Root

Fly (Insect)

Nuisance, or "bugging" others to get what you want or need. Vision, or the power of observation. Vigilance. Flitting from one thing to another. Finding and taking advantage of opportunities. Finding value in other people's discards, or where other people can't. Dreaming of this insect can represent too much or not enough of one of those qualities, or someone or something you associate with the quality. Consider also the insect's actions, context, and your feelings about it. *See also:* Maggots; Insect

Flying

Rising above (such as above your challenges or the mundane). Freedom from the limitations of your own mental, emotional, and physical challenges (or a wish for such). Spiritual transcendence or self-realization. An opportunity to connect with your inner joy or love. A higher perspective or understanding. Greater insight into the world around you. Using your abilities well, or to your advantage. **A pilot** can represent someone in your real life whom you've allowed to guide you or influence your life direction. **Piloting an airplane (or other vehicle)** can represent the way you're "running your life" or handling your responsibilities (for example, flying well could represent feeling that you're doing well in life, while crashing could represent difficulty handling things or a fear of trouble). *See also:* Levitating; Floating; Bird; Traveling; Driving; Airplane

Fog

Confusion or lack of clarity. The unknown or a mystery. A lack of understanding about something in your past. A foggy memory. **Getting lost in a fog** could represent feeling unclear about your direction, the next steps in your life, or how to "return home." *See also:* Confused; Smoke; Cloud; Wet

Folder

A container or grouping of things (files, pages, ideas, people, projects, etc.). Organization, being organized, or how things are organized. Putting something where it belongs. Remembering something (or a desire to do do). Forming an impression or opinion that compartmentalizes something or someone (such as into a category like "talented artists" or "people I like"). *See also:* Filing Cabinet; Container; Drawer; Organizing; Accumulating

Following a Path

Your life direction, a decision, or a series of choices. The idea of whether you're feeling on-track or off-track in your life. Following in someone else's footsteps somewhere in your life. Making the same choice most other people have chosen or would choose, or taking the "expected" or "tried and true" path. *See also:* Walking; Traveling; Path; Map or Directions; Following (Trailing Behind)

Following a Procedure

Following directions, a procedure, or an example can represent: A guided, step-by-step process in real life (such as instructions or a recipe). A desire for clear guidance. Acting on recommendations from others. Obeying, or complying with rules or an authority figure. Relying on others, or paying more attention to others' input than your own inner guidance. *See also:* Map or Directions; Making or Building; Obeying; Cooking; Text; Authority Figure

Following (Trailing Behind)

Something that follows or trails behind something else can represent: One event that occurred after another event in your life. Your perception of something or someone as a lower priority (than whatever was ahead of it). Being "pulled along" or supported financially, emotionally, mentally, etc. Following rather than leading. Copying someone, tagging along, or "riding their coattails." Following (a leader, a trend, etc.) blindly or without thinking for yourself. Perceiving something as an add-on or accessory, or as an afterthought or nonessential. Your issues or emotional baggage that "follow you" wherever you go. *See also:* Chasing; Obeying; Cart; Following a Procedure; Following a Path

Food

Nourishment for the body, emotions, mind, or spirit. A quality associated with the type of food (peanut butter as basic, caviar as extravagant, etc.). A quality associated with the food's shape (a sandwich representing feeling "sandwiched" between two people in a conflict). A quality associated with the food's texture (a banana representing someone who seems "slippery"). A characteristic associated with the food in traditional culture, such as a particular occasion, setting, time frame, or ethnicity (eggnog representing winter holidays). The time of day the food is typically eaten (pancakes representing the morning). For more clues, consider the context, who's eating the food, when and why, its characteristics, and what comes to mind when you think of that type of food. *See also:* Meal; Eating; Chewing; Tasting; Biting; Cooking; Feeding; Bread; Dessert; Spice; Absorbing

Foot

How you "step out" into the world, make progress in your life, or accomplish things in the world around you. The image you project (as in "putting your best foot forward"). Consider what stood out about the foot or feet, what was going on with them, and how you felt about it. *See also:* Shoe; Sock; Barefoot; Toe; Heel; Ankle

Forehead

Thought or ability to think. Awareness of something, as in having something "at the forefront of your mind." Intuition or knowledge. Connection with Spirit. *See also:* Face; Body Part; Head

Forest

The unknown. Losing your way, or feeling lost. Losing perspective, as in "can't see the forest for the trees." The idea of infinity, wilderness, or the great "out there." *See also:* Thicket; Jungle; Rural; Tree; Outdoors; Darkness

Forgetting

Forgetting something can represent: A fear of failure or of losing control. A fear that you'll forget something (perhaps because you have a lot on your mind). The importance you place on whatever the thing you forgot represents in your real life (such as next week's final exam). *See also:* Losing an Item; Amnesia; Late; Missing an Event

Forgiving

Actual forgiveness occurring during the dream. A desire for or acknowledgment of forgiveness in real life. Willingness to forgive or overlook perceived wrongs (in other words, an opportunity to release a judgment of someone you've labelled as "bad" or "wrong"). *See also:* Apology; Blamed, Being; Blaming; Confronting; Confronted, Being; Denying; Feeling; Decision, Your; Decision, Someone Else's

Fork

A fork (the eating utensil) can represent: Selecting or acquiring things that you want, enjoy, or find useful or inspirational (information, situations, friendships, etc.). The methods, actions, activities, or practices you use to nurture yourself physically (food, vitamins, etc.), emotionally (support from friends, family, etc.), mentally (information, positive environment, etc.), or spiritually (prayer, meditation, loving attitude, etc.). *See also:* Knife; Silverware; Branch; Sharp

Fort

Defensiveness or againstness. Self-defense. Disagreement or an antagonistic mentality. Strength, especially protective strength. Something or someone in your life that you consider a foundation or stronghold, or that helps you feel secure, safe, or well-protected. **Living in a fort** may represent feeling distanced or protected from the world, people, or situations (or a desire for such). *See also:* Protected, Being; Security; Protecting; Building; Cover; Fight

Fountain

Abundance, an infinite amount, or enough. Something that flows from a source. Quenching or satisfying. A source of life, energy. *See also:* Well; Water, Body of; Water; Hose

Four

Order or organization in your life. Solid or sturdy. Balanced, even, or symmetrical. A square, cube, box, or something with that shape. Something else you associate with four, such as a quartet, time frame, someone's age, or your family. *See also:* Number; Age; Time Frame; Square; Rectangle

Fox

Clever or resourceful. Sly or wily. Shifty or elusive. Having a misleading charm or ulterior motive. Dreaming of this animal can represent too much or not enough of one of those qualities, or someone or something you associate with the quality or animal. Consider also the animal's actions, context, and your feelings about it. *See also:* Animal; Dog; Coyote

Fragment

A piece, sliver, or other fragment can represent: Part of a whole (such as one member of a group, or one event in a series). The idea of small. The idea of "not enough" or feeling short-changed. A miniature version, or something that's representative of the whole. **Fragments of an object that's breaking or eroding** can represent: disintegration, destruction, or its aftermath. *See also:* Breaking; Eroding; Size

Fragrance

Fragrance or perfume could represent: Self-image, or the way a person wants to be seen by others. An attempt to gain approval, be seen as more desirable or acceptable, or hide something you consider undesirable. Freshness or pleasantness. Attractiveness. Personality, or a particular characteristic of a person. *See also:* Smell; Cleaning; Deodorant

Frame

A frame (such as surrounding a picture) can represent: Highlighting or drawing attention to something. Defining, outlining, or limiting something. Finishing, embellishing, or adding detail to something. *See also:* Landscape; Artwork; Photo; Limit or Boundary

Freezer

Calming down or cooling off emotionally. Experiencing "coldness" from someone, or feeling "cold" toward someone. Preserving, storing, or keeping something long-term. The idea of putting something on hold or wanting to get rid of it. A restricted or tight space, or a lack of freedom. *See also:* Ice; Cold; Appliance

Friend

Real, imagined, or desired friendship. The same person in your real life. The role the friend plays in your life (such as supporting, inspiring, etc.). The characteristic that stood out about the friend in the dream (a good listener, enthusiastic, etc.). Someone else in real life (for example, a celebrity who's your friend in a dream could represent a real-life friend who reminds you of that celebrity). *See also:* Person You Know; Person Unknown; Liking; Friendly

Friendly

A source of good will, camaraderie, support, encouragement, or something else that feels positive. Someone who's been friendly with you, or whom you wish would be. A desire for or appreciation of good will from others. *See also:* Liking; Friend; Approval; Good; Person You Know; Person Unknown

Frog or Toad

Moving forward in leaps, possibly interspersed among long periods without apparent progress. All-out effort, followed by a period of rest. Indirect or nonlinear progress (as in leaps that form a crooked path). The idea of hidden potential. Dreaming of this animal can represent too much or not enough of one of those qualities, or someone or something you associate with the quality or animal. Consider also the animal's actions, context, and your feelings about it. *See also:* Animal

Fruit

Being productive or making useful things. Creativity or creating. Harvesting, or a reward at the end of a long process. Children or offspring. Reproduction. Femininity. Consider also the fruit's context and what you associate with that kind of fruit, such as the region where it grows or its primary characteristic (color, shape, texture, etc.). *See also:* Apple; Reaping; Seed

Fuel

Fuel (gasoline, coal, firewood, etc.) can represent: The resources (skills, ability, knowledge, contacts, etc.) needed to make progress or move ahead somehow in your life, or in a certain area. Energy (perhaps energy that can be converted into work, effort, or progress). *See also:* Engine; Battery; Feeding; Vehicle; Exhaust; Electricity; Fire; Nuclear

Funeral

An ending (of a phase of life, a phase of a relationship, a job, an activity, etc.). A recognition of the end of a phase, or even a celebration of one (such as a graduation). Honoring or acknowledging a certain person (whether dead or alive). Grief or loss. A feeling of losing a person, relationship, activity, experience, a way of being, etc. The idea of supporting someone who has experienced a loss or challenge. *See also:* Dead Body; Dead Acquaintance; Coffin; Burying; Grave; Cemetery; Cremation; Hearse

Funnel

Controlling or limiting flow or direction (such as of liquid, money, a process, a decision, etc.). Consider also the dynamics of the funnel. For example, a slow-draining funnel might represent a bottleneck, delay, or holdup in a real-life flow or process. *See also:* Liquid; Flow or River; Drain; Slow; Decreasing; Waiting; Canal; Pipe

Fur

Fur, an animal pelt, or animal skin can represent: Protection from or fear of an undesirable social experience or harsh environment. Empty or void of life energy. Death or an ending. A need to feel powerful over your environment or those in it (perhaps based in feelings of inadequacy). A sense of entitlement or self-righteousness. Lack of compassion or reverence for life. An attempt at (emotional or mental) self-preservation. **A real fur coat or other animal-based garment** might represent: Benefitting yourself to the detriment of others; taking from or taking advantage of others; ignorance or indifference to the welfare of others. *See also:* Coat; Skin; Dead Body; Killing; Animal; Fashionable; Cold; Warm

Furnace

A source of heat, energy, life energy, enthusiasm, passion, or creativity (real or desired). Emotional warmth. Stress or pressure. *See also:* Fire; Warm; Hot; Fuel; Ashes; Smoke; Wind; Flow or River

Furniture

If a house represents your life, then furniture might represent certain details, aspects, or activities in your life. For instance, a bed might represent the personal relationship or resting aspect of your life. A kitchen table might represent family life, if that's where your family often interacts. See also the specific furniture item. *See also:* House; Table; Sofa; Seat; Bed; Desk; Drawer; Shelf; Filing Cabinet; Lamp or Light; Decoration

Future

A dream of the future usually doesn't predict the future. More often, it presents your imagined, expected, feared, or desired version of the future. In a dream about the future, the subconscious mind might be playing out a "what if" scenario to explore what a particular situation would be like, and how you might feel about it and handle it. *See also:* Powers; Intuition; After

Game

An experience of or desire for something you associate with a game or sport (such as play, social interaction, competition, or dialogue). The dynamics of a real-life activity or situation (such as between you and your project team at work). Consider also the type of activity, the dynamics between you and the others, and how you felt about what was going on. See also the specific type of activity. *See also:* Competition; Performing; Risking

Gang

A feeling of or desire for camaraderie, belonging, protection, acceptance, or something else. **Being threatened or harmed by a gang** can represent a feeling or fear of being overwhelmed, powerless, or taken advantage of in a particular situation in your life. *See also:* Organization, Membership; Attacking; Attacked, Being; Crime

Garage

Self-improvement, self-care, preparation, motivation, or other activities that enable you to make progress in your life (since a car can represent your ability to make progress). A pointer to a real-life event that happened in a garage. The idea of storing, repairing, preserving, cleaning, or other type of activity you associate with a garage. *See also:* Storage; Vehicle

Garage Sale

A garage sale or yard sale can represent clearing out, cleaning out, or letting go (of things, outdated beliefs, self-defeating patterns, or other things that are no longer working for you). The idea of recycling or letting someone else benefit from what you no longer use (such as sharing your knowledge or skills). The idea of others finding value in what you have to offer (or a desire for such). *See also:* Selling; Sale or Discount; Cleaning; Giving

Garbage

Feeling rejected, tossed aside, not wanted, not needed, expendable (or something or someone you perceive that way). Something you consider distasteful or undesirable. *See also:* Garbage Can; Garbage Dump; Garbage Disposal; Rotten; Smell; Rejection; Inferior; Trash Compactor

Garbage Can

Getting rid of or cleaning out. Rejecting or rejection. Denial. Someone or something that you feel gets "dumped on" with unwanted things, responsibilities, tasks, toxic emotions, or other "garbage." Neglecting or avoiding a responsibility by trying to "throw it away" (for example, throwing away a bill that's due or a report card you don't like). **Secretly throwing things away** can represent shirking responsibilities, being dishonest, or thumbing your nose at authority or rules. *See also:* Garbage; Garbage Dump; Rotten; Smell; Inferior; Rejection; Garbage Disposal; Trash Compactor

Garbage Disposal

Getting rid of what you consider unwanted or undesirable (such as judgments, negative thoughts, toxic relationships, or personal habits that don't support your well-being). A person who deals with other people's "garbage" for them (such as fixing their problems or cleaning up messes for them, perhaps denying them the opportunity to take responsibility for their own situations). *See also:* Appliance; Garbage; Destroying; Rejection; Inferior; Smell; Breaking; Trash Compactor; Garbage Dump

Garbage Dump

A person or place that gets "dumped on." The idea of "discovering a diamond in the rough" or "one person's trash is another one's treasure." **Picking through a junkyard** can represent: having to do something you really don't want to do in real life; feeling like you're getting someone else's seconds or rejects; looking for opportunity in an unexpected place. *See also:* Garbage; Garbage Can; Rotten; Smell; Inferior; Rejection

Garbled

Something garbled or muddled (such as words you can't read) can represent: An actual or imagined communication problem. A desire to understand something, get an answer, or get help somehow in your life (such as from others or from God). Frustration with a real-life problem, process, or relationship. *See also:* Confused; Words; Mentally Unstable; Text; Voice; Communication; Language

Garden

Your life or your consciousness, and all the different aspects of it. The idea of productivity, nurturing, managing, or doing good work. Consider also the state of the garden and anything that stood out or felt significant. **A vegetable garden** can represent: physical, emotional, mental, or spiritual nourishment; benefitting from hard work; the rewards of patience during a long process. **A garden overrun by weeds** could represent neglecting responsibilities or challenges. *See also:* Orchard; Plant; Leaf; Weed; Planting; Seed; Field

Gatekeeper

Permission. An authority figure who gives or denies permission. Someone or something that determines what you can and can't do (such as a person, organization, government, rules or laws, or your own internal decision maker). **Being a gatekeeper** can represent having a sense of control or authority in your own life, or the importance you place on that. **Having trouble getting past a gatekeeper** can represent someone or something you feel is limiting you or holding you back somehow; the idea of placing blame on someone else rather than taking responsibility for yourself and your life. *See also:* Security; Door or Entrance

Gay

The idea of acknowledging every person as a "human" first and foremost, regardless of anything else about them. Appreciating whatever you consider feminine or masculine about yourself or another person. Dreaming that you're gay or with someone of the same gender doesn't necessarily mean you're gay in real life. For example, it could represent a close friendship or other platonic relationship (since physical intimacy in a dream often represents mental or emotional intimacy in real life). *See also:* Female; Male; Self; Person You Know; Person Unknown; Romance

Gem

Something of value (such as wisdom or truth). Consider the characteristics of the gem (including color) and its context in the dream. **A gem as a gift** can represent: something you or the giver values; love, commitment, appreciation, or good will; an attempt by the giver to make a good impression or to influence the receiver. *See also:* Treasure; Stone; Jewelry

Genitals

A private or personal matter. Intimacy, such as a real-life conversation about a personal matter. Personal boundary issues. Keeping private matters private. Self-identity or sexual identity. *See also:* Female; Male; Body Part; Privacy; Sex

Germs

A perceived mental, emotional, or physical threat, especially a small threat that could become larger or multiply. A perceived lack of hygiene (physical, emotional, or mental). A feeling of disgust or distaste. Something you consider unwanted, undesirable, or threatening. *See also:* Insect; Dirt; Infection; Health; Mold or Fungus; Illness; Virus; Invaded, Being

Ghost

Someone you knew (or wish you'd known) in real life who is now dead. Something that has changed or doesn't exist any longer (such as a former relationship or former job). **A scary ghost** can represent a fear about something in your life, or it can be an indication that you were having a Toxic Dream (p. 320). *See also:* Dead Body; Monster; Zombie

Gift

Receiving a gift can represent: A desire to receive something tangible or intangible in real life. Feeling fortunate somehow in your life. Real or imagined generosity. Something of value to you (such as time, energy, a favor, a characteristic, or a talent). *See also:* Opening; Giving; Inheritance

Giraffe

Reaching or stretching (for what you want, toward a goal, etc.). Reaching beyond (beyond a perceived limitation, beyond what others can see or do, etc.). An ability to see things differently (differently than others, from a higher perspective, seeing both sides of an issue, etc.). Being, feeling, or doing things differently than others. Dreaming of this animal can represent too much or not enough of one of those qualities, or someone or something you associate with the quality or animal. Consider also the animal's actions, context, and your feelings about it. *See also:* Animal

Girl

A particular characteristic that stood out about the girl. A stereotypical characteristic of girls. A responsibility in your life. Your inner child. Your playfulness or need for fun. A child or adult you know in real life, or the role that person plays in your life (friend, girlfriend, daughter, etc.). Your vulnerability or need for support or empathy. Consider also the context of the girl and your feelings about her. *See also:* Child; Baby; Daughter; Person You Know; Person Unknown; Female; Woman; Romantic Partner

Giving

Giving (a gift, money, time, effort, etc.) can represent: A time in your real life when you gave someone something (tangible or intangible). Feeling generous in real life, or a desire to give or share. The idea of investing time or effort (such as in a relationship or at work). Consider also the recipient, and your motivations and feelings about giving. *See also:* Paying; Sharing; Gift; Feeding; Supporting; Receiving

Gland

The intention to change yourself or your environment. Expressing yourself (such as creativity, thoughts, or emotions). Productivity, or producing effective results in your life. The idea of getting rid of limiting or toxic factors in your life (such as self-defeating beliefs or external negativity that you've internalized). See also the particular gland. *See also:* Secretion; Lymph; Body Part

Glass

Glass (such as a window pane) can represent: Awareness or clarity, especially of things out in the world (situations, events, people, dynamics, etc.). Ability to see or be seen. Transparency, such as a person's thoughts or feelings being obvious. Communication, openness, or honesty. An invisible barrier (such as a "glass ceiling") through which you can see something but not get to it, or see someone but not communicate with them. **Something being behind glass** (such as jewelry in a display case) can represent protection, security, or the idea of value, desirability, or preservation. *See also:* Window; Mirror; Glass, Drinking; Sharp; Reflective Light

Glass, Drinking

A drinking glass or other drinking vessel can represent the idea of abundance (as in "my cup runneth over"), or lack thereof. The opportunity to satisfy a yearning, thirst, craving, or desire (such as a thirst for knowledge or a hunger for life). *See also:* Dish; Drinking; Container; Glass

Glasses (Eyeglasses)

Enhancement of vision or clarity (physical, emotional, mental, or spiritual). Your mental "filter" mechanism (your biases, assumptions, or how you view situations, events, people, etc.). Willingness to see, acknowledge, or deal with the truth or a particular situation in your life. Ability or willingness to understand. Ability to perceive (such as to be aware of what's happening around you). Ability to receive information or perceive cues from the world around you. *See also:* Vision; Eye; Sunglasses; Glass

Gleam

A gleam (such as from a very clean object) can represent the following perceptions about the object that's gleaming: Newness or cleanliness. Lack of problems, flaws, or complications. The result of hard work or good work. Consider also the meaning of whatever is gleaming. *See also:* Reflective Light; Sparkle; Light (Illumination)

Gloomy

A gloomy setting, character, or mood can represent: Your mood at the time of the dream. Your feelings about something in real life (gloomy, sad, hopeless, etc.). The perceived gloominess of a particular person, group, or environment in your life. *See also:* Feeling; Hurt, Being; Color; Weather

Glove

Self-protection, as in protecting yourself from harshness or threats (since gloves protect a person from cold temperatures, germs, etc.). The masking of a person's identity or motivations (as gloves mask a person's fingerprints). A person's denial of their own humanness or unique self (such as trying to feel no compassion or trying to act anonymously). Hidden or undiscovered abilities or strengths (represented by hands). Disguised or hindered potential to achieve (as gloves can decrease dexterity). *See also:* Hand; Finger; Fingernail; Protected, Being; Cover; Interfering; Bothered, Being; Clothes

Glowing

Something glowing can represent life energy, hope, goodness, or assistance, especially when it appears in the darkness. **A glow around a dream symbol** could also invite you to pay closer attention to whatever that symbol represents. **Something glowing eerily** can represent a person or force with unknown or perceived negative intent. *See also:* Light (Illumination); Reflective Light; Fire; Gleam; Halo; Life Force

Gluttony

A feeling of abundance (physical, emotional, mental, or spiritual), or a desire for such. A feeling or fear of emptiness, lack, or not having enough. Feeling deprived of the good things in life, or a desire for more of the "sweetness" of life or the "spice" of life. "Stuffing" your feelings instead of expressing them. Actual hunger or cravings. *See also:* Food; Hunger; Famished; Eating

Goat

Resourcefulness or the ability to "make do." Security in your own self. Agility or the ability to "climb" or make progress. Acceptance. Lack of pickiness or discretion in what you allow into your life or your personal space. Dreaming of this animal can represent too much or not enough of one of those qualities, or someone or something you associate with the quality or animal. Consider also the animal's actions, context, and your feelings about it. *See also:* Animal

God

Dreaming you are in the presence of God (the Divine, holiest of holies, creator, source of pure love, or whatever name you prefer) can represent: Your actual experience of God's presence during the dream. A desire to feel connectedness with or received assistance from God. Your idea of God or interacting with God (the way you think or hope it would be). A desire for belonging, connectedness, or meaning. **An imagined god or mythological god** (such as Zeus) can represent real, imagined, or desired help; guidance or comfort from an authority figure somehow in your life; feeling vulnerable or powerless somehow; a reminder of how an authentic spiritual connection compares to the emptiness of a pseudo-spiritual icon or "lower-level god." Consider also what the idea of the deity in the dream means to you, its context in the dream, your feelings and intent, and whether you experienced the overwhelming peace and love that signifies God's presence. *See also:* Love; Peace; Light (Spiritual); Religion; Authority Figure; Help, Calling for; Heaven

Gold

Feeling fortunate. Experiencing or desiring happiness or abundance. Something you consider valuable (such as knowledge, money, friendship, or memories). **The color gold** can also represent richness, autumn, or something of personal significance (a wedding ring, team colors, etc.). *See also:* Yellow; Color; Metal; Jewelry; Autumn

Golf

The idea of moving toward a goal (represented by making focused progress toward the hole). Evaluating your progress or being evaluated (represented by the scoring). A real-life interaction or relationship with the other players in the dream. An activity, hobby, or pastime (golf or otherwise) in your life. A competition, or comparing yourself to others. A respite from everyday life, or a desire for one. Consider what was going on in the golf game, who you were playing with, what stood out about the situation, and your feelings. *See also:* Game; Competition; Ball; Performing; Walking

Good

Considering a person or their actions to be good can represent: Recognizing or admiring their positive attributes. Feeling good will toward the person. The idea that the person meets your own standards or they're doing what you want them to do. Comparing them to others or yourself (good vs. bad, better vs. worse). Aspiring or relating to their qualities you consider to be good. **An event you consider to be good** can represent something (real or imagined) that you consider desirable; a wish for a particular experience in your life. For more clues, consider the context of the event and the experience it provided you in the dream (or that you think it would in real life). *See also:* Liking; Respecting; Superior; Approval; Right or Wrong; Obeying; Luck; Expensive

Goodbye

Saying goodbye can represent: a real or imagined ending (of an interaction, relationship, project, phase, school year, etc.). A temporary ending or a parting, as in "goodbye for now." A mock-up or "what if" scenario as played out by your subconscious mind, perhaps providing greater insight into your feelings about the person you're parting with in the dream. *See also:* Leaving a Person; Leaving a Place; Distance; Divider

Goose

Returning home, or to a feeling of "home" inside yourself. Dependence on someone else (including a willingness to accept help from others). Strengthening your own independence and identity. Endurance or persistence. Dreaming of this animal can represent too much or not enough of one of those qualities, or someone or something you associate with the quality or animal. Consider also the animal's actions, context, and your feelings about it. *See also:* Bird; Duck

Gorilla or Ape

Brute force, or possibly gentle strength. Imitation, copying, or aspiring to be like someone else. Nonverbal communication or unspoken language. Basic human skills. Humanity or human-like qualities (such as sentience or compassion). Dreaming of this animal can represent too much or not enough of one of those qualities, or someone or something you associate with the quality or animal. Consider also the animal's actions, context, and your feelings about it. *See also:* Animal; Monkey; Chimpanzee; Orangutan

Gossiping

A desire to feel a connection with the person with whom you're sharing gossip. A desire for acceptance, feeling included, or feeling more important. Crossing someone's boundaries (as in trying to "get into their business"). Using information as a currency or weapon. Trying to gain power (or take power away) from others through revealing secrets, information, or misinformation. A judgment of the person you're gossiping about. A desire to be closer to the person you're gossiping to. **Someone gossiping about you** can represent a feeling or fear of judgment, hostility, or a loss of privacy. *See also:* Interfering; Telling on Someone; Lied To, Being; Lying

Graduation

A completion or ending. An accomplishment or achievement. Official approval or permission, or feeling qualified to do or be a certain thing in your life. The idea of having complete knowledge or understanding of a certain topic or area, or of a part of your life. Completion of an inner process, project, or something else that has a natural cycle with an ending. Completion of a life phase or transition (such as "graduating" from childhood to young adulthood). *See also:* Ritual or Tradition; Succeeding; Ending; Special Occasion

Grandparent

Your real-life grandparent. An authority or caretaker figure. Unconditional love and support, wisdom, understanding, maturity, or something else you associate with a grandparent. A spiritual authority figure or wise elder in your life. *See also:* Family; Person You Know; Authority Figure

Grasping

Holding or grasping an object can represent: Keeping or saving something (control, your job, etc.). Trying to stop something from being taken away from you. Trying to take or get something. An attempt to maintain power or control. Continuing a process or maintaining your effort. *See also:* Holding; Taking From; Carrying; Holding a Person

Grasshopper

Making a huge leap of progress. Making a leap within your mind (such as an assumption, conclusion, or leap of logic). Using multiple talents or multitasking (as a grasshopper can jump and fly with his wings at the same time). Dreaming of this insect can represent too much or not enough of one of those qualities, or someone or something you associate with the quality or insect. Consider also the insect's actions, context, and your feelings about it. *See also:* Insect; Cricket

Gratitude

A real, imagined, or desired expression of thanks. Feeling particularly fortunate or glad, either in general or regarding a particular situation or person in your life. Feeling that you or someone else is deserving of thanks. *See also:* Feeling

Grave

An ending, such of a phase. A sense of loss or grief. Fear of the unknown. Denying or "burying" something, such as a secret or your feelings (or a desire to do so). *See also:* Cemetery; Burying; Coffin; Dead Body; Dead Acquaintance; Death of You; Safe or Vault; Funeral

Gray

The color gray can represent: Neutrality. Modernity. Gloominess, or another mood or emotion. Dullness or lifelessness (the opposite of vividness). *See also:* Color

Green

The color green can represent: Life or new life. Vigor. Growth. Nature. Freshness. Coolness. A relaxing environment or relaxed mood. *See also:* Color

Grim Reaper

Fear of death. Acknowledging your own mortality. A feeling or fear of something in real life trying to take something from you (time, attention, energy, focus, etc.). A feeling or fear of an ending or a change in something (such as a phase, project, or relationship). Fear of an impending threat or ending (real or imagined). *See also:* Evil; Death of You; Dying

Groom

A groom in a wedding can represent: A commitment or connection (romantic or otherwise). The beginning of a new phase, process, or lifestyle. The idea of a wedding, party, or other gathering. A desire for, fear of, or curiosity about being in a committed relationship or marriage. Reflecting on a certain romantic relationship (past or present). *See also:* Wedding; Relationship; Marriage; Man

Ground

A foundation, such as a set of beliefs, values, relationships and other factors that form the basis of the way you think and experience things. The beginning, as in building something "from the ground up." Something that's obvious, visible, or known to others (whereas something underground is not obvious or could be secret). "Where you stand" or "how things stand" (such as your opinion or the status of a process). *See also:* Dirt; Mud; Earthquake; Underground

Groundhog

Keeping to yourself. Cycles or seasons. Sleep or dreaming. Something that's subconscious or that happens without your awareness. Low-key activity or "staying under the radar." Dreaming of this animal can represent too much or not enough of one of those qualities, or someone or something you associate with the quality or animal. Consider also the animal's actions, context, and your feelings about it. *See also:* Animal; Mole (Animal); Hedgehog

Group

A real or imagined group of people or things. Belonging, acceptance, or connectedness. Security or protection. Abundance. Plurality, or the idea of strength in numbers. Anonymity (as in "getting lost in the crowd"). Pay attention to what is symbolized by the individual items in the group, and the purpose or motivation of the group. *See also:* Organization, Membership; Band; Class; Many; Accumulating; Variety; Organizing

Guest

An interaction or visit with someone, or a desire to have company or interact with certain people (or with new people). The idea of supporting or honoring the person who is your guest. **Being someone else's guest** can represent (experiencing in real life or imagining): a new or different experience of a temporary nature; feeling or being new to a particular environment or situation; feeling welcomed, supported, or honored by others. *See also:* Party; Special Occasion; Event; Visiting; Traveling; Trip or Vacation; Holiday; Appointment; Meeting; Arriving; Returning

Gum, Chewing

Idle or pointless talk. Busy work, or doing an activity just to fill your time. Indecisiveness, or "going around and around" while trying to decide. A problem or "sticky situation." A process that's yielding no progress or results. A perceived characteristic of the gum chewer in the dream (such as carefree, casual, insecure, or disrespectful). **Blowing a bubble with bubble gum** might represent: fun or playfulness; creativity; a process; a tangent or distraction. *See also:* Chewing; Bubble; Mouth

Gym

A real-life place to meet or interact with others, or the process of doing so. A real-life setting for self-improvement (physical, emotional, or mental), or the process of doing so. **A gymnasium where groups gather** (such as in a school) can represent: a community gathering place for activities or events; a specific group event (such as a game, show, or dance). *See also:* Exercising; Gymnastics; Muscle; Martial Arts; Arena or Auditorium; Audience; Game

Gymnastics

Complexity, such as having to "jump through hoops" to solve a problem or meet a goal. Flexibility, or ability to adapt in various situations or environments. Self-discipline, or self-improvement over time. Mental, emotional, or physical activity or a particular pursuit in your life. *See also:* Exercising; Performing; Competition; Muscle

Hail

A feeling fear of a challenge or adverse circumstance somewhere in your real life. The idea of someone or something "going cold." Transformation (since hail is rain transformed into ice). Abundance or punishment in your life (real, perceived, desired, or feared). *See also:* Cold; Ice; Rain; Storm; Weather; Cloud

Hair

Hair or hairstyle can represent: Personality, style, or the perceived role the person plays in your life. The state of the person's body, emotions, or mind (the way you perceive it). A characteristic that reminds you of a certain person or something else your real life. **Something that's "off" about a person's hair** (weird color, missing, too much, in the wrong places, etc.) may reflect a problem or situation you feel or fear that person having in real life (for example, being covered in hair could represent feeling overwhelmed or out of balance). **Pulling out your hair** could represent frustration, or rejecting something about yourself or your situation. **Losing your hair** can represent a feeling or fear of you, your life, or your identity being compromised or not being what you expect; a negative state of mind; a fear of vulnerability or lack. **Hair loss as part of the aging process** could represent a particular time frame, or the idea of getting older or associated changes. **Hair color or other characteristics** may provide clues to what the person represents (for example, gray hair representing older or experienced, or a short and neat haircut representing well-organized or conservative). **Trimming hair to make it neater** can represent taking care of details in some area of your life.

172

Drastically cutting hair (such as shaving your head or cutting hair very short) can represent freedom or loss (such as of self-identity, femininity, or masculinity). For more clues, consider your feelings about the hair and its characteristics. *See also:* Beard; Shaving; Wig; Comb; Tangle; Hair Product; Salon; Attribute; Body Part

Hair Product

Hairspray, hair gel, or other styling product can represent: Support. Something or someone (a tool, catalyst, person, etc.) who supports or helps you accomplish what you want. Something or someone who provides structure or a framework. For more clues, consider the particular product, its role, context, and characteristics. For example, hairspray might represent a wish to keep something the same, make something last, or put something "on hold." *See also:* Hair; Controlling; Organizing

Halo

A figure with a halo can represent: Your desire for spiritual guidance, comfort, support, or something else. Perceived goodness, holiness, or saintliness. *See also:* Angel; Glowing; Light (Spiritual); Good

Hammer

Force, power, or strength. Building or constructing. Work or effort. Aggression. *See also:* Tool

Hamster

A hamster, gerbil, or other similar animal can represent: The idea of "storing up" or "saving for later" (such as memories or money). Isolating yourself, or having time to yourself. Nosy, or "sticking your nose into things." Cuteness, or someone or something you consider cute. Dreaming of this animal can represent too much or not enough of one of those qualities, or someone or something you associate with the quality or animal. Consider also the animal's actions, context, and your feelings about it. *See also:* Animal; Mouse; Rat

Hand

A person, humanness, or humanity in general. The ability to get things done, being "handy," or "handling things." The idea of holding on or letting go (physically, emotionally, or mentally). **A hand coming toward you with ill intent** could represent a feeling or fear of persecution, hostility, aggression, criticism, or being taken advantage of by someone or by people in general. **Holding hands or other positive interaction** with hands can represent good will or affection you feel toward someone (or that you believe someone feels toward you, or that you wish they did). Consider the context, whose hand it was, and what it was doing. *See also:* Finger; Touching; Fist; Body Part

Handshake

A greeting or welcome. An introduction, such as when meeting a new person or encountering a new idea or subject matter. Cooperation. An agreement, contract, commitment, or promise. *See also:* Hand; Touching; Meeting Someone; Agreement

Hard Object

Solid, definite, or for "for sure." Strong or enduring. Strict. Inflexible. Unfeeling, cold, or lacking compassion. *See also:* Rigid; Dry Up; Stone; Metal

Hat

A role you play, want to play, or want others to think you play. The impression you want to give to others, or your self-image (for example, wearing a top hat representing your desire for others to think you're wealthy, or a jester's hat representing your identity of yourself as funny). Disguising your identity, or a desire to. Protection (such as protecting yourself from others' influence or opinions). Hiding, distancing or isolating yourself (physically, emotionally, or mentally). *See also:* Head; Clothes; Costume; Cover; Crown

Hawk

The power of observation. A visionary perspective. Watchfulness, protectiveness, or vigilance. Taking from others. Agility. Ability to maneuver in changing conditions or to cope with volatile situations. Dreaming of this animal can represent too much or not enough of one of those qualities, or someone or something you associate with the quality or animal. Consider also the animal's actions, context, and your feelings about it. *See also:* Bird; Eagle; Falcon

Head

A head or skull can represent: A person's identity, self, personality, life, mood, or state of mind. Authority over yourself, or the authority figure of a group (such as the president of a company). Pay attention to whose head it was, how and where the head appeared, and what stood out about it. **A decapitated head** can represent the idea of losing your identity, effectiveness, potential, or life. **Discovering a disembodied head or a headless body** could represent an ending, or the idea that you see that person as no longer effective in the same way (such as no longer helpful or no longer a threat). *See also:* Brain; Forehead; Face; Scalp; Body Part

Headache

A problem or challenge. Overwhelm. Thinking too hard (or feeling like you are). A feeling or fear of something threatening your self-identity or sense of self (such as a lapse in personal integrity). *See also:* Head; Ache; Pain; Brain; Face; Forehead

Headlight

The ability to see things clearly. Seeing your way forward in life or in a certain situation (or a desire for such). Intuition, or clarity of inner vision. Strategizing or planning how to proceed. A person (whomever the headlight's vehicle represents in your life). *See also:* Light (Illumination); Vehicle; Car; Road

Healer

Real or imagined healing or assistance (physical, emotional, mental, or spiritual). The idea of fixing a problem. Feeling unclear or seeking answers. Assistance from a spiritual source (real or desired). *See also:* Medical Treatment; Repairing; Healing; Health; Doctor; Therapist; Problem; Medical Office

Healing

Physical healing (such as a wound that healed) can represent: Inner healing. A pointer to an area within your consciousness that's ready to heal. Recovery. Renewal or a fresh start. Forgiveness or releasing a grudge. Peace. A need for support or help. **Healing powers** can represent: compassion for others; the idea of Divine healing; desired, imagined, or a past instance of helping yourself or someone else, solving a problem, a spiritual experience, feeling special, or positive attention. *See also:* Repairing; Health; Healer; Problem; Medical Treatment; Scab; Scar; Salve; Powers; Paranormal

Health

A real or imagined issue regarding of your well-being (physical, emotional, mental, or spiritual). The "health" of a situation, project, environment, etc. (such as a "healthy" bank account). *See also:* Condition; Healing; Healer; Illness; Infection; Well; Medical Treatment; Life Force; Life

Hearing

Hearing something (a sound, voice, words, noise, etc.) can represent: Real, imagined, desired, or feared communication. A willingness (or unwillingness) to hear or accept information, news, a change, etc. For more clues, consider what you heard, its context and source, and how

175

you felt about it. See also the particular type of sound. *See also:* Listening; Eavesdropping; Ear; Noise; Communication; Voice; Words; Quiet; Sensory Cues (the category)

Hearse

A transition (such as from one phase into another). A catalyzing event somewhere in your life, or the means by which you made (or are making) a change in your life. A sense of loss or grief. *See also:* Funeral; Cemetery; Grave; Dead Body; Coffin; Vehicle; Driving

Heart

Love, compassion, or caring. Connection with a loved one, God, or the Divine in other people. Life. Soul. Human essence, or the humanity within a person. Passion or enthusiasm. Personal strength. Desire or emotional attachment to someone or something (as in "the heart wants what it wants"). *See also:* Shape; Chest; Breast

Heart Attack

Fear of having a heart attack. A feeling or fear of a sudden crisis that's out of your control. A "crisis of the heart." *See also:* Heart; Pain; Chest

Heartburn

Feeling unable to accept or "digest" something, or the idea that something "doesn't sit well" with you. Emotional or mental upset. Fearing, dreading, or imagining negative outcomes. A feeling or fear of stress. *See also:* Indigestion; Stomach; Chest; Pain; Heart

Heaven

Heaven (or a heaven-like place) can represent: The idea of heaven or the afterlife. Feeling a connection with God during the dream. Spirituality. Spiritual peace and love. A positive or happy feeling. *See also:* God; Light (Spiritual); Love; Peace; Religious Figure; Death of You; Dying; Religion

Heavy

Something heavy or dense can represent: A burden, or a feeling of being burdened. Great substance or strength. Great significance (as in a "weighty matter"). Seriousness or solemnity. Full of meaning, richness, or some other attribute. An imagined or real-life obstacle or challenge. Something difficult to move or change. *See also:* Big; Carrying; Fat; Measure

Hedgehog

Self-protection through avoidance, personal boundaries, abrasiveness, or using negativity to distance yourself from others (as in a hedgehog rolling up into a spiny ball to protect itself). Rest or a rest cycle. Dreaming of this animal can represent too much or not enough of one of those qualities, or someone or something you associate with the quality or animal. Consider also the animal's actions, context, and your feelings about it. *See also:* Animal; Porcupine

Heel

Ability to gain momentum or gain traction (such as to make progress or move forward in life). Tenacity or stubbornness (as in "digging your heels in"). **An injured heel** can represent: a feeling or fear of losing your ability to make progress; a need to slow down or stop trying so hard, perhaps for your own well-being. *See also:* Foot; Walking

Helicopter

Ability to "lift above" (as "rising above" a situation, problem, or others' pettiness). Observation from a higher perspective, literally or figuratively. Ability to see the "big picture" or the "grand plan." Personal mobility or autonomy in life (such as the ability to make your own decisions, or to work toward goals and dreams on your own). The idea of a pursuit or being pursued. *See also:* Flying; Levitating; Traveling; Engine; Fuel; Airplane

Helmet

A helmet, hardhat, or other protection for the head might represent: Self-protection. Protecting something personal (thoughts, feelings, decisions, identity, etc.) from others or from outside influences. The idea of protecting yourself from mental, emotional, or other attack. *See also:* Armor or Shield; Protecting; Cover; Head

Help, Calling for

Calling for help (police, a friend, God, etc.) can represent: A particular time you called for or wished for help in real life. A current desire for help. A feeling or fear of a threat, helplessness, confusion, or inability to take action. **Not being able to call for help (such as yell or dial the phone)** can represent: a feeling or fear of not being able to get help, an overwhelming situation, or an obstacle to getting help (such as feeling too ashamed to ask). *See also:* Communication; Rescued, Being; Rescuing; Voice; Phone; Misdialing; Paramedic; Emergency Room

Helpless

Being or feeling helpless or vulnerable can represent: An actual feeling of helplessness or vulnerability or a desire for help in a particular aspect of your life. Losing power or control somehow in your life (or a fear of such). A focus on the unpredictable nature of life. *See also:* Can't Move;

Can't Speak; Attacked, Being; Abandonment; Left, Being; Feeling; Illness; Disabled; Paralysis.

Hero

The idea of help, rescue, or bravery. Good will or other admirable qualities in action. **Dreaming that you're a hero** can represent a characteristic or action you associate with heroism; a desire to help others (or someone in particular), feel more powerful in the face of a challenge, or feel better about yourself through helping someone else. *See also:* Rescuing; Rescued, Being; Superhero; Supporting; Sacrificing; Character

Heron

Being partially involved in an issue or situation (since herons are often seen wading). Trying something out, or stopping short of full commitment. Gathering physical, emotional, mental, or spiritual nourishment. A higher perspective. The ability to identify and achieve something you want. Dreaming of this animal can represent too much or not enough of one of those qualities, or someone or something you associate with the quality or animal. Consider also the animal's actions, context, and your feelings about it. *See also:* Bird; Crane; Flamingo; Stork; Pelican

Hesitating

A hesitation in real life, such as due to: Uncertainty. Fear. Shyness. Insecurity. Overwhelm. Feeling flustered. Feeling at a loss (such as a loss for words). A desire or need to think things through or figure things out. *See also:* Interrupting; Quitting; Waiting; Last Minute; Confused

Hiding

Keeping a secret (or wanting to). Stealth, or not wanting to be seen or noticed. Feeling or fearing a threat, or a feeling a need for self-protection. Perceived or feared manipulative, misleading, or dishonest action (such as lying). A desire to remain anonymous. A fear of admitting or taking responsibility for something. A desire for privacy. Consider the motivation for hiding. *See also:* Privacy; Cover; Under; Burying; Secret; Quiet; Avoiding; Costume

High

Being elevated, at a great altitude, or looking down on a scene can represent: A higher or more insightful perspective, or an ability to see the "big picture." Feeling more spiritual or more in touch with a higher power. "Rising above" a problem, challenge, pettiness, or immaturity. The idea of being or feeling: superior, more powerful, having greater knowledge, or better qualified; wiser, more mature, more evolved, more experienced, or further along in your process than others. Consider the context and your feelings about whatever was high. *See also:* Above; Superior; Flying; Climbing; Upstairs; Big; Falling; Air; Sky; Measure; Elevator; Drug

High School

Dreaming that you're in high school if you aren't in real life can represent: Revisiting the past, perhaps to learn a real-life lesson. Entering a new stage of learning or personal development. A person, activity, characteristic, or something else you associate with high school. *See also:* School; Class; Group; Time Frame; Age; Location; Building

Hill

A mountain, hill, or slope can represent: A challenge, hurdle, or obstacle. A project or task to be done. Overwhelm, exaggeration, intimidation, or dread. The beauty or strength of nature. Endurance or constancy over time. **A downhill slope** can represent something you perceive as easy or as declining somehow. *See also:* Ledge or Cliff; Ramp; Climbing; Descending; Sliding; Slipping

Hip

A hip (the body part) can represent: Balance (or lack of it) in your life. Physical, emotional, or mental flexibility. The ability to move forward through your life or some aspect of it, maneuvering well and maintaining balance as you go. *See also:* Buttocks; Joint; Pivoting; Rotating; Leg; Sitting; Body Part

Hippopotamus

Large or bulky. Obvious. Hiding aspects of yourself (thoughts, opinions, motives, physical self) or not communicating or revealing everything about yourself (as hippos are sometimes seen submerged in water.) Dreaming of this animal can represent too much or not enough of one of those qualities, or someone or something you associate with the quality or animal. Consider also the animal's actions, context, and your feelings about it. *See also:* Animal; Rhinoceros

Hit by a Vehicle

The idea of a sudden challenge in real life (such as a feared, expected, or imagined change or crisis). A feeling or fear of someone harming or endangering you, infringing on you or your personal space, or compromising your boundaries (physically, emotionally, or mentally). *See also:* Accident; Attacked, Being; Car; Vehicle; Injured; Pain; Rear Ended; Driving

Hitchhiking

A request for help, especially help with moving ahead, change, or accomplishing a goal. The idea of relying on others for assistance. An issue of trust, or a question of trusting someone you don't know well. *See also:* Requesting; Traveling; Sharing; Receiving; Supporting; Vehicle; Road; Thumb

Holding

Holding an object can represent the following relative to whatever the object represents: Continuation or maintenance. Ownership or control. Responsibility or caring for. Affection or liking. *See also:* Holding a Person; Restrained; Grasping

Holding a Person

Holding a person close (as in a hug) can represent the following with regard to that person or whatever they represent: Affection. Wanting. Possessiveness or controlling. Wanting to keep or maintain. For more clues, consider the context and how you felt about the holding. *See also:* Grasping; Holding; Hug; Restrained; Cuddle

Hole

The idea that something is missing or something has been lost. A flaw, irregularity, or the idea that something is not quite right. An opening or opportunity for something to pass from one area to another (such as in a dam, fence, or computer network). **A hole in clothing** can represent: a threat to your personal boundaries; vulnerability; perceived shabbiness or inferiority. **Being down in a hole** can represent: "feeling down"; a feeling or fear of being stuck somehow in your life. *See also:* Door or Entrance; Empty; Vacuum; Well; Underground; Vent; Depleted; Bursting; Leaking; Broken Object; Breaking; Keyhole; Problem; Opening

Holiday

Dreaming of a specific holiday can represent: A past, expected, imagined, or feared event around that time. A celebratory (or other holiday-related) mood or setting for the dream. Something or someone you associate with the particular holiday or time of year. *See also:* Dates on a Calendar; Special Occasion; Party; Festival or Carnival; Trip or Vacation; Time Off; Event; Guest; Time of Year; Time Frame

Homeless

A feeling or fear of losing your quality of life, security, social support, personal or financial well-being, or something else. The idea of losing an aspect of your personal foundation or something you take for granted (such as a loved one, a life perspective, or a belief system). A feeling or fear of being left out, abandoned, or rejected by others. Rejecting yourself or not feeling "at home" in yourself or your body. Feeling like you don't have a "spiritual home" (not feeling a connection with God). The idea of living outside accepted society or its norms. *See also:* House; Losing an Item; Scarcity; Nomad

Homework

An assigned task or a responsibility. The idea of practicing something in order to learn or improve. An extra load or an increased number of tasks on a to-do list. Something extracurricular, "in the margins," or outside the scope of a primary activity. *See also:* Working; Text; Math; Task

Honey

The deep, rich sweetness of life. A sweet reward resulting from hard work. Nourishment for body, emotions, mind, or spirit. Health or well-being. *See also:* Bee; Food; Nest or Dwelling

Honeymoon

The early part of a social process (relationship, teamwork, etc.) when participants are on their best behavior or trying to make a good impression, often before any major problems arise. An actual honeymoon. A trip or vacation. The idea of connecting with or spending time with someone you're close to (romantically or platonically). *See also:* Trip or Vacation; Wedding

Horn

Horns or antlers can represent: Self-defense or self-preservation. Aggression. Masculinity. Someone or something you perceive as having animal- or devil-like characteristics (depending on the type of horns and your feelings about them). *See also:* Animal

Horse

Power or strength. Working or work activity. The ability to work or make progress in life. Freedom. Transportation or a journey. Perceived masculinity or femininity. Dreaming of this animal can represent too much or not enough of one of those qualities, or someone or something you associate with the quality or animal. Consider also the animal's actions, context, and your feelings about it. *See also:* Animal; Riding; Carrying; Traveling; Donkey; Mule

Hose

A communication channel, connection, route, pathway, or process. **A hose with a strong, focused stream of water** could represent focus, aim, working toward a goal, or staying on track in some aspect of your life. **A leaking hose** could represent an unanticipated problem or complication. **Spraying someone with a hose** could represent playfulness, a desire to change or get rid of the person, a desire to "clean" or remove something from their character or life. **A neatly-wound hose** might represent organization or a task well done. **A tangled hose** might represent disorganization or a problem. *See also:* Flow or River; Pipe; Passageway; Water; Watering; Flood; Fountain; Drain; Squirting; Funnel

Hospital

The idea of dealing with a crisis or fixing a problem. Feeling vulnerable or desiring help somewhere in your life. A fear of something happening that's out of your control. A source of help, or a place or person you went to when you needed help. **Being in the hospital** can represent a desire for help, or not feeling your usual self (mentally, emotionally, or physically). **Someone else being in the hospital** can indicate your concern about the person, or your opinion that they need extra care or attention. **Working in a hospital** (when you don't in real life) can represent giving, good will, or demands from people in your life who need help. *See also:* Illness; Injured; Medical Treatment; Surgery; Doctor; Nurse; Emergency Room; Medical Office; Medicine

Host

A hostess or host (such as at a restaurant or party) can represent: Managing, coordinating, or welcoming (or a person who does these things). Directing or providing guidance. Hospitality. Representing a group. *See also:* Invitation; Party; Restaurant; Server; Crowd; Flow or River

Hostage

Being taken hostage can represent a feeling or fear of: Someone trying to control, coerce, manipulate, or deprive you of free will (physically, emotionally, or mentally). An authority in your real life (a person, organization, habit, pattern, limiting belief, etc.) that has power over you or that feels overbearing or oppressive. *See also:* Abduction; Taking From; Attacked, Being; Attacking; Restrained

Hot

Heat or something hot can represent: Energy. Increased activity (as heat involves molecules vibrating faster), or a need for decreased activity.

Pressure or stress. Excitement. **Being too hot** can result from actually feeling too hot physically while sleeping, or it can represent a feeling or fear of oppression, a challenging or uncomfortable situation, or not feeling well (physically, emotionally, or mentally). *See also:* Warm; Fire; Weather; Landscape; Tropical; Desert; Location; Feeling

Hotel

Yourself or your life. Your own bedroom or house. Somewhere away from home where you've spent time. The idea or feeling of being a guest, being waited on, or cleaned up after. The feeling of being on vacation or taking a break from the usual. A mental, emotional, or spiritual "home away from home" (such as a person you feel as comfortable with as your own family). *See also:* Building; Room; Visiting; Trip or Vacation

House

A house, apartment, flat, or any place of residence often represents you or your life, even if it doesn't resemble your current home. The events in the house may represent real or imagined events in your life. Each room may represent a different area of your life (such as your bedroom representing your personal life). Each level may represent a level of your consciousness (such as a basement representing your subconscious mind or attic representing spirituality). A house can also represent security, comfort, protection, familiarity, or belonging (as in the idea of "home"). Also consider the mood and condition of the house and anything that stood out about it (for example, a dreary house might represent sadness, or a house missing its curtains might represent personal boundary issues). **Your childhood home** might represent you or your current life, or a time in your past. **Someone else's home** might represent that person or their life, your relationship with that person, or a real-life situation in which you were both involved. *See also:* Building; Nest or Dwelling; Room; Floor; Basement; Main Floor; Upstairs; Furniture; Mansion; Porch; Backyard; Roof; Hut; Homeless; Location

Hug

Familiarity or closeness. Affection. A feeling of being surrounded or enveloped. **An unwelcome hug** could represent a feeling or fear of unwelcome (physical, emotional, or mental) intimacy or your boundaries being compromised. *See also:* Touching; Holding a Person; Handshake; Kissing; Arm; Romance; Goodbye

Hummingbird

Tasting the "sweet nectar" of life. Endurance. Quick progress, erratic changes in direction, or pausing or "hovering in place" while waiting or evaluating (based on the way hummingbirds fly). Protection of self, others, property, or what you consider to be yours. Dreaming of this animal can represent too much or not enough of one of those qualities, or someone or something you associate with the quality or animal. Consider also the animal's actions, context, and your feelings about it. *See also:* Bird; Levitating

Hunger

Feeling deprived of the good things in life. Feeling deprived (or depriving yourself) of basic emotional nourishment, such as love or support. A search or wish for something. Actual hunger or cravings. *See also:* Famished; Wanting; Eating; Food; Thirst

Hunting

Hunting for wildlife (or something else) can represent: Looking for something you lack, such as information, knowledge, enlightenment, power, self-confidence, self-esteem, a relationship, or a job. An attempt to feel more powerful by dominating those you consider less powerful (perhaps based on feelings of powerlessness, denial, or lack of awareness). A desire for an experience or a feeling unrelated to killing (such as solitude or relaxation). For more clues, consider your feelings, your motivation, and the context. *See also:* Searching; Killing; Killed, Being; Chasing; Chased, Being; Net; Attacking; Abuse

Hurricane

A feeling or fear of overwhelm, threat, victimization, loss of control, chaos, or unpredictability. The idea of timing, such as the need to make a good decision, or the need to take action now to avoid harm or unpleasantness later (as in evacuating before a hurricane arrives). *See also:* Disaster; Weather; Storm; Wind; Flood

Hurt, Being

Remembering, experiencing, imagining, or fearing hurt (physical, emotional, or mental). A pointer to an opportunity for inner healing. *See also:* Injured; Pain; Feeling; Accident; Weapon; Inferior; Attacked, Being; Disabled; Illness; Scar; Hurting

Hurting

Hurting someone else can represent: Feeling vulnerable or the need to protect yourself. Fear of threat or harm. Unexpressed anger or other feelings that indicate an opportunity for inner healing. **Hurting yourself** can represent: judging or punishing yourself; being overly strict or harsh with yourself; a sign that you may be holding yourself to unhealthy and unrealistic rules, standards, or beliefs; a reminder of the opportunity to love or be more gentle with yourself. *See also:* Injured; Feeling; Bully; Abuse; Judgment or Disapproval; Offensive or Ugly; Scar; Problem; Advice or Opinion; Hurt, Being; Attacking; Ache

Hut

A hut or any other small, simple residence can represent: You or your life (or that of the owner's). Simplicity, or a desire for it. Protection or self-protection. Lack (or a feeling or fear of it). Having or needing only the basic necessities. *See also:* House; Building; Storage; Barn

Hyena

Unpredictability. Self-protection. Criticism or "biting" comments (due to hyenas' very strong jaws). Watching, observing, or vigilance. Laughter or taunting. Dreaming of this animal can represent too much or not enough of one of those qualities, or someone or something you associate with the quality or animal. Consider also the animal's actions, context, and your feelings about it. *See also:* Animal; Wolf; Dog; Bear

Hypnosis

A feeling or fear of giving your power over to someone else in your real life, or of shirking your responsibility. A tendency to live without true awareness, deep thought, relishing the moments, or appreciating the small things (in other words, an opportunity to be more present in your life or a certain aspect of it). The idea of a subconscious action or pattern (or something else that happens without your awareness).

Ice

Ice or something frozen can represent: Arrested progress or halted activity (since freezing visibly stops water's movement). Freedom or ease of progress (since it's easy to slide across the ice). Rigidity, stubbornness, or unchangeability. Brittleness or fragility (such as of someone's feelings or character). A perceived risk (as in the risk of slipping on or falling through ice). Cold-heartedness or unwelcoming. Dormancy, a rest period, or putting something "on hold." **A wintry, icy landscape** could represent hopelessness, bleakness, harshness, a temporary lack of progress in your life, or a setting for fun and adventure (depending on your feelings about it). Consider also the context and your feelings about and relationship to the ice. *See also:* Cold; Weather; Winter; Time of Year; Condition; Decreasing; Sparkle; Freezer

Ice Cream

A feeling of or desire for fun, an enjoyable activity, or a special occasion. Happiness or other feelings (for example, eating ice cream with a certain person could represent the feelings you experience when you're with that person in real life). *See also:* Dessert; Sugar; Food; Cold; Milk

Ice Skating

Making progress easily somewhere in your life. Freedom of movement or an abundance of choices. Fun or recreation. **Having difficulty skating** could represent feeling challenged, insecure, or unsupported in some aspect of your life. *See also:* Sliding; Traveling; Falling; Slipping; Ice; Winter; Game

Ignoring

Avoidance. Not wanting to hear or accept something. Judging or distancing yourself from someone or something. **Being ignored** can represent a feeling or fear of being overlooked, disrespected, or invisible in some aspect of your life. **Ignoring a warning** can represent a feeling or fear of authority or consequences, or neglecting a responsibility or your better judgment. *See also:* Turning; Watching; Distance

Iguana

The power of observation or perceptiveness. Accuracy (such as when aiming for and meeting a goal). Quick response. Warmth, warm weather, or a warm mood. Ability to blend in, or at least to not stand out. Dreaming of this animal can represent too much or not enough of one of those qualities, or someone or something you associate with the quality or animal. Consider also the animal's actions, context, and your feelings about it. *See also:* Animal; Lizard

Illness

Vulnerability. Feeling under the weather or not your usual self mentally, emotionally, or physically. **Someone else being sick** can represent your feeling that they're more vulnerable than usual, or that they could benefit from positive attention. Also consider the symbolism of the particular illness (such as an infection representing something invading your personal space, or diabetes representing an inability to enjoy the sweetness of life). See also the specific illness, symptoms, or the body part involved.

See also: Immune System; Virus; Infection; Pain; Ache; Vomiting; Diarrhea; Tired; Germs; Coughing; Heart Attack; Arthritis; Seizure; Tumor; Injured; Disabled; Health

Immune System

Defense or self-defense. A feeling or fear of (physical, emotional, or mental) invasion, attack, or compromise. A response to a real or imagined threat. A combative environment somewhere in your life (or in a movie, the media, or a video game). Your own inner mental or emotional conflict. A real or imagined situation that triggers self-righteousness or againstness. A feeling or fear of something you perceive as "foreign" or different. An actual or imagined immune system battle against an infection or something else. *See also:* Allergy; Inflammation; Infection; Invaded, Being; Attacked, Being; Attacking; Lymph; Body Part

Increasing

The idea of "more." Improvement (or the desire for it). Worsening (or a fear of it). Exaggerating or amplifying. Something becoming more important or urgent. For more clues, consider the context and what was increasing. *See also:* Swelling; Climbing; Bigger, Getting; Many; Extra; Infinite

Indigestion

Inability to accept or "digest" something in your life (such as a change, event, situation, or realization). Something real or feared that "doesn't sit well" with you. *See also:* Heartburn; Diarrhea; Illness; Pain; Digestion; Food; Eating; Absorbing

Infection

A feeling of intrusion or invasion somehow in your life. A challenge. An inner conflict. An "infectious" thought or attitude (as in judgment, kindness, or hope). An actual or imagined immune system battle against an infection or something else. A perceived imbalance of some kind on the physical, emotional, or mental level. *See also:* Invaded, Being; Immune System; Germs; Virus; Rash; Illness; Coughing; Health; Invading

Inferior

The idea of comparing one thing to another. Comparing yourself to someone else or to a standard. A judgment of something or someone as "less than," bad, or wrong. *See also:* Judgment or Disapproval; Bad; Low; Under; Broken Object; Cheating; Right or Wrong; Offensive or Ugly; Injured; Hole; Bottom; Sparse; Scarcity

Infinite

Infinity (or something that seems infinite) can represent: The idea of no limits or no end. Freedom somewhere in your life. An extreme idea, feeling, or place (such as "the best," "the most," or "the brightest"). *See also:* Many; Big; Space; Limit or Boundary; Extra; Increasing; God

Inflammation

Protection or self-defense, perhaps through anger or "heating things up." Anger, provocation, or a nuisance somewhere in your life. A reaction to a perceived threat or something foreign, unrecognized, or questionable. *See also:* Pain; Swelling; Allergy; Infection; Warm; Fight; Invaded, Being; Feeling

Inheritance

Something inherited, passed on, or gifted from one person to another, perhaps from one generation to another (such as a characteristic, habit, role, way of thinking, tendency, or belief). *See also:* Gift; Money; Finances; Enough; Rich

Injection

The idea of someone introducing something into your personal space or consciousness (such as animosity, criticism, or their own belief). Direct or quick action (such as to correct a problem). A particular health care experience, or receiving assistance in general. **Receiving a beneficial injection** (with your permission) could represent strengthening or improving yourself, or protecting yourself from a future threat. **An injection against your will** could be an indicator of a Toxic Dream (p. 320), or it could represent a feeling or fear of someone forcing their opinions or expectations onto you, or "injecting" themselves into your life or consciousness somehow. Consider the context and purpose of the injection, and your feelings about it. *See also:* Vaccine; IV; Invading; Invaded, Being; Vein; Blood; Doctor; Sharp

Injured

A feeling or fear of vulnerability, weakness, tiredness, threat, attack, or pain (physical, emotional, mental, financial, or otherwise). An indication of a Toxic Dream (p. 320). See also the part of the body that was injured. *See also:* Hurt, Being; Accident; Pain; Ache; Broken Bone; Attacked, Being; Disabled; Scar

Ink

Communication, message, meaning, expression, or creativity that is visible or obvious. Permanent, unchangeable, or difficult to change (such as an agreement). *See also:* Pen or Pencil; Writing; Communication; Tattoo

Insect

An insect or other bug can represent: Something that's "bugging" you in real life. A certain quality of the insect that's significant to you right now. Think about what that type of insect symbolizes to you personally, and traditional ideas about the insect (for example, ants are often thought of as industrious or well-organized). Notice what the insect is doing and how (for example, a bee gathering nectar might represent enjoying the sweeter things in life, whereas a bee buzzing angrily around your head could represent a nuisance or threat). **A swarm of insects** can represent feeling overloaded or pestered by many small things (such as to-do list items or problems). See also the specific type of insect. *See also:* Animal; Insects (the category)

Integrity, Compromising

A compromising activity or situation can represent a feeling or fear of such an activity in real life (one through which you compromise your integrity or allow yourself to be used, taken advantage of, your boundaries crossed by others). Consider what's behind those feelings or fears (beliefs, judgments, lack of support for self, or other issues), and look for an opportunity to work through any underlying issues. **Someone else compromising their integrity** could represent: the way you're perceiving, labelling, or judging that person (for example, as self-sabotaging or insecure); you compromising your own integrity somehow. *See also:* Lying; Cheating; Agreement, Breaking an; Sabotaging; Dishonest; Betraying; Betrayed, Being

Interfering

A feeling or fear of interference in your real life (such as by a person, the weather, etc.). Consider what process was interfered with, what the process represents (a relationship, project, communication, etc.), and the motivation behind the interfering. *See also:* Interrupting; Bothered, Being; Invaded, Being; Sabotaged, Being; Betrayed, Being; Telling on Someone; Bothering; Invading; Sabotaging; Blockage or Obstacle; Gossiping; Privacy

Internet

The internet, web, or "online" can represent: Communication. Connection, community, or network. The idea of the whole being greater than the sum of its parts. The human collective, or shared human consciousness. **Connecting with people or companies** over the internet can represent a need to express, be heard, feel validated, or feel connected. **Searching the internet** can represent a desire for information, an answer, clarity, or help. **Not being able to access the internet** can represent a feeling of isolation, or a communication or productivity disruption somewhere in your life. For more clues, consider your activity and your motivation for accessing the internet. *See also:* Communication; Wire; Computer; Phone; Login; Technology

Interrupting

A real-life situation or process in which you were interrupted or are afraid of being interrupted. Perceived lack of respect or courtesy on the part of the interrupter (or whatever the interrupter represents in your real life). A feeling or fear of a crisis or sudden problem. A real-life intrusive environment (such as noise, wind, or visual distraction). For more clues, consider who was interrupting, why, and how you felt about it. **Someone constantly interrupting you by dropping by to visit** can represent a perceived lack of thoughtfulness, bad timing, or desire to connect with you. **Being interrupted when you're speaking** can represent a feeling or fear or not being heard or respected. *See also:* Quitting; Hesitating; Interfering; Ending; Blockage or Obstacle; Cut Off; Bothered, Being; Bothering; Privacy

Interview

An actual, expected, or imagined interview. An application process or competition (such as for a job or university admission). A feeling or fear of being questioned, evaluated, or "put on the spot" by others. A desire to understand or learn about something or someone. Getting approval from or making a certain impression on someone (or a desire for such). *See also:* Talk Show; Job; Workplace; Meeting; Test; Audition; Appointment; Decision, Someone Else's

Intuition

Something that feels like intuition (direct knowledge of something, independent of rational thought) can represent: An actual intuitive insight (be sure to evaluate it thoroughly when you're awake). A desire to know or understand something. Feeling curious or in the mood to learn. Feeling very clear-headed at the time of the dream, or wishing that you were. *See also:* Discovering; Communication; Future; Paranormal; God

Invaded, Being

Being invaded or intruded upon can represent an actual, feared, or imagined: Compromise of your boundaries (physically, emotionally, or mentally). Interruption. A person "getting into your business" or insinuating their way into a situation. *See also:* Fight; Interfering; Bothered, Being; Attacked, Being; Violence; Privacy; Controlled, Being

Invading

Invading or intruding on others (such as invading their privacy or intruding into their personal space) can represent: Insensitivity. Self-righteousness. An intention to help or rescue. A desire for more power or control. A desire to retrieve something you've lost (such as your dignity). Feelings of hostility. A desire for revenge. Consider also your motivation for invading, and others people's reactions. *See also:* Bothering; Interfering; Interrupting; Attacking; Privacy; Controlled, Being; Fight; Violence; Invaded, Being

Investigator

An investigator or detective can represent: A desire to know or understand someone or something. The idea of solving a mystery. A desire for a secret to be revealed (or a fear of that). Locating or recovering something that's missing (such as an object, information, or relationship), or a desire for that. *See also:* Secret; Police; Searching; Finding a Lost Item; Crime; Criminal; Discovering; Catching Someone; Question; Stalking; Missing Person

Investment

A physical, emotional, or mental outlay (such as of money, time, or effort) in order to receive a future benefit. Examples include investing in a child's education for the benefit of their future success; spending time and effort in a relationship that provides love and security; acting generously and then being able to feel good about it. *See also:* Finances; Loaning; Buying

Invincibility

Self-empowerment or self-protection (or a desire for it). The experience of your "true" state of being, without limiting beliefs or self-judgments. **Being invincible against harmful people** can represent: not letting others' judgments or negativity "get to you" in real life; a feeling or fear of too many demands on you (or on your time, energy, autonomy, privacy, etc.) *See also:* Powers; Superhero

Invitation

Being invited or receiving an invitation can represent: An invitation, welcome, or request in real life (or a perceived or desired one). The idea of being included or accepted by others. Connecting or interacting with others or with someone in particular (or a desire for that). *See also:* Requesting; Server; Guest; Visiting

Iron

An iron (or ironing clothes) can represent actual, desired, or imagined: Change or transformation. Neatening, straightening, or improving yourself or something else. Repairing or resolving a situation (as in "ironing out" a problem). Preparing the way for or making things easier (as in "smoothing the way"). Pressure, or the experience of being under pressure. *See also:* Wrinkle; Clothes; Cleaning

Island

Separation, isolation, or independence. **A remote, deserted island** can represent freedom (from responsibilities, society, etc.), or physical, emotional, or mental isolation or deprivation. **A lush, tropical island** can represent abundance, adventure, or pleasantness. **A beautiful resort island** could represent relaxation, fun, or a break from day-to-day life. *See also:* Stranded; Distance; Trip or Vacation; Sand; Tropical; Water, Body of

Isolating

Isolating yourself from others might represent: A need for more time to yourself. Focusing on yourself, your own needs, or other aspects your personal process. Independence, or a desire for more or less independence. Not wanting to participate in society, or wanting to act against it (perhaps due to beliefs or issues with authority). Needing a break from the day-to-day activity around you. **Someone who purposely chooses isolation** (such as a hermit or a loner) can represent your perception of that person (or whomever they represent) in one of the ways previously mentioned. *See also:* Leaving a Person; Leaving a Place; Rejection; Divider; Abandonment; Left, Being; Stranded; Distance; Breaking Up

Itch

A desire, urge, or compulsion. A nuisance or something nagging at you, in your environment or within yourself. Something in your life that needs attention. *See also:* Skin; Problem; Allergy; Infection

IV

Being given an IV (intravenous drip) could represent: Feeling "not quite yourself" physically, emotionally, or mentally. A feeling or fear of lack, deprivation, or needing help. The idea of someone trying to affect you very directly, with or without your permission (as in "getting under your skin"). Consider also the context and the contents of the IV. *See also:* Injection; Skin; Liquid; Water; Sharp; Invading; Invaded, Being; Vein; Blood; Doctor

Jackal

Opportunism, or ready to take advantage of an opportunity. Scavenging, or making use of what's available, whatever you can find, or others' work (since jackals are scavengers). Alone time, or contentment with being alone. Dreaming of this animal can represent too much or not enough of one of those qualities, or someone or something you associate with the quality or animal. Consider also the animal's actions, context, and your feelings about it. *See also:* Animal; Dog; Coyote

Jaguar

Quick and effective in reaching goals. Tenacity, or sheer energy for the long-haul. Taking from or receiving from others. Excelling in an area or environment where others don't (since jaguars do well in water, while other cats do not). Dreaming of this animal can represent too much or not enough of one of those qualities, or someone or something you associate with the quality or animal. Consider also the animal's actions, context, and your feelings about it. *See also:* Cat; Animal

Jaw

Talking, or other forms of communication. Communicating well or with strength. Ability to "take in," process, or break down events or information from the world around you. Perceived masculinity or femininity, depending on the characteristics of the particular jaw. *See also:* Communication; Chewing; Face; Chin; Body Part

Jay

A blue jay or other jay can represent: Assertiveness, standing up for yourself and your needs. Power, or the use (or abuse) of power. Intrusion into others' space or business. Dreaming of this animal can represent too much or not enough of one of those qualities, or someone or something you associate with the quality or animal. Consider also the animal's actions, context, and your feelings about it. *See also:* Bird

Jealousy

Feeling envy or jealousy in a dream can represent actual envy or jealousy in your real life (past or present). Consider how you can better support yourself, work through and validate unexpressed feelings, and make positive changes within yourself in terms of how you view yourself and the situation. *See also:* Feeling; Judgment or Disapproval

Jellyfish

Dangerous beauty, or the dangers of the temptation of beauty. A nuisance or pest in your life. Something that you feel or fear is a quiet, lurking threat in your life (perhaps a subconscious dynamic such as a judgment or self-defeating belief). Dreaming of this animal can represent too much or not enough of one of those qualities, or someone or something you associate with the quality or animal. Consider also the animal's actions, context, and your feelings about it. *See also:* Animal; Sting

Jewelry

The way you think the wearer wants to portray themselves to the world. A characteristic or gift you perceive the wearer to have. Something of value to you, such as love, acceptance, sentimentality. A commitment, treasure, or remembrance given from one person to another. A treasured memory, touchstone, or commitment that's important to the dreamer. **Wearing jewelry** can represent embellishing yourself, your image, a story, or something else. **Someone else's jewelry** can represent something you know, perceive, or assume about that person. **Jewelry you're wearing (or would like to wear)** can represent: something valuable or meaningful to you in real life; an attempt to boost your sense of self-value. **Losing jewelry** can represent a feeling or fear of: losing touch with a certain aspect of yourself or your life (depending on the type of jewelry); neglecting a commitment or responsibility (such as to someone else or to yourself); underestimating your unique value as a person. See also the specific type of jewelry. *See also:* Decoration; Ring (Jewelry); Earrings; Bracelet; Necklace; Gem; Fashionable; Clothes

Job

Productivity. Adding value, contributing to society, or making a difference in the world. An agreement, commitment, or arrangement. An ongoing process or activity. An activity that feels like work, but isn't or shouldn't be. A feeling or fear of being forced to do something or help out. *See also:* Working; Workplace; Interview; Promotion or Raise

Joining

Joining with another person or with a group can represent an actual or desired: Commitment to the other person or people (such as joining in marriage or joining a community). A commitment to a shared cause or goal (such as joining a workers' union or philanthropic organization). Acceptance of a creed or philosophy, or a set of beliefs, intentions, values, etc. (such as when joining a religion or political party). Interaction with others who share your interests. A feeling of belonging or acceptance by others (or a desire for it). The idea of "strength in numbers," or a desire for more power or help. Feeling that you belong or are a part of a whole. *See also:* Joining Together; Organization, Membership; Meeting; Agreement; Rejoining

Joining Together

Joining two or more things (objects, ideas, people, etc.) together can represent an actual, perceived, or desired joining together (such as a relationship, interaction, partnership, agreement, or attachment). *See also:* Joining; Attached; Joint; Repairing; Rejoining; Reuniting; Mixing; Meeting Someone; Cooperating; Next To; Tight

Joint

A body joint (such as an elbow or knee) can represent: Flexibility, or ability to change directions as needed. Adaptability to situations or challenges. An ability to take things in stride or go with the flow. See also the particular joint. *See also:* Pivoting; Rotating; Joining Together; Sharing; Body Part

Journal

Expressing yourself, listening to yourself, or being heard (or a need or desire for such). Tuning into your inner wisdom. An inner flow or process (such as creativity or expressing emotion). *See also:* Writing; Notebook

Judge

An ultimate or final authority or judgment. A feeling of guilt, or worry about being accused or punished. A feeling or fear of others determining your future, perhaps based on your past, their opinions, or a even a whim. *See also:* Authority Figure; Decision, Someone Else's; Blaming; Blamed, Being; Judgment or Disapproval; Justice; Trial; Court; Jury; Crime; Fairness

Judgment or Disapproval

A feeling or fear of being judged or experiencing disapproval somewhere in your life. A desire for acceptance or approval. Anger, shame, jealousy, or other related feelings. **You judging someone or something** (considering them bad or wrong, or assigning another judgmental label) can represent: judging the aspect in yourself that you're judging in the other person; an attempt to distance yourself from whatever or whomever you are judging; anger at the person or situation represented in the dream; an opportunity to accept or forgive. Be careful that your judgments and limitations aren't keeping you from seeing the true meaning or value of the thing you judged (such as the real person behind the action, or the lesson in the situation). *See also:* Blaming; Blamed, Being; Arguing; Rejection; Decision, Someone Else's; Decision, Your; Right or Wrong; Advice or Opinion; Bad; Hurt, Being

Jumping

Making great or sudden progress. Acting quickly or hastily. **A risky jump** can represent a risk you took in real life, that you're considering, or that you were imagining during the dream. *See also:* Jumping Off; Falling; Diving

Jumping Off

Giving up, quitting, leaving, or abandoning (such as jumping off a bus full of people). The end of a process or beginning of a new one. Avoidance. **Jumping off to avoid a dangerous situation** can represent escaping from a perceived or feared threat (or a desire to do so). **Jumping off for fun** (such as bungee jumping or skydiving) can represent excitement or freedom (or a desire for it.) *See also:* Jumping; High; Falling

Jungle

A rich or stimulating environment in your life or imagination. Overwhelm or chaos (physical, emotional, or mental). A perceived threat or a threatening situation. A wilderness or the unknown. A feeling or fear of being lost or uncertain about personal direction. For more clues, consider the jungle's characteristics, the events there, and your feelings. *See also:* Forest; Thicket; Tropical; Outdoors

Junkyard

A perceived ending. Abandonment. An issue regarding purpose or meaning. Something or someone you consider "on hold" or waiting for a new beginning. A setting, situation, or environment where you spend time while waiting for a new start. Finding value in something that someone else has finished with (such as an old idea or a seemingly obsolete product). Discovering a new purpose, or desire to do so. **See also:** Garbage Dump

Jury

A jury can represent: A feeling or fear of scrutiny or judgment by others. A desire for fairness or "due process." A feeling of guilt about something you've done or you considered doing. **See also:** Court; Trial; Justice; Judgment or Disapproval; Blamed, Being; Blaming

Justice

Justice or symbols of justice (court, judge, legal system, etc.) can represent: The idea of "right and wrong." Integrity or "doing what's right." Your conscience (or someone else's). An authority or a final judgment, or your feelings about one in your life. A need to take more responsibility in your life. Guilt, or something you fear could get you into trouble. An issue regarding punishment or a penalty. **See also:** Attorney; Trial; Judge; Court; Courtroom; Jury; Blaming; Blamed, Being; Crime; Rule or Law; Suing; Revenge

Kangaroo

A bond between mother and child, or the idea of keeping loved ones close physically, emotionally, or mentally (as a mother kangaroo keeps her babies in her pouch). Ability to make progress or move forward. Moving forward in leaps (as opposed to gradual, steady progress). Self-defense, assertiveness, or pushing someone away (as in a kangaroo's kicking skills). Dreaming of this animal can represent too much or not enough of one of those qualities, or someone or something you associate with the quality or animal. Consider also the animal's actions, context, and your feelings about it. **See also:** Animal; Opossum

Key

Permission or access. Power or authority. The (real or imagined) answer to a problem, puzzle, or something else you'd like to "unlock." **Your personal set of keys** (such as car and house keys) can represent your self-identity, personal power, access, or abilities in life. **Losing your keys** can represent compromising yourself or giving away your personal power somehow, or possibly neglecting your responsibility for yourself. **See also:** Door or Entrance; Lock; Keyhole; Unlocking; Starting an Engine

Keyhole

A puzzle, riddle, or something else you'd like to "unlock." Imagining or wanting to access something forbidden or not allowed. A boundary, or an obstacle that denies access. **Peeking through a keyhole can represent** curiosity or awareness (or a desire for such). *See also:* Lock; Unlocking; Hole; Key; Door or Entrance

Kidney

Removing toxicity from or maintaining a balance within yourself, your life, or your consciousness. Filtering out what you don't want (as from other people's opinions or feedback), and keeping only what benefits you. *See also:* Urinating; Blood; Liver; Garbage; Body Part

Killed, Being

You being killed can represent: A feeling or fear of ill will, victimization, manipulation, or someone or something taking power away from you (physically, emotionally, or mentally). Something of yours (such as a project or process) coming to an end, perhaps earlier than you expected. An ending within yourself, mentally or emotionally (such as a certain event changing the way you see the world, "killing" your old outlook on the world). *See also:* Dying; Attacked, Being; Killing; Execution; Death of You; Violence; Life Force; Hunting; Shot, Being; Weapon

Killer

A perceived threat. A fear of attack, manipulation, or being taken advantage of (physically, emotionally, or mentally). A general threat, such as violent crime or terrorism in the world (for example, a killer breaking into your house could represent your fear of ill will "intruding" into your life somehow). *See also:* Killing; Attacking; Killed, Being; Shot, Being; Attacked, Being

Killing

Killing or wanting to kill can represent: a desire for power or control, perhaps based on feelings of anger or powerlessness (thus indicating an opportunity to work through an underlying issue). Emotions being expressed during the dream state. Feeling unwilling or unable to deal with the problems you feel the person causes you in real life. **Killing in self-defense** can represent a feeling or fear of being attacked (mentally, emotionally, physically), or the need to stand up for yourself. **Killing someone accidentally** can represent a feeling or fear of accidentally hurting that person (perhaps their feelings), or your subconscious mind wanting to avoid hurting them. *See also:* Attacking; Killer; Killed, Being; Execution; Violence; Chased, Being; Hunting; Weapon

Kissing

Non-romantic kissing (such as from your grandma or a friend) can represent perceived affection, approval, connection (or a desire for such). **Romantic kissing or other romantic interaction** can represent: emotional intimacy (emotional trust or openness), an interaction (a dialogue or shared process), or a feeling of closeness with someone; remembering when you felt close to someone; liking the person or wanting to know them better (not necessarily romantically). **Unwelcome romantic kissing** can represent unwelcome emotional intimacy (such as a stranger telling you their secrets) or a feeling that someone is interacting in too familiar a way (such as acting like they're your close friend when they aren't). *See also:* Lips; Hug; Cuddle; Romance

Kitten

Responsibility. Innocence. Your inner child or playfulness. Taking time for yourself, having fun, or nurturing yourself or your sense of play. Dreaming of this animal can represent too much or not enough of one of those qualities, or someone or something you associate with the quality or animal. Consider also the animal's actions, context, and your feelings about it. *See also:* Cat; Pet; Baby Animal

Knee

The ability to move forward, take action, or make progress in life. The ability "take things in stride" or "cushion the bumps" along the way in your life (as knees do while walking). **An injured knee** can represent an impediment to moving forward, getting in your own way, or feeling a need to slow down for your own well-being. *See also:* Joint; Shin; Leg

Knife

Your ability to make the best use of your environment or make a situation work better for you. Independence or "dividing and conquering." Transforming something into a more useful form (such as delving into someone's criticism to find the constructive part). Trying to get to the bottom of a problem or figure something out (perhaps through examining small details). Consider also the context, motivation, and the item being cut. **Someone threatening you with a knife** can represent perceived or feared invasion, victimization, criticism, or compromise of your personal boundaries or integrity. *See also:* Tool; Silverware; Sword; Scissors; Sharp; Weapon

Knight

Honor or chivalry. Rescue, defense, or bravery. Loyalty, duty, or service to the highest leader (such as a cause, or God). Self-defense (such as by armor). Good will, integrity, or honesty. Someone or something you perceive as powerful or dangerous. For more clues, consider the characteristic or action that stood out, and the meaning you associate with a knight in general. *See also:* Soldier; Armor or Shield; Royalty; Character

Knitting

Knitting, crocheting, or other similar craft can represent: An actual hobby or pastime (needlecraft or otherwise). A particular project. A creative or productive process that converts ideas or raw materials into something else. A certain age group, such as grandmas (who often knit) or babies (who often have things knitted for them). Complicated or convoluted. *See also:* Making or Building; Weaving or Spinning; Yarn; Sewing

Knob

A knob that functions as a handle (such as on a cabinet) can represent: Access or accessibility (physical, emotional, etc.). The idea of handling or "getting a handle on" something in your life. Action, or intention toward action. Beginning a process. Searching. **Turning a knob (such as to control an appliance)** can represent control, change, or variety (or a desire for it). Consider also the context and function of the knob, and the type of action involved. *See also:* Opening; Pulling; Doorknob; Drawer; Cabinet; Lock; Appliance; Turning Off; Turning On

Knock, Hearing a

A knock on your door (or your doorbell ringing) can represent actual, desired, or feared: The idea of someone wanting to communicate with you. Someone trying to get access to you (such as to interact with you, understand you, or get information or something else from you). Someone wanting you to "open up," be honest, or connect with them in a real way. An opportunity, or a desire for one. Someone or something threatening to "invade your space" (such as to compromise your integrity or take advantage of you). *See also:* Door or Entrance; Knocking; Ringing; Hearing

Knocking

Knocking on a door or ringing a doorbell can represent (real or imagined): Attempting to gain admission or surpass a barrier (such as to attain a new experience, certain knowledge, or acceptance by a certain person or group). Progressing forward, or moving into a new phase. Trying to communicate with or gain access to someone, perhaps to make a request or convey information. Searching for or exploring an opportunity. *See also:* Door or Entrance; Ringing; Hearing; Passageway; Knock, Hearing a; Explosion; Lock; Entering

Knot

A particularly tough challenge or problem whose solution is not obvious. Security or control. Stress. Complexity or complication (as in "a knotty situation"). A joining of one or more objects or people (as in "tying the knot" by getting married). *See also:* Problem; Tying; Holding; Restrained

Koala

Gentleness. Resting or moving slowly. Grasping or holding on. A bond between mother and child, or the idea of keeping loved ones close physically, emotionally, or mentally (as a mother koala keeps her babies in her pouch). Isolation from others. Dreaming of this animal can represent too much or not enough of one of those qualities, or someone or something you associate with the quality or animal. Consider also the animal's actions, context, and your feelings about it. *See also:* Animal; Panda

Laboratory

Your workplace. Curiosity or questioning. A desire for understanding, knowledge, or answers. Testing an idea. An experiment or experimental approach. A mystery to be solved. Science, scientists, logic, or a logical approach. **Someone running a laboratory** can represent power, control, or an authority figure in your life. *See also:* Science; Chemistry; Test

Ladder

The ability to make progress, go to the next level, or "rise above" a certain situation (or a desire for such). The idea of making progress by taking one step at a time. A real or imagined escape from a particular situation or threat. *See also:* Climbing; High; Stairs

Ladybug

A perception of or wish for "good luck." Friendliness or helpfulness. Femininity. Charm or beauty. Dreaming of this insect can represent too much or not enough of one of those qualities, or someone or something you associate with the quality. Consider also the insect's actions, context, and your feelings about it. *See also:* Insect; Beetle

Lamp or Light

Experiencing or desiring insight, clarity, understanding, or discovery (as in "shining some light on the subject"). The idea of finding your way in some aspect of your life. Feeling lost or needing guidance. Something that is "known" (as opposed to dark representing "the unknown"). **See also:** Light (Illumination)

Landscape

Landscape or scenery can represent: A real-life setting or scene. Elements that create a particular setting or scene for dream action (such as a dark forest to convey a setting of remoteness or confusion). Decoration, creative expression, or improvement (as in landscaping around a house). The real-life people or things you encountered along the way in the part of your real life portrayed in the dream (similar to encountering different kinds of scenery on a trip). The idea of being or feeling inconsequential (as the scenery in a play is often not part of the central action). See also the specific type of landscape and any elements of it that stood out. **See also:** Location; Plant

Landslide

A feeling or fear of: Losing your footing or foundation (such as your beliefs, things you could always count on, or things you've tended to take for granted). Sudden, unexpected change. Loss, or loss of control. Overwhelm. **See also:** Flood; Disaster; Cover; Trapped; Escaping; Descending; Water; Storm; Avalanche

Language

Hearing or reading a language you don't understand can represent: The idea of not being able to understand something you need to know. Communication trouble in real life (or a fear of such). **See also:** Writing; Words; Text; Garbled; Accent

Larva

A beginning, or the early stage of a process. The period before a transition or metamorphosis, or the "before" part of a "before and after." Infancy. Potential. An early sign of a threat or problem, before it becomes a big one. **See also:** Maggots; Parasite; Worm; Caterpillar; Cocoon; Insect

Last Minute

Putting something off until the last minute can represent: Real-life or imagined procrastination. A desire to avoid whatever the activity represents. Fear that you'll end up having to rush something at the last minute. Feeling passive-aggressive toward an authority figure, perhaps the one who assigned you the task. The importance you place on the real-life task that was represented by the "last minute" task in the dream. A desire for more challenge or excitement in your life. **Something coming**

through at the last minute (such as finding a solution or being rescued) can represent: waiting or hoping for something in real life; wanting things to work out. *See also:* Waiting; Late; Hesitating

Late

Arriving late for something can represent: The idea that the event you're late for represents something very important to you in real life. Conscientiousness, or fear of punishment. Neglecting a responsibility. Fearing or wanting to avoid the thing you're late for. Fear of failure. Passive-aggression toward an authority figure. Feeling disorganized, or feeling overwhelmed by your schedule. **Feeling bad about being late** can represent a feeling or fear of letting someone down, missing something, or "messing up." **A late time frame** (such as late in the day) can represent a point that's late in a real-life process, or the time frame of a real-life event. *See also:* Missing an Event; Schedule; Last Minute; Time Frame

Laughing

Happiness, joy, fun, humor, compassion, or another positive feeling somewhere in your life (or a desire for it). A feeling or fear of being laughed at, made fun of, or alienated somehow in your life. Feeling like someone is trying to get the "last laugh" somehow in your life. For more clues, consider the context and your feelings about the laughter. *See also:* Feeling; Voice; Bully; Clown

Lavender

Relaxation. Aroma. Freshness, natural, or herbal. Femininity. A particular geographic region. A feeling you associate with lavender (such as with the scent or the color). *See also:* Flower; Plant; Smell; Purple

Lawn

Home. A feeling of expansiveness or no limits. Recreation or playfulness. Consider also the condition of the lawn (such as a neatly trimmed or neglected lawn representing your perception of someone's attitude or habits) and its context (such as a wide lawn around a house representing well-established personal boundaries). *See also:* Backyard; Outdoors; Thicket

Leader

A leader can represent an authority figure, such as someone or something in your real life you allow to have power over you, or someone whose opinions you care about. **You as a leader** can represent: your ability or potential to lead or influence others; a desire to be a leader in some way. *See also:* Authority Figure; Manager; Teacher; Steering; Driving; Design or Plan

Leaf

Life, or an aspect of your life. Personal growth or development. Also consider the condition of the leaf. **A new leaf** could represent a beginning or fresh start in your life. **A wilted leaf** could represent a feeling or fear of lack, neglect, or sadness. *See also:* Tree; Vine; Plant; Sprout

Leaking

Something leaking (such fluid out of a container) can represent a feeling or fear of: Loss, or loss of control. Something dwindling, disappearing, or being lost. Information or secrets being leaked. Depleting someone's energy, patience, or other supply. Integrity or security being compromised (such as a person's or an organization's). For more clues, consider what's leaking, why, and the resulting effects. *See also:* Depleted; Overflowing; Container; Liquid; Hole; Betrayed, Being; Telling on Someone

Leaving a Person

A real or imagined ending in your life. The idea of abandonment (such as physically leaving, or neglecting a responsibility). **You leaving someone** can also represent: a decision (perhaps a decision to end a process); standing up for yourself to make needed changes in your life. **Someone leaving you** can also represent: a feeling or fear of being abandoned, alone, or left behind in real life. *See also:* Abandonment; Leaving a Place; Betrayed, Being; Betraying; Rejection; Escaping; Goodbye; Distance

Leaving a Place

Leaving a place or situation can represent: The end of a phase, project, or something else in your life. A desire to escape or avoid a real-life situation. A feeling that you're neglecting a responsibility or promise. A desire to be done with something or to leave something behind in your life. *See also:* Escaping; Leaving a Person; Distance; Setting Down

Ledge or Cliff

Risk, danger, or fear. A boundary, edge, or limitation (real or perceived). The end of something (such as a situation or process). *See also:* Limit or Boundary; Edge, Coming to an; High; Hill; Valley

Leech

Dependence, neediness, or relying on someone. Being taken from by others, whether willingly or not. Giving something away. Giving up your energy, time, attention, money, or something else. The idea of wasting or leaking (such as wasting time or effort). Dreaming of this animal can represent too much or not enough of one of those qualities, or someone or something you associate with the quality or animal. Consider also the animal's actions, context, and your feelings about it. *See also:* Parasite; Animal; Sucking; Blood

Left, Being

Being left alone or behind can represent: A feeling or fear of being abandoned, forgotten, alone, or left behind in real life (by a specific person, yourself, God, etc.). The importance of the person or thing being left, or of something it represents (such as the importance of a particular responsibility). *See also:* Abandonment; Betrayed, Being; Rejection; Leaving a Person; Lost, Being; Losing an Item; Orphan; Helpless

Left Side

The left-hand side (or something appearing on the left or coming from the left) can represent perceived or imagined: Receiving or taking. Intuition. Creativity. Femininity. "Going with the flow." Liberal political views (as in "the left"). Negativity. Something else you personally associate with the left side. Also consider the context and meaning of whatever's on the left side. **Doing something left-handed when you're actually right-handed** can represent challenging yourself (perhaps unnecessarily); trying something new or in a new way; looking at something from a different perspective. *See also:* Right Side

Leftovers

Abundance or plenty. Too many or too much. Something that's being repeated. A situation similar to another recent one. A feeling of "being in a rut" or experiencing a lack of variety. Something or someone extra. Being last, or being considered last. Consider also how you felt about whatever was left over. *See also:* Food; Meal; Extra; Big

Leg

Ability to move forward, take action, or make progress in life. **A broken leg can represent:** A perceived or real impediment to your progress in life; a feeling or fear of your progress being slowed; a need to slow down for the sake of your well-being. *See also:* Shin; Ankle; Branch; Broken Bone

Leopard

Action, decisiveness, or quick results. Being well-suited to a particular environment. Tending not to be seen or noticed. Opportunity or opportunism. Dreaming of this animal can represent too much or not enough of one of those qualities, or someone or something you associate with the quality or animal. Consider also the animal's actions, context, and your feelings about it. *See also:* Cat; Animal; Jaguar

Letter (Alphabet)

A word that starts with that letter. A person whose name begins with that letter. A grade or other evaluation. The shape of the letter, or something that shape represents (such as a capital "A" representing an arrow). A priority, level, or sequence (such as "Plan A, then Plan B"). The feeling you get from that particular letter. For more clues, consider the context of the letter. Sometimes a letter doesn't convey any useful meaning to interpret. *See also:* Communication; Text

Letter (Message)

A past, expected, desired, imagined, or feared communication (perhaps to or from someone specific in your life). The idea of expressing yourself to someone or wanting to be heard by them. *See also:* Communication; Email; Giving; Receiving; Delivery; Mailbox; Address

Levitating

A feeling of or desire for freedom, love, or "lightness" (feeling happier, without burdens, etc.). The power to change your own attitude or state of mind to be more positive. An indicator that you were feeling great happiness or joy during the dream. Rising above a challenge (or a desire to do so). Rising above "the everyday," the mundane, pettiness, etc. Experiencing great clarity, insight, or a "higher perspective." A special ability or characteristic that you feel puts you "above the crowd." *See also:* Flying; Floating; Powers

Library

A specific real-life place where you interact with or work alongside others (such as your workplace or school). An environment with a characteristic of a library (such as quiet, authority figures or experts, learning or studying, books, or information). Browsing, shopping, or picking things out. Information or knowledge. Organization, or an information system (such as your files on your computer). Shared resources, or a setting that includes community resources. The idea of borrowing or lending. The idea of responsibility or being penalized for not following through on a promise (as in late fines). For more clues about meaning, consider what stood out about the library, the events there, and your feelings about them. *See also:* Book; Building; Room; Quiet

License

A license (such as a marriage, medical, or business license) can represent: Permission or approval. Official permission from someone or something you consider an authority. Access or accessibility. The ability to conduct a certain activity. *See also:* Driver's License; License Plate

License Plate

A license plate (such as on a vehicle) can represent: Permission from or approval by an authority. Your unique identity as you feel it's seen by others, or as you choose to display it. Your unique identifying characteristics, as you see them. An issue of validation or recognition by others, or the idea of self-validation. **Your license plate being stolen** can represent a feeling or fear of losing your identity or reputation. **Purposely driving without a license plate** could represent trying to hide your identity or go unnoticed. *See also:* License; Vehicle; Car; Driver's License

Licking

Trying or "getting a taste of" whatever is represented by the object you're licking. Trying to understand or discover information about something. Evaluating or trying to decide what you think about something. *See also:* Tasting; Eating; Tongue; Mouth

Lied To, Being

Someone lying to you can represent: A feeling or fear of someone being dishonest in real life. Viewing people as generally dishonest or untrustworthy. Being in denial, or having lied to yourself in some way. *See also:* Betrayed, Being; Catching Someone; Dishonest; Lying; Fake; Pretending; Gossiping; Trickery

Life

Your life, existence, life experience, or history can represent: Feelings, thoughts, or fears about your past, present, or future. Your life path or direction. The scope of your life or variety of activities. Your affect on others in your life (or some aspect of it). **Dreaming that you never existed** may involve recognizing the difference you've made so far in your life. *See also:* Alive or Exists; Past; Life Force; Light (Spiritual); Person You Know; Person Unknown; Animal

Life Force

Your life force, life energy, chi, or the part of you that constitutes "life" can represent: Your existence. Your soul. Your will, ego, or consciousness. Your identity. The idea of being alive. **Your life force flowing out of you** can represent feeling: tired, weak, or drained by something in real life; disappointed or apathetic; out of touch with your sense of purpose or the meaning in your life; disconnected with God. *See also:* Life;

Alive or Exists; Dying; Death of You; Killed, Being; Dead Acquaintance; Death of a Loved One

Light (Illumination)

A light (such as from a lamp or unknown source) can represent: Clarity or understanding (as in "shedding some light" on a particular subject). Hope, goodness, or assistance, especially when it appears in the darkness (such as a lighthouse). **A spotlight** can represent the idea of being focused on, seen, or recognized by others; an indication of something you consider important or worthy of attention. *See also:* Lamp or Light; Glowing; Sun; Candle; Fire; Reflective Light; Gleam; Sparkle; Light (Spiritual); Turning On; Turning Off; Furniture

Light (Spiritual)

Dreaming that you're in the presence spiritual Light (or God) can represent: A desire to experience a deeper connection God, assistance from God, or another kind of spiritual experience (such as clarity or enlightenment). Feeling connected with God during your dream. Consider whether during the dream you experienced the overwhelming peace and love that signifies God's presence. *See also:* God; Love; Peace; Heaven; Angel; Religious Figure; Light (Illumination)

Lightning

A feeling of or fear of punishment. A perceived or imagined uncontrollable force. God, or other authority figure. An insight or realization. A rare event, or an event that seems against all odds. A sudden change (such as something that changes your outlook or way of thinking). Danger, especially from an unpredictable threat. Targeted destruction. A feeling or fear of bad luck. Fate. Randomness. Electricity or excitement (as in "there's "electricity in the air"). *See also:* Electricity; Storm; Cloud; Electrocute

Lightweight

You or something else being lightweight can represent: Airiness. A "light" or carefree attitude. Without burden. A perceived lack of substance or strength. *See also:* Levitating; Floating; Size; Measure; Skinny

Liking

Positive feelings toward the thing or person you liked in the dream, or whatever they represent. Good will. Familiarity. Attraction. Respect. Approval. For more clues, consider the context and nature of your feeling of "like." *See also:* Love; Friendly; Respecting; Approval; Superior; Good; Romance; Crush, Having a

Lily

Beginnings or endings. Spring, a fresh start, or renewal. A particular feeling (such as celebration or mourning). *See also:* Flower; Flower Bulb; Plant

Limit or Boundary

A limit, boundary, or edge can represent: A challenge or obstacle in your life. A limitation put on you by others, society, circumstance, environment, or something else outside yourself. A perceived personal limitation, or perhaps some you're limiting yourself. A beginning or ending. An extreme, or something "far out" (such as "the edge of the world," "the edge of reason," or "the limit of your patience"). "The best," "the most," or another superlative concept. For more clues, consider the context of and your feelings about the limit or boundary. *See also:* Edge, Coming to an; Ledge or Cliff; Divider; Restrained; Top; Bottom; Infinite; Frame

Lion

Protectiveness. Aggression. Ruling or being in charge. Power, strength, or strength of character. Commanding respect through personal character, rather than through violence or manipulation. Dreaming of this animal can represent too much or not enough of one of those qualities, or someone or something you associate with the quality or animal. Consider also the animal's actions, context, and your feelings about it. *See also:* Cat; Animal

Lips

Communication. Expression of feelings. Sensitivity or sensuality. Secrets. Consider what the lips were doing (for example, pursing your lips might represent indecision, and biting your lips might represent nervousness). *See also:* Mouth; Communication

Liquid

Ability to adapt or accommodate (as a liquid takes on the shape of its container). Pervasiveness, or an ability to have far-reaching effects (as a liquid naturally spreads into its surroundings). **Liquid flowing or changing shape** can represent change, transformation, or movement forward in your life (possibly beyond your control). *See also:* Water; Wet; Flow or River; Water, Body of; Drinking; Bottle; Leaking; Air

List

Organization or the need to be organized. Analyzing or trying to figure something out. Tasks or chores (such as your to-do list weighing on your mind). A group of something (such as reasons, people, objects, or things you want to remember). A plan or strategy. *See also:* Organizing; Task

Listening

Listening to someone or something can represent: Interest. Compassion or understanding. Respect. Advice, or taking advice. Obedience. A desire for information or to understand. Communication. Spying. Consider the context, who's talking, who's listening, and their motivations. *See also:* Communication; Hearing; Eavesdropping; Music; Ear; Watching; Obeying

Liver

Emotion (especially anger). Passion, "the fire within," or enthusiasm about life. The ability to process what's around you and reject what you don't need or could hurt you. The ability to process input from other people, using what's beneficial and letting go of the rest. *See also:* Kidney; Body Part

Living with Someone

Someone who shares your home can represent: Someone who's a part of your life, interacts with you often, or seems familiar to you (perhaps because you know or knew them well, or because they've been on your mind lately). Exploring what it would be like to spend time (or more time) with that person. *See also:* House; Person You Know; Person Unknown; Relationship

Lizard

The power of observation and perceptiveness. Quick response. Acting or reacting automatically or without conscious thought (such as a reflexive mental or emotional reaction). Instinct or a basic dynamic (such as human bonding, fear, or aggression). Dreaming of this animal can represent too much or not enough of one of those qualities, or someone or something you associate with the quality or animal. Consider also the animal's actions, context, and your feelings about it. *See also:* Animal; Salamander; Iguana

Llama

Having the strength to carry a responsibility or burden. Carrying baggage. Expressing your opinions, preferences, or distastes. Standing up for yourself. Dreaming of this animal can represent too much or not enough of one of those qualities, or someone or something you associate with the quality or animal. Consider also the animal's actions, context, and your feelings about it. *See also:* Animal

Loaning

Lending something to someone can represent: Feeling that you've given something (tangible or intangible) to that person (and perhaps you expect them to return it or give you something in return). Feeling that someone is indebted to you. Helping someone ("lending" them your knowledge or expertise). *See also:* Investment; Owing; Money; Finances; Borrowing

Location

A location can represent something you associate with a real-life location, event, person, memory, desire, fear, or something else in real life. A location can also convey a mood or characteristic that consistent with whatever that location's events represent (such as the happiness of a theme park representing your happiness on the first day of summer, or a peaceful lake representing the calmness of your quiet house). Consider your feelings about the location and anything that stood out about it. See also the specific type of location. *See also:* Places (the category)

Lock

An obstacle to getting what you want in a certain area of your life. Security (physical, emotional, or mental), or a desire for more. A need to focus on personal boundaries (such as strengthening them or allowing yourself to become more open with others). **Something that is locked** can represent experiencing an obstacle in some area of your life, or feeling the need to look for an alternative way forward. **Locking something** can represent an issue of trust or a concern about someone taking advantage of you. *See also:* Door or Entrance; Key; Security; Privacy; Closed; Knob; Opening; Unlocking; Keyhole; Closing

Locker

A locker (such as at school or the gym) can represent: Security, especially of tangible or intangible things that are important to you or your success. Privacy or ownership. Having authority over one small area within a larger area (such as being responsible for one aspect of a group project). **Looking for something in your locker** can represent a desire for something (answers, information, etc.) or searching for something you're missing or you've lost (your identity, motivation, etc.). **Cleaning out or organizing your locker** could represent cleaning out or re-prioritizing some aspect of your life (or a desire to do so). **Not being able to unlock your locker** can represent feeling stressed, afraid things won't go well, wanting to do well, or holding yourself back somehow. *See also:* Cabinet; Storage; Lock; Security; Privacy; Unlocking

Locomotive

Power, momentum, or massiveness. The power to make progress in your life. A feeling of overwhelm. Something that seems unstoppable or unavoidable, or the idea of control being out of your hands. *See also:* Engine; Driving; Train; Tracks, Railroad; Traveling

Logic

Using logic (such as to solve a problem or figure something out) can represent: The idea of applying your logic to something in real life. Feeling argumentative. Feeling a need to make a case for something or defend yourself. Searching for an answer or solution. Curiosity about something. *See also:* Problem; Arguing; Math; Science

Login

Security. A point of access or entrance (such as a door or starting point). A test or verification of someone's identity. A question of authenticity or honesty. A test for whether a person should be allowed into something (such as a group, restricted area, or area of knowledge). *See also:* Unlocking; Password; Computer; Door or Entrance; Internet

Loon

Mental clarity. Insight into deeper levels within. The surfacing of a memory. The idea of accessing your subconscious mind. A willingness to "dive in" or "go deep." Skill at accomplishing what you want or need. Dreaming of this animal can represent too much or not enough of one of those qualities, or someone or something you associate with the quality or animal. Consider also the animal's actions, context, and your feelings about it. *See also:* Bird

Losing an Item

A feeling or fear of losing whatever that item represents in real life, or a feeling that you've been neglecting it or taking it for granted. An issue of responsibility, or a reminder of an important responsibility. **Losing your seat or your place in line to someone else** can represent: the idea of someone "taking from you" in some way (such as stealing your limelight, taking advantage of you, or ignoring your rights or needs somehow). See also the item you lost. *See also:* Forgetting; Missing Person; Left, Being; Finding a Lost Item; Setting Down; Seat; Cheating; Waiting; Lost, Being; Failure

Lost, Being

A feeling or fear of being lost, without power, or without direction in your life or some aspect of it. A sense of not knowing which way to go or where to start. Feeling lost within yourself (such as feeling you've lost your identity). *See also:* Missing Person; Left, Being; Losing an Item

Lotus Flower

Inner peace. Perfection. Spirituality. A personal process of opening, unfolding, or evolving. Consider its context and anything that stood out about it. *See also:* Flower; Plant

Loud

Exaggerated, such as someone making an extra effort. Anger or other intense emotion. Importance or urgency. Aggressiveness or intrusion into your personal space, such as someone encroaching on your personal boundaries or integrity. For more clues, consider the context of and intention behind whatever was loud. *See also:* Noise; Music; Hearing

Love

Good will, empathy, respect, care, comfort, support, or adoration. Spirituality. The experience of loving others or being loved (or a desire for such). Altruism or giving. Attachment or wanting. Idolizing or objectifying. Consider the context, your feelings, intent, and motivation during the dream. *See also:* Light (Spiritual); Peace; Liking; Giving; Feeling; Wanting; Romance; Crush, Having a

Low

Down-to-earth, practical, or grounded. Starting at the beginning, or from the ground up. Feeling down or depressed. The idea of "the lowest" or "the least." A limited perspective or lack of clarity. Base instincts. Relating to something immoral or unethical. *See also:* Inferior; Under; Bottom; Descending; Basement; Underground; Soft

Lubricant or Catalyst

Something (a person, thing, action, event, situation, etc.) that encourages something else, makes it easier, or helps a process go faster or more smoothly (or a desire for such). For example, oil lubricating two gear wheels might represent humor making last week's job interview go more easily. *See also:* Salve; Engine; Fuel; Chemistry

Luck

The idea of good luck or bad luck (or an event that you consider as positive or negative) can represent: Your subconscious mind's effort to explain a coincidence or random event. Feeling grateful or fortunate (or ungrateful or unfortunate) about something in your life. Hope or fear regarding future events, as you imagine them. An attempt to disengage yourself from your responsibility for your life, your actions, and their consequences (by attributing an event to "bad luck"). *See also:* Magic; Bad; Good; Blaming; Event; Winning; Symbol

Lung

Breathing or flowing. Life, or being alive. Survival. A cycle. Ebb and flow. An activity or process that happens automatically or subconsciously. *See also:* Breathing; Rib; Chest; Surviving

Lying

A feeling or fear of dishonesty in real life (yours or someone else's). Perceiving the world as generally dishonest or untrustworthy. Lying to yourself in some way, or being in denial. *See also:* Betrayed, Being; Lied To, Being; Dishonest; Fake; Gossiping; Cheating; Trickery

Lying Down

Peace. The idea of resting physically, emotionally, or mentally (or a desire to do so). "Sitting it out" or not participating somehow in your life. Not standing up for yourself in a certain situation. "Lying down on the job" or not fulfilling responsibilities somehow in your life. *See also:* Resting; Asleep; Bed; Setting Down

Lymph

Cleanup or removal of (physical, emotional, or mental) toxins from your life. The ability to discern what's useful from what's not. Self-protection within yourself (such as by letting go of toxic thoughts or self-defeating beliefs). The essence of your physical existence. The ability to deal with the aftermath of conflict (including taking responsibility for your part in it). *See also:* Immune System; Gland; Blood; Allergy

Lynx

Solitary, or comfortable being alone. Silent or secretive. The idea of nonverbal communication. Instinctive. Independent. Dreaming of this animal can represent too much or not enough of one of those qualities, or someone or something you associate with the quality or animal. Consider also the animal's actions, context, and your feelings about it. *See also:* Cat; Animal

Machine or Robot

Someone or something you perceive as lacking human characteristics such as emotion, compassion, discernment, responsiveness, or warmth. The idea of doing things automatically or without thinking, or being on "auto-pilot." A servant, or someone you consider to be in a subservient role. Power. Repetition or monotony. For more clues, consider what the machine or robot was doing and how you felt about it. *See also:* Electric; Technician or Mechanic; Factory; Engine; Puppet

Maggots

Physical, emotional, or mental: Festering or rotting, as when a situation or feeling that needs attention has not been dealt with. The results of a messy or "stinking" situation. Something you consider undesirable or unclean. Making "treasure out of trash" (being resourceful, or using what you have to your best ability). Dreaming of this creature can represent too much or not enough of one of those qualities, or someone or something you associate with the quality or creature. Consider also the animal's actions, context, and your feelings about it. *See also:* Parasite; Fly (Insect); Worm; Larva; Insect

Magic

A wish or desire. A feeling or fear of illusion (that something "is not what it seems"), trickery, or manipulation in your life. Acknowledgment of the existence of a higher power (or at least of something beyond your understanding). **Doing magic** can represent: a desire to change or control situations or people around you; the idea of accomplishing a task so challenging that it seems "like magic." **Someone else doing harmful magic against you** can represent: a feeling or fear of being disliked, victimized, or manipulated; feeling a lack of power. *See also:* Spell; Curse; Powers; Luck; Trickery; Witch

Magnet

A perceived force or energy of some kind. Attraction. The idea that "opposites attract" or "opposites repel each other." Polarities (such as right and wrong, black and white, good and bad). The electromagnetic field of a living creature, or environmental effects on it (such as effects from another person's negativity). The idea of an invisible force, magic, illusion, or an unexplained phenomenon. Control, or keeping someone or something under control. Automation. Manipulation. *See also:* Battery; Liking

Mailbox

Actual or imagined communication. **Receiving mail in a mailbox** can represent the idea of receiving communication from someone, whether you want it or not (since you have no say over what gets put into your mailbox). **Mailing a letter** can represent something you'd like to say to someone else (written, spoken, etc.), a message you've sent in real life, or one you'd like to send. *See also:* Letter (Message)

Main Floor

The main floor in a house or building often represents your current life and the experiences and activities in your life. *See also:* Floor; Room; Basement; Upstairs

Makeup

Makeup such as foundation, lipstick, or eye shadow can represent: Feeling the need to enhance or change yourself somehow to increase acceptance by others or yourself. An issue regarding perfection, judging an aspect of yourself, or an unwillingness to accept yourself. Routine, especially morning routine. The idea of preparing yourself or "protecting" yourself to go out into the world. Femininity, as defined by society. Feeling the need to go along with peer pressure or societal tradition. Wanting to "put on a different face" or portray an image other than who you are. Creating an emotional or mental facade. The idea of a special occasion. Something that comes to mind when you think of that particular type of makeup or part of the face. Consider the context and your motivations. *See also:* Face; Decoration; Fashionable

Making or Building

Creativity or ingenuity. Productivity. Making use of what's available. Motivation for change or progress. Evolution, development, or maturation. *See also:* Design or Plan; Factory; Mixing; Woven; Technician or Mechanic; Creativity; Shaping; Support, Architectural

Male

Someone or something that's male can represent: A person in your real life. Masculinity. Male self-image, or a related issue. Fatherhood or your relationship with your father. Your inner child (whether you're male or female). Stereotypical male characteristics, emotions, or dynamics. Something you personally associate with being male. **A problem with the male reproductive system** can represent a perceived issue with one of the above topics. *See also:* Man; Person You Know; Person Unknown; Body Part

Man

Someone you know in real life, or the role he plays in your life (supervisor, father, friend, doctor, etc.). A characteristic that stood out about the man (such as strength, humor, or intelligence). Stereotypical masculine characteristics, personality traits, interests, abilities, etc. For more clues, consider the context of the man and your feelings about him. *See also:* Male; Person You Know; Person Unknown

Manager

Your actual manager or supervisor. Someone or something in your real life whom you allow to have power over you in some way. Someone whose opinions you listen to. A desire to rebel against authority. Your ability to manage yourself or an aspect of your life. A need for more (or less) self-discipline. Real or imagined assistance or guidance, or someone who "keeps you in line." A tendency to go along with someone else's expectations or opinions rather than following your own true path. *See also:* Leader; Superior; Authority Figure; Design or Plan; Coworker; Obeying

Manatee

Gentle, docile, unassuming, innocent, or harmless. Feeling contented with the simple things in life. Vulnerability, or susceptibility to others or the surrounding environment. Dreaming of this animal can represent too much or not enough of one of those qualities, or someone or something you associate with the quality or animal. Consider also the animal's actions, context, and your feelings about it. *See also:* Animal

Manicure

Improving your ability to get things done well or to deal with the details in your life. Attention to detail in improving yourself. Getting yourself or your mind in order. Pampering or taking care of yourself (or the importance of doing so). A desire to control how others view you, or a fear of being judged. Increasing your self-esteem in some way (or a desire to do so). *See also:* Salon; Fingernail; Toe; Decoration

Mansion

A mansion, palace, or castle can represent real, desired, or imagined: Power or status. Abundance or wealth (monetary or otherwise). Opulence or luxury. Attainment of an experience you desire or something you've always wanted. If the mansion is yours in the dream, it might represent you or your current life. *See also:* House; Big

Manure

Something you consider undesirable (such as an aspect of yourself or your personality, a habit, a tendency, etc.). Undue disrespect from someone else. A feeling or fear of being affected by someone else's problems or issues. Finding value in someone else's discards, such as using someone's rejection of you to "springboard" into a positive new process (since manure contains rich nutrients for growing plants). *See also:* Feces; Garbage

Many

The idea of "many" can represent abundance or overwhelm, depending on your feelings. Consider what led to having "many" of something and how you felt about it *See also:* Group; Increasing; Variety; Bigger, Getting; Infinite; Big; Rich

Map or Directions

Guidance or direction, or a desire for it. **Trying to figure out directions** (with a map, compass, recipe, etc.) can represent trying to figure out a solution, achieve certain results, or answer a question. **Being unable to figure out directions** can represent feeling stuck, confused, overwhelmed, or feeling a need for guidance somewhere in your life. *See also:* Following a Path; Following a Procedure; Steering; Path; Road; Driving; Traveling; Direction

Marching

Marching can represent how the marcher in the dream goes about their life or a certain activity in their life. **Marching with others or in formation** (as in a marching band or military ranks) could represent conformity or compliance; unity; a shared purpose, intention, or set of beliefs; teamwork; a desire to convey power or ability. *See also:* Walking; Parade; Band; Soldier; Fight

Marriage

An agreement, partnership, or ongoing arrangement (whether related to a romantic relationship or not). The idea of a commitment, promise, or contract. A real or desired relationship (such as a romantic relationship, friendship, business partnership, etc.). **Being married when you're not in real life** can represent: a particular relationship in your real life, since most relationships involve the same basic dynamics as in marriage (trust, communication, etc.); exploring what it might be like to be married (in general or to a certain person); experiencing the demands of commitments or responsibilities in your life. For more clues, consider the people involve, their dynamics, and what stood out about the marriage. *See also:* Wedding; Relationship

Martial Arts

Defending your mental, emotional, or physical boundaries or interests. Arguing or defending your beliefs, opinions, or convictions. Personal power or assertiveness (or a desire or more). Discipline or self-discipline (perhaps too much or too little). Practice and improvement. Your ability to focus or concentrate. Inner peace or balance. For more clues, consider the context, participants, motivations, and your feelings. *See also:* Competition; Game; Exercising; Nationality; Attacked, Being; Attacking; Weapon; Gymnastics

Masked or Hooded

A masked or hooded figure can represent: A fear you're too afraid to face (but when you do face it, it may lose its power to scare you). Mystery, or mysterious motives or identity. The unknown. Hiding from something or someone. Self-judgment. *See also:* Hiding; Costume; Cover; Coat; Cape; Secret; Clothes

Massage

The idea of receiving help, support, therapy, or medical treatment. Actual, imagined, or desired pampering (physical, emotional, or mental). **Massaging someone else** can represent: Giving to, supporting, or soothing someone (or wanting to do so); helping someone solve a problem or work through an issue. *See also:* Touching; Medical Treatment; Pampering Yourself

Math

A real-life problem or challenge that's on your mind. Being in the mood for problem solving and mental challenges. An "echo" or continuation of a similar kind of activity you were doing earlier in the day. Concern about an upcoming math test or other event. An indicator of a high level of stress or a Toxic Dream (p. 320). *See also:* Problem; Puzzle; Calculator; Homework; Chemistry; Number

Maze

A complex or challenging path or process. Confusion (such as a confused state of mind, or confusion about a certain decision). Overwhelm. A perceived challenge, puzzle, or problem in your real life. Feeling unsure how to achieve a certain goal or create a certain situation in your life. *See also:* Puzzle; Confused

219

Meal

Nourishment for the body, emotions, mind, or spirit. Relaxing, socializing, bonding with others, or something else you associate with mealtime. Characteristics you associate with a particular meal (hurrying at breakfast, socializing at lunch, bonding with family at dinner, arguing at holiday dinners). Actual hunger while you're sleeping. *See also:* Food; Eating

Measure

Measuring, weighing, or gauging something can represent: An attempt to evaluate or observe (possibly to determine what further action is needed or what choice to make). An attempt to understand, study, or figure something out. Tracking progress. Comparing one thing to something else, or to a standard. Consider also what's being measured and why. *See also:* Lightweight; Heavy; Size; Big; High; Inferior; Superior; Balancing

Media

"The media" or media sources (television, radio, newspapers, or online sources) can represent real or imagined: Communication. News or new information. Gossip. "The establishment," as perceived by you. The interests of the media as perceived by you (such as honesty, disclosure, spin, or financial or political motivations). *See also:* TV; Show or Movie; Internet; Newspaper; Radio

Medical Office

A workplace, environment, or organization where problems are fixed or solutions are found (such as your workplace, a customer service department, etc.). Consider also your motivation for and feelings about visiting the medical office. *See also:* Medical Treatment; Healer; Doctor; Nurse; Healing; Health; Illness; Injured; Hospital; Medicine; Rescued, Being; Rescuing; Problem

Medical Treatment

Addressing a physical, emotional, mental, or spiritual problem (or a desire to do so). A desire to find an answer, solution, or source of help (perhaps due to feeling overwhelmed, helpless, or uncertain about what to do). **Receiving first aid** can represent: a real-life or feared crisis, threat, or other situation needing urgent attention; the importance of getting help from others. *See also:* Doctor; Nurse; Medicine; Surgery; Rescued, Being; Rescuing; Paramedic; Healer; Healing; Illness; Injured; Health; Problem; Medical Office; Hospital

Medicine

A real or desired solution. A means of creating a desired experience or quality of life. Making a change in the "cause" part of a "cause and effect." **Taking medicine** can represent a real-life attempt to fix a problem (physical or otherwise), or a desire to do so. **Losing or forgetting to take your prescription medicine** may represent neglecting a particular responsibility (perhaps involving self-care); the importance you place on self-care. *See also:* Drug; Medical Treatment

Meeting

A real or imagined interaction among the meeting attendees in the dream (or whomever or whatever they represent). A group decision-making process. Collaboration or sharing of information. Productivity or a productive process. Something else that meetings represent to you (being put on the spot, boredom, duty or responsibility, leading or following, etc.). For more clues, consider the meeting's purpose, context, dynamics, attendees, and your feelings during the meeting. *See also:* Working; Workplace; Class; Interview; Appointment; Visiting; Joining; Organization, Membership; Meeting Someone; Person You Know

Meeting Someone

The idea of meeting that person or someone they represent in your life, whether a real or imagined meeting (for example, meeting your mother for lunch might represent yesterday's meeting with a motherly coworker, and meeting Abraham Lincoln could represent a desire to know what he was like). **Meeting someone new** can represent: something new in your life (such as a new person, idea, or solution), real or imagined; the beginning of a process (such as a relationship or phase); a fear of change or of something unknown. For more clues, consider the context and whom or what the person might represent. *See also:* Handshake; Meeting; Person Unknown; Seeing

Menacing

Being threatened by someone or something menacing can represent a feeling or fear of a threat somewhere in real life (mentally, emotionally, or physically). A recent threatening experience you witnessed (in person, on TV, etc.). *See also:* Attacking; Bully; Criminal; Violence; Evil

Menstruation

Femininity or womanhood. A cycle, or something that follows a cycle. An ending, or the preparation for a new beginning. Something that comes and goes repeatedly. Preparation for what's to come. *See also:* Female; Pregnancy; Blood

Mentally Unstable

Dreaming that you're mentally unstable can represent a feeling or fear of: Not being able to think clearly or logically. Others not accepting you. Being unable or unwilling to deal with your life right now (as in frustration, overwhelm, or a low tolerance for problems or responsibilities). **Someone else being mentally unstable** can mean you're attributing to them one of the things just mentioned, or you feel that a situation or person seems unpredictable or "off" somehow. This could also be an indicator of a Toxic Dream (p. 320). *See also:* Unstable; Confused; Disabled; Weird

Menu

A decision, a set of choices, or the opportunity to make a choice somewhere in your life. Availability of options. Abundance. Consider the context, what stood out about the menu, and how you felt about it. *See also:* Decision, Your; Food

Mermaid

A mermaid or merman can represent: A sense of magical, mystical, fantasy, or other-worldly. The combination of two "ways of being" (such as both feminine and masculine), or being "of two worlds" (such as work life and home life). Support, assistance, or kindness. A desire to be different than you are. A desire to fit in or excel in a different or new environment. Femininity or masculinity, or your feminine or masculine ideal. Someone or something you feel is different or unusual. A real-life friend, or a desire for friendship. *See also:* Fish; Mythological Character

Merry-Go-Round

The idea of a repeating cycle. Going around and around (such as circular logic, or repeating a process or lesson). Participating in a process or activity with others in real life. A feeling or fear of "getting nowhere." A desire for more "simple fun" in your life. For more clues, consider your feelings (feeling delighted about choosing a horse might represent your delight about a recent real-life decision). **Not being able to get off the merry-go-round** might represent feeling stuck in a never-ending situation or pattern. **Not being able to get on the merry-go-round** could represent feeling like you're not being allowed to participate somehow in your life. *See also:* Ride; Playground; Amusement Park; Ferris Wheel; Festival or Carnival

Messenger

Real or imagined: Communication or message, or the person who sends or delivers it. A mode of delivery (such as through a particular person, delivery service, or the news media). *See also:* Delivery; Communication; Representative; Carrying; Letter (Message); Angel

Metal

Cold. Strength, or strength of character. Rigidity or rigid thinking. Modern, minimal, or sleek. Persevering or enduring. Someone or something that's malleable (influenceable) only when "warmed up." Consider also the context of the metal in the dream. *See also:* Gold; Hard Object; Rigid

Microphone

The idea of "amplifying" or "broadcasting" who you are, your expression, thoughts, or opinions. Self-expression in a big way. The idea of being heard or spotlighted by others. For more clues, consider how you felt about the microphone. *See also:* Voice; Increasing; Stage or Screen; Performing; Singing; Communication

Midday

A particular midday occasion in your real life. Taking a break or a rest. Experiencing or needing physical, emotional, mental or spiritual nourishment. Consider also what midday means to you personally, and what you typically do during that time of day. *See also:* Time of Day; Time Frame

Milk

Basic or essential nourishment or sustenance (physical, emotional, mental, or spiritual). Motherly support or encouragement. The sweetness of life. Childhood, childlike qualities, or innocence. *See also:* Drinking; Food; Breast; Cow

Mirror

Self-awareness, examination of self, or looking inward. Self image or the image you project to the world (or the difference between them). Self-consciousness, vanity, or insecurity. Physical, emotional, or mental superficiality. A focus on "the surface" or on only what can be observed (such as the appearance of a situation rather than the full reality of it). *See also:* Reflective Light; Glass; Self

Miscarriage

The (possibly unexpected or premature) end of a phase, process, or endeavor. Loss or grief. Issues involving responsibility for self or others. Rejecting your inner child, your playfulness or creativity, or belief in self.

A feeling of something in your life not happening in the right timing or not being "meant to be." Consider the context and how you felt about the situation. *See also:* Fetus; Ovum; Baby; Birth, Giving; Female

Misdialing

Having trouble dialing the phone (or repeatedly pressing wrong digits) can represent: Frustration in communicating something (such as a message or a need). A perceived or feared inability to communicate with a particular person. A feeling or fear of being isolated or cut off from others, or of not being able to get help when you need it. An indication of a Toxic Dream (p. 320). *See also:* Communication; Problem; Failure; Phone; Help, Calling for

Missile

A feeling or fear of: Victimization, aggression, being targeted, or other negativity in your life. A disagreement, war, or other hostility. An attack, possibly originating from an unknown or anonymous source. Power being taken away from you (or a desire to take power from others). An attack from a distance or from a protected position. *See also:* Bomb; Rocket; Flying; Violence

Missing an Event

Missing an event or time frame (an exam, appointment, bus, scheduled payment, etc.) can represent a missed opportunity or neglected responsibility, or a fear of such. Consider also the reason you missed or were late for the event (for example, missing an appointment because you forgot about it could represent feeling disorganized in real life). *See also:* Late; Failure; Failing a Test; Feeling

Missing Person

A feeling or fear of neglecting or taking that person for granted. Exploring your feelings about how much that person means to you. An imaginary worst-case scenario. Recognizing that you're missing something that person represents (fun, spontaneity, being organized, spirituality, etc.). *See also:* Lost, Being; Losing an Item; Abduction; Killed, Being; Escaping

Mixing

Mixing things together (or something that's already mixed) can represent: The idea of mixing whatever is represented in real life by the mixed things, and the results that would follow (such as mixed jelly beans representing the beauty of uniting people with different personalities or backgrounds). Real or desired creativity, where individual elements or

224

ideas are combined to create something new. An activity or procedure that involves mixing (such a baking, painting, or composing music). Synergy, cooperation, or compatibility among two or more elements, people, or groups (or a desire for such). *See also:* Chemistry; Making or Building; Agreement; Woven; Cooking; Joining Together; Quilt; Variety; Food

Mockingbird

Being inspired by others, or by the world around you. Copying from others. Leading your life "out loud" or celebrating yourself in the world (rather than being what others expect or want). The idea of "singing your song" or expressing yourself with confidence. Dreaming of this animal can represent too much or not enough of one of those qualities, or someone or something you associate with the quality or animal. Consider also the animal's actions, context, and your feelings about it. *See also:* Bird; Cuckoo

Model, Fashion

An ideal. The concept of measuring "perfection" according to society's or someone else's standards. An example, or someone who serves as an example. A role model, or a perceived characteristic that you admire or you'd like to emulate. Insecurity, superficiality, or a preoccupation with appearance or image (perhaps indicating an opportunity to work through underlying judgments or self-defeating beliefs). *See also:* Celebrity; Performing; Clothes; TV; Show or Movie

Mold or Fungus

Something you perceive as "something good gone bad." Neglect or lack of use. Lack of hygiene (physical, emotional, mental, etc.). Opportunism or using whatever resources you have. A parasitic relationship. Abundance or thriving. *See also:* Virus; Infection; Germs; Rotten

Mole (Animal)

Adept at improvising or navigating "in the dark" (without information or cues for guidance). A subconscious activity or process. Secret or stealthy activity, perhaps leading to surprises for others. Keeping your actions or feelings to yourself, perhaps until they erupt to the surface. Dreaming of this animal can represent too much or not enough of one of those qualities, or someone or something you associate with the quality or animal. Consider also the animal's actions, context, and your feelings about it. *See also:* Animal; Groundhog; Hedgehog

Money

Money (currency, bills, coins, a check, etc.) can represent: Value or "currency" of some kind. Something of value that you've given or received in your life, or that you'd like to give or receive (such as money, love, respect, or good will). Something you treasure (such as a relationship or memories). Investment or saving. **Being given money** can represent receiving: something valuable (tangible or intangible) in real life; feeling someone's generosity (or a wish for such). **Paying money** can represent giving something valuable, perhaps in return for something valuable. **Winning money** can mean you'd like for this to happen in real life, or you're feeling fortunate. **Someone demanding money** can represent a real or feared demand in your life (monetary or otherwise). **Someone owing you money** can represent feeling the person is indebted to you somehow, or that you've done more for this person than they've done for you. *See also:* Finances; Rich; Check (Money); Loaning; Borrowing; Paying

Monk

Denial of worldly things, or freedom from worldly things. Peace. Solitude. Isolation, or being out-of-touch with events in the world. Spiritual dedication. Religious vigilance. A singular focus. Repression or suppression (such as of self, expression, needs, etc.). Something mysterious or hidden (a person, activity, motive, talent, tendency, etc.). *See also:* Religious Figure

Monkey

Intelligence, understanding, or thoughtfulness. Playfulness. Physical, emotional, or mental agility. Adaptability to environment or circumstances. Companionship or community. Imitation, copying, or aspiring to be like someone else. Basic human skills. Humanity or human-like qualities (such as sentience or compassion). Dreaming of this animal can represent too much or not enough of one of those qualities, or someone or something you associate with the quality or animal. Consider also the animal's actions, context, and your feelings about it. *See also:* Animal; Chimpanzee; Gorilla or Ape; Orangutan

Monster

A subconscious fear or imagining. A real-life situation in which you felt threatened or pursued. A person or thing with whom you associate a certain characteristic of the monster (such as a monster's red color representing the red pick-up truck that hit your car last week). **A monster coming after you** can represent: a physical, emotional, or mental threat (or fear of one); an indicator of a Toxic Dream (p. 320). *See also:* Deformity; Werewolf; Vampire; Zombie; Ghost; Mythological Character

Month

A particular month (May, August, etc.) can represent the actual time frame of a real-life event portrayed in the dream, or it can set a mood or context that you associate with that month or time of year (such as January representing a new beginning or June representing your friend who has a June birthday). *See also:* Time of Year; Dates on a Calendar; Time Passing; Time Frame; Spring (Season); Summer; Winter; Autumn

Moon

Nighttime or darkness (or something represented by those). A "light in the darkness." Illumination or "shedding light on" something. Intuition. Creativity. Inspiration. Perceived femininity or feminine energy. Consider the context and how you felt about the moon's presence. *See also:* Night; Time of Day; Light (Illumination); Darkness

Moose

Steady movement forward through life. Exploration of or sensitivity to your environment. Unassuming. Large (in size, presence, personality, etc.). Feeling clumsy, or the idea that clumsiness is okay as long you "get the job done." Dreaming of this animal can represent too much or not enough of one of those qualities, or someone or something you associate with the quality or animal. Consider also the animal's actions, context, and your feelings about it. *See also:* Animal; Elk

Morgue

A "look back" or a post-mortem analysis of something that has ended (such as a project, process, event, or relationship). The end of a phase. A setting of solemnity or seriousness. A place where it's quiet or where people sleep. *See also:* Dead Body; Ending

Morning

A beginning. A fresh start or clean slate. An awakening (physical, emotional, or mental). New insight or clarity. Part of a recurring cycle. Also consider what mornings mean to you personally (such as whether or not you're a "morning person"). *See also:* Time of Day; Sunrise

Mosquito

The idea of taking something (time, energy, integrity, etc.) or being taken from, perhaps without permission. Stealth. A nuisance, or feeling "bugged" by something. Dreaming of this insect can represent too much or not enough of one of those qualities, or someone or something you associate with the quality. Consider also the insect's actions, context, and your feelings about it. *See also:* Blood; Sucking; Insect

Moth

Feeling drawn to something or someone. Attraction. An instinct or desire, or acting on one. A nuisance or bother. Focusing on the "light," God, your higher purpose, optimism, or something else that's "light " or that attracts your attention. Activity during what would usually be a period of rest. Dreaming of this insect can represent too much or not enough of one of those qualities, or someone or something you associate with the quality. Consider also the insect's actions, context, and your feelings about it. *See also:* Insect; Butterfly

Mother

Your real-life mother. An authority or caretaker figure (such as your employer). A feminine role model or inspiration. The idea of motherhood, motherly qualities, or parenthood in general. Your spiritual parent (God). *See also:* Family; Person You Know

Motorcycle

The means by which you move forward in your life, the context within which you grow personally and learn your life lessons. Independence or autonomy. Vulnerability or lack of protection (physical, emotional, or mental). Openness to or connection with your environment. Taking action in a risky or exposed way, or proceeding without protecting yourself very well. *See also:* Vehicle; Traveling; Driving

Mountain Lion

Strength in action, especially through stealth. Personal power. Decisiveness, the attitude of "act now, think later." Being in touch with your basic instincts. Smoothness in action. Capability, possibly with an edge of unpredictability. Dreaming of this animal can represent too much or not enough of one of those qualities, or someone or something you associate with the quality or animal. Consider also the animal's actions, context, and your feelings about it. *See also:* Cat; Animal; Leopard; Jaguar

Mouse

Quiet, shy, or staying hidden (unnoticed, unseen, or unheard). Curious, or tending to get into everything. The idea that focusing on the small things or actions can bring big results. The power of understatement. Pestering or "gnawing away at" (as in something bothering you, or trying to get what you want). Dreaming of this animal can represent too

228

much or not enough of one of those qualities, or someone or something you associate with the quality or animal. Consider also the animal's actions, context, and your feelings about it. *See also:* Animal; Hamster; Rat

Mouth

Expressing yourself or your opinions. Need, want, or lack. The ability to nourish yourself (physically, emotionally, mentally, or spiritually). An opening or a beginning. Consider also the context and what the mouth is doing. *See also:* Lips; Tooth; Tongue; Eating; Communication

Moving Around

Someone or something moving around energetically can represent: Feeling active or high-energy. The desire for activity, excitement, or interest. Life or being alive (where movement indicates the presence of life). **Chaotic movement** can represent the idea of a person or situation seeming unpredictable or out of control. See also the particular type of movement. *See also:* Alive or Exists; Exercising; Chaos; Trembling; Carrying; Pulling; Can't Move; Relocating

Mucus

Defense or a protective measure. Cleansing or clearing out. An aspect of yourself or someone else (personality, actions, habits, etc.) that you consider undesirable. *See also:* Secretion; Nose; Coughing; Virus; Illness

Mud

A "sticky" or "dirty" mess, such as a challenge or problem. Feeling stuck, or feeling the potential to get stuck somehow in your life (as in "stuck in the mud"). The idea of someone you feel is unadventurous or rigid in their ways (as in "a stick in the mud"). The idea of something rigid or difficult that becomes either easier or messier (as when water converts hard dirt to mud). Consider also the context, such as whether the mud is being used as a building material. *See also:* Ground; Dirt; Wet

Mule

Stubbornness, single-mindedness, or tenacity. Work, productivity, or tirelessness. The idea of thankless work. The result of combining two things that are different (as a mule is the offspring of a horse and a donkey). Inability to multiply or create something new (as mules are generally sterile). Dreaming of this animal can represent too much or not enough of one of those qualities, or someone or something you associate with the quality or animal. Consider also the animal's actions, context, and your feelings about it. *See also:* Animal; Donkey; Horse

Muscle

Physical, emotional, or mental strength or power. Movement. Motivation. Progress in life, or the ability to make progress or get things done. Endurance or perseverance. See also the particular part of the body involved. *See also:* Body Part

Museum

The past. Things from your past that are preserved or still lingering (memories, emotions, judgments, etc.). The importance of whatever is represented by the museum's contents. The idea of being unused, untouched, untouchable, or unattainable (like the items in a museum). The idea of something being perceived as out of date or obsolete (or a fear of such). Reverence for (or even "worship" of) people or things from the past. *See also:* Antique; Past; Time Frame

Music

Expression, communication, or a message. **Hearing music** can represent the idea of someone (or your own intuition or spiritual guidance) trying to give you a message. Think about what the lyrics and mood of the music convey, its context in the dream, your feelings about the music, and what it reminds you of in real life. (A song you've heard recently repeating in your head all night may not have any significant meaning other than perhaps your subconscious mind enjoys it.) **Playing a musical instrument** can represent: a desire to express or say something; a need for a creative outlet; your potential to express yourself or accomplish things in the world. *See also:* Song; Singing; Performing; Band; Listening; Hearing; Radio; Creativity

Mustache

Masculinity, masculine personality characteristics, or maturity. Someone in your life whom you feel tends to hide their feelings or to not communicate very openly (as a mustache can obscure the mouth). An attempt to hide or alter one's identity. **A manly mustache on a woman** can represent your perception (or imagining) of the woman as having a physical, emotional, or mental trait you associate with masculinity; the idea of someone (or of women in general) not conforming with societal "feminine" norms; a blurring or overlooking of gender boundaries. **A mustache on a man** can represent: someone you know who has a mustache; your attitude or preference about men having mustaches (consider how you felt about the mustache). *See also:* Hair; Beard; Shaving

Mythological Character

A mythological character or creature (such as Hercules or a unicorn) can represent: Whatever comes to mind when you think of that character or creature in real life. The traditional symbolism of that character, such as what it's known for, its typical characteristics, context, actions, and role (such as a leprechaun representing luck). Its primary characteristic (such as a unicorn's peacefulness or Ares' combativeness). Consider also what stood out about it in the dream, and your feelings about it. *See also:* Character; Mermaid; Dragon; Werewolf; Vampire; Monster; Mythological Place

Mythological Place

A location from myth or legend (such as Camelot or the Land of Oz) can represent: Something that comes to mind when you think of that place (consider the characteristics, mood, context, characters, and events you tend to associate with it). The traditional symbolism associated with that location (such as an event, story, character, characteristic, or mood). Something that stood out about your particular dream version of the place, perhaps something different than the traditional version. *See also:* Mythological Character; Location

Naked

Openness, honesty, or emotional availability. Feeling vulnerable or exposed (physically, emotionally, or mentally) somehow, perhaps to other people's opinions or judgments. A feeling or fear of being too forthcoming in relationships, or of rushing things in a certain relationship. Something that's basic, simple, or unadorned (such as "the naked truth"). **Being naked in a public place and feeling embarrassed** can represent: a fear of being embarrassed, singled out, or judged in a social situation; feeling it's important to fit in, maintain appearances, or be accepted. **Being naked in a public place on purpose** can represent: feeling comfortable with yourself, having nothing to hide, or not tending to let others' opinions limit you (or a desire for such); lack of respect for others and their feelings; sharing too much or burdening others (such as sharing your feelings, problems, or secrets inappropriately). *See also:* Undressing; Exposed (Body)

Name

Seeing or hearing a name can be just an inconsequential dream event. If the name seems to have significant meaning, consider the context and what the name means to you personally. **Saying someone's name** can mean you're focusing on that person for some reason, perhaps with the intent of communicating with them. **Someone saying your name** can represent perceiving or imagining them communicating with you or their focus being on you in real life. **Someone calling you an unpleasant name** could represent a feeling or fear of being disrespected or rejected somehow. *See also:* Words; Communication

Napkin

An attempt to clean up a "mess" or problem in your life, or a means of doing so. The idea of being careful how you nourish yourself physically, emotionally, mentally, or spiritually. *See also:* Cleaning; Eating

Nationality

Nationality, ethnicity, or culture can represent the actual country or continent, its people, its culture, or anything you personally associate with that area of the world. Consider its context in your dream and what comes to mind when you think of that nationality. For example, an object that is Chinese might represent Eastern culture, ancient origin, a particular philosophy, alternative medicine, or a person with whom you've interacted that you perceive to be of Chinese origin. *See also:* Country; Region; Nomad; Telescope

Neck

A bottleneck or slowdown in a process. Support. A means to an end. Vulnerability. Sensitivity or sensuality. Beauty or grace. A significant connection, or something that connects two significant things. The ability or willingness to revisit your past or issues from the past, or to "look behind" you. *See also:* Jaw; Throat; Body Part

Necklace

The idea of adornment. Having certain expectations about personal appearances. A perceived attempt to control or "own" someone. **Someone giving you a necklace** can represent perceiving or imagining they have positive feelings toward you; something tangible or intangible you received from them in real life (or a desire for such); feeling or fearing that they want to influence you or have more power in your relationship (as in people putting collars on dogs for control and proof of ownership). *See also:* Jewelry; Neck

Negotiating

An actual negotiation, disagreement, or argument in your life. A focus on the balance between giving and taking somewhere in your life. A focus on worth, value, or getting a good deal. An area of your life that involves an agreement, or an opportunity to make one (with others or with yourself). *See also:* Arguing; Agreement; Sale or Discount

Nerves

Nerves or the nervous system can represent: Interaction. Communication or inner communication. Connections. A network. *See also:* Body Part; Feeling

Nest or Dwelling

A dwelling (nest, hive, birdhouse, doghouse, etc.) can represent: A house. A resting place. A feeling of security or home. Settling down or staying in one place. Making a home more comfortable or livable. Family, or a setting for family connection or bonding. *See also:* House; Bird; Shell

Net

The idea of catching, intending to catch, or being caught. **Being caught in a net** can represent a feeling or fear of being accused, cornered, or victimized. **Being in a high place with a net below** can represent: safety (or a desire for it); the idea of moderated risk; feeling open to taking a risk, but only within reason; the idea that someone "has your back" or is watching out for you. *See also:* Catching Something; Catching Someone; Hunting; Internet

New

Newness or cleanliness. A beginning, fresh start, or clean slate. Perceived perfection. The perception that whatever the new object represents in your life is lacking problems, flaws, or complications. **Something that's trendy, modern, or cutting-edge** can represent: feeling that you're "ahead of the curve" or ahead of the times (or a desire for such); keeping up with others or wanting their approval. **Something unknown or unexplored** might represent: an opportunity to learn or discover; something in your real life that feels new or unfamiliar to you (such as a new workplace or project); being open to new possibilities; feeling confused, unsure, or lost; things seeming strange or "not as they should be" somewhere in your life. *See also:* Starting Over; Unknown Thing; Person Unknown; Fashionable; Creativity; Different; Discovering; Changing; Weird; Location; Unknown Thing

New Year

A new beginning or new start. A new promise, agreement, or direction. Resolving old issues before moving on to new things. A past, expected, imagined, or desired event that you associate with the New Year or that time of year. *See also:* Holiday; Party

Newspaper

News, new information, change, or a message or update. A source of information (a person, website, social media, etc.). Communication in general. The media, "the establishment," or a particular media institution. *See also:* Media; Communication

Next To

Something that is next to something else could represent: Your feeling that the two belong together, are involved with each other somehow, or have something in common. Things that are close together spatially in real life. Events that are close to each other in time. People who are emotionally close to each other. Companionship, or a desire for it. *See also:* Touching; Staying; Distance; Almost

Night

Mystery or uncertainty. Stealth or sneakiness. An action or activity of a questionable nature. Rest, sleep, or peace. **Something happening at night** can represent: something in your real life happening without others finding out; an action with stealthy motives; something you keep to yourself and do not tell others about. *See also:* Time of Day; Darkness; Black; Evening; Twilight; Sunset; Moon; Star

Nightclothes

Your personal, private, or home life. Relaxation, casualness, downtime, or being off-duty. Evening or nighttime. Sleep or other nighttime events. **Feeling embarrassed about being seen in your nightclothes** can represent a feeling or fear of being vulnerable or exposed (physically, emotionally, or mentally). *See also:* Clothes; Night; Underwear

Nine

Full or well-rounded. Well thought-out and planned. Done to perfection (as in being "dressed to the nines"). An ending. Finality or ultimate decision. The idea of "almost" (as nine is "almost ten"). Something else you associate with nine, such as a nonet, nonagon, time frame, someone's age, or your family. *See also:* Number; Age; Time Frame

Nipple

Nurturing or support (physical, emotional, mental, spiritual, etc.). **A female nipple** can represent: femininity; female sexuality; mother or motherly love. **A male nipple** can represent: masculinity; femininity; strength; macho or bravado; unfulfilled potential. *See also:* Breast; Chest; Baby; Body Part

Nodding
Agreeing, supporting, listening, or other communication (or the desire for such). *See also:* Head; Turning; Asleep

Noise
The presence or action of someone else. Activity. Celebration. Chaos or stress. Anger or other feelings. **When ongoing noise stops, the silence can represent** the completion of a phase, or the end of whatever the noise represents (activity, intention, persistence, etc.). **A specific noise** (such as a bell ringing or gunshot) can signify an important event or symbol in the dream. For more clues, consider the type of noise, how you felt about it, and its context. See also the specific type of sound. *See also:* Loud; Soft; Quiet; Words; Hearing

Nomad
Freedom. Random or irregular. Feeling ungrounded, uncentered, or without a strong foundation or inner sense of "home." An ability to adapt to various situations and environments. A focus on aspects of life other than material possessions. *See also:* Traveling; Homeless; Erratic

Nose
Self, or a person (as in "counting noses"). The boundary between self and the world (since the nose is a boundary between air outside the body and inside the body). Nosy, meddlesome, or a feeling or fear of someone being that way. The idea of interrupting or butting in. *See also:* Smell; Mucus; Body Part

Notebook
A collection of thoughts (possibly whatever has been on your mind lately, or matters you've been "studying" in your life). Work, a process, or a project in your life. Paying attention (as in noticing things and taking mental notes). The idea of the written word, writing, or authorship. School, education, or learning somewhere in your life. For more clues, consider the owner, purpose, and context of the notebook. *See also:* Journal; Writing; School; Book

Nuclear
Power, or out-of-control power. A perceived threat. A thing or situation you feel could easily become destructive or spiral out of control. *See also:* Fuel; Bomb; Hot

Numb

An unwillingness or inability to feel emotion. Feeling disconnected from life or the world. Communication problems. Being in denial. A refusal or inability to acknowledge or accept something. **Numbness in a certain body part** can represent feeling weak or "off" somehow in whatever that part of your body represents. See also the specific body part. *See also:* Can't Move; Nerves; Unfeeling

Number

A specific number can be significant itself (such as "1" representing being alone, or "4" representing stability), or it might represent something specific (such as an age, a year, or a number of people or objects). Dreaming about numbers or math can also mean that your logical mind was working hard, perhaps trying to understand or solve a challenge in your life. For more clues, consider the number's context, your feelings about it during the dream, and any personal meaning it has for you. Sometimes numbers show up when you're dropping off to sleep or waking up that can seem important at the time, although they often have no significant meaning. See also the particular number. *See also:* Text; Math; Words and Numbers (the category)

Nun

Purity. Benevolence. Religion or religious practice. Dedication to a certain lifestyle, cause, or set of beliefs. Femininity. Strictness or discipline (with others or yourself). Repression, abstinence, denial of self or a certain aspect of self. *See also:* Religious Figure; Religion; Church; Monk

Nurse

Caregiving, support, nurturing, or healing. The idea of responsibility for or authority over others (such as an actual responsibility or a feeling of being overburdened). Knowledge, especially of a practical nature. **A nurse or caretaker helping you** can represent a desire for healing or assistance right now. *See also:* Medical Treatment; Healer

Oar

Your ability to "get places," navigate, or change direction in your life. **Losing your oars while in a boat** can represent: a particular real-life situation in which you feel unempowered; a feeling or fear of not being able to change direction in your life. *See also:* Propeller; Steering

Oasis

An oasis in a desert can represent: Relief, or a desire for it. A break from something challenging in your life or mind (a situation, worrying, etc.). Rest or relaxation. Abundance, or receiving plenty of what you need. *See also:* Desert; Water; Resting

Obeying

An issue of personal power or control. A question of who is in charge of you, or who you're allowing to be in charge of you. Respect for the person you're obeying, their ideas, or their opinions. Consider the context of and your feelings about the obedience. (Be careful not to confuse obeying a person with loving that person. Requiring obedience of an adult can indicate an imbalance of power, whereas love does not control or place conditions on others). **Choosing to obey against your will or against your better judgment** can represent: a feeling or fear of giving your power away; a personal boundary issue; confusion; lack of trust in yourself. **Being forced to be obedient** can represent: a feeling or fear of pressure to comply (such as with rules, another person's expectations, or your own self-limiting expectations); an indicator of a Toxic Dream (p. 320). *See also:* Good; Agreement; Quitting; Manager; Authority Figure; Demanding; Listening; Following (Trailing Behind)

Object

Something in your real life that the object resembles in some way, or of which the object reminds you. A particular characteristic you associate with the object. Consider what stood out about the object, your feelings about it, its context, and how and when it appeared (for example, a new wedding ring might represent a new relationship, or a bright blouse might represent cheerfulness). See also the specific kind of object. **An object that appears bigger than expected** might represent something that seems overwhelming or important to you. Seemingly random objects can appear when you're dropping off to sleep or waking up that can seem important at the time, although they often have no significant meaning. *See also:* Unknown Thing; Objects (the category)

Octopus

Busy-ness or multitasking. Going in many directions at once (lots of different thoughts, activities, etc.). Approaching a problem from many different angles. Grabby (literally or figuratively). Dreaming of this animal can represent too much or not enough of one of those qualities, or someone or something you associate with the quality or animal. Consider also the animal's actions, context, and your feelings about it. **See also:** Animal; Squid

Off

"Away from" or "different than." Distancing, or a desire for distance. A feeling or fear that something is "off" or not quite right. **Running off of something** (such as a road or bridge) can represent: a fear of making a mistake or of losing control; a need to pay more attention to your responsibility for yourself or to "watch where you're going" in some aspect of in life. **See also:** Accident; Slipping; Falling; Jumping Off; Weird; Rotten; Turning Off

Offensive or Ugly

Perceiving something as: Undesirable or unwanted. Unacceptable. Outside societal norms or non-standard. Be careful that your judgments and shortcomings aren't keeping you from seeing the true meaning or value (the real person behind the appearance, the usefulness of the object, the lesson available to you, etc.). **See also:** Judgment or Disapproval; Inferior; Weird; Hurt, Being; Smell

Old Person

A particular person in your real life (whether or not the person is elderly in real life). An authority figure. Someone you respect or look up to. Wisdom. Experience, or knowledge gained from experience. Something that has existed a long time. The later portion of a phase or process, perhaps one that has taken a long time. **See also:** Age; Aging; Person Unknown; Person You Know

One

Single or solitary. A beginning or first step. Perceived as best, superior, or perfect. First priority. Independent or strong. Unique or special. Unified (as in "two become as one" or "one for all and all for one"). Purity. A starting point for a process, or returning to the starting point. Something else you associate with one, such as a time frame or someone's age. **See also:** Superior; Winning; Number

Onion

A multilayered situation in your real life, where you need to look beyond the obvious. A personal growth process in which you work through each layer of an issue as you delve down toward its root. Something that has a strong presence. The idea of "fake tears." **See also:** Food; Spice

Opening

Opening something (such as a door or box) can represent: Curiosity. A desire for understanding or information. A search for something (an object, person, opportunity, etc.). Beginning something, or a desire to do so. Clarity, or openness to the truth. Honesty with yourself. Receiving something tangible or intangible, or a desire to receive. A matter regarding personal boundaries or personal space (such as feeling "open" or "closed," or too much one way or the other). **An opening that serves as a point of access** (such as an entrance) can represent a perceived opportunity or vulnerability. *See also:* Door or Entrance; Hole; Bursting; Pulling; Unlocking; Discovering; Exposed (Object); Helpless; Closing

Opossum

Using inaction or pretending as a self-defense strategy, or in a wise way (as opossums pretend to be asleep when threatened). The idea of faking, hiding the truth, hiding your feelings, or "playing opossum." Refusing to argue or fight. Slow and steady progress. A bond between mother and child, or the idea of keeping loved ones close physically, emotionally, or mentally (as a mother opossum keeps her babies in her pouch). Isolation from others. Dreaming of this animal can represent too much or not enough of one of those qualities, or someone or something you associate with the quality or animal. Consider also the animal's actions, context, and your feelings about it. *See also:* Animal; Kangaroo

Orange

The color orange can represent: Bold, outgoing, or assertive. A happy mood. Invigorated. Warmth. Autumn, or the "winding down" of a phase or cycle. *See also:* Color

Orangutan

Intelligence. An elevated perspective or living in a lofty way (since orangutans spend time in trees). Independence or separation. Basic human skills. Humanity or human-like qualities (such as sentience or compassion). Dreaming of this animal can represent too much or not enough of one of those qualities, or someone or something you associate with the quality or animal. Consider also the animal's actions, context, and your feelings about it. *See also:* Animal; Monkey; Gorilla or Ape

Orca

Power, or the responsible use of power. Authentic personal power or strength of self. An issue of freedom or personal choice. The ability to make your life the way you want it to be. The idea of magical, spiritual, or unknown. Dreaming of this animal can represent too much or not enough of one of those qualities, or someone or something you associate with the quality or animal. Consider also the animal's actions, context, and your feelings about it. *See also:* Whale; Fish; Animal

Orchard

Productivity. Delayed gratification or long-term gain. A result or benefit from hard work or other investment. Growth or maturation. Abundance or life. *See also:* Fruit; Tree; Plant; Garden; Planting; Field

Organization, Membership

A membership organization (such as a club or association) can represent: A shared experience or interest among certain people. A community or circle of interaction. Mutual support. Inclusion, approval, or belonging (such as of people who meet membership criteria). Exclusion or rejection (such as of people who do not meet membership criteria). *See also:* Group; Business; Church; Religion; Cult; Gang; Joining; Meeting

Organizing

Organizing things (such as into categories, stacks, containers, or folders) can represent: Control or organization. A logical mental process. Trying to make sense of or understand something. Prejudging or labelling people or things. Breaking down an idea or situation to make it more manageable in your mind. Putting things away or trying to get rid of things, literally or figuratively (such as possessions, outdated beliefs, or memories). Feeling disorganized or needing to organize your thoughts, your life, or a certain aspect of your life. *See also:* Container; Folder; List; Group

Orphan

Dreaming that you're an orphan when you're not in real life can represent: Feeling left out, abandoned, unsupported, or like you don't belong somehow in your life (or a fear of such). Something for which you feel there's no match (as with an "orphaned" sock). Loneliness or aloneness. Finding "strength in one" or strength in self. *See also:* Left, Being; Extra

Ostrich

Avoidance or denial. Hiding as a defense strategy. Independence. Well-grounded, practical, or earthy. Having what you need to make progress easily or quickly. Vision (such as clarity about the past or preparation for the future). Dreaming of this animal can represent too much or not enough of one of those qualities, or someone or something you associate with the quality or animal. Consider also the animal's actions, context, and your feelings about it. *See also:* Bird; Emu

Otter

Light-heartedness, playfulness, or joy. Activity or productivity. Curiosity. Well-adapted to a particular environment (perhaps one you consider to be outside the norm). Ability to maneuver through situations or around obstacles. Dreaming of this animal can represent too much or not enough of one of those qualities, or someone or something you associate with the quality or animal. Consider also the animal's actions, context, and your feelings about it. *See also:* Animal; Beaver

Outdoors

A physical location in your real life. The public or social aspect of your life. The "public" aspect of yourself, meaning the "self" you make visible to others (your image, thoughts you share, observable actions, etc.). Interactions with others. The idea of what's beyond yourself or beyond your inner experience. A particular feeling from your real life, depending on the outdoor location (such as a cemetery representing grief, or wilderness representing feeling free or vulnerable). *See also:* Lawn; Backyard; House; Location; Landscape; Forest; Jungle

Overflowing

Something overflowing its container (such as liquid overflowing a glass or a river overflowing its banks) can represent: Abundance (desired or not). The idea of "too much." A feeling or fear of an accident, catastrophe, or loss of control. *See also:* Leaking; Bigger, Getting; Flood; Many

Ovum

Fertility. The potential for something great. The very beginning of a process. Something you need in order to begin a process. Femininity. The need to nurture or to be nurtured, or to protect or be protected. *See also:* Fetus; Baby; Birth, Giving; Pregnancy; Body Part

Owing

Owing (money, a favor, etc.) can represent: A sense of gratitude for something you received. A feeling or fear that you owe someone something, or that they could demand something from you. **Someone owing you something** can represent: feeling that person "owes you" or is indebted to you somehow, or that you have given more to this person in your relationship than you've received from them; the attitude of giving only in order to receive something back (perhaps giving conditional rather than unconditional love). *See also:* Loaning; Finances; Bills; Debt; Borrowing; Money

Owl

Wisdom or understanding. Excellent vision or forethought. An ability to see what others have difficulty seeing. Stealth or quietness (or their advantages). Dreaming of this animal can represent too much or not enough of one of those qualities, or someone or something you associate with the quality or animal. Consider also the animal's actions, context, and your feelings about it. *See also:* Bird

Ox

Strength or fortitude. Hard work. Ability to make progress. Reliability. Service or servitude. The idea of thankless work. Oppression or repression (by self or others). Dreaming of this animal can represent too much or not enough of one of those qualities, or someone or something you associate with the quality or animal. Consider also the animal's actions, context, and your feelings about it. *See also:* Animal; Bull; Cow; Bison; Buffalo

Package

An arrival or something new (such as a person, object, responsibility, situation, etc.). Something mysterious or unknown. Something tangible or intangible that you perceive to be of value (such as a gift, respect, or love). **Receiving or waiting for a package** could represent an expectation, fear of, or desire for the arrival of something tangible or intangible (communication, support, etc.). *See also:* Rectangle; Square; Container; Delivery

Packing

A preparation phase (such as for a project). Preparing for a recent, expected, imagined, or desired journey or change. A ending (as in packing in preparation to go home). Portability or mobility. Storing or saving. Prioritizing or selecting among many things (items, people, options, etc.). Choosing what you'll carry forward with you in life, and you'll leave behind (relationships, agreements, beliefs, judgments, etc.). *See also:* Suitcase; Bag; Tight

Pain

Physical or emotional pain (imagined or from real life). An imbalance in the body or its electrical field. A real-time reaction to a dream event during which you were hurt. Also consider which part of the body hurts in the dream (for example, a painful neck might represent something in real life that you consider "a pain in the neck"). *See also:* Injured; Problem; Ache; Inflammation

Painting

Painting (such as a wall or a craft item) can represent: A real or imagined change in your surroundings, your life, a situation, your outlook, or something else within or around you. "Covering over" the old with the new. Making a fresh start. Creativity or expression (perhaps of your current feelings or mood). **Someone painting graffiti on your property** can represent: a feeling or fear of invasion, threat, or your boundaries being violated somehow (mentally, emotionally, or physically). *See also:* Cover; Creativity; Artwork; Photo

Pale

Paleness of color can represent: A slight amount of whatever the color represents (for example, pale yellow might represent a mellow kind of happiness, while bright yellow could represent abundant joy). Weakness of whatever the color represents (for example, a pale face might represent a low-energy person). *See also:* Color; Soft

Pampering Yourself

A feeling of or desire for pampering or special treatment. Calling attention to a specific need, want, or desire. A desire to focus on yourself and your needs more in general. A need to focus less on yourself and more on others or situations around you. *See also:* Massage; Gift

Pancreas

Maintaining balance, such as having enough (but not too much) activity, energy, or heat. Control, stability, or a thermostat-like function in your life or in a certain process. Issues involving "sweetness" or the sweet things in life (such as happiness, enjoyment, or fulfillment)—perhaps the idea of "too much" or "not enough" sweetness, or an inability to enjoy yourself. *See also:* Gland

Panda

A relaxed disposition. Good natured. Non-aggression as a strategy. The appearance of friendliness or good will. Peaceful, or focused on peace. Vegetarianism. Dreaming of this animal can represent too much or not enough of one of those qualities, or someone or something you associate with the quality or animal. Consider also the animal's actions, context, and your feelings about it. *See also:* Animal; Bear

Pants

Being prepared to go out into the world, interact with others, or be seen. Ability to make progress or achievement. A sense of authority or being in charge. Maturity or adulthood. Consider also the type of pants. For example, dress pants might represent the workplace. Expensive or designer pants might represent status or an attempt to convince others that the wearer is important. Old or dirty pants might represent hard work, a focus on areas of the self other than appearance, or neglected self-care. *See also:* Clothes; Leg

Parachute

A safety mechanism or escape route (such as for escaping an uncomfortable situation, conversation, or relationship). A catalyst or circumstance that makes a process easier or gentler. Conquering a fear or meeting a goal (or a desire for such). *See also:* Skydiving; Falling

Parade

An actual parade, procession, festival, or celebration or other group activity in your real life. A series of events in your past, if the different units in the parade seem to parallel certain events in your real life. A flow or process (since a parade "flows" down the street and has a beginning, middle, and end). A key characteristic you associate with the parade (such as community, participation, volunteerism, a religious rite, or a certain time of year). Also pay attention to what stood out about the parade. For example, a marching band in neat rows might represent organization or teamwork, while a float covered with flowers might represent creativity in nature. *See also:* Festival or Carnival; Flow or River; Event; Marching

Parakeet

Curiosity. Joyful chatter. A "whistle while you work" attitude. Talking without really saying anything. Companionship. Dreaming of this animal can represent too much or not enough of one of those qualities, or someone or something you associate with the quality or animal. Consider also the animal's actions, context, and your feelings about it. *See also:* Bird

Paralysis

Being paralyzed when you aren't in real life can represent: Feeling unable to make progress of your own accord in your life, or in a particular situation. Feeling held back or self-sabotaged. Feeling indecisive, ineffective, or overwhelmed. The idea of acknowledging the true value of something that you've tended to take for granted. **A body part that is paralyzed** can represent feeling less than fully functional in the area represented by that body part. See also the specific body part. *See also:* Helpless; Can't Move; Can't Speak; Disabled; Numb; Nerves

Paramedic

Attending to a crisis, or a perceived need to do so. **Receiving treatment from a paramedic** can represent: a desire for help with a problem in your life (physical or otherwise); a situation that urgently needs attention that could become urgent if not addressed; a subconscious fear of something going wrong or a crisis developing. **Being a paramedic (when you aren't in real life)** can represent: helping with a real-life crisis or problem; a desire to help others; a tendency toward rescuing others or even codependency. *See also:* Hospital; Doctor; Help, Calling for; Emergency Room; Firefighting; Rescued, Being

Paranormal

The paranormal or supernatural can represent: The unknown, mysterious, or unexplained. A desire or attempt to understand. The idea of "the other side" or something other-worldly. A possible indication that you were having a Toxic Dream (p. 320). *See also:* Powers; Healing; Intuition; Angel; Astrology

Parasite

Dependence. Someone else taking something from you (energy, time, attention, money, etc.) without your permission. A relationship in which one individual takes from the other one. A feeling or fear of being sabotaged. Allowing something (an activity, habit, etc.) to sap your energy or time. The idea of you doing one of the previously mentioned things to someone else. *See also:* Insect; Sucking; Leech; Mosquito; Maggots; Larva

Park

A certain public place in real life. A break or getaway from day-to-day life. A feeling of play, recreation, or freedom. A real life "safe place" for your inner child (such as a trusted friend or supportive group). **A lush, green park** could represent abundance, peace, or other pleasant feeling or real-life experience. Consider also the type of park and its context in the dream. *See also:* Playground

Parrot

A person who speaks without really understanding what they're talking about. Mimicking, repeating, or learning by rote rather than through true understanding. Persistence or perseverance. Enjoying a good challenge. Playfulness. Dreaming of this animal can represent too much or not enough of one of those qualities, or someone or something you associate with the quality or animal. Consider also the animal's actions, context, and your feelings about it. *See also:* Bird

Party

A real or imagined group event or situation where you interacted with others. The people in your social circle. **A dinner party** might represent your close circle of friends, other people with whom you interact regularly, or an imagined group interaction. **Enjoying a holiday party** can represent: being in a social or festive mood; your interactions with people around you during the holiday season (past, imagined, or expected). **Someone throwing you a surprise party** could represent: a real-life surprise or gathering you've experienced; a desire for more positive attention from others. *See also:* Special Occasion; Festival or Carnival; Holiday; Guest

Passageway

A passageway or hallway can represent: A transition from one phase to another in your life. A change or new beginning. A connection from one dream area (or one point in time) to another. A part of your life in between other major parts of your life (such as your commute home from work representing the "passageway" between work life and home life). *See also:* Entering; Door or Entrance; Stairs; Alley; Tunnel; Vent

Passport

Permission from an authority figure. Permission to "come and go" as you please or to access different areas, people, information etc. Giving yourself permission to do something or feel a particular way. **Losing your passport** can represent: losing your identity; feeling like an outsider, "unofficial," or unaccepted; losing permission or access to a certain kind of experience. *See also:* License; Approval

Password

Access or entrance. A mystery or a secret code. Protection or security. A weakness or point of vulnerability. A test for whether a person is allowed into a group, restricted area, area of knowledge, or something else. A test or verification of identity. *See also:* Lock; Security; Code; Door or Entrance; Login; Computer; Secret; Privacy

Past

The past in a dream could be: A memory of something from your past, or your current thoughts and feelings about it. An attempt by the subconscious mind to review, remember, explore your feelings about, or make sense of past events. An opportunity to reconcile, resolve, or heal an issue within yourself regarding something in your past (such as grieving, reaching closure, forgiving, coming to terms, letting go of, or reaching inner peace with your past). *See also:* Before; After; Time Passing; Time Frame; Life; Dates on a Calendar

Path

A journey. A path you've taken through your life or a portion of it (past, present, or imagined future). A course of action you've chosen. The characteristics of a certain process (such as a winding path representing a convoluted process in real-life). A series of events you've experienced or you're imagining. *See also:* Following a Path; Road; Traveling; Walking; Trip or Vacation; Map or Directions; Direction; Crossroads

Paving

Paving a surface such as a road could represent: Fixing a problem, or the desire to do so. The idea of "covering over" something (such as the truth). Avoiding or hiding something (problems, issues, a messy situation, something old or outdated, etc.). Feeling the need to smooth things out or make things easier somehow. Having or wanting a fresh start in some area of your life. *See also:* Road; Painting; Cover; New

Paying

Paying someone can represent (real or imagined): Owing, or feeling that you owe. Living up to a commitment or promise. A consequence, or "paying the price" for a past action or decision. Paying something intangible (such as in paying your dues, paying respect, or paying tribute). **Someone demanding payment** can represent a real or imagined demand on you (such as for money, work, attention, or help). **Someone paying you for your efforts** can represent: getting results; cause and effect; reward for work done or time invested; receiving what you feel you've earned or you deserve (such as money, recognition, admiration, or gratitude), or a desire for such. **Someone giving you money when buying something from you** can represent an exchange of something valuable for something else valuable (money, time, energy, support, etc.). *See also:* Money; Check (Money); Owing; Giving; Buying; Receiving; Finances; Bills

Peace

Experiencing something calm (such as a inner feeling or a real-life situation). Your acceptance of "what is" right now (although you still have the option to make changes in the future). An indication that you have released a feeling of againstness within yourself (such as a judgment, self-defeating belief, or something else that was disrupting your inner peace).

Healing or upliftment. A spiritual experience or reminder. *See also:* Love; God; Light (Spiritual); Heaven; Quiet

Peacock

Expressing (yourself, your thoughts, your feelings, etc.) fully and without reservation. Pride in self, or celebrating who you are. Bragging, showing off, or an attitude of feeling superior to others. A tendency to be vocal or noisy. Dreaming of this animal can represent too much or not enough of one of those qualities, or someone or something you associate with the quality or animal. Consider also the animal's actions, context, and your feelings about it. *See also:* Bird

Pelican

Gathering. Collecting. A large capacity for something (such as for knowledge, information, or empathy). Taking in a lot something (information, advice, etc.) and then sorting through it to find what's useful to you. Carrying a lot (such as responsibilities, emotional or mental baggage, etc.), or a willingness or tendency to do so. Dreaming of this animal can represent too much or not enough of one of those qualities, or someone or something you associate with the quality or animal. Consider also the animal's actions, context, and your feelings about it. *See also:* Bird; Crane; Heron; Flamingo; Stork

Pen or Pencil

Communicating, or the ability to do so. A means or channel of communicating (such as through art, music, the media, politics, or activism). Self expression. Creativity or creative freedom. Problem solving. A thought process. Consider the context and intention behind what's being written or drawn. *See also:* Typing; Writing; Ink; Notebook

Performing

The idea of attention being focused on you, or your efforts being highlighted. A desire for attention (to motivate others, share your expression, receive validation, etc.). A fear of attention, either in a particular situation or in general. A feeling or fear of being observed or evaluated. A concern about others' opinions of you. *See also:* Audience; Stage or Screen; Music; Choir; Show or Movie; Dancing; Singing; TV, Being On; Audition; Applause; Song; Creativity; Microphone

Person Unknown

A person you don't know in real life can represent: A person you know in real life (perhaps who shares a characteristic with the dream person). A particular person's role in your life (such as a friendly stranger representing one of your real-life friends). A characteristic or a general type of person (such as a helper or critic). A type of person you would (or wouldn't) like to know. A problem, challenge, issue, to-do list item, or something else on your mind. A religious figure or helper (real or imagined). **A threatening stranger** could represent a feeling or fear of a threat somewhere in your life. Consider also the person's characteristics, actions, what stood out about them, and your feelings about them. *See also:* Man; Woman; Girl; Boy; Character; Shadow; Alien; Hiding; New; Unknown Thing; Person You Know; People (the category); Menacing

Person You Know

A person you know can represent: That actual person in real life. Your perception or opinion of that person, or a characteristic you attribute to them (for example, your disciplinarian eighth-grade teacher might represent the discipline you need to finish a particular project on time). For more clues, consider the person's actions, manner, context, your feelings, and anything that stood out about the person in the dream. *See also:* Man; Woman; Girl; Boy; Family; Friend; Character; Person Unknown; People (the category)

Pet

Responsibility. Unconditional love or acceptance. Innocence or other childlike qualities. Dependence. Your own inner child. **Your pet being in trouble or sick** can represent a feeling or fear of neglecting a responsibility such as taking care of yourself or something in your life; your love for your pet and desire for their well-being. See also the specific type of animal. *See also:* Animal; Petting an Animal

Petting an Animal

Connection. Communication. Expression of positive feelings. Love, compassion, or good will. Support or reassurance. Companionship or togetherness. **Petting an animal you don't know** could represent: chatting with someone new; exploring a new situation; showing good will; showing positive intentions in a social situation. *See also:* Pet; Animal

Phase or Process

The same phase or process in your real life (or that you fear, expect, or imagine). A totally different phase or process (such as collecting postage stamps representing "collecting" money in your savings account). For more clues to meaning, consider the nature of the phase or process, anything that stood out about it, and how you felt about it. See also the specific type of process (saving, working, growing, etc.). *See also:* Task; Working; Activity; Event; Beginning; Ending; Interrupting

Phone

Communication. Connection. A real or imagined interaction between two people. A desire for or fear of receiving a particular message (or sending one). Expressing yourself or being heard. **A cell phone** can represent personal or private communication (since it's usually owned and used by only one person). **Calling for help** (for example, 911) could represent a desire for help; a feeling or fear of victimization. Consider your motivations and feelings about the phone during the dream. *See also:* Communication; Voicemail; Help, Calling for; Misdialing; Problem

Photo

The person, place, or thing shown in the photo, or your thoughts and feelings about it. A memory, or the way you remember an event. The idea of a mock-up or fake version of what's in the photo (since a photo is a representation rather than the real thing). **Taking a photo** can represent wanting to remember something, enjoy a particular moment, or save something for later (literally or figuratively). Consider also the context, the subject portrayed, and how you felt about the photo. *See also:* Video; Artwork; Camera

Picnic

An actual or imagined social interaction, meal, or gathering. Nourishment for your body, emotions, mind, or spirit (perhaps obtained from sources outside yourself, such as in nature). For more clues, consider the type of picnic, what was happening, who was involved, and anything else that stood out. *See also:* Food; Eating; Outdoors; Party; Meal; Holiday

Pig

A feeling of freedom from rules. Not worrying what others think. Nourishment (physical, emotional, mental, or spiritual). Intelligence. Happiness. Dreaming of this animal can represent too much or not enough of one of those qualities, or someone or something you associate with the quality or animal. Consider also the animal's actions, context, and your feelings about it. *See also:* Boar; Animal

Pigeon

Returning home, or to a feeling of "home" within yourself. A perceived nuisance, or needing to "be a nuisance" to get what you want. Being or feeling underrated. The idea of commonness or pervasiveness. Hiding your specialness. Finding the specialness in yourself or others. Dreaming of this animal can represent too much or not enough of one of those qualities, or someone or something you associate with the quality or animal. Consider also the animal's actions, context, and your feelings about it. *See also:* Bird; Dove

Pink

Fun, playfulness, or spontaneity. Lightness. Your inner child (or someone else's). Childhood. Femininity, or stereotypical feminine qualities. *See also:* Color; Red

Pipe

A communication channel. A connection between people, places, or things. A route, pathway, or delivery method. Movement from one place to another. A process or something else that flows. Progress through time. **A leaky pipe** could represent an urgent problem or loss of control (or fear of such); a surprise; something not going as expected. *See also:* Passageway; Hose; Water; Flow or River; Drain; Vent; Funnel; Flood

Pivoting

Pivoting or turning (such as pivoting on your foot, or the action of a hinge or lever) can represent: A turning point or change in the course of events (such as a decision, or an event that "changes everything"). Flexibility or adaptability, such as to various situations. Changing your mind or taking a different position. Changing the subject or redirecting an interaction (such as to avoid a particular truth). Alternating your focus (such as between different areas in your life). Movement (literal or figurative). *See also:* Turning; Circles, Going in; Joint; Between; Rotating

Plant

Growth, development, evolution, or refinement. A person, their life, or their quality of life. Life force, nature, or a higher power. Doing good work, or producing good or useful things. Consider the plant's characteristics, context, and what that stood out about it (for example, a sick plant might represent a perceived imbalance in your life, and a thriving plant might represent vibrancy). If a particular part of the plant stood out, consider its individual meaning. Consider also the type of plant. **A palm tree** might represent a warm climate or a relaxed feeling (or a desire for such). **A fruit tree or flowering plant** might represent productivity or creativity. **A prickly cactus** might represent a threat, obstacle, or irritable person. *See also:* Planting; Seed; Sprout; Root; Stem or Trunk; Branch; Leaf; Garden; Lawn; Field; Tree; Flower; Vine; Farming; Landscape

Planting

Planting seeds, bulbs, or cuttings can represent: A new beginning. An investment for long-term results, the idea of "reaping what you sow," or looking forward to results from effort you've invested. Nurturing (a person, project, etc.) or participating in the process of life. Patience to allow a process to take its natural course. *See also:* Plant; Farming; Seed; Sprout; Garden

Playground

Play or having fun. A place or group in which you tend to have fun (for example, playing on the different equipment at a playground might represent the different conversations you had with people at a real-life party). *See also:* Park; Sliding; Merry-Go-Round; Seesaw; Amusement Park

Poetry

Expression (such as of ideas, emotions, etc.). Creativity. Telling a story (in any form). Pattern or organization. Romance. Sentimentality. An interpretation or way of perceiving a certain situation. *See also:* Story; Song; Words; Book; Creativity

Poison

A poison or toxin can represent actual or imagined: Mental or emotional negativity. Ill will. Threat or danger. Something seeming "off" or not quite right in your life. *See also:* Drug

Police

A real or imagined authority. Your own conscience. Protection or security, or a desire for more. Rules or requirements (yours, a group's, society's, etc.). Laws (a country's, nature's, scientific, spiritual, etc.) or an issue regarding them (dislike, a desire for better enforcement, etc.). A need to take responsibility for your actions. Being asked to live up to an agreement you've made. **Calling the police** can represent: a feeling or fear of threat or overwhelm; a need for protection or help. **Being afraid of the police** can represent; fear of a real-life authority (the tax collector, your supervisor, etc.); fear of being falsely accused. **The police catching you breaking the law** can represent: a feeling or fear of being accused, watched, or scrutinized; feeling a need to take more responsibility for yourself and your actions. *See also:* Security; Protected, Being; Rule or Law; Authority Figure; Investigator; Blamed, Being; Catching Someone; Criminal; Crime

Pool

Swimming or floating in a pool can represent: Freedom from your usual limitations (or a desire for it). Taking a break, or a desire to escape from your responsibilities for a while. The lifting of a burden. Recreation, play, or fun. **Being pulled underwater** can represent overwhelming circumstances in real life. **A calm pool** can represent peace, relaxation, or a calm situation. *See also:* Water, Body of; Swimming; Diving; Floating; Underwater

Porch

A public or social aspect of your life. Your personal boundary, or the boundary between your personal life (represented by the house) and your public life (represented by the outside world). *See also:* Door or Entrance; Backyard; Outdoors; House

Porcupine

Self-defense. Protecting yourself in a harsh environment or social situation. Distancing yourself from a perceived threat (physical, emotional, mental, etc.). "Bristling" or putting up emotional walls. Brashness or bravado as a defense mechanism. Dreaming of this animal can represent too much or not enough of one of those qualities, or someone or something you associate with the quality or animal. Consider also the animal's actions, context, and your feelings about it. *See also:* Animal; Hedgehog

Possessed

Dreaming that you've been possessed (that some other entity has inhabited your consciousness) can represent: An experience or fear of your boundaries being compromised, or of losing control. An indicator of a Toxic Dream (p. 320). *See also:* Controlled, Being; Exorcism; Evil

Powers

Special powers or superpowers can represent having or desiring: Power. Control. Ability. Self-empowerment. Change. Freedom or autonomy. The experience of your "true" potential state of being (such as living without limiting beliefs or self-judgments). For more clues, consider the type of power. For example, **the power of invisibility** could represent a desire to know or understand, or to "disappear from" a responsibility. **Invincibility against harm** can represent your ability to not let other people's judgments or negativity influences "get to you" in real life. **Someone else having special powers** can represent a feeling or fear of them having power over you, harming, or manipulating you. *See also:*

Witch; Disappearing; Future; Paranormal; Healer; Hypnosis; Invincibility; Muscle; Superhero

Praying

An experience of connecting with God (or a desire for such). A certain time you received or needed help (or a desire for such). Consider who was praying and the context and nature of the prayer. *See also:* God; Light (Spiritual); Religious Figure; Religion

Pregnancy

The beginning of a new phase, process, or project. A responsibility (perhaps a new one) in your life, real or imagined. Creativity or the desire to create something new. A curiosity about pregnancy. *See also:* Baby; Fetus; Ovum; Birth, Giving; Bigger, Getting

Pretending

Pretending, or something that is pretend (such as a "pretend game" or an imaginary friend), can represent: Something or someone in real life that you perceive as pretend or fake. Pretending in your real life (such as role-playing, performing, or pretending as a means of avoiding reality). Imagination or creativity. A desire for more excitement, entertainment, or adventure. **Creating a pretend scenario or game with someone else** might represent: friendship, interaction, or camaraderie; a group or shared goal. *See also:* Game; Performing; Show or Movie; Character; Fake

Prison

Lack or loss of freedom (real, perceived, or imagined). Punishment. Discipline. A feeling or fear of an authority having too much control over you, or allowing them too much control. *See also:* Trapped; Restrained

Privacy

An issue of (physical, emotional, or mental) personal boundaries. Feeling that you need more personal space somehow in your life, or perhaps more time to yourself. Consider also the context and your motives for wanting privacy. *See also:* Hiding; Interfering; Watching; Divider; Curtain; Invaded, Being; Controlled, Being; Stalking; Cover; Security; Lock; Secret; Quiet; Avoiding

Problem

A particular problem (real-life, feared, or imagined). A feeling or fear of being challenged somehow. Feeling held back or encountering an obstacle in real life, or a fear of such. **Trying to solve a problem** can represent a desire for a real-life solution; feeling stressed; being in "problem solving" mode (perhaps due to your activity earlier in the day); experiencing extra energy during the dream state. Consider also whether this could have been a Toxic Dream (p. 320), which often involves dealing with a stressful problem. *See also:* Blockage or Obstacle; Disaster; Chaos; Accident; Test; Bothered, Being; Decision, Your; Crime; Injured; Can't Move; Hurt, Being; Bad; Disobeying; Math; Puzzle; Riddle; Creativity

Processing

Processing an input into a modified output can represent: Transformation or change. Creativity. Renewal or rebirth. Resourcefulness. Personal healing or growth. **A factory that reshapes metal into a final product** might represent a novice becoming an expert or a baby growing up into an adult. **A plant that refines raw ingredients** (such as a mill or oil refinery) might represent refinement (such as of character, skills, or discernment). **A plant that recycles old materials into new products** might represent transforming an outdated belief into an updated one. *See also:* Making or Building; Factory; Workplace; Business

Promotion or Raise

Real or desired: Validation or recognition. Reward for hard work. Abundance. Progress. *See also:* Job; Money; Increasing; Workplace; Superior

Propeller

Power to move forward (such as on a project or in your life). Something that propels you forward (motivation, enthusiasm, desire, ambition, encouragement from others, etc.). *See also:* Accelerator; Fuel; Oar

Proposal

A real or desired proposal, suggestion, or offer (such as for a certain agreement, commitment, or shared process). The idea of working with someone as a team or beginning a process together (romantic or otherwise). **A marriage proposal** can also represent a milestone in a romantic relationship (or a desire for one); the closeness in a certain romantic relationship (past or present); a platonic proposal (such as for a business partnership); feeling "put on the spot" somehow in real life. **Writing a proposal** can represent a real or imagined challenge (for example, the resume you sent out last week "proposing" that a certain company hire you). *See also:* Engagement; Marriage

Protected, Being

Feeling or fearing that you need protection from a person, situation, or event in your life. Actual protection or support from others. The idea of too much protection, being sheltered from reality, or feeling "smothered." Consider who or what is protecting you and why. *See also:* Security; Armor or Shield; Police; Protecting

Protecting

Protecting someone or something can represent real or imagined: Feelings of protectiveness or empathy. Responsibility or duty. Secrecy or keeping secrets. Consider whom you're protecting and why. *See also:* Rescuing; Cover; Armor or Shield; Security; Police; Protected, Being

Pulling

Desire, want, or need (such as wanting someone's attention). A desire to change something in your life (as in pulling things in a different direction). **Pulling an object away from someone** can represent: taking from someone; a desire for power or control (or to regain it); a desire for whatever the object being pulled represents; reclaiming something you feel belongs to you; feelings of self-righteousness or revenge. **Backing away or pulling back from someone** can represent rejection, abandonment, caution, or fear of whatever that person represents. *See also:* Taking From; Towing; Carrying; Opening; Reaching For; Moving Around

Puppet

Someone or something you consider powerless or unempowered, perhaps who lets others speak for them or make decisions for them. Childhood. Perceived childishness. Imagination, playfulness, or creativity. Something or someone you consider to be a fake or a mock-up. *See also:* Toy; Machine or Robot; Doll

Puppy

Responsibility. Innocence. Playfulness. Optimism. Unconditional love. Dreaming of this animal can represent too much or not enough of one of those qualities, or someone or something you associate with the quality or animal. Consider also the animal's actions, context, and your feelings about it. *See also:* Dog; Pet; Baby Animal

Purple

Fun. A sense of individuality, or the freedom to be yourself and express yourself. Richness (of life, personality, etc.). A sense of royalty or distinction. *See also:* Color

Pushing

Evidence of intention. Power, force, or control (actual, feared, or desired). **Pushing something toward someone** can represent giving; trying to convince someone to accept or receive something. **Pushing someone** can represent: being pushy with opinions or ideas; encouraging the person to do something or to do a good job; aggression or ill will. **Pushing someone away from you** can represent rejection, aggression, maintaining boundaries, self-defense, or a need for space. For more clues, consider who or what was pushing and why. *See also:* Giving; Attacking; Attacked, Being; Heavy; Swelling; Carrying; Pulling

Puzzle

A real-life problem or challenge. Feeling stressed, perhaps from real-life problem solving. **Working on a puzzle for fun** might mean you're in the mood for problem solving or mental challenges, or that you're experiencing some extra energy during the dream state. *See also:* Problem; Math; Riddle

Quail

Independence (perhaps from parental influence and support). Thriving on group interaction, support, and interdependency. Camouflage or hiding. Being well adapted to or receding into a particular environment. Dreaming of this animal can represent too much or not enough of one of those qualities, or someone or something you associate with the quality or animal. Consider also the animal's actions, context, and your feelings about it. *See also:* Bird

Quarry

A quarry or mine can represent: The idea of looking beyond the obvious and digging beneath the surface to find valuable meaning or insight. A desire for or search for something (information, money, answers, etc.). Abundance. A desire for or ability to "sift through" and extract the value from something (such as information, an experience, or someone's feedback). *See also:* Digging; Searching

Quest

A real-life challenge. A desire for more adventure, meaningful challenge, or being helpful to others in your life. The idea of achievement or doing good work, and the associated sense of satisfaction. *See also:* Searching; Test; Problem

Question

Desire or intention. **Asking a question** can indicate a desire for guidance, understanding, information, or a solution to a problem in real life. **Someone else asking you a question** can represent: a feeling that someone's trying to understand or get something from you (information or otherwise); a desire for others' interest in or involvement with you. **Being interrogated** could represent a feeling or fear of being accused, taken advantage of, or intruded upon somehow. *See also:* Investigator; Police; Requesting

Quicksand

A real or imagined challenge that seems difficult to escape or recover from. A perceived "losing situation" in your life, or one that seems to keep getting worse. *See also:* Problem; Unstable; Swamp; Mud; Ground

Quiet

Peacefulness. Emptiness. Anticipation. Stealth. **The silence after noise stops** can represent the completion of a phase, or the end of activity, chaos, or stress. **When a person is silent while interacting with you,** their silence could represent contentment, an inability to communicate, secrecy, shyness, anger, resentment, or guilt. Consider the context and how you felt about the quiet. *See also:* Secret; Whisper; Hiding; Cover; Noise; Soft; Evenness

Quilt

Comfort, reassurance, or the feeling of home (or a desire for such). A puzzle or problem that's solved. The idea of being "well put together," organized, or balanced. Logic or organized thinking or planning. Creativity or its results. The idea of complexity, depth, or having multiple layers. *See also:* Cover; Mixing

Quitting

Feeling tired or ready to move forward in some area of your life (for example, quitting your job could represent being tired of your job, ready for a new job, or exploring how it would feel if you really quit). The idea of giving up, or giving up on something or someone. Perceiving or imagining failure somehow in your life. For more clues consider the context and your motivation for quitting. *See also:* Interrupting; Ending; Phase or Process; Hesitating; Obeying

Rabbit

Vulnerability. Sensitivity. Running from a perceived threat. Protecting yourself by leaving (a situation, relationship, etc.). Fertility. Abundance or proliferation (such as of ideas, opportunities, or to-do list items). Dreaming of this animal can represent too much or not enough of one of those qualities, or someone or something you associate with the quality or animal. Consider also the animal's actions, context, and your feelings about it. *See also:* Animal

Rabies

Anger or rage. Emotion that seems to be "contagious" or out of control. A (real or perceived) hidden danger of getting involved with someone or something. **Getting rabies** can represent a feeling or fear of being invaded by an outside force or having your boundaries compromised, perhaps in a way that triggers anger. *See also:* Infection; Mentally Unstable; Illness; Chaos

Raccoon

Disguise, misleading appearances, or masking your true personality. Stealth or hiding. Opportunism. Hygiene (physical, emotional, mental, or spiritual). Dreaming of this animal can represent too much or not enough of one of those qualities, or someone or something you associate with the quality or animal. Consider also the animal's actions, context, and your feelings about it. *See also:* Animal; Opossum

Radio

An actual radio or another type of media (TV, audio player, etc.). Connection or interaction (with the world, people, places, experiences, etc.), especially in a detached way (as a with radio). A real or imagined communication, or desire to hear something specific (such as a message or answer). A communication channel (such as "the grapevine" or a website). *See also:* Communication; Music; Media

Rain

The idea of assistance, abundance, or a gift (from a person, God, etc.). Nourishment or replenishing. Cleansing. Washing away the old and starting new. Spiritual presence. **Unwelcome rain** can represent: a feeling or fear of a challenge, punishment, bad luck, or untimely circumstance in your life; nuisance, frustration, challenge, criticism, or someone's perceived attempt to "rain on your parade"; "dark" emotions such as anger or despair. *See also:* Wind; Cloud; Weather; Flood; Storm; Watering; Water, Body of; Wet

Rainbow

A feeling of hope or optimism. A perceived or imagined promise of luck or good things (or a desire for such). The idea of a higher power. A different experience or world (as in a world "over the rainbow" or "at the end of the rainbow"). Celebrating your uniqueness or the differences among people (as in different colors in a rainbow). A wide range or full spectrum of something (such as of emotions or choices). "Shining a light" on someone or something in a way that reveals more about them, such as their many facets (based on how a rainbow is created). *See also:* Color; Light (Illumination)

Ram

Strength or force. Aggressiveness, conflict, or confrontation (or being able to handle these things). Strong offense or defense (such as through sheer force, an airtight argument, etc.). Standing up for yourself or your opinions or beliefs (and sharing them with others). Dreaming of this animal can represent too much or not enough of one of those qualities, or someone or something you associate with the quality or animal. Consider also the animal's actions, context, and your feelings about it. *See also:* Sheep; Animal

Ramp

A transition, such as into or out of a process or activity. Something that makes progress or a process easier. A beginning or ending. *See also:* Bridge; Hill; Descending; Climbing

Rash

Irritability. A mental or emotional reaction to something in your life, such as a situation or person. A feeling or fear of something intruding physically, emotionally, or mentally. A fear of something or someone that you perceive to be different from you. Attempting to maintain effective personal boundaries or stand up for yourself (or having trouble doing so). A judgment against yourself for maintaining personal boundaries. *See also:* Allergy; Immune System; Inflammation; Infection; Skin; Acne; Virus

Rat

Your fears. Something you judge as negative or unwanted (such as a person or an aspect of yourself or your life). Stealth. Hidden motives or actions (since rats are nocturnal). Resourcefulness, adaptability, or a self-preservation. "Gnawing away at" something (getting a project done bit by bit, spending your savings little by little, guilt that's "eating at you," etc.). Dreaming of this animal can represent too much or not enough of one of those qualities, or someone or something you associate with the quality or animal. Consider also the animal's actions, context, and your feelings about it. *See also:* Animal; Mouse; Hamster

Raven

A message or message bearer (real or imagined). A perceived "alert" to pay attention to something in your life. A feeling of foreboding. A fear of death or endings. The end of one thing (phase, project, relationship, etc.)

before a new one begins. Dreaming of this animal can represent too much or not enough of one of those qualities, or someone or something you associate with the quality or animal. Consider also the animal's actions, context, and your feelings about it. *See also:* Bird; Crow; Blackbird

Reaching For

Reaching for something or someone can represent: Wanting or needing something that the reached-for object or person represents. An intention toward a certain action or direction. For more clues, consider the intention behind the reaching. *See also:* Pulling; Wanting; Arriving

Reaping

Reaping or harvesting something (such as produce or a crop) can represent: The results of work or effort. The "effect" part of "cause and effect." The idea of justice or getting what you deserve. The idea of karma, or of "receiving back what you give" in life. *See also:* Grim Reaper; Farming; Fruit; Result

Rear Ended

Someone colliding into the rear end of your vehicle can represent a feeling or fear of: Someone causing you harm (through negligence or on purpose). Someone "sneaking up behind you" or backstabbing. Being surprised by a new problem or challenge (or a fear of such). *See also:* Accident

Receiving

Receiving something (money, gifts, time, effort, etc.) can represent: A past situation in which you received something. The idea of receiving whatever the item represents (or a desire for or fear of such). Experiencing or desiring abundance. Feeling open to receiving tangible or intangible gifts from others. Feeling fortunate or grateful for someone's generosity in your life. *See also:* Winning; Borrowing; Giving

Rectangle

A foundation or platform. Balanced. Sturdy. Secure. A box or container. Consider what the shape means to you personally and the context in which it appears in the dream. *See also:* Shape; Square

Red

Stimulating or exciting. Anger. Passion. Heat. Exotic. Full of life or vigor. Red can also appear in a dream to highlight something important. *See also:* Color

Referee

An authority figure or mediator in your life. A desire for fairness or an impartial opinion. Someone whose opinions you listen to, especially in terms of making decisions or settling arguments. Someone or something by whose decisions you must abide (your supervisor, a judge, etc.) *See also:* Judge; Decision, Someone Else's; Authority Figure; Rule or Law

Reference Source

A reference book (dictionary, thesaurus, etc.) or other reference source (librarian, consultant, etc.) can represent: Something or someone you perceive as an authority or source of information. Seeking or finding answers or understanding (or a desire to do so). A quest for knowledge or greater intellect. A desire to be correct or to do something correctly. *See also:* Authority Figure; Rule or Law; Book

Reflective Light

A reflection or glimmer of light can represent: Insight or understanding. An indirect effect, influence, or action. The suggestion that whatever is glimmering is special or important. The idea of an illusion. A representation of something or someone (rather than the actual thing or person). *See also:* Mirror; Light (Illumination); Lamp or Light; Glowing; Fire; Gleam; Sparkle; Communication

Region

A real or imagined region (state, continent, etc.) can represent: An actual physical place. A real or imagined environment or situation. A nonphysical place (such as a mental or emotional "place" within you, an imaginary place, or a place in a story or movie). For more clues, consider what the region brings to mind for you, what stood out or felt familiar about it, and your feelings about it. *See also:* City; Country; Nationality

Reincarnation

Dreaming that you've died and reincarnated might represent a fresh start or new beginning somehow in your life (or a desire for one). Depending on what kind of life you reincarnated into, your dream may indicate how you feel about the way you've been leading your life (such as grateful or guilty). *See also:* Death of You

Rejection

An issue involving boundaries, personal power, authority, or preference. **Being rejected** could represent: a feeling or fear of rejection, being let down, or being left out; rejecting or judging yourself in some way. **Re-**

jecting someone can represent judgment or a desire to distance yourself. For more clues, consider the motivation of the person doing the rejecting. *See also:* Feeling; Abandonment; Judgment or Disapproval; Leaving a Person; Denying

Rejoining

Rejoining or reconnecting something that has broken apart can represent an actual, perceived, or desired repair of whatever the object represents in your real life. See also the item that's being rejoined. *See also:* Joining Together; Reuniting

Relationship

A real, imagined, or desired relationship. The relationship person in the dream can represent a different relationship person in real life (for example, in a dream where you're back with an ex-boyfriend, he might represent your current boyfriend, a new person you're curious about, or a general desire to be in a relationship). A relationship in a dream can also represent a different kind of relationship in real life (for example, dreaming that you're married to a coworker might represent your platonic, day-to-day workplace relationship with that person). *See also:* Romantic Partner; Ex; Breaking Up; Two; Marriage; Romance

Relative

A member of your real family (whether or not the dream relative looks like one of your actual relatives). Someone who feels like family to you. Someone whom you (subconsciously) associate with a family member or a certain family role (such as a father representing your boss who's a great fatherly role model). Someone whom you interact with regularly (such as a coworker). *See also:* Mother; Father; Son; Daughter; Grandparent; Aunt; Uncle; Cousin; Person You Know; Person Unknown

Religion

The general idea of religion or philosophy. A specific religion. Your inner spiritual experience (real or imagined). A specific religious reference in your life (a certain religious authority or location, a symbol, an event, a memory, etc.). A (religious or non-religious) group with something in common (such as shared beliefs, philosophies, goals, attitudes, or leadership). An organization that holds authority. A setting in which teaching takes place, such as school. Feeling "preached to" or pressured to adopt certain beliefs. *See also:* Church; Light (Spiritual); Religious Figure; Religious Symbol; Organization, Membership; Authority Figure; Rule or Law; Ritual or Tradition; Cult

Religious Figure

A religious figure or deity can represent: A religious figure that has meaning to you. Your desire for a spiritual connection (such as for guidance, clarity, or comfort). A reminder of how an authentic spiritual connection compares to a representation of God or representative to God. Also, consider the context and personal meaning of the particular religious figure. *See also:* God; Religion; Religious Symbol; Statue; Angel; Monk; Nun; Help, Calling for; Authority Figure

Religious Symbol

A religious symbol can represent: A desire for spiritual guidance, comfort, or connection of some kind. A touchstone for a connection with God. A reminder of how an authentic spiritual connection compares to the emptiness of a "lower-level god" or pseudo-spiritual symbol. A real-life religious setting (such as a place of worship). Something in your real life that feels religious or sacred. *See also:* Religion; Symbol; Church; Religious Figure; Statue; Star; Symbol; Fish; Sign

Relocating

Moving from one home to another can represent an actual or imagined: Change or transition in your life or in your mind. Fresh start or new beginning. Escaping, or a desire to do so. *See also:* House; City; Location

Repairing

A feeling of or desire for: Repairing something (a situation, relationship, problem, etc.). Healing or improvement. A fresh start. Peace. *See also:* Healing; Joining Together; Technician or Mechanic; Sewing; Closing

Repeating

An emphasis or focus on whatever you're repeating. Correcting a mistake, or a desire to do so. The idea of trying again or getting another chance. **Something repeated over and over** can represent: feeling stuck in a cycle, pattern, or rut; monotony or boredom; learning, or a chance to learn; the idea of practicing in order to improve. *See also:* Circles, Going in; Returning; Copying; Ritual or Tradition; Altering; Starting Over

Representative

Something that represents, supports, or stands for something else (such as you, a specific group, a person, a cause, etc.). The deliverer of a message (real, desired, or feared). A substitute or stand-in for someone or something in your life. *See also:* Messenger; Selling; Leader

Requesting

Asking for something can represent: A want, need, or desire for the actual thing or something it represents. A desire for power, control, attention, assistance, or something else. Authority or responsibility (real or imagined). A feeling of lack. Consider also the context and the motivation behind the request. *See also:* Question; Demanding; Wanting; Invitation

Rescued, Being

A feeling or fear of needing help or needing to be rescued (physically, emotionally, or mentally). Receiving good will or support, or a desire for such. The idea of letting others rescue you or clean up your messes too often. The idea that you could benefit by being more open to accepting help from others. Consider who's rescuing whom, why, and your feelings about it. *See also:* Hero; Paramedic; Firefighting; Ambulance; Rescuing

Rescuing

Rescuing someone or something can represent: Good will toward others, compassion, or a sense of humanity. The idea that you've been doing too much (or not enough) helping others. The idea of rescuing or taking responsibility for others as a relevant theme in your life somehow. For more clues, consider who's rescuing whom, the dynamics involved, and your feelings. *See also:* Hero; Protecting; Ambulance; Firefighting; Digging; Rescued, Being

Respecting

Respecting someone else can represent real-life respect for that person, for someone they represent in your life, or for a certain characteristic you associate with them (for example, respecting your intelligent calculus professor could represent your respect for intelligent people in real life). *See also:* Liking; Love; Good

Restaurant

A source of nourishment (physical, emotional, mental, or spiritual), such as a place, situation, activity, relationship, person, etc. A real or imagined group activity or gathering place. *See also:* Eating; Food; Meal; Business; Server; Host; Bakery

Resting

Dreaming that you're resting or you need to rest (when you're actually sleeping already) can represent: A particular time in real life when you were resting or needed to rest. The idea of resting too much, or not enough. Taking a break, or wishing you could. Being extra tired or feeling mentally or emotionally drained. *See also:* Lying Down; Tired; Asleep; Time Off

Restrained

Being physically restrained can represent: Feeling or fearing a lack of freedom or power (physical, emotional, or mental). Feeling unable to maneuver, escape a situation, or make progress somehow in your life. *See also:* Tormented; Hostage; Prison; Holding; Holding a Person

Result

A result, effect, or consequence often represents a real, imagined, or feared result in your life or mind. Consider the relationship of the action to its result in the dream, then look for a parallel set of events in your real life, fears, or imagination. For example, harvesting apples after a long growth cycle might represent your desire for a long-term stock payoff, or receiving a parking ticket while parked illegally might represent a fear of getting in trouble for breaking a rule. *See also:* Cause; Reaping; After

Returning

Someone returning (to you, to a place, etc.) can represent a real or imagined: Reunion. Returning to the past, or situation similar to a past one. Restoring, recreating, or revisiting something from the past. Resuming a process that's been interrupted. A feeling of missing someone or something, or of wanting them back. The idea of going home again or of feeling the security of "home." **Revisiting a place** can represent: a desire for familiar surroundings; a need or desire to repeat a past activity (perhaps due to unfinished business). **Returning an item you've purchased** can represent: dissatisfaction; rejection; judgment, criticism, or the feeling of "not good enough"; getting rid of things (such as relationships or beliefs) that you feel don't work for you. **Returning an item someone gave you** can represent an ending, a refusal, or discontinuing a commitment. *See also:* Backward; Repeating; Rejoining; Reuniting; Joining Together; Finances; Visiting

Reuniting

An actual, desired, or imagined reuniting. Repairing a problem (such as ending an argument or repairing a broken object). A fresh start or new beginning. An ending (such as of a long period of separation). The idea of peace, unity, or harmony after a period in which there was none. *See also:* Joining Together; Rejoining; Returning

Revenge

A feeling or fear of being wronged or "taken from" somehow. A perception that someone has broken a real or imagined rule. Blaming your feelings of anger, resentment, or hurt on someone else rather than taking responsibility for your own feelings. An opportunity to release a judgment or grudge from the past that's still weighing you down. Self-righteousness, or getting caught up in judging someone else as "wrong" or "bad." *See also:* Enemy; Blaming; Justice; Rule or Law; Violence; Crime; Debt; Feeling

Revolving Door

A passage from one phase to another in your life. A new beginning, change, or momentum in your life. Efficient flow (of a crowd, a process, your work, etc.). The idea of being in and then out of an activity quickly, a lack of perseverance, or fickleness. **A revolving door that's jammed** can represent feeling stuck or blocked in some aspect of your life, or something not going forward as expected. **Being stuck going around and around in a revolving door** could represent feeling unable to escape a particular pattern, habit, or situation. **Getting hurt by a revolving door** can indicate a need to pay more attention to a transition, a decision, or the effect that others' behavior is having on you. *See also:* Door or Entrance; Turning; Rotating

Rhinoceros

Well protected or shielded (physically, emotionally, or mentally). Determination and follow-through. Momentum. A show of strength (or even overreaction) in response to provocation. Lacking delicacy, gentleness, or diplomacy. Dreaming of this animal can represent too much or not enough of one of those qualities, or someone or something you associate with the quality or animal. Consider also the animal's actions, context, and your feelings about it. *See also:* Animal; Hippopotamus

Rib

The ribs or ribcage might represent: Breathing or something you associate with it (life, cycles, or ebb-and-flow). Vulnerability or protection. An enclosure or something that maintains your integrity (physical, emotional, or mental). A support, or something that provides structure. **A pain in the ribs** might represent someone or something you consider a "thorn in your side." *See also:* Chest; Breathing; Lung; Food

Rich

Dreaming that you're rich can represent: An experience of (or desire for more) abundance somewhere in your life, such as terms of money, experience, love, support, time, energy, etc. A mindset of abundance (such as practicing gratitude or choosing to "see the glass as half-full rather than half-empty"). Focusing on superficial value (such as based on appearances) and missing the inner value, experience, and meaning. *See also:* Buying; Finances; Money; Many; Expensive

Riddle

Applying logic to figure out something in your real life. Curiosity about something real or imagined. A desire for an answer or solution. Confusion about what course of action to take in some area of your life. Experiencing stress or high energy during the dream state. *See also:* Problem; Puzzle

Ride

A ride (such as at an amusement park or carnival) can represent: Fun, diversion, or adventure (or a desire for such). A process or activity, especially one in which you feel you have little or no control. **A thrill ride** (such as a roller coaster) can represent: experiencing too much (or too little) of "ups and downs," changes, unpredictability, excitement, or adventure; following someone else's "path," expectations, or orders; a journey or a certain series of real-life events with something new happening around each turn. *See also:* Amusement Park; Festival or Carnival; Merry-Go-Round; Ferris Wheel

Riding

Participating in a real-life or imagined process. For example, riding a bus with other passengers might represent working with teammates toward a shared goal (represented by the direction and destination of the bus) with a leader who's in charge of direction (represented by the bus driver). **If you're not helping control the direction** (for example, as a passenger on a train), riding could represent "just going along for the ride" in a group activity. **If you're controlling the direction** (for example, when riding a motorcycle), riding could represent leading or being in charge of a process, yourself, or your life. See also the type of vehicle. *See also:* Traveling; Driving; Vehicle; Ride

Right Side

The right-hand side (or something appearing on the right or coming from the right) can represent perceived or imagined: Giving or pushing.

Logic or rationale. Masculinity. Rigidity. Conservative political views (as in "the right"). Positivity. Something else you personally associate with the right side. Also consider the context and meaning of whatever's on the right side. **Doing something right-handed when you're actually left-handed** can represent challenging yourself (perhaps unnecessarily); trying something new or in a new way; looking at something from a different perspective. *See also:* Left Side; Enemy

Right or Wrong

Seeing someone as right or wrong can represent: A judgment you're making against that person. Having trouble seeing things from that person's perspective or empathizing with them. Feeling insecure or threatened by the person, their actions or viewpoints, or something else about them. Feeling that the person has broken a rule of some kind. An opportunity to release a similar kind of judgment you're making against yourself. *See also:* Judgment or Disapproval; Inferior; Superior; Disobeying; Advice or Opinion; Evil; Good; Bad; Weird

Rigid

Fixed, unbending, or unchanging (personality, opinion, outlook, attitude, etc.). Strict about rules. Unable or unwilling to adapt to new situations. Stability over time, strength, endurance, or perseverance. Perceived as unfeeling, cold, lacking compassion. *See also:* Hard Object; Metal; Disobeying; Steady

Ring (Jewelry)

Something personal, meaningful, or significant about the owner (or giver) of the ring (for example, your grandmother giving you her ring might represent her giving you her love). Commitment (such as an engagement ring representing a commitment to be married). Belonging (such as a high school ring representing being part of a certain school and graduating class). Authority or a role (such as a queen's ring representing her royal authority, or a mother's ring with children's birthstones representing her role as mother). *See also:* Engagement; Jewelry; Circle

Ringing

Communication. **A phone ringing** can represent: a real, imagined, desired, or feared communication (or other contact) with another person; a request for your time or attention. **A bell ringing** can represent: a message being delivered (such as a school bell announcing the end of a class period or church bells signaling a special event); a message to pay attention to in the dream or in real life. *See also:* Communication; Phone; Chimes; Loud; Noise; Warning

Risking

Taking a risk or gamble can represent: A particular real-life risk, or your thoughts and feelings about one. The way you relate to risk in general. Fear of losing something. A desire to make a wise decision. For more clues, consider how you felt about the dream risk and its results. *See also:* Game; Dice

Ritual or Tradition

A milestone that marks a person's progress. A transition from one phase to another. A recognition or celebration (such as of an event, person, or achievement). Something that is repeated due to tradition, custom, habit, or compulsion. Something done by rote, or in an unfeeling or "empty" manner. *See also:* Religion; Church; Baptism; Wedding; Repeating; Organization, Membership

Road

A way to get from one place to another, literally or figuratively (such as a specific path or direction you take, one event leading to another, or an action leading to a result). Your life path or journey, or a portion of it (past, present, or future). A connection or route between two things (people, places, situations, etc.). An experience you participated in with others. The way you or someone else chose to go about something (as in taking "the high road" or "the road less traveled"). **Being stranded on a highway** can represent feeling stuck, alone, or helpless somehow in your life. **Accidentally running off the road** can represent: a feeling or fear that you're off-track somehow in your life; neglecting responsibility for yourself or others; a need to pay more attention somewhere in your life. **Being hit or injured on a road** can represent a feeling or fear of vulnerability or harm. For more clues, consider anything that stood out about the road and events there, where you were traveling to and from, and your feelings about it. *See also:* Path; Passageway; Tollway; Alley; Traffic; Driving; Traveling; Ramp; Map or Directions

Robin

Reliability. Happiness or cheerfulness. The beginning of a cycle. The idea of new beginnings, starting fresh, or freshness. Early (such as early enough, or too early). Dreaming of this animal can represent too much or not enough of one of those qualities, or someone or something you associate with the quality or animal. Consider also the animal's actions, context, and your feelings about it. *See also:* Bird

Rocket

A rocket or spacecraft can represent: Power (such as to make progress toward a goal). Achievement, perhaps despite overwhelming challenges (as a rocket overcoming the force of gravity). Something that's complicated, hard to understand, or difficult to maneuver. The idea of space or traveling a long way (literally or figuratively). The idea of going somewhere "foreign" (a foreign country, a "different world," etc.) *See also:* Airplane; Starting an Engine; Leaving a Place; Space, Outer; Astronaut; UFO; Bomb; Missile

Romance

Actual, desired, or imagined closeness (mental, emotional, or physical) with another person. Your feelings of sentimentality, meaning, intimacy, or tenderness regarding another person. A desire to feel valued, approved of, or liked by another person. Looking outside for validation, happiness, or for your needs to be met. The day-to-day dynamics of a particular platonic relationship in real life. *See also:* Relationship; Love; Kissing; Sex; Liking; Hug; Attractive

Romantic Partner

Your current romantic partner, or a quality you'd like to experience more of in your current relationship. Your idea of an ideal romantic partner or qualities. The idea of a relationship in general. A real-life platonic relationship (such as with a coworker or friend). Pay attention to what's happening in the dream for clues about your thoughts and feelings toward your real-life partner, relationship, or the relationship area of your life. **Dreaming that someone is your romantic partner who never was in real life** can mean: your subconscious mind was exploring what it would be like to be closer to that person (romantically or otherwise); perhaps you just like this person, think they're nice, or find them interesting; you've noticed qualities you like or admire in this person. *See also:* Relationship; Ex; Breaking Up; Person You Know; Person Unknown

Roof

Protection from the world or from "the elements" (harsh conditions, challenging situations, etc.). A finishing touch or last step in a process (since a roof might be the last part of house construction). Something that seems unattainable or "over your head." A lid, cap, or perceived limitation on how high you can go or how much progress you can make.

Something you perceive as the greatest, highest, or utmost. A higher or insightful perspective (as a rooftop provides a higher view). *See also:* House; Building; Ceiling; Main Floor; Floor; High; Top

Room

A room in a house or building can represent: A certain aspect of your life you associate with that room (such as a family room representing your family life). A type of activity (such as a kitchen representing nourishment of body, emotions, mind, or spirit). A setting, time frame, or characteristic (such as a bedroom representing nighttime, a playroom representing recreation, etc.). The setting for an event that represents a specific real-life event or feeling that happened in that kind of room (such as an attic that represents the time you rediscovered a childhood toy in your attic). Also consider what comes to mind when you think of the type of room. *See also:* Space; Door or Entrance; House; Building; Floor

Rooster

Persistent vigilance. Virility. Alarm. Noisy or intrusive. Bravado. Helping others, purposely or inadvertently. Dreaming of this animal can represent too much or not enough of one of those qualities, or someone or something you associate with the quality or animal. Consider also the animal's actions, context, and your feelings about it. *See also:* Chicken; Bird

Root

A foundation or anchor (such as a set of beliefs or a person you can count on). A beginning or basis for something (such the motivation behind a social movement). A precursor or point of origin (as in a person's "roots" or background). A reason behind something (as in the "root cause" or the "root of the problem"). A sense of security, stability, or consistency (as in "to put down roots"). Strength (or perhaps hidden strengths, since roots are underground). Something that lies hidden or outside of your (or others') awareness. A means of obtaining physical, emotional, mental, or spiritual nourishment. *See also:* Underground; Ground; Root Vegetable; Plant; Tree; Flower Bulb

Root Vegetable

A root vegetable such as a carrot or potato (where the food portion of the plant develops underground) could represent: An activity that is mostly unseen or unknown. The idea of methodically accumulating or stashing things away (such as money or ideas). Something invested or planted that grows or becomes bigger, possibly without your awareness (such as your love for your child, money invested in stocks, or a problem). *See also:* Root; Food; Flower Bulb

Rope

Rope that is connecting or binding things together can represent: A relationship. A mental or emotional bond. An agreement, commitment, or vow. Communication, or a communication network. A feeling or fear of being constricted or restrained (as in "feeling tied down," not having room to maneuver, or otherwise lacking freedom). A means of control (such as a cowboy's lasso representing a CEO's control over the company). *See also:* String; Yarn; Thread

Rose

Sentiment or feelings (real, perceived, desired, or imagined). **A yellow rose** might represent friendship, good will, or kind thoughts. **A white rose** might represent purity, innocence, pure love, a new beginning, or making peace with someone (or the desire to do so). **A pink rose** might represent closeness, familiarity, appreciation of the receiver's specialness or uniqueness. **A red rose** might represent admiration, affection, romantic attraction, love, or celebration. *See also:* Flower; Thorn

Rotating

Rotating (such as a spinning top or a person spinning in circles) can represent: Repeating the same action or pattern over and over. Having enough energy or momentum to keep going in a process. A broad or 360-degree view, or the ability to see all sides of a situation. *See also:* Circles, Going in; Weaving or Spinning; Pivoting; Turning; Curve; Dizzy

Rotten

Neglect, or problems caused by neglect or avoidance. Shirking a responsibility, especially for something that needs ongoing maintenance, upkeep, or "tending to" (relationship, finances, health, job, etc.). A person whom you feel or fear has ill will or a neglectful or uncompassionate attitude. *See also:* Garbage; Eroding; Deterioration; Inferior; Mold or Fungus; Smell

Royalty

Status, respect, specialness, wealth, power, popularity, approval, or something else you personally associate with royalty. **Dreaming that you're a member of royalty** can represent feeling or desiring one of the qualities listed above. **Being with someone who is royal** can mean: you're curious about that person; you'd like to be in their social circle (or feel you deserve to be); your subconscious mind considers the real-life royal to be your acquaintance because of their familiarity from media appearances. *See also:* Celebrity; Authority Figure

Rule or Law

A rule or law can represent: A rule set forth by an authority in your real life. A societal norm, or a rule you feel is generally accepted by others. A self-guiding principle or other rule you've chosen to use yourself. A feeling or fear of a threat or punishment. Authority, or a specific authority figure in your life. *See also:* Authority Figure; Blaming; Blamed, Being; Judge; Police; Religion; Justice; Crime; Decision, Someone Else's; Disobeying; Demand

Running

Quick progress (such as on a project, in life, or along your life path). A desire to move forward more quickly. A perception of time passing quickly (or not quickly enough). Feeling rushed somehow in your life, or making a "dash to the finish line." A real-life intense activity or exertion. *See also:* Traveling; Escaping; Fast; Chasing; Chased, Being

Rural

A rural setting (such as the countryside or a remote desert) could represent: An actual place that shares characteristics with the rural dream setting. A feeling of peace or serenity. Distancing yourself from chaos or unpleasantness (or a desire to do so). A feeling of isolation or escape. Nature, God, or spiritual beauty. A place, region, characteristic, feeling, or mood you associate with the rural dream scene. *See also:* Field; Forest; Desert

Sabotaged, Being

A feeling or fear of sabotage or betrayal. Feeling a lack of trust for a particular person in your life. Feeling like people or things are against you or not supporting you. Sabotaging yourself somehow in real life. *See also:* Interfering; Betrayed, Being; Interrupting; Telling on Someone; Blockage or Obstacle; Sabotaging

Sabotaging

A desire to stop something (a person, process, etc.), perhaps because you disagree or feel threatened. Feeling hostility toward or fear of whatever is represented by the thing you're sabotaging in the dream. Passive aggression or resistance to authority. A desire to compensate for a feeling of powerlessness. Sabotaging yourself somehow in real life. *See also:* Interfering; Interrupting; Betraying; Betrayed, Being; Disobeying; Sabotaged, Being

Sacrificing

Making a sacrifice in order to benefit another person can represent: The idea of making a sacrifice in real life somehow. Care, concern, or love for the other person. Generosity. Co-dependence or a related issue or pattern. **A ritual sacrifice** can represent: betrayal; doing "evil" or harm in the name of "good"; fear of harm or victimization; cold-heartedness or lack of compassion (pointing to an opportunity to resolve an underlying issue within yourself); an indicator of a Toxic Dream (p. 320). *See also:* Hero; Ritual or Tradition; Killing

Safe or Vault

Security or protection of something you value (tangible or intangible). **Putting something into a safe** can represent: concern about someone crossing your boundaries, taking advantage of you, or taking something from you; wanting to keep a secret or certain information private. **Unlocking or taking something out of a safe** can represent: revealing a secret; trusting, opening up, or feeling more relaxed in a certain area of your life; pondering a secret or something that's of value to you. *See also:* Hiding; Security; Storage; Grave

Salamander

The power of observation and perceptiveness. Quick response. Skittishness. Sensitivity or vulnerability to your environment. Dreaming of this animal can represent too much or not enough of one of those qualities, or someone or something you associate with the quality or animal. Consider also the animal's actions, context, and your feelings about it. *See also:* Animal; Lizard

Sale or Discount

A situation you perceive as offering you an advantage, opportunity, or good deal. The idea of getting more for what you give, or desiring such (such as more for your money, more results for your effort, etc.). A beneficial offer (such as a generous proposition or an offer of help). An offer of something extra (such as to "sweeten the deal"). *See also:* Buying; Selling; Store; Negotiating

Salivating

Desire. Hunger. Feeling prepared for or looking forward to what's coming next. A subconscious or conditioned response. *See also:* Mouth; Eating

Salon

The idea of improving the impression you make on others or the version of yourself you show the world (or a desire for such). A makeover or fresh start in your life (or a desire for it). Help from an expert, or assistance to do something you feel you can't do yourself (or feeling a need for such). A place or activity where others focus on or pamper you. Consider also the context, events, and your feelings about them. *See also:* Hair; Scissors; Manicure; Shaving; Comb; Dyeing; Hair Product

Salt

Interest, excitement, or enthusiasm. **Adding salt to food** might represent making things more interesting or "spicing things up" somehow in your life. **Salt used to melt ice or snow** could represent: dissolving or getting rid of something unwanted (problems, nuisances, etc.); the ability to "get traction" to make progress somehow in your life (or a desire for such). *See also:* Tasting; Spice; Food

Salve

Comfort, relief, soothing, healing, calm, or control (or a desire for such). The idea of decreasing a problem, its effects on you, or your reaction to it. *See also:* Lubricant or Catalyst; Healing

Sand

Abundance, or the idea of infinity (as in a seemingly infinite number of grains of sand). A particular location or type of location. **A warm, sandy beach** could represent an actual or desired vacation, or a warm, happy mood. **Tiny grains of sand** could represent the small things in life, or lots of things that make up a larger whole. **Sand through an hourglass** could represent the passage of time. **Sand in your shoe** could represent a small nuisance that's wearing on you. *See also:* Beach; Water, Body of; Ground

Saving (Keeping)

Saving or keeping something can represent: The value or good memories you associate with whatever you're saving in the dream. Abundance (or a desire for it). A fear of scarcity. Preparedness for the future (or lack of it), or the idea that in the future you may need whatever you're saving. For more clues, consider the meaning of the item you're saving and your motives for saving. *See also:* Storage; Shelf; Container; Finances; Money; Increasing; Many; Past; Rescuing

Saw

A saw (or the act of sawing) could represent: Division, separation, or destruction. The process of dividing something into smaller pieces or sections (such as deconstructing a problem in order to analyze it). Breaking down something in order to build something new from its pieces (such as reorganizing a large group into several more specialized ones). Splitting things apart (such as in the breakup of a relationship, or the parting of friends at the end of a school year). For more clues to meaning, consider the context, how the saw was being used, and how you felt about it. *See also:* Scissors; Tool; Cut Off

Scab

Protection. Self-defense or "putting up a wall" due to a real or perceived harm or threat. The process of physical, emotional, mental, or spiritual healing. *See also:* Injured; Healing; Cover; Scar

Scalp

The source or root of something (since a scalp is the source of hair growth). A covering or a protective measure (since a scalp covers the skull). For more clues, consider the context and your feelings. *See also:* Head; Skin; Hair; Brain

Scar

A physical or emotional wound. Your memory of a past emotional challenge. The results or consequences of hostility or ill will somewhere in your life. Healing, recovery, or renewal. *See also:* Healing; Scab

Scarcity

Lack or a perception of lack (physical, emotional, mental, spiritual, financial, social, etc.). One kind of scarcity or poverty in a dream might represent another kind in real life (for example, dreaming that you have no money could represent feeling spiritually empty). *See also:* Depleted; Empty; Sparse; Famished; Debt; Wanting; Dry; Skinny

Scarf

Protecting, obscuring, or disguising whatever is represented by the body part the scarf is covering. Your perception of the wearer (such as their self-expression, characteristic, mood, etc.). Perceived femininity or masculinity. For more clues, consider the context of the scarf (such as who was wearing it and which body part it covered), its role in the dream, and how you felt about it. *See also:* Tie; Clothes; Decoration; Cover

Schedule

A schedule, deadline, or issue regarding time in your real life. The idea of efficiency, inefficiency, or time management. An authority figure, rules, expectations, or other outside pressure to which you feel subjected in real life. *See also:* Calendar; Time Frame; Late

School

Your actual school. The period in your life when you went to the school in your dream, or something you associate with it (a person, event, activity, feeling, etc.). The idea that you're learning or being presented with lessons in your real life, or that you could benefit from learning something. A similar situation or feeling in your real life that reminds you of when you attended the school in your dream (such as a class you attended at work). *See also:* High School; Class; Group; Homework; Teacher; Time Frame; Age; Location; Building

Science

Knowledge or understanding. A desire to understand something or how things work in nature, the world, yourself, or your life. A desire to figure out why certain events happened the way they did, why a person said or did a certain thing, or how an action led to a particular result. A characteristic associated with the particular science (such as archeology representing the idea of digging through layers of information to discover meaning). Feeling particularly curious or having a lot of mental energy during the dream state. *See also:* Chemistry; Laboratory; Therapist; Technology; Math

Scissors

The process of dividing something into smaller pieces (such as to understand it better or to separate it into more manageable pieces). Splitting something apart (such as two people going separate ways or splitting something in order to share it). **Cutting something out of something else** (such as out of fabric or a newspaper) could represent focusing on something you want in your life, or a desire to remove something unwanted from your life (and keep only what you want). *See also:* Sewing; Tool; Sharp; Knife; Hair

Scorpion

Self-defense. Fear or anxiety (of attack, judgment, criticism, "stinging words," etc.). The advantage of being quick. The idea of hiding or not drawing attention to yourself. The idea of having a "hidden gift" (as scorpions glow under ultraviolet light). Dreaming of this creature can represent too much or not enough of one of those qualities, or someone or something you associate with the quality or creature. Consider also the creature's actions, context, and your feelings about it. *See also:* Insect; Sting

Seagull

Persistence, even to the point of pestering. Brazen exploration, especially where there are likely to be rewards. Capable in more than one "world" or environment (as the seagull is capable on land, in the air, and at sea). Dreaming of this animal can represent too much or not enough of one of those qualities, or someone or something you associate with the quality or animal. Consider also the animal's actions, context, and your feelings about it. *See also:* Bird

Seahorse

Magical or ethereal. The advantage of being different or unique in your environment. Copying, borrowing, or building on ideas from others (since the seahorse "copies" the appearance of a horse). Dreaming of this animal can represent too much or not enough of one of those qualities, or someone or something you associate with the quality or animal. Consider also the animal's actions, context, and your feelings about it. *See also:* Animal; Fish; Horse

Seal

A seal or sea lion can represent: Cleverness. Playfulness, imagination, or creativity. Knowing when to rest, and doing it well. Maneuvering well in a "fluid" or changing environment. Dreaming of this animal can represent too much or not enough of one of those qualities, or someone or something you associate with the quality or animal. Consider also the animal's actions, context, and your feelings about it. *See also:* Animal

Searching

Looking for something (help, understanding, information, etc.) or someone (someone for whom you're responsible, someone you've lost, someone you love and therefore fear losing, etc.). A desire to regain something physically, emotionally, or mentally (such as a past experience or a sense of well-being). **Searching for something you've lost** can represent feeling that you've lost (or are afraid to lose) whatever that item represents. For example, searching for your car because you forgot where you parked it could indicate feeling you've lost touch with yourself, your self-identity, or your personal integrity (represented by the car). **Looking for something in a drawer** can represent revisiting the past or trying to retrieve something (such as memories or your algebra skills from high school). *See also:* Losing an Item; Discovering; Rescuing; Digging; Investigator; Telescope

Seat

A place to rest (mentally, emotionally, physically, or spiritually). Your place in the world, a community, group, family, workplace, or otherwise (since a seat can represent your place in a room). **Not being able to find a place to sit** can represent: feeling like there's no opportunity to rest or take a break in real life; feeling challenged in figuring out where you "fit in" right now. *See also:* Sitting; Sofa; Bench; Buttocks; Stolen Item

Second Place

Winning something other than first place (such as second or third) can represent excelling or doing well (or a desire to do so). **Being unhappy about winning something other than first place** might mean you're feeling "less than," criticizing yourself, comparing yourself to others too much, being too competitive or hard on yourself, or focusing too much on outer accomplishments. *See also:* Winning; Failure

Secret

A secret (or being asked to keep a secret) can represent: An issue of trust or trustworthiness. An attempt to withhold the truth, hide something, or lie. The idea of "protecting" someone from the truth. Using secrecy as a strategy to accomplish something you couldn't accomplish otherwise (such as throwing a surprise party). **Secret or stealthy actions** can represent a feeling or fear of someone gaining power or control using stealth, or of you doing so yourself. *See also:* Confiding; Privacy; Cover; Hiding; Quiet; Code; Password; Investigator; Underground; Trickery

Secretion

A secretion (such as from a gland) can represent: Being productive, or producing results somewhere in life. Producing something specific (such as a creative idea). Self-regulation, maintaining balance in your life, or managing your life. See also the specific gland or body part. *See also:* Gland; Mucus; Milk

Security

An issue of safety (physical, emotional, mental, financial, etc.). Protection against a real or perceived threat or undesired situation (such as invasion of your personal boundaries, abandonment, etc.). A desire to feel safe, protected, or reassured somehow in your life, or someone or something that helps you feel that way. Stability, or a desire for it (people and things you can count on, rules that don't change, financial security, etc.).

Consider the context, motivations, and your feelings about the security. *See also:* Police; Safe or Vault; Privacy; Protected, Being; Protecting; Armor or Shield; Lock; Invincibility; Fort

Seed

An idea. A beginning or early stage of a process. Potential to become something greater. Something or someone whom you feel will thrive if they receive nurturing. Wisdom. The essence or essential aspect of something. *See also:* Flower Bulb; Fruit; Sprout; Plant; Planting; Garden; Food

Seeing

Seeing things or people in a dream can mean they're on your mind for some reason right now. Watching or witnessing an event can represent a real or imagined event, perhaps one in which you were a passive bystander. Consider the context, what you were seeing, and how you felt about seeing it. *See also:* Watching; Discovering; Vision; Turning; Audience; Visiting; Meeting Someone; Relationship

Seesaw

Indecision, or "going back and forth" about something. The idea of "give and take" between two people or groups. **Two people cooperating on a seesaw** might represent cooperation or teamwork in real life (or a desire for such). **Two people working against each other** could represent you experiencing or creating hostility, selfishness, or sabotage in your life. *See also:* Playground; Balancing

Seizure

A sudden, temporary shift in someone or something (a demeanor, situation, activity, etc.). Experiencing or fearing a temporary loss of control or an absence from your usual state of mind (such as a lapse in judgment). A feeling of being overtaken temporarily by something out of your control (such as a disruption or illness). A perceived crisis of some kind. *See also:* Illness; Condition; Disabled

Self

You in a dream usually represent yourself, whether you were an active participant in the dream events (from a first-person perspective) or you were observing a version of yourself taking part in the dream (from a third-person perspective). Sometimes you in a dream can represent: your life experience; a role you play; your desires, fears, or imagination; some other aspect of yourself.

Selling

Selling or a salesperson can represent: The idea of an exchange or trade between two people for mutual gain (an exchange of ideas, collaboration, etc.). An offer or proposition. Persuasion, having a personal agenda, or representing a certain cause or interest in an interaction (such as persuading someone to vote a certain way, or "presenting your case"). A feeling or fear of (mental or emotional) manipulation or aggression. *See also:* Representative; Store; Buying

Server

A server (such as a waiter or bartender) can represent: The idea of catering to someone else (to their requests, opinions, expectations, etc.), voluntarily or otherwise. A role, responsibility, or job that involves fulfilling others' needs or requests. Providing a service for a payment in return (such as money or something intangible such as gratitude, meaning, or approval). Serving or giving to others out of generosity. Carrying or delivering things (such as objects, information, or messages). *See also:* Restaurant; Host; Carrying

Setting Down

Setting down an object in a certain location can represent: Setting aside a matter or activity until later. A desire not to have to deal with or acknowledge something. Actual or perceived rejection or neglect. Feeling or imagining that you're finished with something specific in your life, at least temporarily. *See also:* Losing an Item; Leaving a Place; Leaving a Person; Lying Down; Location; Sitting

Seven

Perfection (such as the idea of spiritual perfection or strength). The idea of luck or good fortune (or the desire for such). A feeling that something in your life is reaching its potential, completion, or perfection (or a desire for such). Something else you associate with seven, such as a septet, heptagon, time frame, someone's age, or your family. *See also:* Number

Sewing

A creative process. Productivity. A productive phase, process, or project. Design or engineering. Converting raw materials into something else (such as a list of basic points into a speech). Repairing, fixing, or healing (or a need to do so). A domestic task or mindset. A particular stereotypically feminine or masculine role. **Sewing a seam** could represent joining things together (such as getting married, creating a friendship, combining ideas, or collaborating with a partner). *See also:* Design or Plan; Repairing; Joining Together; Fabric; Thread; Scissors; Knitting; Weaving or Spinning; Sharp

Sex

Mental or emotional intimacy (such as an emotionally sensitive conversation or a close friendship), or a desire for or fear of such. A particular experience of feeling close to someone emotionally, mentally, or physically (in the past, in your imagination, etc.). Liking the person or wanting to know them better (platonically or otherwise). **Unwelcome sexuality** might represent a feeling or fear of an unwelcome attempt at emotional intimacy from someone else (such as a stranger sharing too much information) or a feeling that someone is trying to act inappropriately familiar (such as someone acting like they're your close friend when they're not). *See also:* Relationship; Romance; Communication; Bond

Shadow

Seeing a shadow (an unrecognizable or dark object or figure) can represent: Mystery. An anonymous force or feeling. A particular person, or the idea of someone unknown. A subconscious issue or other dynamic. Fear or another feeling. Consider the context of the shadow, what it brings to mind, and how you felt about it. See also the meaning for the specific type of shadow (such as a person or specific object) and whatever stood out about it (such as its action or perceived intention). *See also:* Person Unknown; Shape; Darkness

Shamrock

Perceived luck you've had or you desire. The idea of blessings or gratitude. Lightheartedness or optimism. Something else you personally associate with shamrocks or with the particular one in the dream. *See also:* Symbol; Plant

Shape

A shape (circle, square, triangle, etc.) can have many different meanings depending on its context in the dream. Consider what stood out about the shape, and what the shape brings to mind. See also the meaning of the item that exhibits that shape. Seemingly random shapes can appear when you're dropping off to sleep or waking up that can seem important at the time, although they often have no significant meaning. *See also:* Person Unknown; Square; Triangle; Symbol; Circle; Rectangle; Diamond Shape; Heart; Erratic; Sign; Shaping; Curve

Shaping

Shaping or molding a substance (such as manipulating clay into a certain shape) can represent: Making or overseeing changes (such as to yourself or to a plan). Transformation or metamorphosis. Influencing a process, situation, outcome, person, or something else. Having power or control somehow in your life (or desiring more). *See also:* Changing; Controlled, Being; Controlling; Making or Building; Artwork; Creativity; Design or Plan; Shape; Clay; Soft

Sharing

Communication. Connection. Generosity or kindness. Physical, emotional, or mental intimacy (real, feared, or desired). **Willingly sharing something** (such as sharing your lunch with a friend) can represent fairness, generosity, good will, or another positive dynamic. **Being forced to share** (such as having to share an office at work) can represent: a feeling or fear of deprivation in your life; an opportunity to work through a personal issue (such as a judgment or resistance to authority); an opportunity to appreciate the inner rewards of generosity and camaraderie. *See also:* Communication; Giving; Joining Together; Joint

Shark

Attack or aggression. Strength. Tenacity. Acting with stealth or anonymity. The unknown. The subconscious mind or something within it. The idea of something "suddenly coming out of nowhere," or your ability to react to unpredictable events. A fear of or focus on something that may never happen or that may not exist. The idea of going directly after something you want. Feeling vulnerable in a situation in which you feel "out of your element" (as humans may feel in water because they're typically land dwellers). Dreaming of this animal can represent too much or not enough of one of those qualities, or someone or something you associate with the quality or animal. Consider also the animal's actions, context, and your feelings about it. *See also:* Fish; Animal

Sharp

A perceived physical, emotional, or mental threat in your life. The idea of an intrusion into your personal boundaries or space. The idea of piercing or breaking through (such as breaking through a symbolic glass ceiling in your career) or experiencing a personal breakthrough (such as seeing things in a new light). The idea or threat of a puncture or hole in something, allowing something to escape (such as letting a secret out or "losing steam"). See also the meaning of the particular type of sharp object. *See also:* Knife; Injection; Scissors; Shaving; Sewing; Glass; Fork; Tool; Spine; Edge, Coming to an

Shaving

Shaving as part of normal grooming can represent: Your daily routine, or a specific part of it. Taking care of yourself or attending to your needs physically, emotionally, mentally, or spiritually. Paying attention to the way you present yourself to the world (your actions, words, demeanor, etc.). Acknowledging what you've accomplished lately. Getting rid of what you no longer need (such as letting go of stress or judgments). **Shaving off a mustache, beard, or hair completely** can represent: freedom from whatever the hair represents to you; revealing yourself or an aspect of yourself; directness or authenticity; simplicity; neatness; a fresh start; a desire to return to a younger age (or a younger image); a perceived loss of masculinity or femininity, individuality, or freedom of self-expression. For more clues, consider your feelings and motivation for shaving. *See also:* Hair; Beard; Mustache

Shedding

Shedding (or flaking or peeling skin) might represent: Releasing the physical, emotional, or mental things that are outdated or that you no longer need (outdated beliefs, judgments, etc.). Feeling as though you're "losing" an aspect of yourself or your life. Part of a cycle. Renewal or re-generation. A new beginning or a second chance. *See also:* Skin; Decreasing; Washing Yourself

Sheep

Belonging, or finding where you belong. One of the crowd. The idea of being a "follower" or going along with others. Benign. Minding your own business. Fitting in or "blending in" with others. Dreaming of this animal can represent too much or not enough of one of those qualities, or someone or something you associate with the quality or animal. Consider also the animal's actions, context, and your feelings about it. *See also:* Animal

Shelf

Saving or storing (memories, ideas, money, objects, etc.), or a desire for such. A feeling or fear of being "shelved" or set aside. An aspect of yourself or your life that you "put on display" to others (a talent, your sense of humor, etc.). Certain details or aspects of your life (such as the books on a shelf representing your interests, hobbies, or areas of knowledge). *See also:* Storage; Container; Accumulating; Furniture

Shell

Protection or self-protection (physical, emotional, or mental). Hiding, or something that is hidden. Fear, or some other reason for hiding. Distancing yourself from others, the environment, or a specific feared experience (or a desire to do so). *See also:* Armor or Shield; Nest or Dwelling; Weapon

Shin

Vulnerability. Taking a risk. The idea of putting your best foot forward. A willingness to take a chance or make progress, despite the risk or vulnerability. *See also:* Leg; Bone; Body Part

Shipwreck

A mishap, crisis, or disaster (or fear of such). Something in your real life you perceive as a disaster or huge disruption. Something that ended in an abrupt or unexpected way (such as a phase, project, activity, or relationship). Evidence of something gone awry (or a fear of such). *See also:* Broken Object; Disaster; Accident; Boat; Descending

Shirt

Your perception of: The wearer's mood or state of mind. The image of the real-life wearer, or one you think they try to project. A role the wearer plays or would like to play (as in a uniform shirt or business blouse). A shirt can also convey the setting of the dream (such as summertime or a formal setting). *See also:* Clothes

Shoe

Your ability to move forward easily as you achieve or make progress in the world (as shoes can facilitate easier walking). Your ability to protect yourself or maintain your integrity (as shoes protect your feet and ability to stand up). The image you present to others. *See also:* Foot; Sock; Clothes

Shoelace

Preparedness. Taking care of details. Feeling secure about making progress in your life. **Tying a shoelace** can represent organizing, preparing, or "neatening up" yourself or your life; self-evaluation, self-improvement, or self-correction; recovering from a challenge and starting over again. *See also:* Shoe; Foot; Tying

Shopping Center

A shopping center can represent your life or your current life experience. Each store or area may represent a different aspect of your life, such as an activity, relationship, or project. Consider your feelings about the places in the shopping center and the events there, and look for parallels with feelings and events in your real life. *See also:* Store; Business; Crowd; Buying; Selling

Shot, Being
A feeling or fear of attack, persecution, judgment, or other hostility in your life. **A bullet wound** can represent feeling victimized, wounded, or taken advantage of in your life (physically, emotionally, or mentally). *See also:* Attacking; Killer; Weapon; Killed, Being; Attacked, Being; Injection

Shoulder
Carrying a heavy load or responsibility, or the ability to do so. Pushing your way forward (such as toward a goal or toward something you want). Comfort or support (as in "a shoulder to cry on"). Rejection or betrayal (as in someone giving you "the cold shoulder"). *See also:* Joint; Body Part

Shovel
A desire or need to delve deeper, search for, understand, uncover, discover, or recover. *See also:* Digging; Ground; Underground

Show or Movie
A show or movie might represent: Something you observed recently (such as events in real life, on TV, or online). A desired or feared event or series of events. A situation in which you felt distanced from or removed from what was going on (perhaps as an observer). *See also:* TV; Stage or Screen; Theater; Audience; Arena or Auditorium; Performing; Talk Show; Celebrity; Video Recorder; Media

Sign
Guidance, information, or insight (or a desire for such). Something that you perceive as pointing you in a certain direction or confirming whether you're "on track." A quality or meaning associated by you or by cultural traditions (for example, a yield sign might represent being more thoughtful of others, and a "slippery road" sign might represent a fear of risk). A label you place on something in your mind (such as a perception, interpretation, or judgment). Consider what the particular type of sign brings to mind and your feelings about it. *See also:* Communication; Shape; Symbol; Future; Rule or Law; Stop Sign; Religious Symbol; Astrology; Artwork

Silverware

The means by which you support, nourish, or nurture yourself (physically, emotionally, mentally, or spiritually). Your ability to access and use your environment (nourishment, relationships, situations, resources, information, etc.) wisely in a way that supports and nurtures you. **A fork** might represent selecting or acquiring specific things you want or like, or experiences that nourish you on some level. **A spoon** can represent gathering up things (activities, practices, inspiration, etc.) that nourish you. **A serving spoon or ladle** might represent serving or nourishing yourself or others. *See also:* Fork; Knife; Tool

Singing

Self-expression. The essence of yourself, your personality, or your spirit. The idea of having a voice in the world. Creativity. Communication. Freedom or inhibition. A desire to experience more of one of those things. *See also:* Voice; Song; Performing; Music

Sink

Transformation or renewal (as in from dirty to clean). Removing things that are unwanted or harmful from your consciousness or life (such as judgments, self-defeating beliefs, or toxic relationships). Because a sink is where you clean up after yourself or your family, it can represent "cleaning up after" (such as taking responsibility for past decisions, direction, and actions, and "cleaning up" any resulting "messes"). **A kitchen sink filled with dirty dishes** can represent a catch-all (such as someone who takes on other people's problems), or neglected responsibility. **A bathroom sink** might represent: your mental or emotional "cleanliness" (such as conscientiousness, integrity, or a non-judgmental attitude); a personal process; your way of thinking, relating to yourself, making decisions, etc. (since the bathroom sink is used for day-to-day personal maintenance). *See also:* Cleaning; Water; Faucet; Soap; Drain; Bathtub or Shower; Bathroom

Sitting

Resting or taking a break. Physical, emotional, or mental tiredness or exhaustion. **The action of sitting down** can represent taking a break, taking a less central role, quitting, or giving up. **A seated position** can represent watching or "sitting it out" rather than participating. *See also:* Buttocks; Watching; Standing Up; Seat; Bench; Setting Down

Six

Balanced (as in two sets of three, or three couples). Something that has been started but needs more work before it is finished. An age or time frame. Something else you associate with six, such as a sextet, hexagon, time frame, someone's age, or your family. *See also:* Number

Size

The relative size of something (for example, if something seems larger or smaller than you'd expect) can have significant meaning. Size can represent: perceived power, strength, importance, or prominence in your mind (the larger the object, the more you may feel it has these qualities); a particular point in a process (such as a tiny sapling representing an early point in a process, or a huge, dead tree representing the end of a process). *See also:* Big; Small; Measure; Bigger, Getting; Smaller, Getting

Skating or Boarding

Skating or skateboarding can represent: Making progress smoothly, quickly, or well in somewhere your life (possibly due to your talents or another advantage represented by the skates). Moving past or around obstacles easily. Skimming over the surface rather than delving into details. Creativity. Sports or competitiveness. Taking a risk (since it's easy to fall during this activity). Also consider the context (for example, skating with another person could represent a friendship or other relationship). *See also:* Vehicle; Riding; Driving

Skiing

Skiing or other winter downhill activity can represent: Making quick or smooth progress, perhaps due to external circumstances or risk-taking. Also consider the context. **A pleasant downhill experience** could represent fun, relaxation, or conquering a challenge (or a desire for such). **An out-of-control experience** could represent a feeling or fear of losing control in a particular area of your life. *See also:* Sliding; Descending; Competition; Snow; Cold; Winter; Hill

Skin

Protection or self-protection. Your personal boundaries or integrity. **Someone or something threatening your skin** can represent a feeling or fear of someone threatening your integrity or your emotional, mental, or physical boundaries. *See also:* Scalp; Body Part; Cover

Skinny

Someone who appears too thin can represent: Deprivation of emotional, mental, or spiritual nourishment. A feeling or fear of not having enough. The idea of depleted resources, loss of energy, or waning strength. Fear of loss. Feeling a need to do less (or more) somewhere in your life. Feeling or fearing that something is not quite right. *See also:* Depleted; Empty; Small; Scarcity; Inferior; Hunger; Fat

Skunk

Self-protection. A hidden strength or means of self-defense. Self-confidence or feeling self-secure. The idea of "making a stink" (such as standing up for yourself or others, or bringing attention to something). Suppressed anger, or the idea of transforming anger into something productive. Dreaming of this animal can represent too much or not enough of one of those qualities, or someone or something you associate with the quality or animal. Consider also the animal's actions, context, and your feelings about it. *See also:* Animal

Sky

Potential. Infinity. The idea of "above." A higher power. **A blue sky** can represent optimism, possibility, limitless potential, hope, or freedom. **A gray sky** can represent a state of mind or emotion (sad, irritable, wistful, reflective, etc.), or a dampening of optimism. **A dark, threatening sky** can represent a real or feared challenge or problem in your life, or "dark" emotions (anger, despair, etc.). **A night sky** can represent infinite possibilities, awe of nature, infinity, or existence. *See also:* Weather; Air; High; Sun; Star; Moon; Cloud

Skydiving

A feeling or fear of taking a risk. Facing or conquering a fear. Accepting or succeeding at a challenge. Beginning a process. "Jumping into" an activity or process with full commitment. *See also:* Parachute; Falling

Sliding

Sliding, sledding downhill, or a slide at a playground can represent: An easy process (or easier than expected). A path from one point in life to another. Working hard or taking a risk (climbing up) in order to experience something you desire (sliding down). Skimming over the surface rather than delving into details. Play, childhood, freedom, or a carefree attitude. A particular event or time frame you associate with this activity. *See also:* Playground; Ice; Slipping; Hill; Ice Skating; Lubricant or Catalyst

Slipping

Slipping (whether or not it leads to falling) can represent: "Losing your footing" or stability during a particular process (or a fear of such). Losing a solid foundation (such as a firm belief being shaken, losing faith in an ideal or a person, or losing a feeling of security or dependability). *See also:* Falling; Off; Sliding; Hill; Tripping

Slow

Moving or traveling slowly can represent: A desire for something to happen more quickly. A feeling or fear of being slowed down or restricted. A belief that it's important to proceed slowly or cautiously in some area of your life. **Trying to run away but only being able to move slowly** might mean you were having a Toxic Dream (p. 320), or your subconscious mind was exploring a worst-case scenario (perhaps to help avoid a problem in real life). *See also:* Brakes

Small

Something that is small (perhaps smaller than you would expect) can represent: Something you feel lacks power, strength, importance, or effectiveness. Something you perceive as vulnerable or overlooked. Something that seems "under control" in your life (or that you'd like to have more control over). "A lesser amount" or "lesser degree" of whatever the object or person represents (or example, if a car represents personal power, an undersized car might represent feeling unempowered in your life). **Something in miniature form** can represent something you'd like to study, control, keep, or try out on a small scale. For more clues, consider the meaning of the object or person that's small. *See also:* Size; Smaller, Getting; Measure; Toy; Sparse; Skinny

Smaller, Getting

Something or someone getting smaller or shrinking can represent: A perception of that person or thing having less power, strength, influence, importance, or presence in the world. A matter that has become less important or less prominent within your mind. The idea of "less of" whatever the thing or person represents. *See also:* Small; Size; Deflating; Decreasing

Smell

A particular smell or odor can represent: The thing or person emitting the smell. Something else you associate with the smell (such as a setting, person, or event). An idea typically associated with the smell (such as the scent of a rose representing beauty or garbage representing rot). An attempt to change a perception, situation, or environment. **An unpleasant odor** can represent something you consider undesirable (dishonesty, neglect, etc.) or toxic (ill will, festering emotions, etc.). **Someone else's body odor** might represent your judgment of that person, or a perception of ill will or lack of self-care. **You having body odor** could represent a concern about your image or your (verbal or nonverbal) communication, or a feeling or fear of being judged by others. *See also:* Fragrance; Deodorant; Garbage; Rotten; Flower; Offensive or Ugly; Nose; Sensory Cue (the category)

Smoke

A perceived warning or sign of trouble. A real or imagined precursor to a problem, destruction, loss, or an ending. Something you consider an illusion, meaningless, fake, or of no consequence somewhere in your life (as in "smoke and mirrors"). Emotion (perhaps that feels dark, destructive, or toxic). A real, desired, or feared communication (as in a "smoke signal"). Consider also the context, your feelings about, and the source of the smoke. *See also:* Fire; Ashes

Snake

Perceived threat or ill will. The advantage of stealth. Defense. Self-defense or standing up for yourself. Toxic emotion or thoughts. Dreaming of this animal can represent too much or not enough of one of those qualities, or someone or something you associate with the quality or animal. Consider also the animal's actions, context, and your feelings about it. *See also:* Animal; Worm; Eel

Snow

The idea of covering up, blanketing, hiding, or obscuring what lies beneath. A fresh or new appearance (at least temporarily). The idea of the whole being comprised of many unique elements (such as people in an organization or humankind). A certain time frame, event, or memory you associate with snow. **A snowflake** can represent temporariness, uniqueness, perfection, or the unseen facets of a person. *See also:* Winter; Cold; Ice; Weather; Storm; White; Sparkle; Avalanche

Soap

Getting rid of unwanted things (problems, worries, guilt, unpleasant memories, self-defeating beliefs or habits, etc.), or a desire to do so. The idea of renewal or starting fresh. Someone or something that makes it easier to get rid of what's unwanted. Cleanliness of body, mind, environment, or of a particular aspect of your life or consciousness. The idea of slipperiness (such as a "slippery slope" or questionable motive). *See also:* Cleaning; Sink; Bathtub or Shower; Washing Yourself; Bubble; Deodorant; Bleach

Sock

Protection. Comfort or warmth, or a feeling of such. Preparation for or ability to make progress in your life. Something or someone that acts as a buffer to mitigate potentially harsh conditions. **A single sock** could represent something or someone you perceive as missing its partner. *See also:* Clothes; Foot; Shoe

Sofa

Rest or relaxation, or a desire for such. The idea that you've been resting too much or need to be more active. The social aspect of your personal life. Your "alone time," or a desire for more of it. Time spent in front of a screen (TV, computer, etc.). *See also:* Furniture; Seat; Bench; Sitting

Soft

Gentle or compassionate. Comfortable or cozy (as in something pleasant like a blanket). Undefined or undecided. Primordial, yet to be determined, or yet to form. **Something soft that you'd expect not to be** (such as an apple or basketball) can represent someone or something that seems tired, "down," neglected, or deteriorated. **Something that's pliable** can represent someone or something that's changeable, easily adaptable, naive, or easily convinced. **A soft sound** can represent gentleness or soothing, perceived weakness, or lack of clarity or certainty. Pay attention to the context and meaning of the object that was soft, and your feelings about it during the dream. *See also:* Shaping; Changing; Deterioration; Stretchy; Shape; Quiet; Whisper; Noise, Pale

Soldier

A soldier or warrior can represent: Power. Authority. Aggression. Protection, security, or defense. Pay attention to the role the soldier played in the dream, and how you felt about the soldier. **Feeling protected by a soldier** can represent feeling or desiring protection in your life. **Feeling threatened by a soldier** can represent a feeling or fear of abuse or a threat by an authority. **Being a soldier (when you're not in real life)** can represent: feeling powerful or wishing for more power somehow in your life; feeling a need to fight or to protect yourself, others, your rights, your well-being, etc. *See also:* Attacking; Attacked, Being; Fight; Armor or Shield; Knight

Son

Your real-life son. Someone who feels like a son to you. Someone whom you feel protective of or parental toward. *See also:* Family; Child

Song

An expression (such as of ideas, feelings, thoughts, opinions, or meaning). Feelings of expressiveness or sentimentality. A real or imagined story or scenario. A person's identity, essence, uniqueness, individuality, or specialness. Consider also the characteristics, lyrics, and mood of the song, and your feelings about it. **Hearing a song** can represent an actual or desired message (such as guidance, information, or an expression of feelings). (A song going through your head repeatedly throughout the night because you've heard it recently may have no useful meaning to interpret.) *See also:* Music; Singing; Performing; Writing; Poetry

Space

Freedom, permission, or possibility. **Having plenty of space** can represent the idea of having time to yourself or having healthy personal boundaries. **Space away from others** can represent distance or isolation. *See also:* Room; Space, Outer; Distance

Space, Outer

New experiences or "unexplored territory" in your life. Adventure. A strange or new situation. Remoteness or isolation. *See also:* Sun; Star; Alien; UFO; World; Rocket; Astronaut, Infinite

Sparkle

Something that sparkles (such as sequins, glitter, or sunlight on the ocean) can represent: Richness. Liveliness. Effervescence. Activity or busy-ness. Playfulness. See also the type of object that was sparkling. *See also:* Reflective Light; Gleam; Light (Illumination)

Sparse

The idea of lack or of having to do without something (or a fear of such). Simplicity. **A sparse environment** can represent: a perceived lack of abundance somewhere in your life; a desire for more simplicity in your life; the idea that you could benefit from thinking in simpler terms. *See also:* Scarcity; Empty; Small; Decreasing; Inferior; Desert; Skinny

Special Occasion

A past or expected special occasion. A desire, expectation, or fear of what a certain occasion represents to you. A need for more fun, celebration, excitement, or a change of pace in your life. Consider also the meaning of the type of occasion. *See also:* Party; Event; Birthday; Graduation; Wedding; Baptism; Holiday

Spell

Power, control, or escape (or a desire for such). **Someone putting a spell on you** can represent: a feeling or fear that someone would like to control, manipulate, or take advantage of you; feeling powerless in a certain context (such as in a certain situation or relationship). *See also:* Magic; Curse; Witch; Attacked, Being; Attacking

Spice

The idea of making an experience more interesting or bringing more excitement or intensity to it. *See also:* Salt; Food; Condiment

Spider

Fear or anxiety (perhaps related to something specific in your life). Power, or perceived power. The element of surprise. The idea of "catching" opportunities, experiences, or other things you want (as in a spider's web). Creativity. Femininity. Maneuverability in various situation (because spiders have eight legs). Dreaming of this creature can represent too much or not enough of one of those qualities, or someone or something you associate with the quality or creature. Consider also the creature's actions, context, and your feelings about it. *See also:* Insect; Web; Bitten

Spine

Your ability to support yourself (physically, emotionally, or mentally). The idea of standing up for yourself, what's right, or something you believe in. Inner strength. Perseverance. Maintaining integrity. *See also:* Bone; Neck; Body Part

Spring (Season)

A new beginning, fresh start, birth, rebirth, or awakening. Hope, promise, or potential. Creation or fertility. Planting, sowing, or investing in the future. Consider also what spring means to you personally, and how you felt about it during the dream. *See also:* Time of Year; Time Frame; Weather

Sprout

A sprout or seedling can represent: New hope. A beginning or a fresh start. Life or growth. Progress (especially early progress). Potential. Youth or immaturity. The most basic form or smallest version of something or someone (such as a baby or an organization). *See also:* Leaf; Vine; Plant; Seed; Planting; Farming; Garden; Bigger, Getting

Square

Balanced or solid. Logical. Symmetry. Consider also what the shape means to you personally and its context in the dream. *See also:* Shape; Four; Rectangle

Squid

Multitasking or coordination. Overwhelm. Feeling "consumed" by something (an activity, relationship, etc.). Invisibility. Hiding as a self-defense, or knowing when it's advantageous to be seen and when it's not. Vision or ability to see or understand. Perceived sliminess or ill will. Dreaming of this animal can represent too much or not enough of one of those qualities, or someone or something you associate with the quality or animal. Consider also the animal's actions, context, and your feelings about it. *See also:* Animal; Octopus; Fish

Squirrel

Activity or overactivity. Preparing or being prepared. Gathering, collecting, or saving. Self-protection in a harsh or challenging situation (since a squirrel can keep warm by wrapping its tail around itself). Dreaming of this animal can represent too much or not enough of one of those qualities, or someone or something you associate with the quality or animal. Consider also the animal's actions, context, and your feelings about it. *See also:* Animal; Chipmunk

Squirting

A liquid squirting (such as out of a hose or pipe) can represent: A result of (physical, emotional, or mental) pressure, overwhelm, or overload. Taking action, extending, or reaching out (especially while keeping a distance or protecting yourself). *See also:* Bursting; Rejection; Hose; Flow or River

Stage or Screen

A setting where life events take place, or a context for the action in the dream. **Watching events on a stage** can represent feeling that you're a passive observer rather than a participant in some aspect of your life. **Being on stage** can represent a feeling of self-consciousness, being observed, or feeling especially concerned about others' opinions about you. *See also:* Theater; Audience; Curtain; Arena or Auditorium; TV, Being On; Show or Movie; Performing

Stairs

The means by which you make progress, improve, or move upward in life (represented by walking up the stairs), or the means by which you lose progress or make things worse (represented by walking down the stairs). The boundary or passageway between the levels of consciousness (such as mental and spiritual). *See also:* Climbing; Descending; Ladder; Passageway; Basement; House; Building

Stalking

Stalking something or someone can represent: Curiosity, obsession, or fascination about whatever that thing or person represents. A desire for power or control over what is being stalked, perhaps due to a feeling of powerlessness. A desire to have some kind of connection with or wanting something from that thing or person. Expecting or imagining that a certain experience will result from encountering that thing or person. *See also:* Investigator; Watching; Controlling; Chasing; Privacy

Standing Up

Waiting. Persevering. **Standing up from a seated position** can represent: an intention (such as to act or participate); honor or respect; a desire to be noticed, heard, or considered; an intention to end a process or distance yourself from a situation. Consider the person's motivation for standing. *See also:* Sitting; Leaving a Place; Leaving a Person; Applause

Star

A star in the sky can represent: A goal, dream, or lofty idea (as in "shooting for the stars"). A sense of connectedness across space and time. A source of insight, knowledge, or direction. A higher power. Awe, a magical feeling, or a pleasant mood. Optimism. Peace, or feeling that everything is as it should be. **A star shape** can represent: recognition for a job well done (as in a gold star emblem); authority or permission (as in a sheriff's badge); certain religions or practices. Consider also what the specific star brings to mind and its context in the dream. *See also:* Night; Sky; Space, Outer; Light (Illumination); Shape; Symbol; Religious Symbol; Celebrity

Starfish

Multifaceted or multitasking. Sacrificing something in order to survive or benefit (as a starfish can lose an arm when escaping a predator). Regeneration or rebirth, such as after a loss. The idea of radiating out or expanding into multiple directions. Self-protection (as in the starfish's spiny surface). Dreaming of this animal can represent too much or not enough of one of those qualities, or someone or something you associate with the quality or animal. Consider also the animal's actions, context, and your feelings about it. *See also:* Star; Fish

Starting an Engine

Starting a car or other engine can represent: The beginning of a process. An intention, decision, or desire to act. Transforming energy into action. "Going somewhere" or making progress in your life (such as toward a certain person, situation, or goal). Leaving or escaping, or a desire to do so. *See also:* Beginning; Accelerator; Key; Keyhole; Engine; Vehicle

Starting Over

A past, expected, or imagined situation that involves something starting over. A desire for a second chance or a fresh start. Fear of having to repeat or redo something (perhaps due to fear of doing something wrong or of getting caught cheating). Fear of failing. If you are the one starting over, consider your feelings and reasons for starting over in the dream. See also the specific type of process that started over. *See also:* Beginning; Entering; Changing; Altering; Ending; Repeating; New

Station

A train, bus, or other travel station can represent: A past or imagined trip. The beginning or end of a process, phase, or journey in your life (or a point in the middle of one of those). A milestone in your life. A real-life public place. A group or process you participated in with other people. For more clues, consider the events at the station and how you felt about them. *See also:* Airport; Train; Traveling

Statue

A particular person or a public figure, or your feelings about them. A particular attribute of the subject portrayed (such as grace or authority). An idea the statue conveys (such as freedom or determination). Something that seems significant about the statue or its condition (such as being immovable, broken, or incomplete). **You being or turning into a statue** might represent a feeling or fear of being unable to respond, move, or make progress somewhere in your life. *See also:* Artwork; Religious Figure; Religious Symbol; Fake; Can't Move

Staying

Staying in a place or situation (such as staying in the same job) can represent: Resistance to change, wanting to keep things the same, or preferring familiar situations or environments. Feeling hesitant (perhaps hesitant to leave). Demonstrating loyalty. An expectation that something interesting will happen or things will improve. **Staying with someone or remaining in their presence** can represent: love, care, or support; a bond with that person; patience or tolerance; a perceived debt to that person or feeling that you "owe them." Consider your motivation for staying. *See also:* Waiting; Surviving; Relationship; Visiting; Next To; Love

Steady

Sturdy, sound, or secure. Someone or something in your life that you feel you know or can count on. Mental or emotional sturdiness (such as a solid argument, logical point, valid idea, reliable person, or wise action). *See also:* Balancing; Muscle; Trust; Rigid; Hard Object; Infinite

Stealing

An issue involving personal boundaries, power, or control. Intention or desire. Self-righteousness. A feeling of lack. **Someone stealing from you** can represent others' demands on you; a feeling or fear of being disrespected, invalidated, or undervalued somehow. **You stealing from someone else** can represent a feeling that they "owe you" somehow, or that you need their attention, time, effort, etc. *See also:* Cheating; Thief; Stolen Item; Abduction; Taking From; Attacked, Being

Steam

Anger or other urgent emotion. Energy or power. A by-product of a process or event. Fogginess or lack of mental clarity. *See also:* Water; Cooking; Hot; Engine

Steering

Decisions, management, or authority. The way you "steer" yourself through your life or "steered" yourself through a particular process in the past. Your responsibility for guiding and managing yourself in the context of your life. **Steering to stay on the road** can represent a feeling of being or staying "on track" in your life. **Steering to turn a corner** can represent deciding to make a change or go in a new direction in your life. **Steering a vehicle that contains passengers** can represent a feeling of responsibility for those people in real life, or for their experience in a particular situation. **Losing control of steering** can represent a feeling or fear of neglecting responsibility, losing control, or letting things get out of control. *See also:* Driving; Leader; Vehicle; Riding; Road

Stem or Trunk

A plant stem or tree trunk can represent: A person or thing that supports or is a main source of support (physical, emotional, mental, or spiritual). An area of growth, experience, or progress. A point of origin that leads to other things or events. A cause or reason behind something (as a result that "stems from" a particular cause). The center or "heart" of something (a person, organization, etc.). *See also:* Plant; Tree; Branch; Wood

Stick

A part of a greater whole (since a stick is part of a tree). A tool or means of accomplishing a desired task. Motivation. Being or feeling nudged to do something. **A stick that has fallen off of a tree** might represent: an ending or new beginning; something in your life (such as a person, situation, object, phase, or project) that you feel you're finished with. **A stick used as a weapon** could represent a feeling or fear of aggression. *See also:* Branch; Leaf; Tool; Weapon

Sting

Being stung can represent a feeling or fear of: Being attacked or acted on in a negative way (physically, emotionally, or mentally). An unpleasant surprise. Being overburdened by external circumstances. Betrayal. Intrusion, or someone crossing your personal boundaries or taking advantage of you. See also the insect or animal that stung you. *See also:* Bitten; Insect; Attacked, Being

Stingray

A stingray or manta ray can represent: Fluidity of movement (such as progress through your life). Agility (such adapting to situations or maneuvering around obstacles). The idea of laying low, remaining unseen, or camouflaging yourself (or your emotions). Reacting to an intrusion into your personal space. Dreaming of this animal can represent too much or not enough of one of those qualities, or someone or something you associate with the quality or animal. Consider also the animal's actions, context, and your feelings about it. *See also:* Animal

Stolen Item

The idea of a person having or using something (tangible or intangible) that doesn't belong to them or that you feel they don't have a right to. A feeling or fear of being taken advantage of. See also the particular item. *See also:* Stealing; Thief; Losing an Item

Stomach

The ability to accept or "stomach" something (a situation, person, comment, etc.). The courage or ability to handle a situation. Thinking things over or mulling a situation (as in "letting a problem digest" or "chewing on" an idea). *See also:* Digestion; Indigestion; Eating; Fat; Body Part

Stone

A stone or rock can represent: A challenge or obstacle. A weight or burden. Fixed, rigid, or unchanging. Stubbornness or rigidity. Coldness, hardness, or harshness. A means of attacking someone, such as with criticisms or judgments (as in "throwing stones"). **Multiple stones** can represent a group of things (such as people, ideas, thoughts, or to-do list items). See also the form that the stones took, if any (such as a wall or mountain). *See also:* Boulder; Hard Object; Cold; Gem; Problem

Stop Sign

A delay or pause in a process. A question of whether or not to stop doing something. A real or perceived attempt by an authority to stop you from doing something or from "getting somewhere" in your life. An issue regarding rules or laws. A perceived need to stop, think, or wait in a particular aspect of your life, or to stop trying to do so much. *See also:* Brakes; Traffic; Sign

Storage

A storage area (such as a storage room or warehouse) can represent actual or desired: Saving or storing (such as of objects or memories). Procrastination or postponing. Accumulating (such as ideas, or beliefs). Holding onto things emotionally (such as grudges, blame, or judgments). Inactivity or dormancy in some area of your life, or things that are "on hold." Hoarding or keeping things for yourself (such as money) or to yourself (such as secrets). *See also:* Container; Cabinet; Safe or Vault; Accumulating; Drawer; Locker; Shelf; Extra; Hiding

Store

A store or other shopping site can represent: A real-life public place. An area of your life (such as your work life or home life). Abundance or availability. A particular store can also represent a different store in real life (for example, a supermarket could represent an electronics store you visited recently). For more clues, consider your feelings about the store and the events there during the dream. *See also:* Shopping Center; Buying; Business; Sale or Discount; Bakery

Stork

Motherhood or fatherhood. A new "birth," responsibility, or fresh start somewhere in your life. The idea of delivering, transporting, giving, or receiving. "Wading through" something (such as a difficult time, a mess, or lots of information). Dreaming of this animal can represent too much or not enough of one of those qualities, or someone or something you associate with the quality or animal. Consider also the animal's actions, context, and your feelings about it. *See also:* Bird; Pelican; Crane; Heron; Flamingo

Storm

Challenges, rough times, or turbulence (in life, in a relationship, etc.). Anger, frustration, or other upset feelings. A feeling or fear of danger or disruption. A physically, emotionally, or mentally harsh environment. The idea of an outside force affecting you or a process in which you're involved. *See also:* Weather; Rain; Wind; Thunder; Lightning; Cloud; Hail; Waves; Hurricane; Tornado; Flood; Disaster; Chaos

Story

An event or series of events in your life, as portrayed by your subconscious mind. A lesson, moral, or some other kind of insight. A wish or desire (such as an adventurous tale pointing to a wish for more adventure in your life). Your imagination or creativity at work. *See also:* Book; Text; Writing; Communication; Lying; Lied To, Being; Main Floor

Stove

A real-life activity involving cooking or food preparation. The effort you put into mentally, emotionally, or spiritually nourishing yourself or your family. The idea of things "heating up" (such as getting exciting or combative). *See also:* Appliance; Cooking

Stranded

A feeling or fear of being abandoned or of lacking support somehow in your real life. *See also:* Left, Being; Abandonment

Straw

Something that provides cushioning or protection against unpleasantness (such as someone mediating an argument). A filler (such as busywork or telling stories to fill spare time). Something perceived as playing a secondary role, benign, or having little value. A fake or mock-up (as a "straw man"). A situation relating to making decisions fairly or randomly (as in "drawing straws"). Being fed up (as in "the last straw"). The end or by-product of a process. *See also:* Farming; Plant; Straw, Drinking

Straw, Drinking

A want, need, or desire. A tube or conduit. The means by which something gets from one place to another. *See also:* Drinking; Sucking; Passageway

Stretchy

Something that stretches and then returns to its original form (such as elastic or a rubber band) might represent: Resilience. Responsiveness. Adaptability. An ability to handle crisis or stress well. *See also:* Soft; Changing; Shaping

String

String connecting or binding things together can represent: Relationships, bonds, or communication. Feeling constricted or restrained (as in "feeling tied down"). **String coming unwound** can represent: a situation you perceive to be coming undone or "falling apart"; the idea of getting to the bottom of a problem or figuring something out. **Winding string or tying things together with string** can represent putting things in order, or getting things under control or organized (or at least trying to appear that way to others). *See also:* Thread; Rope; Tying

Stuck

You or your vehicle being stuck can represent a feeling or fear of: Being unable to make progress in your life (or in a particular aspect of it). Being or feeling stuck in a certain situation, or "stuck in a rut" or routine somehow in your life. **An item being stuck** can represent feeling stuck or challenged in whatever area that item represents. *See also:* Can't Move; Blockage or Obstacle; Broken Object

Succeeding

Feeling successful somehow in real life, or a desire for that. Feeling like you could do better than you're doing now. Mentally preparing yourself for a challenge ahead. Real or imagined approval from others. Feeling happy in general or acknowledging that life is good right now. *See also:* Test; Winning; Competition; Arriving; Surviving; After

Sucking

An attempt to get or take something, or to pull something toward you (a desired feeling, experience, object, etc.). Manipulating something or someone for a desired benefit. Taking time, energy, attention, money, or something else from someone else. Need, or a feeling or fear of lack. *See also:* Drinking; Taking From; Lips; Mouth; Parasite; Scarcity

Sugar

Emotional sweetness (such as camaraderie or caring). "Sweet times" or the sweetness of life. Happiness, or the desire for more of it. Actual hunger or a craving for sweets. *See also:* Dessert; Drug

Suing

Accusation, blame, anger, or revenge (or fear of such). **Someone suing you** can represent: a feeling or fear of making a mistake, neglecting a responsibility, or being falsely accused; feeling guilty about something you've done or something you're contemplating. *See also:* Justice; Blaming; Blamed, Being

Suitcase

Something you're carrying with you (such as emotional or mental "baggage," or unfinished business). A real-life or imagined a trip. A symbolic journey (such as through a learning process or a life phase). A temporary situation, perhaps one that's unfamiliar or "foreign" to you. Possessions, or the idea of ownership. Necessities, essentials, or the bare minimum you need to get along. Portability, mobility, or transferring something from one environment to another (such using design found in nature to inspire an engineering design). *See also:* Bag; Packing; Traveling

Summer

Actual or desired: Happiness or fun. Relaxation or a break from work. Warmth or heat. A particular warm-weather activity. Consider also the role summer plays in the dream and your feelings about it. *See also:* Time of Year; Time Frame; Sun; Sunny; Warm; Hot; Weather

Sun

Life or existence. Someone or something you consider a critical source of physical, emotional, mental, or spiritual support. A higher power. Illumination or insight. Daytime (as a setting for the dream events). A perceived or imagined source of danger, stress, or other mental or emotional "heat." *See also:* Light (Illumination); Time of Day; Sunny; Suntan; Sunburn; Space, Outer

Sunburn

A feeling or fear of: The results of neglecting a responsibility or a detail of self-care (such as overindulging in food and then feeling sick). The effects of negativity from someone else, or from the world in general. Others trying to cross your boundaries or take advantage of you. Being "burned" by someone or something. *See also:* Inflammation; Sun; Red

Sunflower

A sunny or cheerful mood (or desire for such). Quick and direct progress towards a goal (as in a sunflower's growth and orientation toward the sun). Achievement, or perhaps exceeding expectations. A personal or spiritual growth process. Abundance or harvest. A particular time frame (a season, occasion, etc.). *See also:* Flower; Sun

Sunglasses

Viewing things in an altered way due to your internal filters (perceptions, assumptions, judgments, biases, preferences, etc.). "Shading" or protecting yourself (such as from others' judgments or from facing reality). Distancing yourself from people or social interactions. A desire for privacy, hiding yourself or your feelings. Mystery. Anonymity or questionable identity. Feeling insecure. An attempt to project a certain image or type of personality. Consider also the context of the sunglasses and how you felt about them. *See also:* Glasses (Eyeglasses)

Sunny

A sunny day can represent: A happy or carefree mood. A positive outlook. A lack of problems or complications. *See also:* Sun; Light (Illumination); Warm; Hot; Weather

Sunrise

A literal or figurative awakening. The beginning of a phase, project, relationship, or something else with a life cycle. Preparing for activity or productivity. Nature, or an appreciation of natural beauty. God or spirituality. Consider also how you felt about the sunrise. *See also:* Time of Day; Morning; Sun

Sunset

The end of a phase, project, relationship, or anything that has a life cycle. Finishing or completing something. Winding down or relaxing. Romance or sentimentality. Nature, or an appreciation of natural beauty. God or spirituality. Consider also how you felt about the sunset. *See also:* Time of Day; Evening; Twilight; Night; Sun

Suntan

Self protection (perhaps on a subconscious level). Ability to adapt to a situation or environment. A particular time you spent outdoors in real life. **Purposely getting a suntan** can represent: a desire to project a certain image or control what others think about you, even to your own detriment (such as losing too much weight); exposing (or overexposing) yourself to dangers or toxins (physical, emotional, or mental); the idea of becoming less susceptible to negativity from others (as a suntan increases melatonin in skin). *See also:* Sun; Beige; Sunburn

Superhero

Good will or rescuing (or a desire for such). Ability, power, empowerment, or authority (or a desire for such). Feeling very good about yourself, or you wishing did. *See also:* Hero; Character; Powers; Rescuing; Rescued, Being

Superior

The idea of comparing one thing to another, or yourself to something else (another person, a standard, etc.). A judgment of something or someone as "more than," "better than," "good," or "right." *See also:* Right or Wrong; Good; Liking; High; Above; One; Manager; Promotion or Raise

Support, Architectural

A pillar, beam, or other architectural support can represent: Physical, emotional, mental, or spiritual support (or a desire for it or dependence on it). Resources, or sources of support (people, information, etc.). Reliability, strength, or steadiness. A person's character. Personal integrity, morals, or values. Basic beliefs or understandings. *See also:* Supporting; Rescuing; Rescued, Being; Building; House; Making or Building

Supporting

Assistance, good will, or the way you relate to others. **Physically supporting someone** (such as helping them walk) can represent the idea of supporting them physically, emotionally, mentally, or spiritually in real life (or a desire to, or a fear of having to). **Physically supporting something** (such as carrying an object) can represent feeling or fearing a responsibility or burden. **Supporting someone by paying their expenses** can represent generosity, responsibility, or obligation; value or self-worth; helping too much or helping too little. **Supporting a candidate, cause, or team** can mean you like, agree with, feel connected with, or identify with them. **Feeling supportive or having good will toward someone** can mean you feel that way in real life. *See also:* Giving; Paying; Feeding; Leader; Hero; Feeling; Support, Architectural

Surgery

A real or imagined problem. A feeling or fear of something being "off" physically, emotionally, or mentally. Assistance from a source outside yourself (or a desire for it). The idea of someone crossing your personal boundaries with or without your permission. A feeling or fear of some-

306

one taking advantage of you, forcing their opinion on you, or "getting into your business." Surgery without your permission can indicate a Toxic Dream (p. 320). *See also:* Illness; Doctor; Hospital

Surprise

Preparing yourself for something you imagine might happen. Your thoughts and feelings about a surprise that happened in real life. An imagined version of a surprise you'd enjoy or you want to avoid. *See also:* Discovering; New; Opening

Surviving

Surviving a challenge or threat can represent: A real-life success. Imagining how it would feel to face a challenge and succeed. Fear of a particular threat or hardship. **Fighting for your own survival** can represent a perceived struggle in your real life (such as financial survival or survival to maintain your identity). *See also:* Alive or Exists; Staying; Succeeding; Winning; Fight

Swallowing

Accepting something (such as reality, a fact, a situation, a suggestion, advice, or a decision). Deciding to believe something. "Taking something in," as in trying to understand it or to realize that it has happened. Internalizing something mentally or emotionally (such as taking on someone else's problem or internalizing a belief from an external source). *See also:* Eating; Drinking; Neck; Mouth; Tongue

Swamp

Lack of "solid ground," foundation, or beliefs (or a fear of losing such). Not knowing how to proceed or what to believe. A challenging area or phase of your life. A feeling or fear of hidden challenges or messiness. *See also:* Water, Body of; Mud; Problem; Descending; Quicksand

Swan

Grace. A connection with your own inner beauty. Staying afloat (such as financially or emotionally). The ability to reach or stretch yourself to get what you want in life. Dreaming of this animal can represent too much or not enough of one of those qualities, or someone or something you associate with the quality or animal. Consider also the animal's actions, context, and your feelings about it. *See also:* Bird; Goose

Swearing

The strength or depth of emotion, expression, or commitment. **Swear words** can indicate something you wanted or needed to express at the time of the dream (emotion, thoughts, excitement, etc.). **Swearing to tell the truth or taking an oath** can represent an intention to be honest, a desire to convince someone, or a wish for someone else to be honest. *See also:* Communication; Feeling; Words; Agreement

Swelling

Dealing with emotional or mental injury or toxicity in your life. A tendency toward being reactionary or easily triggered. **Something that's swollen** (such as a river or a risen loaf of bread) can represent abundance or the idea more of whatever the swollen item represents (such as a swollen river representing more of a threat, or risen bread representing greater volume). *See also:* Increasing; Bigger, Getting; Many

Swimming

Moving forward or making progress in your life. Effort toward achieving a goal. Freedom from your usual limitations. Excelling at an activity or in an environment that doesn't come naturally to you (since humans are typically land-dwellers). **Swimming with swim fins** can represent a great ability to make progress, especially in a new, different, or challenging situation or environment. *See also:* Traveling; Floating; Water, Body of; Diving; Underwater

Swirl or Eddy

A swirl, eddy, whirlpool, or vortex can represent: A disturbance. A variation from the usual. A force of nature that poses a real or imagined threat. Something or someone that "sucks you into" something (such as into an activity, habit, way of thinking, etc.). A perceived opening between levels or worlds. *See also:* Flow or River; Tornado; Waves; Door or Entrance; Circles, Going in

Sword

A challenge or potential threat. A dramatic conflict. Honor or dignity. A flourish or gesture. Ritual or tradition. *See also:* Knife; Weapon; Sharp

Symbol

A particular quality or meaning associated with the symbol by you or by cultural traditions. A quality associated with the shape of the symbol (for example, a diamond shape representing excellence). Something specific, either in your real life or your imagination (an object, person, place, activity, etc.). A stand-in for something unknown to you. A desire for information, clarification, or understanding of something. Consider your feelings about the symbol during the dream, and what it brings to mind for you in general. *See also:* Shape; Sign; Religious Symbol; Code; Arrow; Shamrock; Star; Flag; Map or Directions

Table

Physical, emotional, mental, or spiritual nourishment. Interaction, conversation, or negotiation. Postponing or setting aside a certain matter (as in "tabling" an agenda item). Consider the type of table, its context, and the activity taking place at the table (for example, a kitchen table could represent your relationship with family, or a coffee-shop table might represent a recent conversation with friends). *See also:* Furniture; Eating

Taking From

Taking something from someone can represent: A need, demand, or desire. Taking from that person in real life (such as wanting their time, energy, attention, or money), or a desire to do so. An issue regarding personal boundaries (such as an attempt to take without asking). *See also:* Thief; Pulling; Abduction; Stealing

Talk Show

Being on a talk show, or being friends with a talk show host, can mean that your subconscious mind considers that person a friend because you've "interacted" with them often in the past by watching their show. (The subconscious mind may not see much difference between encountering a person on TV and encountering them in person.) *See also:* Show or Movie; TV, Being On; Interview; Celebrity

Tangle

Complication. Chaos or the absence of order. A feeling or fear of a problem somewhere in your life. The idea of neglect, or a need for maintenance. *See also:* Knot; Thicket; Wrinkle; Fight

Task

A task, chore, or other item to accomplish can represent: A real-life task that's on your mind. An attempt to handle a full schedule or large to-do list. Stress due to a busy life or mind. A plan or strategy. A worry, need, or something else you feel you need to act on. *See also:* List; Homework; Working; Activity

Tasting

Testing, trying, or sampling something (such as an experience). Trying out something during the dream (such as a "what if" scenario, or an imagined result of making a particular choice in real life). A desire to try something new (such as a new hobby or different environment). Evaluating an idea or situation and developing an opinion about it. Physical hunger while you're sleeping. **Tasting something you're cooking** can represent checking your progress or evaluating your results in some area of your life. *See also:* Biting; Eating; Food; Sensory Cues (the category)

Tattoo

Your perception of the tattoo owner's image, identity, or self-expression. A permanent "mark" (such as on the owner's reputation or personality). Belonging to a certain group or crowd. The idea of letting someone or something "get under your skin" (such as getting close to you or triggering your emotions). Consider also the content and characteristics of the tattoo. *See also:* Ink; Skin; Injection; Decoration

Tax

The idea of participating in or contributing to society or the world. A requirement by an authority figure in your life. Rules. A commitment, agreement, or arrangement (financial or otherwise). A demand on you. A challenging situation. An issue of responsibility or personal integrity. *See also:* Paying; Money; Giving; Tollway

Teacher

Authority. Assistance. Information or understanding. The idea of taking on a role. **A teacher who's not a teacher in real life** can represent: an authority figure in your life; someone whose opinions or advice you listen to; someone who has taught you something, or from whom you think you can learn something. **You being a teacher when you're not in real life** could represent: feeling you have something valuable to share; teaching or explaining something to a certain person or group (or a desire to do so); a desire to feel respected or looked up to; curiosity about being a teacher. *See also:* Authority Figure; Leader; Class; School

Technician or Mechanic

Repairing, fixing, mending, rebuilding, or healing, or a person whom you feel is an expert in such. A desire, need, or curiosity regarding one of the previously mentioned items. *See also:* Repairing; Making or Building; Technology; Machine or Robot

Technology

Applied knowledge. An ability to accomplish something, or applying that ability somehow in your life. Getting things done efficiently or quickly. Something or someone that makes things easier or offers convenience (or a desire for such). The idea of "working smarter," or a result of doing so. **The era of the technologies in the dream** (such as vintage cars or modern phones) can indicate which time frame in your life the dream represents (past, present, or imagined future). *See also:* Machine or Robot; Science; Design or Plan; Electric; Technician or Mechanic

Telescope

A telescope, binoculars, or other device that magnifies can represent the following: Examining something in real life that's represented by the object being magnified (such as to clarify the facts or your feelings about it). Observing or studying (perhaps based on a desire to understand or gain knowledge). The idea of bringing closer something or someone who seems remote. A perceived invasion of privacy. Consider also who was using the telescope and their motivations. *See also:* Investigator; Searching; Secret; Watching; Stalking; Privacy

Telling on Someone

Rules. The ideas of "right" and "wrong." Justice. Your general intention to "do the right thing." An attempt to maintain order somewhere in your life. Fear of being told on by someone else. A feeling of self-righteousness. **Someone telling on you** can represent: someone in your life whom you feel or fear you can't trust; feeling guilty about something you've done or you're considering doing. *See also:* Interfering; Warning; Gossiping; Betrayed, Being; Sabotaged, Being; Trust

Ten

Perceived perfection. Complete. Achievement. A goal, end point, or end of a cycle. Being neat, organized, or "even." The underlying basis for a pattern (as in our numbering system being based on the number ten). Something else you associate with ten, such as a decagon, dectet, time frame, someone's age, or your family. *See also:* Number; Relationship; Second Place

Termite

Activity of which you're not aware (such as judgments or other dynamics within in your subconscious mind). Gradual change through very small changes over time. "Eating away" at something (such as completing a large task bit by bit). The idea of an intrusion on your personal boundaries. Erosion (such as of a foundation, belief, or moral). Action that's beneficial on one hand but harmful on another (as termites' activity benefits them but has detrimental effects for others). Dreaming of this insect can represent too much or not enough of one of those qualities, or someone or something you associate with the quality. Consider also the insect's actions, context, and your feelings about it. *See also:* Insect

Terrorism

A feeling or fear of violence, victimization, or ill will. A reaction to an instance of physical, emotional, or mental aggression. Harmful action in the name of self-righteousness, or asserting one's cause or needs as superior to those of others. Focusing on perceived negativity rather than on positivity in the world or in your personal environment. *See also:* Attacking; Attacked, Being; Violence; Evil; Tormented; Weapon; Threat

Test

A real, expected, feared, or imagined challenge or evaluation. For example, being nervous while taking a test might represent your nervousness about a job interview scheduled later this week. *See also:* Problem; Competition; Succeeding; Failing a Test; Interview; Writing; Laboratory; Medical Treatment

Text

Communication (actual, imagined, desired, or feared). Information (or a desire for or fear of it). **Reading text** can represent: trying to understand something, find information, or solve a problem in real life; a desire for knowledge in general; an academic pursuit. Consider the context and content of the text and your feelings about it. *See also:* Words; Writing; Texting; Book; Story; Language; Communication; Following a Procedure; Garbled

Texting

Communication or connection. A dialogue. News or information. **Sending a text message** can mean you have news, something to ask, or something to express to someone. **Receiving a text message** can represent the idea of hearing from someone or suddenly becoming aware of something. *See also:* Communication; Typing; Words; Text

Theater

The idea of watching others go about their lives, or hearing their stories. Feeling like a passive observer rather than a participant somehow in your life. Considering your life from an objective or unbiased perspective. Drama in your life (or a desire for less drama, or perhaps more drama). *See also:* Stage or Screen; Arena or Auditorium; Show or Movie; Audience; TV, Being On

Therapist

A need or desire to express your feelings, thoughts, or something you're dealing with. A desire to be heard or have someone to talk to. A concern about your well-being or level or happiness. A desire for help (such as understanding something, dealing with a challenge, or solving a problem). Curiosity about the idea of working with a therapist, perhaps regarding a particular topic or challenge. *See also:* Doctor; Advice or Opinion; Communication; Listening; Science

Thicket

Tall or overgrown grass, brush, or shrubbery can represent: Perceived chaos or wildness, or a desire for more order or control somewhere in your life. Neglect, or neglected responsibility. The unknown. Fear of a hidden threat. The idea of hiding or being obscured. Nature or the outdoors. *See also:* Forest; Jungle; Vine; Tangle

Thief

Being taken advantage of, stolen from, disrespected, manipulated, or otherwise victimized (or a fear of such). Consider also the meaning of whatever the thief stole. *See also:* Stealing; Cheating; Taking From; Catching Someone; Criminal

Thigh

Strength or power to move forward, take action, or make progress in your life. Ability to stand up for yourself or stand on your own. Being prepared to act or respond when the time is right. *See also:* Leg

Thirst

A need or desire (such as for knowledge, understanding, satisfaction, or love). A feeling or fear of lack or deprivation. *See also:* Dry; Hunger; Famished; Scarcity

Thorn

A feeling or fear of emotional pain, disappointment, or disadvantage (perhaps which comes as a surprise). The downside of a situation or relationship (as thorns are the "downside" of a beautiful rose). A hidden danger or source of harm, or a fear of such. *See also:* Sharp; Threat; Plant

Thread

Connection. Fastening or securing. Continuity, something that unites, or something in common. **A loose thread on a garment** could represent a perceived imperfection. **A neatly wound spool of thread** could represent organization or order. *See also:* String; Yarn; Rope; Woven; Fabric; Sewing

Threat

A feeling or fear of a physical, emotional, or mental threat somewhere in your life. Feelings about a threat you encountered in person, in the media, in a movie, or in your imagination. Anxiety about something specific or in general. An indication that you were having a Toxic Dream (p. 320). *See also:* Attacked, Being; Evil; Warning

Three

Balanced or solid (as in a tripod). A well-balanced life. A certain time frame. Holiness or a higher power. Something else you associate with three, such as a trio, triangle, time frame, someone's age, or your family. *See also:* Number; Age; Time Frame; Triangle

Throat

The idea of self or expressing yourself. Vulnerability (as the throat is critical for breathing, circulation, and eating). **Throat problems** can represent a feeling or fear of: being unable or hindered in expressing or standing up for yourself; being unheard, ignored, or overlooked; having no say in things that affect you. *See also:* Neck; Voice; Body Part; Funnel

Throwing

An intention or action. **Throwing an object (such as a ball) to someone** can represent: an invitation to dialogue, play, or otherwise participate; giving power or handing something off to the person (as in "the ball is in your court"). **Throwing something at someone with intent to hurt them** can represent: a feeling or fear of losing control; a particular emotion (anger, frustration, jealousy, etc.); a desire to avoid that person. **Throwing an object with intent to scare a person** can represent: feeling a need to defend yourself; a desire for power (perhaps due to feeling unempowered). Consider the intention for throwing and the object being thrown. *See also:* Game; Attacking; Garbage; Breaking; Catching Something

Thumb

The ability to grasp or hold on (such as holding onto money, or persevering in a particular situation). An opinion or expression. **Thumbs-up** can represent approval or self-confidence (or a desire for it). **Thumbs-down** can represent a negative answer or opinion you feel or fear, or a self-judgment. *See also:* Finger; Hitchhiking

Thunder

Fear, or something you fear. Power (or a reminder of it, desire for it, or fear of it). An authority or higher power. The idea of punishment, or a threat of it. *See also:* Storm; Cloud; Noise; Loud

Thyroid

Energy or heat. Endurance. Ability to maintain an energy level, enthusiasm, or motivation. A perceived or imagined physical, emotional, or mental issue. *See also:* Gland

Ticket

Permission. Access to something, someone, or an experience. Official permission by an authority or by society, perhaps to participate or be part of a group (or a desire for such). Consider also what the ticketed event represents. **Losing an admission ticket** could represent feeling like an outsider in some way, or a fear of being denied access to a particular experience. **A penalty ticket** (such as for illegal parking or a traffic violation) can represent a feeling or fear of being caught, accused, or punished somehow. *See also:* Caught, Being; Police

Tie

A necktie can represent perceived or desired: Image. Personality or style. Masculinity. Success or power. **Tying a necktie** can represent preparing, organizing, or "neatening up" yourself or your life (perhaps for an event you're expecting or imagining). *See also:* Tying; Clothes; Scarf; Decoration

Tiger

Strength in action. Assertiveness or aggression. Being pro-active, or taking pre-emptive action to avoid problems before they arise. Personal strength or courage. Dreaming of this animal can represent too much or not enough of one of those qualities, or someone or something you associate with the quality or animal. Consider also the animal's actions, context, and your feelings about it. *See also:* Cat; Animal

Tight

Closeness (as in a tight-knit family). Security or unavailability (as in being "locked up tight"). Neatness or tidiness. **Something that is too tight** can represent feeling restricted or blocked somehow in your life. **Someone wearing tight clothes** may mean you think that person is "too full of himself" or has "too much" of something (ego, "hot air," etc.). *See also:* Joining Together; Blockage or Obstacle; Next To; Bond; Holding; Closed; Lock; Security

Tightrope

Walking a tightrope can represent: Feeling pressure, perhaps to maintain a delicate balance or "walk a thin line" somehow in your life. A feeling or fear of risk, failure, or embarrassment. *See also:* Balancing; Falling; Path; High; Rope

Time

A certain time on the clock might represent: An awareness of time in general, the passage of time, or its fleeting nature. Being late or early, being short on time, or having too much time (or a fear of such). A particular time of day, or a certain event that tends to happen at that time. *See also:* Clock; Alarm Clock; Time of Day; Time Passing; Time Frame; Time of Year; Early; Late; Before; After

Time of Day

A particular time of day (such as morning or evening) can represent an actual time frame when the events represented in the dream really happened, or it can set a mood or context that you associate with that part of the day (such as stressed in the morning or relaxed in the evening). *See also:* Time; Time Frame; Daytime; Midday; Morning; Afternoon; Evening; Twilight; Night; Sunset; Sunrise

Time Frame

The time frame, period, or era depicted in a dream can set the mood (such as the 1800s Wild West depicting your workplace) or point to a certain time of your life (such as a 1970s disco representing your senior year in high school), so look for real-life parallel events and feelings from that time in your past. However, sometimes the subconscious mind uses familiar events from the past to represent current events in your life. For example, your high school graduation 20 years ago might actually represent the promotion you received last week, or a past boyfriend might represent your current romantic partner. *See also:* Time Passing; Time of Year; Time; Dates on a Calendar; Calendar; Holiday; Past; Future; Late; Early; Before; After; Time Frames (the category)

Time Off

Time off work or school might represent: Actual time off you've had or are expecting. An experience of or desire for freedom, fun, relaxation, free time, or a break from responsibilities. A desire for a break from what's going on in your consciousness (worry, self-judgment, etc.). Feeling tired. *See also:* Resting; Trip or Vacation; Holiday

Time Passing

The passage of time or a series of events can represent the same in real life. For example, consider a series of dream events in which you visited a store, then you were chased by a swarm of bees, and then you jumped into your friend's swimming pool. This series of events could represent three separate events in your real life that happened in the same sequence (possibly even months or years apart). In this case, you might look for a time in real life when you went to work (represented by the store), then you were feeling overwhelmed by things "bugging" you (represented by the bees), then you "escaped" with help from a friend (represented by the friend's pool). *See also:* Time; Before; After; Past; Future; Aging; Time Frame

Time of Year

A certain time of year can indicate the actual time frame of the real-life events represented in the dream, or it can set a mood or context. For example, a summertime event in a dream might represent a real-life event that happened in the summer, or something you associate with summer (vacation, nice weather, freedom, etc.). *See also:* Time; Time Frame; Spring (Season); Summer; Autumn; Winter; Month; Weather; Dates on a Calendar; Calendar; Holiday

Tired

Actual tiredness (physical, emotional, or mental). Feeling tired of dealing with life or something particular in your life. A particular mental state (such as boredom) or emotion (such as sadness). *See also:* Illness; Fainting; Resting

Tissue

A tissue, wipe, or handkerchief can represent: Crying or emotion. A desire to get rid of or "wipe away" something in your life or mind. **A tissue or other disposable wipe** can also represent something perceived as dispensable or a "throwaway." *See also:* Cleaning

Toe

Beginning a new journey, phase, or project. Trying or considering something (as in "dipping your toe into the water"). **Stubbing your toe** could represent: a temporary obstacle; getting in your own way; a feeling or fear of failure; a need to pay more attention to where you're going, or to consider each decision or step carefully; unpleasantness, perhaps resulting from something that's against your better judgment. *See also:* Foot; Shoe; Joint; Falling

Toilet

The idea of getting rid of things that are used up, no longer needed, "gone bad," or toxic (such as judgments, self-defeating beliefs, or toxic thoughts or relationships). **An overflowing toilet** (or a toilet that won't flush) can represent: a problem getting rid of something; an unwillingness or inability to let go of things that are polluting your mind, body, or life. **Something you value getting flushed down the toilet** can represent a feeling or fear of loss, grief, waste, neglecting a responsibility, or letting go of something. *See also:* Bathroom; Drain; Urinating; Feces

Tollway

Paying (money, time, effort, respect, etc.) for what you use or take, or your responsibility to do so. Paying as you go. Making progress, but at a price. "Paying your dues" in life or a particular part of it. Choosing an "expensive path" (a course of action that requires a lot of time, money, effort, etc.). Investing time or effort in order to get somewhere or accomplish things. Consider how you felt about having to pay to use the road, and whether you paid before or after you used the road (which may point to a real-life sequence of events). *See also:* Road; Tax

Tongue

Your ability to articulate or express yourself. Communication. Expression of thoughts, feedback, opinion, or criticism. Talkativeness. Trying or "tasting" something. Connecting with or experiencing the world around you. *See also:* Mouth; Communication; Licking

Tool

The means by which you accomplish something in your life (such as with "tools" like abilities, talents, resources, technology, help from others, etc.). Something or someone that makes a task or activity easier. For more clues, consider the type of tool, who was using it and how, how it's typically used, and what stood out about it. *See also:* Hammer; Knife; Scissors; Saw; Appliance; Stick

Tooth

Well-being. Handling of your day-to-day life. Personality or identity. **Someone with tooth problems** (losing teeth, false teeth, cavities, etc.) can represent real or feared issues regarding the person's: physical, emotional, or mental well-being; ability to cope, achieve, or get what they want in the world; self-expression or ability to communicate clearly. **Dental care items** (such as a toothbrush) can represent self-care, responsibility for self (physical, emotional, mental, social, etc.), or a perceived need for more of such. *See also:* Losing an Item; Biting; Eating; Mouth; Cleaning; Pain; Ache; Infection; Dentist; Communication

Top

Being at the top or climbing to the top of something can represent (perceived or desired): Success, or your definition of "success." Achievement or work. Fulfillment or satisfaction. Recognition. Superiority, or feeling superior to others (perhaps based on feeling inferior). The end of a process. *See also:* Roof; Building; Limit or Boundary; Bottom

Tormented

Being tormented or tortured can be a strong indication that you were having a Toxic Dream (p. 320). However, it could also represent a feeling or fear of persecution, hostility, aggression, or criticism, ill will, or lack of compassion. *See also:* Attacked, Being; Abuse; Bothering; Bothered, Being

Tornado

An overwhelming or destructive situation in real life, perhaps outside of your control (or a fear of such). A feeling or fear of being taken advantage of or victimized, especially suddenly or in an unpredictable way. *See also:* Storm; Weather; Disaster; Swirl or Eddy

Touching

Connection. Communication. Expression. Consider the context and motivation. **A caress** might represent caring, affection, compassion, or reassurance. **A quick touch or tap** can represent an alert, reminder, or attempt to get someone's attention. *See also:* Hand; Hug; Cuddle; Next To; Feeling; Sensory Cues (the category)

Towel

Absorbing something mentally or emotionally, or the ability to do so. "Taking something in" or learning. "Cleaning up" after yourself or someone else (problems, neglected responsibilities, etc.). Consider also the context and how the towel was being used (for example, drying yourself after a shower could represent the end of a process, and wiping up a spill could represent solving a problem). *See also:* Absorbing; Cleaning; Wet; Dry; Dry Up; Dryer

Tower

Having a higher perspective (a better understanding, greater awareness, ability to "see the bigger picture," etc.). Separation or isolation, or a feeling of such. Limitation or restraint. Perceived arrogance or ignorance.

Power, perceived power, or a wish for power. Security, vigilance, watching, or being watched (as in a tower lookout). *See also:* High; Above

Towing

Towing or pulling something along can represent: Helping. Taking responsibility for or doing all the work for someone else. Passivity or helplessness of whatever's represented by the thing being towed. *See also:* Pulling; Carrying; Cargo

Toxic Dream

A Toxic Dream is usually a very realistic, upsetting dream that's most likely to occur when your body is overloaded or stressed during sleep. The terrible, nightmarish quality of a Toxic Dream can signal that your body, emotions, or mind were in a toxic state at the time of the dream. This type of dream can result from a number of factors from earlier in the day, including: eating refined carbohydrates (sugar, white flour, etc.), processed or junk food, or additives or preservatives; eating too much too close to bedtime; ingesting drugs or other substances that tax the body; encountering environmental toxins (mold, exhaust fumes, etc.); physical, emotional, or mental stress; toxic feelings (such as going to bed angry); not resting your body and mind enough during the day.

Toy

A child or the idea of children. Your childhood or your inner child. Playfulness, or a desire to be more playful. **A specific toy you had in the past** might indicate the time frame in your life represented by the dream events. Consider also the type of toy (for example, building blocks could represent a desire to solve a real-life problem or express yourself through creative design). *See also:* Puppet; Doll; Small

Tracks

Animal tracks or human footprints can represent: The process of moving forward. The manner or means of moving forward, literally or figuratively (as in the course of action that led to certain results). Your journey or life path, or a portion of it (past, present, or imagined future). Evidence of someone's presence or existence, or what they left behind. **Dirty tracks across a clean floor** can represent: someone's presence; perceived carelessness, disrespect, or hostility somewhere in your life. *See also:* Foot; Path; Walking; Dirt

Tracks, Railroad

Making progress or moving onward to what's ahead in your life. The specific path that you feel will lead you where you want to go, or to whatever's next for you. The idea of being on-track or off-track in your life. A feeling of only having one option or path. Your perspective of where you are now in your life (in the context of where you've been and where you're headed). The idea of going along automatically wherever life takes you, merely responding to circumstances rather than directly taking charge of your life direction. *See also:* Path; Road; Train; Locomotive; Traveling; Driving

Traffic

People around you going about their daily business, or activity around you in your life. **Heavy traffic** could represent having a lot going on around you, or a recent time when you did. **Gridlocked traffic** could represent: overwhelm; everyone wanting the same thing or making the same choice; or an inability to make progress, achieve what you want, or "go places" in life. *See also:* Crowd; Driving; Traveling; Vehicle; Road; Chaos

Train

An actual train or other vehicle (such as one you've traveled on, expect to travel on, or you saw in the media). Feeling on-track (or off-track) in your life. The idea of not being in control of your direction or progress, or not needing to be because someone else is in charge (since a train can travel only where its tracks go). **Riding on a passenger train** can represent: a shared experience or a group in which you're "all in the same boat"; a process or phase; your movement forward through life, or the means by which you do so. *See also:* Vehicle; Traveling; Locomotive; Tracks, Railroad; Riding; Trip or Vacation; Teacher; Class; Repeating

Transparent

Something that's transparent or see-through can represent: Seeming to lack substance, meaning, or importance. The idea of lightness. Easy to figure out or understand. Truthfulness. Feeling exposed or unprotected, or wanting to hide or not be noticed. *See also:* Exposed (Object); Disappearing; Glass

Trapped

A feeling or fear of: Being trapped or cornered (literally or figuratively). Having no options. Being forced into a certain action or decision. **Someone trapping you with an intention to harm you** can be an indicator of a Toxic Dream (p. 320), or of your subconscious mind playing out a fear (such as based on imagined events or something you saw on TV). *See also:* Prison; Restrained; Caught, Being

Trash Compactor

The way you're dealing with things in your life or your mind (represented by the garbage). "Stuffing" or denying your personal issues in an attempt to not have to deal with them or to hide them from others. Judging your issues rather than recognizing them as opportunities to improve or heal. "Crushing" and releasing outdated beliefs or self-defeating thought patterns, or otherwise processing through issues. *See also:* Appliance; Garbage; Garbage Can; Destroying

Traveling

Traveling (movement forward, or movement from one place to another) can represent: The passage of time in your life. Making progress or moving forward through your life. A transition (such as between two events, phases, or places). Progressing through a process or symbolic journey. A change of scene or routine. A real-life activity (traveling or otherwise). *See also:* Driving; Walking; Trip or Vacation; Adventure; Visiting; Holiday; Honeymoon; Following a Path; Road; Carrying; Airplane; Boat; Nomad

Treasure

Something you consider valuable (such as love, family, financial well-being, health, knowledge, insight, happiness, fun, or security). Something you've discovered in real life, or would like to discover. *See also:* Gem; Gold; Expensive; Money; Discovering

Tree

You or your life. The idea of life or existence. Patience, endurance, or persistence through challenges. A long or gradual process. Strength. Branching out. **A tall, healthy tree** can represent a flourishing, vibrant life. **A diseased tree** might indicate a part of your life that needs special attention or seems out of balance. Consider also what comes to mind when you think of the particular tree, and its condition and setting. *See also:* Plant; Farming; Orchard; Root; Stem or Trunk; Leaf; Branch; Forest

Trembling

Trembling or shaking can represent real or perceived: Excitement. Fear or caution. Uncertainty. Sensitivity. Weakness or vulnerability. Delicacy. *See also:* Feeling; Earthquake; Moving Around

Trial

Justice. Authority. Judgment or accusation. Arguing. **Being on trial** can represent feeling or fearing scrutiny or judgment, perhaps due to a particular action you've taken or are considering. *See also:* Court; Court-room; Justice; Attorney; Judge; Jury

Triangle

Caution or yield. Change or transition. Balance, or the importance of it. The idea of three. An arrow indicating something in the dream that's important or worthy of your attention. *See also:* Three; Shape

Trickery

A feeling or fear of trickery or manipulation somewhere in your real life. Perceived questionable tendencies of a particular person. Trust issues (trusting too much or not enough somewhere in your life). A feeling of caution regarding the world or a particular aspect of it. *See also:* Lying; Betraying; Lied To, Being; Betrayed, Being; Fake; Secret; Magic

Trip or Vacation

An actual vacation or trip, or a desire for one (although the location in the dream may be different than in real life). A phase, process, or project in your life. Progress, self improvement, evolution, or another development in yourself or your life. The idea of escaping stress or your usual routine. A desire for adventure or new experiences. **A round-trip journey** can represent: revisiting the past or something from your past; returning to where you started in a process (such as returning to "square one," starting over, or coming full circle); going in circles in terms of your thinking or your actions. *See also:* Traveling; Driving; Adventure; Road; Following a Path; Visiting; Holiday; Honeymoon; Airplane; Boat

Tripping

A feeling or fear of: Being "tripped up." Experiencing a sudden challenge or obstacle. Someone finding a problem with something you're doing or planning. Getting in your own way or sabotaging yourself. Becoming distracted, off course, or neglectful. *See also:* Falling; Slipping

Tropical

A tropical setting can represent actual or imagined: Abundance. Adventure or excitement. The feeling of something or someplace exotic or different. Remoteness. The absence of society or its rules, conveniences, or protections. Consider also what the specific setting brings to mind for you. *See also:* Jungle; Hot; Wet; Weather

Trust

An issue of trust, trustworthiness, honesty, or loyalty can represent: Feeling (or wanting to feel) confidence or good will about a person or situation. Evaluating how trustworthy you think someone is in real life, or how trustworthy the world is in general. Questioning how much you can trust yourself (such as to be ethical, to be honest with yourself, or to follow through on commitments you've made to yourself). *See also:* Confiding; Admitting; Secret; Communication; Betraying; Betrayed, Being

Tulip

A cycle or a life cycle. A process of opening or unfolding. A recurring event or process. A particular time of year. A particular location. *See also:* Flower Bulb; Flower

Tumor

A personal issue that you feel you need to deal with. Something that's "eating at you" or gradually encroaching on you. A dynamic within your consciousness that you'd benefit from releasing (such as a judgment or self-defeating belief). Something problematic you've been holding onto, avoiding, denying, or ignoring a long time (such as a relationship issue or work-related problem). *See also:* Illness; Health

Tunnel

The idea of covert activity, or progress that's unseen by others. Accessing or dealing with issues that exist in your subconscious mind. A secret way to get from one place to another (literally or figuratively). A creative way around an obstacle or challenge (or a desire for one). *See also:* Passageway; Underground; Digging

Turkey

Expressing yourself or your feelings unabashedly. Staying within your social circle. The cycle of life. Gratitude. Celebration. Dreaming of this animal can represent too much or not enough of one of those qualities, or someone or something you associate with the quality or animal. Consider also the animal's actions, context, and your feelings about it. *See also:* Bird

Turning

A decision or decision point. The idea of making a change or a change in direction. **Someone turning their head and looking at you** might represent the idea of that person focusing their attention on you in real life. **Someone turning and looking away** might represent the idea of them taking focus off of you, such as leaving, ignoring, abandoning, or disapproving of you. For more clues, consider the context and the intent behind whatever is turning. *See also:* Corner; Traveling; Nodding; Watching; Rotating; Pivoting; Circles, Going in; Arrow

Turning Off

Switching something off (such as an appliance or computer) can represent: An ending, perhaps leading into a new beginning. An intention (such as to stop communicating or participating). **Turning off a light** can represent a desire to rest, end a process, or change or relax your mental focus. *See also:* Ending; Quitting; Light (Illumination)

Turning On

Switching something on (such as an appliance or computer) can represent: A beginning, perhaps after an ending of something else. An intention (such as to begin communicating or participating). **Turning on a light** can represent taking steps to gain clarity or information (as in "shedding light on" a particular matter). *See also:* Beginning; Starting an Engine; Light (Illumination)

Turtle

Self-protection, or an issue of personal boundaries. Strength of self. Hesitance to show your true self, or being careful whom you choose to trust. Isolating yourself, or a need for more time to yourself. Longevity. Patience, or persistence over time. Dreaming of this animal can represent too much or not enough of one of those qualities, or someone or something you associate with the quality or animal. Consider also the animal's actions, context, and your feelings about it. *See also:* Animal; Shell

TV

An actual TV or another type of media. Public media or mass communication. Your connection or interaction with the world, people, places, or experiences, especially in a detached way (since a TV allows only one-way, passive interaction). A screen on which the dream story plays out, perhaps indicating that what's on the screen is especially important to you right now or that it's a "what if" scenario created by your subconscious mind. *See also:* Watching; Show or Movie; Video; Video Recorder; Media; TV, Being On

TV, Being On

You appearing on a TV show, movie, or video can represent: A feeling or fear of being in the spotlight, vulnerable, or "on display." A feeling of or desire for love, positive attention, respect, validation, appreciation, acceptance, or acknowledgment of your specialness or talents. The idea of connecting with others. Sharing (or over-sharing). Fun, adventure, or a desire to try something new. *See also:* Video; Stage or Screen; Theater;

Audience; Arena or Auditorium; Performing; Show or Movie; Talk Show; Celebrity

Tweezers

Attention to detail, or a situation that demands such. The idea of perfection, or focusing too much on trying to achieve it. The idea of removing nuisances from your life. *See also:* Fragment; Scissors; Size; Eyebrow; Hair; Shaving

Twilight

An ending (of a phase, project, process, relationship, etc.). Finishing or completing something. A beginning (since twilight is the beginning of the night). Darkness, or something it represents to you. *See also:* Sunset; Evening; Night; Star; Time of Day; Darkness

Twins

A bond or feeling of closeness (emotional, mental, familial, marital, friendship, etc.), or a desire for it. A perceived similarity between two people or things (similar qualities, situations, etc.). The idea of "double" or perhaps "too much" (such as of work or responsibility). **Identical twins** can also represent: a copy, or the idea of copying; a mirror image or reflection; something mirrored back to you by someone else (such as your mood, attitude, or a characteristic). *See also:* Two; Many; Copying

Two

A connection or partnership (such as a friendship or other relationship). Companionship or the idea of not being alone. A commitment between two people or parties. Support (personal, spiritual, etc.). Something else you associate with two, such as a time frame, someone's age, or your parents. *See also:* Number; Relationship; Second Place

Tying

Security, or a desire for it. Connecting two or more things (or people) together. Creating a relationship or bond. Organizing or "neatening up" (yourself or your thoughts, life, priorities, etc.). Preparing, or taking care of details. *See also:* Knot; Rope; String; Joining; Joining Together; Attached; Sewing

Typing

Communication (real or imagined). A need to express thoughts or feelings to yourself or to someone else. Having a story you'd like to share. **Typing within a work environment** could represent your real-life work situation, even if typing isn't part of your job. Consider also the context, content, sender, recipient, and motivation. *See also:* Writing; Words; Email; Texting; Computer

UFO

Someone or something who seems different or comes from a different background. Something that you don't know, don't understand, or is strange or new to you. The unknown. An unknown or feared power or authority. *See also:* Alien; Space, Outer; Rocket; Airplane; Unknown Thing

Uncle

A real-life uncle. Someone who reminds you of an uncle (such as older, wiser, kind, protective, or trustworthy). Consider what comes to mind when you think of an uncle or the particular uncle in your dream. *See also:* Family; Person You Know

Under

Below something or someone. Being or feeling subordinate to someone or something. Something judged as inferior or unworthy. Subject to an activity or process (as in "under observation," "under surveillance," or "under investigation"). Covered, obscured, hidden, or secret (as in "under wraps"). More basic, or something that serves as a foundation for something else. *See also:* Low; Cover; Hiding; Inferior; Descending; Bottom

Underground

Hidden or secret. Something of which you are (or someone else is) unaware. A stealthy activity (real or imagined). Hiding or burying (or a desire to do so). An activity or dynamic within your subconscious mind. Discovering or suddenly understanding something. Consider what was going on underground and your feelings about it. *See also:* Under; Hiding; Burying; Basement; Ground; Hole; Digging; Low; Secret

Underwater

Subconscious. Hidden or unknown. "Other worldly" or detached from reality. A desire to escape reality or take a break. The environment of your inner life at the time of the dream (for example, clear water might represent mental clarity, or murky water might represent confusion). Acting or thriving outside your comfort zone (since water is outside of a human's usual air-based environment). **Being able to breath underwater** can represent: an ability to thrive in a challenging environment; a feeling of invincibility, power, uniqueness, or specialness (or a desire for such). **Panicking underwater** can represent a feeling or fear of overwhelm, losing control, or mental or emotional smothering. *See also:* Swimming; Diving; Water; Water, Body of; Flood; Drowning

Underwear

Something that's not intended for public knowledge (personal matters, thoughts, feelings, motivations, etc.). Vulnerability or emotional risk. **Discovering you're wearing only your underwear in public** can represent a feeling or fear of judgment, embarrassment, or other negative attention. *See also:* Exposed (Body); Naked; Clothes; Nightclothes

Undressing

The idea of open and honest communication. The idea of revealing information, feelings, truths, or something else about yourself. Willingness to take an emotional risk or make yourself vulnerable in a beneficial way (such as in the process of building trust). **Someone else undressing in an uninvited way** can represent a real or feared intrusion compromising your boundaries or integrity. *See also:* Underwear; Naked; Clothes; Privacy

Unfeeling

Someone who seems unfeeling or lacking compassion could represent: A feeling or fear of emotional pain. Perceived lack of compassion, humanity, or understanding somewhere in your life (or perhaps within yourself). A desire to not feel emotion (or a certain emotion). Emotional numbness or exhaustion. The idea of hiding your feelings, reactions, or caring. *See also:* Feeling; Hurt, Being; Attacking; Bully

Unicorn

Rarity, or a rare experience. Purity or innocence. Integrity or high personal standards. A magical feeling, or a wish for a magical or enchanting experience. Consider also what unicorns bring to mind for you specifically. *See also:* Mythological Character; Horse

Unknown Thing

Something that is unknown, unfamiliar, or unidentifiable can represent: Something or someone in your real life you'd like to understand better. A vague feeling, thought, or idea within yourself. A perceived or feared threat somewhere in your life. Consider what stood out about the unknown thing and your feelings about it. *See also:* Object; New; Weird; Hiding; Code; Puzzle; Riddle; Person Unknown

Unlocking

Access or permission. Authority, or giving someone authority. Acceptance. Openness. Allowing yourself to become more vulnerable with others. An issue involving personal boundaries. Solving a problem, mystery, or something puzzling. **Secretly unlocking something that belongs to someone else** can represent taking advantage of or not being completely honest with someone in real life (or perhaps you don't trust them). *See also:* Opening; Door or Entrance; Key; Keyhole; Security; Privacy; Login

Unstable

Something unstable (such as quicksand or a rickety bridge) can represent: Risk, or fear of risk. Feeling unsteady or unsure somehow in your life. Something or someone you feel or fear is unpredictable (a precarious situation, unreliable person, etc.). Lacking confidence or understanding. Feeling "shaken up" or upset about something in your life. A sense of mental or emotional unsteadiness (such as doubt, confusion, or a questionable decision). *See also:* Erratic; Earthquake Quicksand; Descending; Feeling; Mentally Unstable

Upstairs

The top floor (or an upper floor) in a house or building can represent: Your spirituality or the spiritual aspects of your life. Higher wisdom. Greater insight or perspective. *See also:* Floor; Stairs; Climbing; Ceiling; High; Above; Top

Urinating

Letting go of what you no longer need. Getting rid of what you consider undesirable or unwanted. The ending of a process. Expressing something outwardly, perhaps to "get it out of your system" (such as feelings or opinions). Channeling negativity or destructive expression (disrespect, hostility, etc.) into the world. *See also:* Toilet; Bathroom; Kidney

Vaccine

Guarding or strengthening yourself against attack or intrusion. Protection or insurance. Preparing for the future. Preemptive action to avoid a problem later. A feeling or fear of attack somewhere in your life. *See also:* Injection

Vacuum

A space that has a reduced internal pressure (such as a depressurized room or a black hole) can represent: Real or perceived lack. The desire for less of something or to keep something out. Emptiness or nothingness (such as the experience of emotional or mental emptiness). *See also:* Empty; Hole; Sucking; Cleaning

Valley

Safety, security, or protection. Peacefulness. Fertility or lushness. Easy progress or passage to the next place or phase in your life. A lull in a process (as in experiencing "peaks and valleys"). *See also:* Bottom; Abyss; Flow or River; Drain; Ledge or Cliff; Waves

Valve

Permission, or control of a boundary (since a valve is what allows or disallows fluid to pass through). Regulation of a flow (such as of emotions or a process). Control of flow, including stopping, starting, or regulating how fast something is allowed to proceed. Consider also the context, role, and condition of the valve (for example, a steam exhaust valve might represent control over one's anger, while a broken valve might represent someone who's ineffectively managing a process). *See also:* Vent; Faucet; Door or Entrance; Flow or River; Water; Controlling

Vampire

A real or feared threat in your life. The idea of someone taking advantage of you or taking something from you (such as your time, energy, effort, attention, personal space, or integrity). Someone taking without giving back. A person or group you perceive as greedy or self-serving. The idea of controlling or possessing. *See also:* Sucking; Attacking; Monster; Mythological Character

Variety

The idea of having a variety or range of things somewhere in your life (people, opportunities, ideas, etc.). Having a number of options to consider. Abundance. A desire for inspiration, newness, adventure, excitement, or stimulation (as in having a variety of experiences). *See also:* Group; Many; Different; Changing; Altering; Mixing

Vehicle

The means by which you move forward in your life (where traveling in the vehicle represents your movement forward through time). **Other people in the vehicle** can represent individuals around you in real life, or just people in the world in general. **Being in a vehicle with other people** can represent a recent or imagined shared situation (for example, a dream about traveling on a bus with a bunch of playful monkeys might represent your child's birthday party last week). Consider also the characteristics of the vehicle (for example, an expensive car might represent abundance or pretense, a damaged vehicle might represent a feeling of vulnerability or carelessness, and a dump truck might represent clearing out your to-do list or handling a messy situation). See also the specific type of vehicle. *See also:* Driving; Traveling; Riding; Trip or Vacation; Wheel; Steering; Accelerator; Traffic; License Plate; Engine; Brakes; Fuel; Headlight; Back Seat

Veil

Hiding or obscuring. Protection. Innocence. Femininity. An issue relating to a particular role, rule, or tradition. Anticipating, desiring, or fearing a particular real-life event. Consider also the type of veil, its context and purpose, and your feelings about it. *See also:* Scarf; Cover; Bride; Wedding Dress; Wedding; Hat; Crown

Vein

A vein or artery can represent: Life force, or the state of being alive. Richness or abundance. Communication. Providing, giving, or nourishing. Interconnection within a group. Your connection with yourself, or your inner awareness. Inner peace or harmony. *See also:* Blood

Vent

An opening that vents (such as to release exhaust or steam) can represent: Your or someone else's process of venting energy, anger, frustration, negativity, etc. (or a need to vent such). The ability to control a process that could otherwise be destructive (as in venting steam to avoid an explosion). The idea of dissipation, loss, or waste. *See also:* Exhaust; Pipe; Hole; Valve

Video

Communication, connection, or attention (real, desired, or feared). A focus on whatever the subject of the video represents (perhaps because you consider it important or you want to remember it). Consider what was going on in the video, its context, and your feelings about it. *See also:* Show or Movie; TV; TV, Being On; Camera; Photo; Internet; Video Recorder; Camera

Video Game

A real-life game. A real-life activity or environment that feels like a game somehow (it's competitive, presents one challenge after another, requires progressive levels of skill, requires concentration, etc.). Fun, excitement, or distraction (or a desire for such). *See also:* Arcade; Game; Pretending

Video Recorder

A video recorder (such as a DVR) can represent: Memory. A need or desire to remember or preserve something for later (perhaps because it's important, you like it, or you want to revisit it later). Delayed gratification. Control of your environment or schedule, or the idea of doing something "on your own terms." Creating environments you like or participating in activities you enjoy. *See also:* Camera; TV; Show or Movie

Vine

An ability to adapt to your environment (as you change, or as it changes). Using external resources to your advantage. Someone or something insidiously creeping, sneaking, or insinuating its way into something (or into everything). Taking over an area, process, etc. Covering up or obscuring (as a vine might cover a building). *See also:* Plant; Leaf; Sprout; Thicket

Violence

Violence (or people who commit violence) can represent: A feeling or fear of threat, persecution, aggression, criticism, your boundaries being violated, or your integrity being compromised. A fear of whatever is being attacked. Perceiving that the attacker feels hostility or intolerance for whatever they're attacking. Feeling or perceiving a lack of compassion, understanding, reverence, or respect of others. Focusing on the negativity in the world. An indication that you were having a Toxic Dream (p. 320). *See also:* Crime; Fight; Killing; Attacking; Invading; Killed, Being; Attacked, Being; Invaded, Being; Bully; Threat; Menacing; Arguing; Revenge

Virus

A feeling or fear of intrusion (into your life, mind, personal space, integrity, etc.). A perceived or feared challenge of some kind. An inner conflict. Something or someone taking over or taking control away from you, commandeering the way you think, or using something of yours against you (such as your tendencies, judgments, etc.). A perceived or imagined imbalance (emotional, mental, or physical). The idea of something "going viral" (such as a video on social media). Something mentally "contagious" (such as gossip, a belief, or a judgment) or emotionally "contagious" (such as anger). *See also:* Illness; Infection; Rash; Wart; Germs

Vision

Vision or eyesight can represent: Observation or watching. The ability to see or understand. Having vision, an elevated perspective, or an ability to see the bigger picture. Inner wisdom or knowing. A connection with God (a higher power). The idea of being a visionary, or planning for the future with creativity or resourcefulness. *See also:* Eye; Seeing; Blinking; Glasses (Eyeglasses); Blind; Sensory Cues (the category)

Visiting

Visiting a place or a person can represent an actual, desired, or imagined experience with that place or person (or with something the place or person represents). For more clues, consider your motivation for and feelings about the visit. *See also:* Guest; Traveling; Trip or Vacation; Staying; Seeing; Meeting; Arriving; Returning; Appointment

Vivid Color

A vivid or intense color can represent a large amount or a strong feeling of whatever the particular color represents. For example, a vivid red could represent extreme rage or a strong sense of danger. An intense yellow could represent intense happiness. See also the specific color. *See also:* Color

Voice

Expressing or communicating, or the ability or willingness to do so. A person's identity, personality, uniqueness, or personal power. *See also:* Communication; Singing; Whisper; Can't Speak; Throat; Mouth

Voicemail

Someone's voicemail answering when you call them can represent: An inability to communicate or difficult communication. Physical, emotional, or mental unavailability of someone. Having trouble being heard, getting a point across, or getting a message through to someone. A need for communication in order to resolve an issue. *See also:* Communication; Phone; Voice; Email

Vomiting

A desire to get rid of something in your life or mind (perhaps because it's overloading you or because it's mentally or emotionally toxic). Unable or refusing to accept something in your life (a situation, change, decision, etc.). Feeling "sick of" something in your life. *See also:* Illness; Rejection

Vulture

Finding and taking advantage of opportunities. Issues regarding receiving from others and taking from others. The cycle of life. The idea of recycling, reusing, or repurposing (an object, an ability, yourself, someone else, etc.). Finding value in what others offer or make available. An ending that makes a new beginning possible. Dreaming of this animal can represent too much or not enough of one of those qualities, or someone or something you associate with the quality or animal. Consider also the animal's actions, context, and your feelings about it. *See also:* Bird

Waiting

A real, imagined, or feared situation that involves waiting or delayed gratification. For more clues, consider the context, what you're waiting for and why, and your feelings about waiting. *See also:* Staying; Last Minute; Hesitating

Waking Up

Dreaming that you're waking up (when you're actually still asleep) can indicate that you're not getting good quality sleep or that you were having a Toxic Dream (p. 320). **Dreaming that it's morning and you're going about the day's activities (when you're actually still asleep)** could mean you're subconsciously "rehearsing" something ahead of time because you're worried or because it feels important. **Dreaming that you're sleeping and can't get yourself to wake up** can be an indication of a Toxic Dream, or it can represent: denial or a hesitance to accept reality; worry about an important task; the importance of waking up on time. *See also:* Alert; Asleep

Walking

Getting from one place to another in your life (literally or figuratively). Moving forward along your life path or along a timeline in your life. The way you progress through a particular aspect of your life (a phase, relationship, project, etc.). "Getting ahead" or achieving. A real-life or imagined activity (such as an actual walk or hiking the Appalachian Trail). Consider the context, the origin and destination, and your feelings about walking. *See also:* Traveling; Visiting; Following a Path; Road; Carrying

Wallet

Your financial responsibility or well-being. Your ability to acquire things or experiences in the world. **Losing your wallet** can represent feeling a need to pay more attention to your financial responsibilities. **Someone stealing your wallet** can represent a feeling or fear of someone trying to take advantage of you (possibly financially) in a dishonest or sneaky way. *See also:* Money; Driver's License; Bag; Key

Wanting

Wanting desiring, or being attracted to something can represent: A desire for something or someone the thing represents. A desire for the experience or the feelings you think the thing would provide you. Feeling deprived or lacking. A desire for power, control, possession, or some other mental or emotional experience. *See also:* Demanding; Scarcity; Attractive; Stalking; Crush, Having a

Warm

Warm weather or feeling warm can represent a feeling of or desire for: Love, compassion, or "good will." Pleasantness, comfort, or good times. Security, safety, or the idea of "home." *See also:* Hot; Friendly; Soft

Warning

A warning or a caution sign can represent: A warning you encountered in real life. A feeling or fear of a threat (physical, emotional, or mental). The idea of proceeding cautiously with a particular decision or course of action in your real life. *See also:* Threat; Future; Telling on Someone

Wart

The idea of accepting yourself as you are, or someone else as they are. Something you find unique or interesting about a person or their personality. A judgment, or labelling something as imperfect. *See also:* Virus; Infection; Rash; Skin

Washing Machine

A fresh start, or a desire for one. The idea of cleaning up your or someone else's mess (a problem, neglected responsibility, etc.). A cycle, or a repeating or circular process. Letting go of the past or reaching closure in some area of your life (as a washing machine removes evidence of the past from your clothing). Repairing a relationship or situation, or making amends for past actions. *See also:* Appliance; Cleaning; Water; Soap; Dirt; Bucket or Basket; Drain

Washing Yourself

A fresh start or a new beginning (or a desire for one). "Washing away" something unwanted (such as nuisances or self-defeating thoughts). A desire or need to "clean house" in your physical house, your consciousness, or elsewhere in your life (such as releasing limiting patterns or destructive habits). *See also:* Bathtub or Shower; Cleaning; Soap; Water; Drain

Wasp

Strong and immediate self-defense. An underestimated or hidden danger. Fear, perhaps of attack or persecution. The power of anger. The power that you allow other people's anger to have over you. Dreaming of this insect can represent too much or not enough of one of those qualities, or someone or something you associate with the quality. Consider also the insect's actions, context, and your feelings about it. *See also:* Sting; Insect; Bee

Watch (Jewelry)

Time, the passage of time, or a concern about time. The idea of limited time or not enough time. The idea of having to wait or having too much time on your hands. The importance you place on being on time. The need to adhere to a schedule, or wishing you didn't have to. Consider also the context and characteristics of the watch, how the wearer was using it, and how you felt about it. *See also:* Time; Time of Day; Time Passing; Jewelry

Watching

Supervising or watching out for someone or something. Observing rather than participating. Keeping an objective or neutral perspective. Curiosity or a desire to understand whatever was represented by what you were watching. **Being watched by someone else** can represent a feeling of self-consciousness; an awareness or fear of being observed by others; a heightened concern about others' opinions or motives somehow in your life; a desire for more privacy or alone time. *See also:* Seeing; Stalking; Listening; Telescope; Babysitter

Water

Satisfaction or quenching. Ability to adapt or accommodate (as water assumes the shape of its container). Pervasiveness or ability to have far reaching effects (as water naturally flows and spreads into its surroundings). Consider also the context and action of the water and how you felt about it. **Water that's flowing or changing shape** can represent change, transformation, or moving forward in your life (whether or not it's under your control). *See also:* Water, Body of; Flow or River; Watering; Wet; Liquid; Flood; Bucket or Basket; Underwater; Drain; Well; Faucet

Water, Body of

A body of water such as an ocean, lake, or pond can represent: The context of your life, "your world," or the setting and situations within which the your life takes place. Your emotions or inner state (turbulence, tranquility, etc.). The unknown. An area that you feel holds secrets (perhaps within yourself). **Swimming or floating in a body of water** can represent freedom from your usual limitations or stresses. **A body of water rising over your head** (or you being pulled under water) can represent a feeling of overwhelm or "trying to stay afloat" in real life. **A calm body**

of water can represent peace or relaxation. For more clues, consider the context and condition of the water. *See also:* Water; Waves; Flow or River; Swimming; Floating; Underwater; Flood; Pool

Watering

Watering plants (with a watering can, sprinkler, etc.) could represent: Abundance. Assistance. Physical, emotional, mental, or spiritual nourishment. Satisfaction. A process that delivers something that's needed. A delivery channel for something tangible or intangible. A connection, route, or pathway. *See also:* Plant; Hose; Water; Wet; Rain; Garden; Lawn

Waves

Waves on a body of water can represent: Power, energy, nature, or the force of nature. Rhythm or cycles. Progress or movement forward. The idea of being carried along in life, making things easy for you. **Regular waves (one right after another)** can represent: repetition, consistency, reliability, or predictability; a series of events in your real life. **Turbulent waves** can represent a feeling or fear of challenges, obstacles, overwhelm, chaos, turbulence, or loss of control due to external forces. **One huge wave** could represent sudden overwhelm or a sudden challenge in your life. *See also:* Water, Body of; Flow or River; Swirl or Eddy

Weapon

A weapon or ammunition can represent power or a wish for power. Consider the context and motivation, which can provide clues to what the weapon represents (powerlessness, fear, insecurity, frustration, self-defense, aggression, a desire to be heard, etc.). **A weapon used with the intent to take advantage of others** can represent a feeling or fear of ill will, disrespect, victimizing, or taking from others tangibly or intangibly (time, energy, effort, etc.), such as your boss using authority as a "weapon" to demand you work extra hours without pay. *See also:* Knife; Sword; Stick; Attacking; Killing; Violence; Terrorism; Fight; Crime; Criminal

Weasel

Cleverness. Resourcefulness. Able to "wiggle away" from danger or talk your way out of a challenging situation. Changing back and forth or taking both sides (as in an argument). Changing according to the situation or needs. Dreaming of this animal can represent too much or not enough of one of those qualities, or someone or something you associate with the quality or animal. Consider also the animal's actions, context, and your feelings about it. *See also:* Animal; Beaver; Badger

Weather

Mood or emotion. The "conditions" in your life or the "climate" within your consciousness, from the point of view of your subconscious mind. Your current feelings about a past, current, or future situation. Your mood during a past real-life event (such as a sunny day representing your "sunny" mood at a party last weekend). The mood in a particular group or social environment (such as a hurricane representing your project team's chaotic mood during last week's crisis). **Unpleasant weather** can represent a challenge in your life or unpleasant feelings (angry, sad, etc.). **Fair weather** can represent well-being or a sense of things going well in your life. *See also:* Sunny; Cloud; Sky; Cold; Warm; Hot; Rain; Snow; Hail; Wind; Storm; Lightning; Thunder; Tornado; Hurricane; Flood

Weaving or Spinning

A process, activity, or project in which something is created (such as art, music, construction, or building a relationship). The idea of making something out of nothing (or out of very little). Complexity, or components that "weave together" or "work together" in harmony. Uniting or joining things together. The idea that the whole is greater than the sum of its parts. *See also:* Woven; Yarn; Knitting; Sewing

Web

A spider web can represent: A desire to "catch," keep, or remember something (an opportunity, experience, etc.). A perceived trap, or a feeling or fear of being trapped or manipulated. A business or money-making endeavor. Random searching (as a web catches anything that comes along). **Cobwebs** can represent neglect, emptiness, unoccupied, unused, or an eerie feeling. *See also:* Net; Spider; Trapped; Hunting; Woven; Weaving or Spinning; Internet

Wedding

A commitment, agreement, or promise anywhere in your life (romantic or otherwise). A wedding, party, family gathering, or other event (real or imagined). A milestone in a romantic relationship. The idea of teamwork, joining two things together, or merging two separate processes. **Participating in someone else's wedding** might represent an actual wedding or other event, or your feelings about the couple's real-life relationship. **You getting married** can represent: the idea of a commitment or new beginning (romantic or otherwise); being in a marriage or other commitment with someone (or an imagined version of that); feeling "put on the spot" or the center of attention; the closeness you have (or had) in a certain relationship. Consider also the context, participants, and your

338

feelings. *See also:* Marriage; Special Occasion; Ritual or Tradition; Relationship; Bride; Groom; Church; Wedding Dress; Ring (Jewelry); Honeymoon; Engagement; Proposal

Wedding Dress

Wearing or trying on a wedding dress (or veil) can represent: The idea of your own wedding (such as remembering or imagining your real wedding, or exploring the idea of marriage and what it means to you). Your role in a marriage or other partnership (romantic or otherwise). A commitment you've made or are considering (romantic or otherwise). Exploring the fullness of being a woman, and all that it involves in your culture (such as women's roles, society's views of women, a partner's expectations, or expectations you have for yourself or for someone in your life). *See also:* Veil; Wedding; Bride; Clothes

Weed

Something you consider unwanted, undesirable, extraneous, or invasive. Something or someone whose value or beauty you're having trouble seeing. Dynamics that are cluttering your consciousness (such as self-defeating beliefs, negative self-talk, or judgments). Unwanted elements cluttering your outer environment (such as noise, objects, or unpleasant people). *See also:* Offensive or Ugly; Garden; Plant; Drug

Weird

Something that seems weird or doesn't make sense can represent: The characteristic that makes it seem odd (such as the crookedness of a crooked road representing a complex process, or a strange language representing difficulty communicating with someone). Something in real life that doesn't make sense to you or that your subconscious mind is trying to understand. Someone or something in real life that you consider weird or different. The unknown, or a fear of the unknown. A fear or judgment of something or someone that seems different. *See also:* Different; Changing; Inferior; Mentally Unstable; Right or Wrong; Abuse; Deformity; Offensive or Ugly; Paranormal; Unknown Thing; Person Unknown; New

Well

A well or cistern can represent: Abundance, or a seemingly infinite supply (of wisdom, patience, money, etc.). Sustenance. A source of something you consider critical for physical, emotional, or mental survival. *See also:* Water; Fountain; Drinking; Hole; Health

Werewolf

A mood or personality shift (or frequent ones). A feeling or fear of losing control, aggression, or attack. Wildness or chaos. *See also:* Monster; Mythological Character

Wet

Wetness (such as on a sidewalk or other surface) could represent: Abundance. Clean. The idea of a fresh start. Slipperiness, danger, threat, or a reason to proceed with caution. Being "brought down to Earth" or to reality. **Dealing with water and trying not to get wet** (such as walking in the rain or carrying a bucket of water) can represent a feeling or fear of messiness, nuisance, or discomfort (physical, emotional, or mental). **Being afraid to get wet or get into water** can represent a fear of trying something new or of getting involved in something (as in afraid of "dipping your toe into the water"). *See also:* Water; Cleaning; Water, Body of; Watering; Rain; Liquid; Hose; Pipe; Flood; Bucket or Basket; Towel

Whale

Wisdom or intuition. A large personality or presence. Grandiosity or a grand gesture. Authentic personal power. Integrity. Good will. The subconscious mind. Dreaming of this animal can represent too much or not enough of one of those qualities, or someone or something you associate with the quality or animal. Consider also the animal's actions, context, and your feelings about it. *See also:* Animal; Fish; Dolphin

Wheel

A wheel or tire can represent: Easy progress. The ease with which you move forward and accomplish things in your life. The things you do day-to-day to "smooth the way" for progress or achievement (such as planning ahead, working efficiently, acting effectively, or making sure you're "on track"). It idea of "where the rubber meets the road" (as in when something is really put to the test, when a plan is implemented, or where the real work gets done). *See also:* Vehicle; Road

Wheelchair

Being in a wheelchair (when you don't use one in real life) can represent: Support or help moving through a period of your life, especially assistance getting through challenges or "making the road smoother." Feeling challenged or "disabled" in making progress somewhere in your life. Using tips, tricks, technology, or other means of making life or a certain process easier. Feeling a need for things to be easier for a while. *See also:* Crutch; Disabled; Can't Move; Walking; Leg

Whisper

Gentleness. Thoughtfulness (so as not to bother or wake someone). Someone or something you perceive as secretive, discreet, stealthy, or hiding something. Caution (or feeling a need for it). Wanting to get someone's attention. A subtle message (whether in spoken, written, or body language). *See also:* Hiding; Secret; Voice; Quiet

White

Purity. Peace or acceptance. Love. Potential (such as to become anything or fit in anywhere). A chance to start again, or a "clean slate." A blank feeling. Pale or weak. A washout or whiteout. Surrender. *See also:* Pale; Color; Bleach; Light (Spiritual)

Wig

A wig, hairpiece, or other fake hair can represent: A desire to feel different than others, the same as others, or better about yourself (depending on the type of wig and why the person is wearing it). The idea of obscuring or covering up your real self or personality (possibly due to shame, feeling inferior, or a desire to be accepted or to project a different image). Disguise or secrecy. An attempt to control others' reactions to you. A desire for fun, adventure, variety, a temporary change, or to express yourself differently than usual. Taking a shortcut or wanting to save time somewhere in your life (since a wig is a hairstyle "shortcut"). *See also:* Hair; Fake; Shaving; Scalp; Cover

Wild

Something wild (such as an animal or a wilderness area) might represent: Untouched or unaffected by society or its rules. Instincts, unpredictability, or other characteristics you associate with being wild. *See also:* Chaos

Wind

A wind blowing can represent: Change. Power, force, or energy. A dynamic or movement within your life or consciousness (real, desired or feared). An action taken in response to pressure (since wind occurs as air flows from a high pressure area to a lower pressure area). Unseen forces that you perceive or imagine to help or hinder (such as God, luck, or fate). Challenging forces or factors in your life (such as frustrations or nuisances). Chaos or a loss of control. Something that's moving forward (such as a process, a series of events, or the passing of time). *See also:* Flow or River; Air; Weather; Storm; Tornado; Hurricane

Window

Your view of the world around you. The way you view or perceive people, events, and situations in your life. **Being in a house full of windows** can represent: feeling vulnerable or exposed; feeling very open to the world around you. **Being in a house with very few windows** can represent: isolation from others or the rest of the world (or a desire for that). **Dirty windows or a window washer** can represent an unclear or limited view of something in your life; an opportunity to improve your interaction with the world or with people around you. *See also:* Glass; Transparent; Curtain; House

Windshield

Looking toward the future in your life. An ability to see what's coming in life (as a windshield allows you to see what's coming on the road ahead). **An obscured windshield** might represent: feeling unclear about your future or the path to take; lacking the information you need to make well-informed decisions. *See also:* Window; Glass; Car; Driving

Winning

Success or recognition (or a desire for such). **Winning a competition** can represent the idea of excelling or doing well, or mentally preparing to do so. **Winning money, prizes, or gifts** can represent: abundance or a feeling of lack; feeling fortunate in your life; recognizing someone's generosity. *See also:* Succeeding; Second Place; Surviving; Event; Receiving; Luck

Winter

Something you associate with winter (a time frame, event, place, person, etc.). Cold or harshness. Challenges, hard times, or having to do without something. Less activity (as cold involves molecules vibrating more slowly), sleep, rest, or hibernation. Indoor activities. Celebration or spirituality (as in winter's many celebrations). Snow- or ice-related activities. Consider also the context, events, and what winter means to you personally. *See also:* Time of Year; Time Frame; Cold; Ice; Snow; Resting; Weather

Wire

Connection. Communication. Joining or binding together. For more clues, consider the type, purpose, and context of the wire. *See also:* Electricity; Communication; Joining Together; Attached; Tying; Metal

Witch

Being a witch or wizard can represent: Feeling powerful or powerless somehow in your life. A particular situation in which you're feeling challenged or you'd like to have more power or assistance. A desire for more freedom or autonomy in your life, perhaps an attempt to rebel against an authority figure. Consider also the type of witch, spells, or powers (for example, correcting a wrong could represent a desire to do the right thing, controlling people or situations might represent a desire for change, and the power to disappear could represent a wish to "escape" a responsibility or rule). **A witch coming after you** can represent a feeling or fear of victimization or manipulation somewhere in your life. **Someone accusing you of being a witch** can represent a feeling or fear of being falsely accused or persecuted. *See also:* Magic; Spell; Curse; Powers; Monster

Wolf

Fearlessness. Tenacity. Being proactive. Loyalty or steadfastness. Family, connection, or mutual support. Wildness or freedom. Spirit, essence, or spirituality. Dreaming of this animal can represent too much or not enough of one of those qualities, or someone or something you associate with the quality or animal. Consider also the animal's actions, context, and your feelings about it. *See also:* Animal; Dog; Coyote

Wolverine

Strength. Ferocity or tenacity. Consumption (such as of food, products, or attention). Ambition. Ability or desire to survive. Dreaming of this animal can represent too much or not enough of one of those qualities, or someone or something you associate with the quality or animal. Consider also the animal's actions, context, and your feelings about it. *See also:* Animal; Badger; Bear

Woman

Someone you know in real life, or the role she plays in your life (supervisor, mother, friend, doctor, etc.). A characteristic that stood out about the woman (such as strength, humor, or intelligence). Stereotypical feminine characteristics, personality traits, interests, abilities, etc. For more clues, consider the context of the woman and your feelings about her. *See also:* Female; Person You Know; Person Unknown

Wombat

"Chewing through" or working through problems. Protection (such as of self, family, home, or work) by keeping out of view or out of others'

343

awareness. The idea of going backward or doing things backward, possibly to your benefit or to the benefit of others. Dreaming of this animal can represent too much or not enough of one of those qualities, or someone or something you associate with the quality or animal. Consider also the animal's actions, context, and your feelings about it. *See also:* Animal; Groundhog; Opossum; Beaver

Wood

A piece of wood or an object made of wood might represent: Nature or the outdoors. The cycle of life. The result or output of a process. Fuel, or an input to a process. Fake (as in a "wooden expression"). A tool or something that could be used as a tool. A substitute for something real (as in a duck decoy). Something perceived as numb, dead, or lifeless. Also consider the condition and characteristics of the wood and what they bring to mind. *See also:* Tree; Stick; Branch; Stem or Trunk; Forest

Woodpecker

Determination. Perseverance. Consistency, or consistent progress toward a goal. Annoying or intrusive behavior. "Looking below the surface" for something meaningful or useful. Dreaming of this animal can represent too much or not enough of one of those qualities, or someone or something you associate with the quality or animal. Consider also the animal's actions, context, and your feelings about it. *See also:* Bird

Words

Seeing or hearing words can mean: Communication is on your mind (perhaps because there's something you want to say or hear). Your mind is in "reading mode" or "busy mode" (such as when you've been reading a lot earlier in the day). Sometimes words show up when you're dropping off to sleep or waking up that can seem important at the time, although they often have no significant meaning. *See also:* Communication; Text; Noise; Name; Garbled; Hearing; Song; Writing; Language; Typing; Words and Numbers (the category)

Working

Working during a dream can represent: Feeling like you've been busy or working hard (perhaps too hard) in real life, even in non-job related activities. A problem, challenge, or project that's on your mind. Wanting or needing to be productive right now. *See also:* Job; Workplace; Manager; Coworker; Task; Meeting; Homework; Phase or Process

Workplace

The "work" aspect of your life. Your real-life work or job (even if the dream workplace doesn't resemble your actual workplace). The idea of working or being productive. The idea of your job status (such as having one, not having one, needing one, or getting one). Your relationships at work, or people you know there. *See also:* Business; Building; Factory; Working; Job; Coworker

World

The world (or another world) can represent: The Earth. The people in the world, or people in general. A particular environment. Your personal world with which you interact regularly (people you know, places you go, etc.), or your experience of it. Another setting within your real or imagined experience. *See also:* Person You Know; Person Unknown; Location; Landscape; Mythological Place

Worm

Something you perceive as a basic or low-level form of life. The ability to conform or adapt to situations. Keeping your head down, or going about your business unseen. Working your way through obstacles or problems, or "biting off" only a little at a time. **A mass of worms** could represent something complicated, or lots of little problems (as in "opening a can of worms"). Dreaming of this animal can represent too much or not enough of one of those qualities, or someone or something you associate with the quality or animal. Consider also the animal's actions, context, and your feelings about it. *See also:* Animal; Parasite; Centipede; Snake; Eel

Woven

In a woven object (such as fabric or a tapestry), the weaving can represent: Something organized or regular in your life. Taking an organized or systematic approach in a particular task or way of thinking. The idea of the whole being greater than the sum of its parts. The idea of focusing on the "big picture" or focusing on the details (as in viewing the whole scene portrayed by a tapestry, or focusing on its individual threads). *See also:* Fabric; Thread; Weaving or Spinning; Mixing; Making or Building

Wren

Resourcefulness, strength in one's own self, or a "can do" attitude. The idea of doing great things or making your voice heard regardless of your life situation. Optimism or cheerfulness. Activity or busy-ness. Dreaming of this animal can represent too much or not enough of one of those qualities, or someone or something you associate with the quality or animal. Consider also the animal's actions, context, and your feelings about it. *See also:* Bird

Wrinkle

A challenge or complication in a process. Something you perceive as an imperfection. A perceived sign of usage (or even neglect). An action that requires further action to undo or fix it. **A person with wrinkled skin** can represent: aging or old age (or your feelings about it) or a specific older person in your life. *See also:* Iron; Problem; Blockage or Obstacle; Age; Aging; Skin

Wrist

Flexibility or adaptability, such as to different situations or requirements. Sensitivity or vulnerability (physical, emotional, or mental). A connection between things (as the wrist connects the hand and the arm). *See also:* Hand; Arm

Writing

Communication. Expression. Creativity. **Writing words** can represent: Expressing something (thoughts, feelings, opinions, etc.), or fearing or desiring the expression of something. Recording or noting something, or a desire to remember or preserve something. **Writing music** can represent: communication; inspiration; expressing yourself (or a desire to do so); creating something where there was nothing; creating something new from existing things or within an existing framework; experiencing freedom through creativity. Consider also what was being written and why. *See also:* Story; Words; Text; Typing; Pen or Pencil; Ink; Language; Communication; Journal; Notebook; Music; Song; Poetry

X

An X-mark or check mark (such as next to a list item) can represent: Completion, confirmation, or validation. The importance you place on finishing or checking up on something. Organizing, categorizing, or figuring something out (perhaps yourself or your life). **An "X" to note something (such as a location on a map)** can represent something you consider important, you want to remember, or that needs your attention right now. *See also:* Ex

X-Ray

Having or wanting more insight into a certain aspect of your life. Getting to know yourself better (such as your needs, values, priorities, or other inner dynamics). A closer look at something in your life (such as a

346

relationship or situation), perhaps to help you with a particular decision. The idea of being honest or revealing yourself (your thoughts, feelings, preferences, issues, etc.) to others. *See also:* Transparent; Camera

Yarn

A situation or problem that's more complex than it first appears (as a strand of yarn is actually made of many smaller fibers). **A ball of yarn coming unwound** can represent: a situation that's "coming undone" or "falling apart"; the idea of getting to the bottom of a problem or figuring something out. **Someone winding yarn** can represent putting things in order, or a desire to get things under control or organized (or to appear that way to others). *See also:* Thread; String; Rope; Weaving or Spinning; Knitting

Yellow

Happiness, joy, or a positive outlook. Personal warmth or charm. Fear or cowardice. **Golden yellow** can represent abundance or good fortune (or a desire for such). *See also:* Gold; Sunny; Color

Zebra

Camouflage, misdirection, or obscuring (perhaps through confusion or overwhelm). The ability to see things "in black and white." Ambivalence or the ability to see both sides of an issue. Fun or fantasy. The idea of being exotic or different. Dreaming of this animal can represent too much or not enough of one of those qualities, or someone or something you associate with the quality or animal. Consider also the animal's actions, context, and your feelings about it. *See also:* Animal; Horse

Zero

The idea of "nothing." Empty or void. Depletion (such as of energy, ideas, or self-esteem). Coldness (as in a temperature of zero) or harshness. Infinite, omnipotent, magical, or otherwise special (like the number zero in math). *See also:* Depleted; Empty; Circle

Zombie

Someone who doesn't seem "alive" mentally or emotionally (such as not in touch with logic or common sense, or with their own humanity, compassion, or feelings). A feeling or fear of threat in your real life. An indication that your dream was a Toxic Dream (p. 320). *See also:* Monster; Ghost

Zoo

Zoo animals, habitats, and activities can represent the variety of things in your real life (such as people, houses in a neighborhood, activities, facets of your life, etc.). A group, community, city, company, or other self-contained organization. Chaos, or the presence of lots of different activities somewhere in your life. Being or feeling confined or imprisoned (physically, emotionally, or mentally). Being or feeling removed from your usual environment. Protecting, conserving, or saving. Observation or control. Pampering or an easy life (but perhaps at a price). The idea of exotic, foreign, or rare. Consider also the events at the zoo, their context, and how you felt about them. See also any particular animal, activity, or habitat (swamp, desert, etc.) that stood out. ***See also:*** Aquarium; Animal; Feeding; Amusement Park; Park

PART IV

SYMBOL INDEX

351

What Did You Think of This Book?

Tell the author what you liked about this book and what you would like to see more of in future books. Nancy welcomes your comments, which you can share by posting them on the website of the book purveyor where you purchased this book, or by visiting TheCuriousDreamer.com and clicking the **Contact Us** link at the bottom of the page.

Keep Exploring

To learn more about dreams and access interpretation tools, explore these additional resources from the author of this book:

Free Bonus Download

For a limited time, get a free bonus download as a thank-you for purchasing this book: *Sleep Well, Dream Well, Interpret Well.* You'll learn:

- How to create an environment for good quality sleep.
- Bedtime tips to fall asleep and sleep better.
- What foods can affect dreams and lead to nightmares.
- Measures you can take to help prevent nightmares.
- Tips to enhance dream interpretation for personal growth.
- Three things you should always do before interpreting a dream.

When you sign up you'll be among the first to receive updates on new dream resources and books by Nancy Wagaman.

Bonus link:
http://eepurl.com/dKpgkE

Books in This Series

Take the mystery out of dream interpretation with The Curious Dreamer book series, which includes the following books:

The Curious Dreamer's Practical Guide to Dream Interpretation
The Curious Dreamer's Dream Dictionary

TheCuriousDreamer.com

TheCuriousDreamer.com is a free online dream dictionary website with more than 15,000 dream symbols defined for personal growth by Nancy Wagaman. Try the convenient dream analyzer tool by typing a short description of your dream and then seeing a list of possible dream symbol meanings. Explore DIY dream resources, including meanings of common dreams, top dream symbol categories, and how to program your dreams using focused dreaming.

MyDreamVisions.com

MyDreamVisions.com is Nancy Wagaman's professional dream services website dedicated to understanding dreams and their meanings. Get a professional dream interpretation from Nancy, and read how her interpretations are helping dreamers. Take advantage of dream interpretation tools, sample dream interpretations, tips for improving dream intuition and recall, and educational dream quizzes.

Social Media

Discover more dream information and inspiration by following Nancy's social media accounts:

Twitter: @CuriousDreamers
Facebook: facebook.com/thecuriousdreamer
Pinterest: pinterest.com/dreammeanings
Instagram: @TheCuriousDreamerOfficial

Submit a Dream for Interpretation

You can submit a dream to be interpreted by Nancy Wagaman by visiting her professional dream services site, MyDreamVisions.com, and clicking **Buy an Interpretation.** Type in your dream information, and Nancy will email you a custom dream interpretation exploring dream meaning. Choose the In-Depth Dream Interpretation and Nancy will also include an analysis of dream messages, subconscious thoughts and feelings, any dream indicators about life direction, and any follow-up actions that may be appropriate, such as steps to resolve issues that came up in the dream.

Clients tend to rate Nancy's dream interpretation services very highly and to report that they're extremely satisfied after receiving their interpretation. Feedback has been overwhelmingly positive, including comments such as:

Wow. I hardly know what to say. Your analysis was incredible!

Your knowledge and interpretations are very inspiring!!

Incredibly insightful in-depth interpretation.

Bravo, Ms. Wagaman!...Thank you for having this service.

WOW!!!!!! All I can say is WOW!!!!!

I have been working with someone...but your work goes to another level.

Great analysis! Right on target!

Thank you so very much...my mind can rest now.

Such an in-depth and fascinating look at my dream.

Praise for This Book Series

Readers have positive things to say about the premiere book in Nancy Wagaman's The Curious Dreamer book series, *The Curious Dreamer's Practical Guide to Dream Interpretation*:

"You will become your own dream expert..."
—*Lesley Jones (Book Reviewer, Readers' Favorite)*

"A valuable resource for dreamwork...This book is very practical and deals with the nuts and bolts on dreamwork, as well as how to take care of your tools."
—*Henry Reed, Ph.D. (Psychologist, "Father of the Dreamwork Movement")*

"Insightful...a great in-depth look into interpreting the content and symbolism of dreams...well-written, well-researched..."
—*Amy Shannon (Writer and Book Reviewer)*

"A fascinating read. I enjoyed learning about dream interpretation and had quite a time analyzing my own!"
—*Holly Senecal (Book Reviewer)*

"Takes the labor out of understanding dreams....made for curious people who want to understand their dreams through a quick and easy reference tool..."
—*James Hart (Poet and Editor)*

"This book is a must for anyone interested in dreams..."
—*V. Nunez (Book Reviewer)*

About the Author

Nancy Wagaman is a human technologies innovator specializing in personal growth and transformation. Her practical techniques enable people to transform self-limitations and improve their lives. Rooted in science and intuition, Nancy's transformative techniques are practical and easy to use. Nancy began developing human technologies during her early career at Bell Laboratories, and she has also consulted and conducted research for corporate, university, and private clients. Her work has been featured in magazines, radio, and television. Nancy holds advanced degrees in applied psychology and communications, and bachelor's degrees in psychology and biology. She is the creator of the dreams site TheCuriousDreamer.com, author of *The Curious Dreamer's Practical Guide to Dream Interpretation* and *The Curious Dreamer's Dream Dictionary,* and has written extensively on applied psychology, intuition, and other personal growth topics.

Made in the USA
Middletown, DE
20 December 2018